THE POOR IN
THE MIDDLE AGES ‡

THE POOR IN THE MIDDLE AGES‡

AN ESSAY IN SOCIAL HISTORY

MICHEL MOLLAT

TRANSLATED BY
ARTHUR GOLDHAMMER

YALE UNIVERSITY PRESS
NEW HAVEN AND LONDON

ORIGINALLY PUBLISHED AS *LES PAUVRES
AU MOYEN AGE*, HACHETTE, 1978

HN 11
.M6413
1986

Designed by Sally Harris
and set in Trump type by
The Composing Room of Michigan, Inc.
Printed in the United States of America by
Halliday Lithograph, West Hanover, Mass.

Library of Congress Cataloging-in-Publication Data

Mollat, Michel.
  The poor in the Middle Ages.

  Translation of: Les Pauvres au Moyen Age.
  Bibliography: p. 313
  Includes index.
  1. Social history—Medieval, 500–1500.   2. Poor—History.
3. Charities—History.   4. Poverty—Psychological
aspects.   I. Title.
HN11.M6413 1986   305.5'69'09   86-1686
ISBN 0–300–02789–3 (cloth)
      0–300–04605–7 (pbk.)

The paper in this book meets the guidelines for
permanence and durability of the Committee on
Production Guidelines for Book Longevity
of the Council on Library Resources.

10 9 8 7 6 5 4 3

CONTENTS ‡

v

REFERENCE MATTER 301

PREFACE ‡

Brief and solid: this, in a nutshell, is what I would like this survey of the subject of medieval poverty to be. These two goals need not be contradictory. The problem is how to be brief and yet do justice to the abundance of information (to put it mildly) that has been gathered on the subject and to the many historians whose research has brought that information to light. The fourteen years from 1962 to 1976 have been years of joint research with my students and colleagues, graced by some 90 seminar papers and 220 articles, to say nothing of several theses. Some of this work has already been collected in the 850 pages of the collection *Etudes sur l'histoire de la pauvreté* (Studies in the History of Poverty) published in 1974 and in ten rather badly mimeographed *Cahiers* in which we reported on work in progress. To mention this work is to acknowledge the magnitude of the debt that I owe my collaborators. All that is best in this book comes from them; any defects that remain are attributable to the interpreter.

The collaborative ventures were of many kinds, and different workers naturally held different points of view. The sources, moreover, were quite disparate. Are these to be regarded as weaknesses of a collaborative approach? Workers came to the Sorbonne from both the New World and the Old, and many different audiences listened patiently to recitals of the historical problems associated with medieval poverty: audiences from Moscow to Lisbon, from Beirut to Harvard, from Rome to Toronto—and I mustn't leave out Assisi, Todi, Prato, Lublin, or Mönchen-Gladbach. Did we achieve consensus? Poverty is an idea as well as a composite of complex, shifting, hard-to-grasp social realities. There is no obvious or constant relation between the concept and the reality. The student of poverty must understand the subtleties of the concept and measure the changes in the reality. He must move constantly from the ethereal realms of theory and feeling to the brutal realities and back again. But the sources are sometimes so deficient that the interaction between life and thought comes to seem crucial. This work can therefore claim to be no more than an essay, an invitation to further research. If it is soon surpassed by other works, it will be gratifying to know that it was not written in vain.

INTRODUCTION ‡ ENCOUNTER WITH THE POOR

Poverty, understood in the usual sense of "destitution," was a permanent feature of the Middle Ages. From classical antiquity through the social and economic regression of more barbarous times, poverty was thought to be inescapable. Not until the Renaissance and Reformation, when contemporaries began to feel ashamed at the sight of people living in a state considered unworthy of human beings, did anyone dream of eradicating it. "Charity never faileth," men repeated after the apostle Paul, but they also heeded the words of Christ, "the poor will always be with you." Yet much is ambiguous in the persistence of charity and poverty. Two currents of protest run through the Middle Ages. One flowed from the unfortunate themselves, who rose in rebellion at oddly regular intervals, in the twelfth, fourteenth, and sixteenth centuries, to mention only the most prominent instances. The other, tirelessly impelled by evangelical preaching and from the thirteenth century on encouraged also by the Franciscan movement, attempted to reconcile the abjection of actual misery with poverty construed as a virtue; this ultimately gave rise to various charitable endeavors. But in the absence of the knowledge or power necessary to strike at the root of the evil, no one in either camp could envision anything other than provision of relief to the poor or inversion of the social hierarchy to benefit them.

Apart from these indications of poverty's endurance, another equally valuable source of evidence concerning attitudes to poverty and the feelings it aroused is the vocabulary used to convey the diversity of its actual manifestations. The catalogue of terms used to describe poverty, many of them ambivalent, is notable for its variety and susceptibility to change. Originally a single Latin word denoted poverty throughout the West, but diversification is evident in various vernacular forms that first appeared in the thirteenth century and multiplied in the fourteenth; thus did the human mind and discourse reflect the spread and aggravation of misery and growing awareness of its effects. A case in point is the semantic evolution of the Latin *paupertas* and *pauper* (and of their derivatives in the Germanic and Slavic languages). In French these became, respectively, either *povreté* or *pauvreté* and *pov-*

1

re or *pauvre;* in Italian, *povertà* and *povero;* in Portuguese and Spanish, *pobreza* and *pobre;* and in English, *poverty* and *poor.* The outward differences between these and, say, the German *Armut, arm* are of small moment, for the semantic developments in each case indicate corresponding changes in attitude. The notions expressed are fundamentally identical, and the experiential realities are similar.

The words functioned as adjectives before being used as nouns. Originally, a person was poor *(pauvre)* but later he or she became a pauper *(un pauvre).* Poverty referred first to the quality, then to the condition of a person subject to some deficiency, regardless of that person's social status. People spoke of a poor man, a poor woman, a poor peasant, a poor serf, a poor cleric, a poor knight, a poor journeyman *(compagnon);* though belonging to different social orders, all were in some way below the condition normally associated with their estate. Inequalities thus emerge within the shared condition of poverty. Poverty was a relative matter, and the use of the same words to cover a multitude of cases concealed a good deal of ambiguity. One person was always more or less poor than another.

Beyond that, the use of *the poor* as a collective noun signified awareness of the existence of a de facto social group whose numbers aroused feelings of pity or anxiety. Still a third stage was reached when the adjective *poor,* the concrete noun *pauper,* and the collective noun *the poor* were supplemented by the use of the word *poor* in an abstract sense to evoke not only an image of the afflicted individual and the state of his or her affliction but also an affective component of compassion or horror, which carried with it considerable potential to provoke rebellion or social fear. Though rather difficult to trace in all its complexity, this process of semantic change continued up to the sixteenth century at an ever accelerating pace closely correlated with the development of pauperism itself.

‡ If the changing usage of the words *poor* and *poverty* reflected gradual and deep-seated alterations in the notions they designate, one would expect to find similar changes in synonyms, antonyms, and other related words. By following the evolution in usage we can assess more accurately the range of conditions subsumed under the word *poverty* and the complex attitudes and responses that poverty evoked. It is worth noting, however, that evidence concerning these attitudes and responses generally exhibits only one point of view, that of the non-poor casting their gaze upon the poor.

When we examine the words used to denote poverty in the Middle Ages, we can identify two distinct periods on the basis of linguistic evidence. The Latin synonyms for *pauper*, like the synonyms in the vulgar tongues, experienced the same evolution from the adjectival to the substantive form. This phenomenon in fact affected all terms denoting membership in a social order or estate. We see it, for example, in the case of the word *nobilis*, which at first denoted a moral quality of nobility and only later referred to seigneurial status. It is possible to construct a typology of words relating to poverty based on type of adversity, judgment of the poor, and nature of the feelings they aroused.

Thus we find words referring to impecuniosity and destitution in general (*egens, egenus, indigens, inops, insufficiens, mendicus, miser*); shortage of food (*esuriens, famelicus*) or clothing (*nudus, pannosus*); physical defects such as blindness (*caecus*), lameness (*claudus*), arthritic deformity (*contractus*), infirmity in general (*infirmus*), leprosy (*leprosus*), injury (*vulneratus*); feebleness due to poor health or old age (*aegrotans, debilis, senex, valetudinarius*); mental deficiency (*idiotus, imbecillis, simplex*); temporary weakness affecting women during pregnancy and childbirth (*mulier ante et post partum*); situations of adversity such as those involving the loss of one's parents (*orphanus*), husband (*vidua*), or liberty (*captivus*); and, finally, banishment and exile (*bannus, exiliatus*). Some words conveyed a shade of positive evaluation stemming from a feeling of compassion (*miserabilis, miserabilis persona*) or admiration for the discretion of the "shamefaced pauper" (*pauper verecundus*); respect for the figure of Christ as reflected in the poor can be seen in the extended use made of the honorific "pauper of Christ" (*pauper Christi*), once limited to monks who had voluntarily chosen poverty for love of God. Certain diminutives suggested a good deal of condescension (*pauperculus, paupertinus*). From condescension one proceeded by degrees to disdain, contempt, and, finally, repugnance. The humility of the pauper (*humilis*) was not always understood as echoing the biblical virtue expressed in the *Magnificat* by the term "the Lord's Handmaid." The weakness of the little man (*impotens*) is close to the vulgarity of the peasant (*ignobilis, vilis*, and even *vilissimus*). Dirty, dressed in rags, foul smelling, covered with sores, the pauper came to be seen as repulsive (*abjectus*). One could easily compile a catalogue of miseries and afflictions whose various names (*abjectio, humilitas*, and so on) derive, like *paupertas*, from the use of the corresponding adjectives as substantives to designate particular individuals so stricken. The nomenclature just described is not merely the result of historical compilation. Contemporaries reflected on this terminology in the twelfth century. Men like Bernard of Clairvaux and Peter of Blois used the pair *egenus* and *pauper;* the two words were not synonymous but had specific and different meanings. *Pauperes,* for these writers, referred to a group of the wretched for whom material assistance was required as a matter of justice. *Egenus* traditionally referred to a category composed of needy individuals, orphans, widows, and pilgrims. *Indigentes* referred to a deficiency of an accidental nature.[1] A similar concept of poverty was formulated, also in the twelfth century, at Grandmont, one of the most celebrated centers of actual poverty: alongside the voluntary poverty (*paupertas spontanea*) of the monks and the simulated poverty (*simulatoria*) of hypocrites who are like dilapidated walls and sepulchers, there is the involuntary poverty (*coacta*) of mendicants forced to take to the road and beg in order to survive.[2]

Certain word associations and contrasts shed further light on the condition of the poor. For example, the frequent association of *pauper* with *agricola* or *laborator,* the one being used at times as a synonym for the two others, says a great deal about the origins of the poor, many of whom were drawn from the ranks of men who worked the earth with their hands to eke out a meager subsistence: La Fontaine's "poor plowman" would recognize his ancestor here. Other words illuminate the struggle for daily bread and suggest uncertainty about the future and vulnerability to calamity, evoking anxiety and distress (*anxietas, augustia*) as well as lack of necessary resources (*carestia, penuria*).

Various antonyms established a contrast between the inferiority of the pauper and the superiority of the man who possessed power (*potens*), military strength (*miles*), civic liberty (*civis, burgensis*), or wealth (*dives*). Each set of antonyms corresponds to a different stage in the evolution of medieval poverty.

By the time the vulgar tongues supplanted Latin, the Latin vocabulary for states of poverty and categories of the poor was fairly extensive. We can learn a great deal about the aggravation of the pauper's lot by examining the kinds of vernacular terms that gradually replaced this Latin vocabulary. New words indicated changed circumstances, and not all reflect a spirit of charity. *Pauper* and *pauvre* retained their religious connotation, but other words acquired new and harsher meanings in the middle 1300s, and hostile or disparaging neologisms came into use. For example, words associated with begging begin to imply presumed laziness on the beggar's part, as in the phrase "sturdy beggar." People began to suspect marginal members of society of delinquency and criminality, with a corresponding increase in the number of words to describe vagabonds and beggars. On the other hand, years of economic hardship pointed up a new kind of indigence with which society now had to contend: the poverty of the man who works hard but still does not earn enough to support his family. Thus economic crisis recruited new men into the ranks of the paupers.

Poverty was quite broadly defined. A pauper was a person who permanently or temporarily found himself in a situation of weakness, dependence, or humiliation, characterized by privation of the means to power and social esteem (which means varied with period and place): these included money, relations, influence, power, knowledge, skill, nobility of birth, physical strength, intellectual capacity, and personal freedom and dignity. Living from hand to mouth, he had no chance of rising without assistance. Such a definition is broad enough to encompass the frustrated, the misfit, the antisocial, and the marginal. It is not limited to any one era, region, or social setting. Nor does it exclude those who in obedience to ascetic or mystical ideals chose voluntarily to live apart from the world or those who out of a spirit of self-sacrifice chose to live as paupers among the poor.

‡ Poverty, being relative, existed in various degrees. Among the factors affecting its severity were social rank, period, cultural level, and economic development. In medieval French it was said of a man that he "fell" into servitude or misery, or that he could not "maintain his estate," much less "rise again." From this it is clear that poverty was a form of degradation; a man could fall only so far before he crossed a dividing line, a threshold at which he passed from mere difficulty into hardship and distress. Above the poverty line everyone was of course vulnerable to "the slings and arrows of outrageous fortune." Below, however, lay irremediable disgrace. *Poverty line* may be a misnomer, however, for the threshold of poverty in fact had several dimensions: economic, social, and biological.

To treat the biological dimension first, a man fell into poverty when he could no longer maintain his health or ensure his survival, whether as a result of congenital or accidental infirmity, incapacity for work, or malnutrition. But at what age did the peasant, in each historical period, discover that he had become unsuited for work in the fields, or the artisan for work in his trade, or the merchant for the journeys necessitated by his business, or the cleric for his ministry, or the noble for the rigors of war? Urban conditions were of course different from rural ones. Poor clothing, dilapidated housing, and above all an inadequate and unbalanced diet left the body vulnerable to disease. The great pandemics acted as catalysts that allowed the constitutent elements of poverty to interact. Infant mortality rates would provide a useful indicator of poverty in the Middle Ages if only they could be determined with any accuracy. To some extent modern medical research can help enlighten us about the constituents of what I shall call the "physiological poverty" of centuries past. With the help of modern medicine, an allusion to diet in the *Roman de Renart*, a physical detail in a character painted by Brueghel, or a sign of rickets in a skeleton dug up in an old cemetery can take on a significance that would otherwise go unnoticed, indicating some physical weakness or defect.

Poor hygiene and health are so often linked to lack of economic resources that it can be hard to distinguish between the biological and economic aspects of poverty. Not only for individuals and families but also for villages, cities, seigneuries, and states, the threshold of economic hardship depended on the availability of provisions, which in turn depended on economic, demographic, and climatic factors as well as on the contingency of natural disasters. In a cash economy we can estimate where the poverty level stands by studying fluctuations in prices for basic commodities and in workers' purchasing power. Another important aspect of the economic dimension of poverty has to do with the various deductions that were made from the meager resources of the poor in the form of seigneurial dues, tithes, and city and state taxes. To top it all off, debt, that poisonous remedy for poverty, reduced many a peasant and his lord to distress. Unfortunately, it is easier to discover the path that led from difficulty to hardship and degradation than it is to learn much about the victims.

Finally, poverty also had a social dimension. In the Middle Ages, to suffer a loss of status meant literally to fall from one's estate, to be deprived of its instruments of labor and of the marks of its condition. For a peasant this meant the loss of farming implements and animals; for an artisan, loss of the tools of his trade; for a merchant, loss of his shop; for a cleric, loss of his books; for a noble, loss of his horse and arms. Without these things a man ceased to be anything, because he no longer possessed the means to carry on a social existence. Stripped of his social position and excluded from the community, he was forced into emigration and vagabondage. The poor man was uprooted and alone.

A person could lose status by being cast out of society or by refusing to participate in it, or again as the result of some misfortune. It remains to be conclusively demonstrated that the eleventh and twelfth centuries were a time of relative overpopulation and that this was a cause of pauperization. We know that the birth rate in Europe was elevated from the eleventh century on. This caused difficulties that were compounded among the nobility by the laws of primogeniture and in the rest of society by the custom of dividing the family property among the heirs. As a result, younger sons of the nobility (*juvenes*) were left without resources and forced to seek their fortunes any way they could, while people of lesser rank left home to seek their livings elsewhere. Economic hardship and war reduced many people to poverty in the fourteenth century. Some who lost their social positions found a home in the mercenary companies, while others sought refuge in the cities.

Society's rejects were joined in their wanderings by criminals and antisocial individuals—rebels before their time—who rejected family, society, and state. Not all vagabonds were criminals, but they were apt to become so. This was true of the "forest men" of the eleventh and early twelfth centuries and also of the well-known thirteenth-century renegade Helmrecht, who rebelled against his father and the peasant life. In this connection I should also mention those free spirits, the Goliards, as well as the "children" (of the 1212 Crusade) and "shepherds" who left the discipline of home and family to set out upon a religious quest of one kind or another. That form of beggary known as *gueuserie*, which dates from the fourteenth century, reached a peak in the fifteenth. *Gueux* were hostile to the established order and lived in communities or bands on the fringes of society; thus they were suspected of heresy and subversion. Recruited from the indigent population and living in indigence, these asocial individuals blackened the reputation of the "true" poor who shared their destitution.

Just how important were such marginal groups during the Middle Ages? How much poverty can a society tolerate? What percentage of marginals can a society support without breakdown or repression? Economic, social, and moral factors all influence the answers to these questions, which when it comes to medieval society remain beyond our reach. Still, it is useful to state the problems clearly.

‡We cannot hope to resolve the ambiguities of poverty simply by analyzing medieval terminology and investigating the various dimensions of the problem. We must also consider people's attitudes. It would be simple enough to do as contemporaries did and characterize the poor as either good and true or bad, false, and rebellious, but this would be a facile oversimplification. The subject calls for a deeper investigation.

There was nothing ambiguous about the "true pauper" who lived on what he earned from some humble trade and supplemented his earnings by alms from the parish or confraternity—a meager but resigned existence. His face was familiar. People knew his relatives. Despite his misfortune he remained, in his suffering, a member of the social group defined by the seigneurie and rural, or possibly urban, parish. No questions were raised about him, and his presence in the community caused no disruption. Ambiguity could arise only in regard to the motives for the condescension of the powerful, the commiseration of the lord, the ostentatious gift of the bourgeois. These were shrouded in the impenetrable mysteries of the human conscience: where does true charity—praised by all and practiced by some—begin and end? Ambiguity attaches to the motives of those who give as well as those who receive.

The ambiguity of poverty becomes clear once we cross the sociological threshold, where we immediately encounter suspicion of the poor. Next to nothing was known about the men and women who lived as vagabonds. Since they had fled their rightful place in society, might they not be rebels? Or disease carriers? Were they really poor, or genuinely ill? Hospices prudently offered shelter to "transient paupers" for only a limited period, and in times of alarm access to the city was denied. It was not long before ecclesiastical theorizing drew a distinction between the deserving and the undeserving poor.

The causuists of charity introduced new and subtle distinctions. Honest, sanctifying poverty was contrasted with sinful poverty. Was poverty a virtue or a curse? Along with other biblical bequests the Middle Ages inherited the distinction between the ascetic and humble poverty of the *anawim*[3] and the pessimistic notion of poverty as punishment for one's own sins or for the sins of one's parents, with which the Pharisees of the Gospels had attacked the infant blind at birth. Another dilemma: was poverty a virtue in itself or a means of perfection?

Saint Benedict favored the second alternative, while some Franciscans argued for the first. Even they left some ambiguity surrounding the choice between absolute and moderate poverty. Was poverty to be practiced individually or collectively? Still other debates revolved around such issues as whether Christ was the model of strict poverty or whether his impoverishment consisted in the fact that God—pure spirit—had made himself flesh, and about the nature of and the possibility of reviving the exemplary "apostolic poverty" of primitive Christianity.

These remarks are not as much of a digression as they might seem from the subject of paupers who involuntarily endured a life of suffering. Indeed, people either praised or blamed poverty in the abstract depending on how they felt about the scandal of actual poverty. Ambivalent attitudes toward poverty stemmed from a divergence between Christian principles and social prejudices. The idea, derived from the Gospels, that the pauper was created in the image of Christ the Redeemer was frequently contradicted by brutal contempt—the contempt of the eleventh-century baron—for the peasant, a contempt that we find also in the open curse on the poor pronounced by the author of the *Roman de la rose*. Was true poverty a form of spiritual sublimation? Or was it a permanent disgrace? Therein lies the essential ambivalence, which was clearly perceived by some contemporaries.

In the final centuries of the Middle Ages, by which time the poor are included in various tax rolls, especially in the towns, we find them described in various ways whose meaning is not entirely clear, such as "paupers" and "have-nothings" (*nihil habentes*). The line that separated those who paid taxes from those who did not, who were too poor to be assessed, is not an accurate indicator of the true poverty line. The tax cutoff varied from one region or town to another, and within a particular city or region from one year to the next and one tax to the next, depending on the needs of the treasury. Changes in the taxable *quantum* increased or decreased the number of people subject to taxation and the number of people exempt. The concept of a "fiscal pauper" is suggestive and can be used to gain some idea of the orders of magnitude involved, but it reflects the influence of political and economic conditions more than the reality of poverty. Though a useful indicator, it should be employed with caution.

‡ Thus difficulties with the sources deepen our ignorance of actual poverty. The concerns of medieval writers and administrators were

not our own. Few sources exist that deal specifically and continuously with the history of the poor: what we have is mainly records of alms-giving, often inaccurate, and hospital archives. The poor, who were drawn from all strata of society though of course primarily from the lower strata, were found everywhere. Hence all kinds of sources must be exploited. (By *sources* I mean anything datable—whether written or not—that can yield information about the poor: public and private documents, literary accounts, administrative, economic, and religious records, physical objects, iconographic evidence.) Obviously, the argu-ment *ex silentio* cannot be used. Still, silence as regards the poor in a document may be the product of indifference or contempt or of the inability of humble folk to express themselves. Shouldn't such silence be taken into account just as much as a piece of factual evidence? Moreover, when any writer—preacher, moralist, chronicler, or art-ist—however benevolent, speaks of or describes a pauper, he sees that pauper from his own point of view and in the light of his own personal concerns; the writer rarely adopts the poor man's point of view.

To be sure, the misery of the pauper is often described dispas-sionately and with the purpose of reminding society of its duties to-ward the poor. But what was proposed? Resignation in anticipation of consolation in the hereafter? A social upheaval that would humble the proud and exalt the humble without changing the structure of society? A balance between rights on the one hand and duties on the other, based on some notion of mutual charity? When the poor did express themselves—at the end of the twelfth century, during the fourteenth century, and during the Peasant Wars in the time of Luther—they and their spokesmen seem not to have had a clear idea of either their fate or their solidarity, because they did not know themselves. Misunder-standing of poverty, therefore, extended to paupers themselves.

It would be useful to estimate the numbers of the poor from century to century: the history of poverty cannot be exclusively qualitative history. But quantitative data are rare, scattered, disparate in value, and ambiguous. Nevertheless, an effort must be made to discover pov-erty's rate of growth. Changes are perceptible but hard to quantify and seem to have occurred in a spasmodic manner. What brought these changes about? Politics, war—feudal, urban, and dynastic—and natu-ral disasters all played an undeniable part in causing short-term varia-tions. But how do we account for the huge waves of poverty that engulfed large numbers of paupers, especially at the ends of the elev-enth, twelfth, thirteenth, and fourteenth centuries, only to recede, though not without leaving traces of their presence? And how do we explain the motives of Merovingian bishops, ninth-century monks, eleventh-century hermits, thirteenth-century mendicant friars, and finally laymen instrumental in works of charity, all of whom worked to alleviate the suffering of the poor? The problems we face are of two types, and the solutions to one type of problem seem hard to carry over to the other.

Admittedly, population growth played a very important role, as did economic and technological development. It is important to stress these in any account of poverty. But the problem of poverty is complex and ambiguous and does not lend itself to simplification. Poverty involved more than just the temporal order—religious thinkers at several points in the preceding centuries had turned their minds to the question of poverty. Although they had not foreseen all subsequent developments (how could they have?), they had managed to combine contradictory aspects of the question in a synthetic account. These attempts had deep and ancient roots. The biblical and gospel traditions, occasionally broken but always revived, retained a kind of latent power, like that of a dormant virus: the metaphor makes clear, I hope, the explosive force in Francis of Assisi's proclamation of the dignity of the poor and of the duty to restore that dignity. This was a new turn in the dialectic of happiness and suffering. But what was the nature of the happiness of which men dreamed? Therein lay yet another ambiguity, one of major significance.

PART ONE ‡ THE WEAK OVERSHADOWED BY THE POWERFUL (FIFTH TO ELEVENTH CENTURY) ‡

CHAPTER ONE ‡
THE LEGACY OF
LATE ANTIQUITY

The miseries of the aging societies of the Roman Empire and the deficiencies of the young barbarian nations were a long way from canceling one another out; rather than mutual regeneration, the result of Rome's collision with the barbarians was an accumulation of ills, the brunt of which fell on the powerless. But there was also a kind of compensation, a legacy of late antiquity that worked in favor of the poor. The philanthropy of the Antonines and the munificence of public gifts had left, if not traditions, then at least traces and souvenirs. Above all, it was not in vain that the century of Constantine had fostered initiatives to improve the lot of the poor, initiatives inspired by the Sermon on the Mount and by reference—opportune as well as inopportune—to the principle of charity. But of course poverty, like weeds, needs no fertilizer to grow, and charity, once its seeds have been sown in the human heart, needs no models. The experience of misfortune can be most instructive.

THE SURVIVAL OF URBAN POVERTY

Urban poverty on the ancient model survived in areas that were untouched or relatively unaffected by the invasions of the Germanic tribes. Was such urban poverty more deeply rooted than its rural counterpart, or is it simply better known to us because its concentration and seriousness made it a matter of more immediate concern to contemporaries? From the time of its founder's reign, Constantinople seems to have attracted large numbers of paupers, as did Antioch in the time of Libanius, as well as Ephesus, Caesarea, Jerusalem, and Alexandria. Estimates of the numbers involved are of doubtful value. Saint John Chrysostom's estimate of fifty thousand indigents living in Constantinople around the year A.D. 400 is surely excessive, yet it gives us some idea of what contemporaries thought and considered scandalous. The shockingly large numbers of the impoverished had already provoked reactions of two kinds: repression and pity. A high official in Constantine's entourage by the name of Zoticos secretly used a large sum of public money for the care of lepers, and this in spite of an order of the emperor who, out of concern for the public health, had condemned the victims of leprosy to expulsion or death. But the leprosarium that Zoticos founded at the very gates of the capital, on the Galatan hills, was reported to Constans, and Zoticos was sentenced to be drawn and quartered by mules. Afterward, however, the emperor repented and transformed the makeshift huts that had been constructed by the martyred Zoticos into a permanent hospice bearing his name, and Zoticos became famous throughout the empire as a "foster-father of the poor." In the meantime, however, rigor had gained the upper hand, and in 382, in order to rid Constantinople of the large numbers of beggars who clogged its streets, checks were made to identify which indigents could work and which could not. Those who could work, regardless of whether their unemployment was voluntary or involuntary, were treated as slackers and returned to their owners if they were slaves or, if they were free, handed over to their denouncers as perpetual coloni. By studying legal and ecclesiastical documents scholars have been able to identify different aspects of poverty and the words used to denote them; the sources also reveal attitudes toward poverty ranging from compassion to hostility.

The influx of indigents into the large cities of the East, especially Constantinople, contrasts sharply with the dispersion of the poor in the rural West during the same period. The process was typical: peasants eked out a precarious existence at best and when their survival was threatened left the land; from vagabondage they then fell into misery. The disinherited were thus of many types. For the peasant, difficulties often began with a lack of seed for planting or with bad weather, catastrophe, or pillage of his farm. Farming implements and equipment were often pledged to usurers, which only aggravated the situation. For the Fathers of the Greek Church, a debtor was always a potential pauper. A Syrian inscription that compares the peasant to an ox in harness says that the peasant "fears the harsh lot of the slave." Usurers were not the only creditors: Gregory Nazianzen and Basil of Caesarea complained about the heavy burden of taxation, the arbitrariness of the ratio between payment in kind and payment in coin, the capricious exactions of landowners, and the excessive service requirements imposed on peasants. They also attacked the patronage system as a usurpation of property disguised as a fair exchange of land and service for protection. It was common for poor peasants to avoid paying taxes and other obligations by fleeing to the cities, where they joined others who had preceded them in the descent into misery.

Some authors maintain that in the sixth century a "tidal wave" of poverty inundated the eastern portion of the old Roman Empire. In chronicles, laws, hagiographies, and sermons we find material that can be pieced together to form a picture of the poor. Laws were promulgated in 535 and 539, for example, to check the influx of peasants to the capital. Two consecutive bad harvests had left peasants without the means to pay their debts, and when their property was seized they came to try their luck in Constantinople. Taking advantage of tax exemptions that dated back to 313, they took up modest trades and were helped by public distributions of food and clothing. Conditions similar to those observed in Thrace also afflicted the Near East, Syria in particular. Attempts were made, without notable results, to prohibit the mortgaging of land and work implements. Lawmakers tried to deal with the social consequences of peasant migration to the cities, seeking in particular to protect young girls that procurers purchased in the countryside from impoverished parents and consigned to city brothels. Strong measures proved necessary: the controls on able-bodied paupers, begun in 382 but later abandoned, were now re-instituted. An inspector was made responsible for turning away newly arrived paupers and for seeing to it that the city's own poor were put to work on public construction or food supply projects. Able-bodied paupers were required "to do their share of working the land . . . and to shun idleness, which may lead to delinquency."

The distinction between able-bodied and non-able-bodied paupers was expressed by the terms *penes* (πένης), or poor worker, and *ptochos* (πτωχός), or indigent person reduced to beggary. Each term subsumed a variety of misfortunes sharing certain common characteristics. Impecuniosity was the lot of most. Evelyne Patlagean has found evidence of undernourishment and malnutrition, although it is difficult to be precise about actual rations. The poor suffered from serious deficiencies of vitamins A, B, and D owing to a lack of bread, an excess of starches, and insufficiency of animal fat in their diet. Associated with these dietary deficiencies are certain characteristic diseases common among the poorest of the poor: parasite infestations, polyneuritis, dropsy, blindness, leprosy (reported by the two Gregories: Gregory of Nyssa and Gregory Nazianzen), and of course plague. We now have a fairly accurate idea of the six major pandemics that occurred between 540 and 600, primarily in the large cities of the Mediterranean.

The poor were particularly vulnerable to disease. Bad hygiene (uncleanliness and open sores on the skin), inadequate clothing, and deplorable housing provided extraordinarily favorable conditions for disease-bearing animals and insects, as Michael the Syrian realized in 541. Even without epidemics the average life expectancy, to judge by inscriptions on tombs, was less than thirty-five.

What about the housing of the poor? *Housing* is hardly an appropriate word. In the cities any public or semipublic building, such as the atrium of a church in Antioch or a monastery in Constantinople or the porticoes of a public square, offered shelter to dozens of tramps. Elsewhere, in Cappadocia for instance, the poor sought refuge in the innumerable natural caves. In Constantinople and Jerusalem archeological excavation has revealed exceptions to this general rule in the form of remains of pauper dwellings. Remains, indeed—to judge by extant texts, such dwellings were never more than rude huts of wood or reeds, barely covered over. It would be misleading to think of anything like a family home in discussing these social marginals.

Byzantine poverty can be defined in many different and complex ways. Under Justinian, the Digest set the legal threshold of poverty at fifty gold solidi. But in reality the poverty line depended on the price level and the value of bronze coin. In Byzantium and elsewhere, the definition of poverty in monetary terms depends on the problem of determining the value of the small base-metal coins that circulated among the common people. Distress is more accurately defined by social and moral criteria.

An obvious question is whether the poor living in the Byzantine cities were aware of their numbers and of the limited but real strength that those numbers would indicate. It is difficult to give a categorical answer to this question. In Antioch Libanius had earlier attacked signs of a growing hostility between the establishment and the underprivileged. A few years before Justinian, between 520 and 530, a seditious hetaeria, or political society, had, according to Procopius, mobilized some number of able-bodied but unemployed paupers from the bottom of Constantinople society. The riot that took place in 533 against a change in the value of small-denomination bronze coins was a veritable revolt of the poor, as were the periodic bread riots that are a constant curse in any underdeveloped society. But there were no class movements because there were no classes, and above all because no one—not government officials or political leaders, much less the poor themselves—could conceive of poverty as anything other than a condition to be endured, whether as a result of some permanent affliction or one of life's accidents. Structural factors affecting poverty were not perceived beneath the veil of accidental circumstance.

What was the dividing line between "able-bodied" and "non-able-bodied?" Byzantine law and morality regarded the capacity for work as the defining criterion. Vagabondage and unemployment were political problems; physical and mental disability were moral problems. Justinian's legislation dealt with some of the political problems. The moral problems were also influenced by a diverse tradition: at issue were not only those who were ill, disabled, or old but also abandoned children, girls who had fallen victim to procurers, and, in times of scarcity and famine, all who were hungry. Each of these categories found assistance in a specific type of establishment, for which the Greek language had specific names. Some of these nouns, such as *ptocheion* (πτωχεῖον), or hospice for the poor, and *xenodocheion* (ξενοδοχεῖόν), or hospice for foreigners, were transplanted to the West. The hagiographic literature contains abundant information about these welfare institutions, responsibility for which was shouldered by the Church.

The reason for this was not that the Basileus took no interest in welfare issues. Public giving was part of the imperial tradition, and it was the emperor's function in part to provide, as Trajan had done, not only for feeding his people but also for overseeing what we nowadays would call recreational facilities and leisure time activities and for generally enhancing the "quality of life." The authorization to receive legacies, granted by Constantine to the Church in 321, had been extended by several of his successors in the fourth and fifth centuries to welfare institutions, and Justinian had further extended measures intended to foster their growth. The ancient system of liturgies had been transferred to charitable institutions; tax exemptions and construction assistance helped to stimulate their growth. The story of how Sampson, a man of high social rank under Justinian, founded the most celebrated of all the hospitals of Constantinople is too well known to be retold here. The fact that Julian thought of setting up pagan charitable institutions shows the extent to which social aid institutions had by this time become firmly established under Christian influence.

In fact, the imperial authorities and the Church cooperated to insure that the unfortunate would receive some kind of aid. The government saw to it that property belonging to the churches and monasteries, along with alms donated by the faithful, was not used for other than charitable purposes, while the Church, thus encouraged in its activities, received alms as a public service and established hospitals, already devoted to particular specialties, in cities and along major roads.

"From the generosity of the ancients to the charity of the Christians" it is therefore possible to see a continuous progression in the eastern portion of what had been the Roman Empire. Poverty and social assistance to the poor there took on characteristic forms. It is interesting, however, to compare the evolution of poverty and social assistance in the two parts of the Christian world. East and West did not develop at the same pace. Byzantium still boasted an urban proletariat at a time when poverty in the West was already essentially rural. Yet the Byzantine Empire too was destined to experience rural poverty, and in the eighth and ninth centuries poverty in both regions connoted not so much inferiority to the wealthy as subordination to the powerful. The Justinian Code served as a model in its provisions concerning poverty as in so many other respects, and its influence was extended to much of eastern Europe by the government of Kiev. In the West, the Merovingian councils reaffirmed the provisions of the Theodosian Code concerning widows, and the *Statuta* repeated other provisions relative to orphans. It is not without significance that Carolingian legislation of 827 (in the collection attributed to Anségis) reproduced, in the form of a capitulary and under the name of Louis the Pious, a chapter of Julian's *Epitome* concerning the prescribed use of Church property for charitable purposes. The Carolingian monarchs drew heavily upon imperial and Christian sources. Thus in order to understand fully the evolution of poverty and related issues up to the end of the first millennium we must pay close attention to the traditions associated with these matters and common to both the eastern and western portions of the empire.

THE DOCTORS OF POVERTY   Among the intellectual traditions common to both halves of Christendom, the thought of the Church Fathers is doubtless the most important. It has even been asserted that everything had been said by the fourth century and that, despite periods when the influence of the Fathers was in eclipse and the realities of life had changed considerably, the writings of the Church Fathers remained a constant reference for all Christians. Shaped as much by secular culture as by Christian inspiration, the patristic writings selectively incorporated much of pagan humanism and adapted it to the principle of charity. Imbued with Old as well as New Testament teachings, they established for the medieval concepts of poverty and mercy firm roots in biblical soil.

The Greek and Latin Fathers used the varied resources of their two languages to express the idea of poverty and its concomitant social reality. Clement of Alexandria, Chrysostom, Basil, Gregory of Nyssa, Gregory Nazianzen, Ambrose, and Gregory the Great were particularly diligent in this regard. Nevertheless, two terms, the Greek πτωχός and the Latin *pauper* tended to displace all others. The shifting meanings of the French word *pauvre* derive from this same evolution and gave rise to ambiguities of the sort discussed above. Two aspects of the meaning of both terms remained constant throughout the Middle Ages in both East and West, among Latins, Greeks, Byzantines, and even Moslems. This observation alone is ample evidence that the "peoples of the Book" shared common attitudes toward poverty. The two aspects to which I refer are, first, the distinction between poverty and indigence and, second, the valuation of poverty as a condition of closeness to God.

The distinction between poverty and indigence had been noticed by such writers as Martial, Cicero, and Seneca, who along with the Stoics regarded the acceptance of material poverty, or "contempt for wealth," as a path to wisdom. The Jewish legacy is in a different, higher key: the Hebrew language has different words for the state of one who is indigent and in need of material assistance (*ebyon*) and for the attitude of one "who does not make an ostentatious display before God" but shows himself to be inwardly humble and ready to do God's bidding. Islam preserved this idea, to which the New Testament added the virtues of patience and love. Made explicit by Saint Paul in II Corinthians 8–9, this attitude is based on the idea that Christ, "though he was rich, yet for your sakes he became poor, that ye through his poverty might be rich."

What proved crucial in the Middle Ages was the fact that ever since late antiquity the Christian concept of charity, which is prior to the concept of poverty, had been enunciated and put into practice by bishops and monks in both the East and the West: the Christian view transformed spiritual humility into an active striving toward God and aimed at alleviating the physical and social humiliation of the poor.

If we accept this interpretation, it is easy to perceive the historic milestones in the education of the Christian people, both Greek and

Latin, by teachers both mystical and pastoral, monastic and episcopal. It is not by chance that the names of the Greek Fathers are associated with large cities in which poverty was rampant. Their homilies were commentaries, some unprecedented in their force, upon such passages from the Gospels as the parables of the young rich man and Lazarus and the Sermon on the Mount. Clement of Alexandria's condemnation of lust as the root of all evil prefigures the condemnation of avarice that was a constant feature of the Middle Ages. Also worth mentioning are Saint John Chrysostom's invectives (at Constantinople and Antioch) against those who shirked the duty to give alms, thereby offending directly against Christ, of whom the pauper was an image. The saint demanded that one tenth of the income of the wealthy should be confiscated on behalf of the poor. In Caesarea Saint Basil organized a hospice and a people's soup kitchen. And it was again Chrysostom who expressed himself in lapidary phrases that might easily be mistaken for those of Saint Bernard: "To give a glass of water is to give a chalice. . . . Honor not the host with garments of silk. . . . It is mockery to honor God in sumptuous churches while reviling him in the poor."

"Let us feed and clothe Christ" were the words spoken in the meantime by Gregory of Nyssa. In Milan Saint Ambrose found words that have often been repeated since: "To revile the poor is to commit murder. Naboth did not kill just one pauper. Each day he reviled one, he killed another." The African Church was no less assiduous in affirming the evangelical meaning of charity in response to misery. Leaving aside Tertullian's commentary on the Sermon on the Mount, let me single out for special notice among Augustine's writings, which were so widely influential in the Middle Ages, his fundamental definition of the rich man's superfluity as the poor man's necessity.

As for the monks, the extreme austerity of the Desert Fathers and, later, of the Cappadocian eremites was more than just an example of personal and communal spiritual poverty, which the West venerated in the figure of Saint Anthony. The same may be said of those monks who sought isolation on islands. Saint Basil's conception of the possession of material goods was to prove influential. For him, as for Thomas Aquinas after him, the Christian is but the administrator of what he possesses. Monks have abdicated even this role, but laymen must assume this responsibility and correct social inequalities by redistributing wealth through alms. For Saint Jerome, the widow who borrowed money in order to give alms was simply following the example of Christ. It was Jerome who issued the famous invitation to "follow naked the naked Christ" (*Nudus nudum Christum sequi*). Through him the ambivalence in the Latin word *pauper*, so heavy with significance in later years, was further accentuated in the Vulgate.

Cassian took advantage of the double meaning of poverty. Few works have been as widely read and copied in the West as his *Conferences*. Through his disciples (that is, the monks of Lérins) Latin Christians learned to adopt and adapt the spiritual perspectives of the East, which later underwent lengthy development. I shall have more to say later on about Saint Caesarius and Benedictine monasticism.

Also of fundamental importance are the spirituality and pastoral experience of Gregory the Great and Isidore of Seville. Before turning to them, however, mention should be made of another great teacher of the first millennium: the sixth-century African Julianus Pomerius, whose work was for many years attributed to Prosper of Aquitaine. Shaped by secular as well as ecclesiastical culture, this North African abbot exerted a great influence on Caesarius and on the churches of Spain and Gaul, and his influence was later revived in the ninth century under the Carolingians. For Julianus Pomerius, the monk's poverty, the collective property of the monastery, and even private ownership by laymen are justified solely by their relation to God, the sole owner of all things, and by their use for the common good. Ownership was not legitimate for oneself only but also, and more important, for others. Once an individual ensured his own survival and the survival of his family he had the duty to give whatever he owned beyond his own needs to the *debiles* and *infimi*, that is, to the poor. Julianus Pomerius thus summed up both a long tradition and the fruits of his own meditation upon things he had witnessed and experienced.

It would be pleasant to be able to gauge the influence of such teaching. Normative laws and learned treatises had only an indirect effect on the Christians of the East and West. It was through homilies, lives of saints, accounts of miracles, exemplary tales, and charitable institutions that served as a model for the rich and a shelter for the poor that awareness of the existence of poverty and of the duty to alleviate its ills gradually—very gradually—took shape. The early Christians left a living model for their successors to imitate, whose memory was honored in the many sanctuaries of which he was patron—the Roman equestrian who at the gates of Amiens sliced his cape in two with the stroke of a sword in order to give half to a beggar: Saint Martin.

CHAPTER TWO ‡
A MISERABLE FATE IN A CHANGING SOCIETY
(SIXTH TO ELEVENTH CENTURY)

The scene in which Saint Martin figures at Amiens is rich in symbolism. It is a sublimation of poverty, in which the needy beggar stands for Christ himself. It is also an invitation to charity addressed by way of Saint Martin to those who, as men who own horses and are armed with swords, possess wealth, power, and strength. The scene takes place at the gates of the city, where town and country meet.

Like the East, the West too experienced centuries of hard times, although the timing and nature of events were different in the two halves of the empire. Urban poverty was less serious in the West, though it is said that in the latter days of the empire Rome was obliged to maintain 120,000 people on public assistance. As late as the end of the sixth century, Pope Gregory the Great had to take heroic measures to alleviate severe poverty in the city. In other parts of the Latin world the Germanic invasions accentuated the decay of urban life. Depopulated and fallen into ruins, many ancient cities dwindled to the status of villages between the fourth and the seventh century. A few, with markets on busy routes, revived in the ninth century. But for six centuries the primary locus of confrontation between rich and poor was the countryside. The wealthy man was no longer the possessor of large sums of cash but the owner of vast estates and stores, while poverty was defined by lack of rights over the soil and dependence on others for food.

There was some diversity from place to place and period to period owing to different forms of land tenure, a different mix between old Romanized settlers and Germanic newcomers, varying density of population, and (to some extent) differences in the level of technological development. The equilibrium of an essentially rural society depends on three factors: land, manpower, and tools. If any one of the three is in short supply, progress is difficult and scarcity tends to affect everyone. Poverty is then the general lot, and the condition of the economy is not the major source of inequalities and relations of dependency. An attempt has been made to map the severity of poverty in different parts of Carolingian territory over the course of the ninth century, based on decisions taken by the Frankish councils to deal with poverty-related issues. The result shows greater diversity than would be the case for the Merovingian period or for the tenth and eleventh centuries, during which depressed conditions seem, sadly, to have been much more widespread.

Recent research has shown not a sharp contrast but still some difference between poverty in the Merovingian and poverty in the Carolingian period, as well as in the means of coping with that poverty. The background remained the same: the world was essentially rural under both the Merovingians and their successors. But the prominent issues of the day had changed. For the Merovingian pauper the problem was survival. By the ninth century the problem had become one of maintaining a place in society. The Merovingian pauper was crushed, the Carolingian merely oppressed. As Michel Rouche has written of the ninth century: "Poverty no longer consisted in not having but in not being."[1]

THE MISERIES OF THE
MEROVINGIAN ERA

The main sources for the history of the Merovingian era are ecclesiastical. Compared with monastic and episcopal chronicles, hagiographies, accounts of miracles and translations of relics, works of theology, sermons, and conciliar canons, the importance of royal charters, formularies, and literary works is only secondary. Clerics were the authors of all the documents, however.

Honor to whom honor is due: it is not by chance that Gregory of Tours, bishop of the city of Saint Martin, was particularly attentive to the miseries of his age. Without his *History of the Franks*, his *Miracles*, and his *Book of the Glory of Confessors*, the talent of Augustin Thierry would not have found such rich material for awakening the sympathies of the Romantic generation to the fate of the humble. The poems of Fortunatus were not so detailed. Bede's *Ecclesiastical History*, a prose narrative, does offer many useful observations as to conditions in the British Isles. Pope Gregory the Great, in his *Dialogues*, and Caesarius, bishop of Arles, offer useful and sometimes profound insights into the social realities of their day, thanks largely to their pastoral concerns. It is a pity for my purposes that the intellectualism of Isidore of Seville's *Etymologies* deprives us of much of what that bishop saw and understood of the social problems of Visigothic Spain. Saint Boniface has more to tell us about conditions in Germany. In every country decisions of the national councils relate to concrete issues. The frequency with which these decisions repeat themselves shows the persistence of the problems with which they deal. Royal decrees are often merely the reflection of such problems. The hagiographic sources are difficult to use but precious. Successive reworkings of these hagiographic texts attest to the importance that was attached to them. If many of the extant texts are the product of later editing (often in the eleventh century), the basic material (brought to light by critical methods developed in the eighteenth century by the Bollandists) sheds an interesting light on the character of the needy, different forms of distress, and charitable deeds attributed to the saintly heroes. By combining all these sources we can attempt to glimpse, if not the poor themselves, then at least their reflection.

In the Merovingian era, such pictures as we have of involuntary poverty are as varied as the causes and circumstances of misery. An inelegant but useful terminology distinguishes between "structural" and "conjunctural" poverty according as the primary cause of distress was institutional or circumstantial. Conjunctural poverty seems to have been particularly common during the so-called Dark Ages.

The most important of the circumstantial factors that engendered or aggravated the misery of the poor in the West, just as in the East, was the recurrence of plague. With its first onslaught in 542–44 the epidemic traveled up the Rhône, Saône, and Moselle valleys as far as Trèves, and in regions bordering the western Mediterranean persisted until the beginning of the seventh century. It is impossible to evaluate the moral and social effects of the plague, whose virulence in Tours and Marseilles is described by Gregory of Tours in terms that, oddly enough, might well have been applied to the epidemic of 1720. The rich and mighty were struck down along with the poor. In some areas, however, the poor, urged on by millenarian prophets (one of them a woodcutter who preached in the country around Bourges in the year 590) rose against the wealthy. Such riots were directed against speculators who took advantage of the famine. A more common popular reaction than these subversive uprisings was the ubiquitous recourse to pilgrimages and processions, the most prominent and widely renowned of which was presided over by Gregory the Great in 590. Every scourge and affliction was regarded as a trial leading to possible redemption or as a punishment, and suffering was always interpreted in terms of sin.

An out-of-the-ordinary but still quite frequent occurrence, plague was not as permanent a scourge as war. Gregory of Tours lavished much pity on the victims of the pillage and arson committed by the Frankish, Burgundian, and Gothic kings in the course of their endless wars. Prisoners of war received the attention of the Council of Orléans in 511. A few years later, Caesarius, while on a mission to Theodoric, discovered in Ravenna several thousand natives of Orange who had been deported there. To buy their freedom he gave away the gifts he had received from the Gothic king with such zeal that he was swindled by one unscrupulous dealer, who sold him the same prisoner twice. Prisoners appear to have been numerous in such widely separated places as Marseilles, Flanders, and the Atlantic coastal region, and bishops and abbots such as Eligius, Amand, and Philibert disbursed funds to purchase their freedom. The lot of prisoners of war was similar to that of refugees, whose numbers were also large in an age of violence. They sought safety in the customary right of asylum. Gregory of Tours cites a number of cases in which this privilege, granted to the churches by kings and reaffirmed by the councils, was violated.

The sick and disabled appear to have been numerous everywhere. Gregory of Tours, Fortunatus, and the hagiographies all refer to large numbers of the feeble-minded and lepers and to whole troops of the blind. Such observations suggest pausing a moment to consider the state of health of an underdeveloped society. What little we know about the physical condition of men of this era is not without significance. By analyzing skeletal remains, cemetery archaeology, a relatively new field of study, has turned up in Lorraine and more recently in Hungary evidence not only of violent death due to crime or war but also of atrophy, rickets, and vitamin deficiency (indicated chiefly by dental signs). Defects of this sort, whether congenital or not, may be related to dietary deficiencies and malnutrition. It is interesting to compare what has been observed recently in the Far East with the results of research into famine in the Carolingian era. The diet that had been handed down from ancient times was not well balanced, being almost totally lacking in vitamins A, D, E, K, and especially C. Since there was little knowledge of how food could be safely stored, people went from eating too much to eating too little, and this no doubt caused digestive problems, diabetes, deficiency diseases, and loss of teeth.

What did the poorest of the poor eat when not aided by public distribution of food? According to Gregory of Tours, their diet consisted of grape pips, hazel flowers, and fern roots, with an accompaniment (*companagium*) of common field grass. A hermit described by Bede refused to eat lard because it was a food unsuited to the condition of a pauper! Fear of hunger was no doubt more persistent than hunger itself. For the hungry, the distribution of balanced rations of bread and legumes, which could fill the stomach temporarily but which often led to morbid hunger, was ultimately not conducive to good health. Paradoxically, it was probably the forest dwellers—the hermits, charcoal burners, swineherds, and social marginals—who compensated for other dietary deficiencies by eating wild fruits and thus lived relatively long lives. Did the poor, then, enjoy the longest life expectancy? I would not presume to make such a suggestion. What was the age of those unfortunate *imbecilles ac decrepitati* who were given shelter at the abbey of Saint-Wandrille, or of those "good old grandfathers" (*non-onnes*) who were treated to the generosity of the church of Saint-Germain d'Auxerre?

Existence was in any case a struggle in which only the most robust could triumph. Although we have no idea what the birth rate was, we can guess from the high proportion of child remains in the cemeteries that the infant mortality rate was quite high. Abandonment of newborn infants was common. The hagiographies tell us of the survival of two orphans: Saint Vincentian, who was adopted by a duke, and Saint Odila, who was abandoned by her father because she was blind. Marble basins were placed in the churches of Tours and Angers to receive babies left by their parents. One of the *Formulae* of Tours tells the moving story of how, one morning at the hour of matins, the church-wardens upon opening the doors of the church of Saint-Martin discovered an infant wrapped in rags (*pannis involutum*), with blood on its lips and in danger of death. For three days they made inquiries in vain as to the child's parents and finally found a man willing to adopt it. A true-life story and a commonplace occurrence: here we have an example of a misfortune due to the prevailing attitudes and social structure.

Also counted among the feeble were widows, apparently in vast numbers. Often young and sometimes not without property, many of them had been married since childhood to elderly men. Subject to kidnapping and rape, some of these women were no doubt among the most pitiful of their sex. Bear in mind, too, that this was a time when marriage in the West, like marriage in the East, had not yet acquired the force of a durable bond: one wonders how many so-called widows were in fact abandoned wives. If a passage interpolated into the testament of Saint Rémi (Remigius) is to be believed, a group of forty widows gathered to beg alms below the porch of that saint's church.

Mendicancy, according to all the available sources, was widespread, and it is scarcely surprising that beggars were regarded as importunate and viewed with suspicion. Watchdogs, traditional defenders of property in hard times, were known to maul the poor, and a declaration by the council of Mâcon in 585 forbade bishops to surround themselves with dogs in order to keep paupers away. The importunity of the beggars must have been vexatious indeed if a Saint Caesarius used it as an excuse for refusing alms and as cause to charge one zealous beggar with a venial sin. It should come as no surprise that discretion on the part of the poor was regarded as cause for praise. Gregory the Great, for example, distinguished between paupers who begged in public and those who dared not beg: from a sum of 330 solidi he proposed giving 30 solidi to the public beggars and 150, five times as much, to their more modest brethren. Perhaps he was allowing for the possibility that the public beggars could supplement their share from other sources.

The indigent either stayed in one place, isolated, or joined together in bands and roamed the countryside. Those who stayed put lived in wretched huts, of which Saint Cuthbert's hermitage as described by Bede is typical: it was circular in form with a central living space and a double stone enclosure—a shepherd's hut (*pastorum tugurium*). What about furniture? The Toledo *Homiliary* states that the pauper has neither wood nor pot. Bede tells us that Kind Oswald, returning to England, had wood placed alongside fountains for the use of the poor who happened by. When the poor banded together, they were often referred to as forming "multitudes." In 536 in Clermont, according to Gregory of Tours, the poor assembled in a mob to demand for their service the priest Cato, who "was in the habit of feeding them." In Metz the poor attempted to prevent Saint Arnulf from retiring to a hermitage. Vagabonds at first roamed from city to city in search of distributions; in a later period they went from monastery to monastery. The Council of Tours (567) recommended that each city distribute sufficient food to keep beggars fixed in one place.

From scattered indications in the sources it can be determined that, along with the sick and disabled, the prisoners of war, and widows and orphans, the poorest of the poor were the rootless vagabonds who were driven from the land by scarcity, epidemic, and debt, by the weight of their burdens and the inadequacy of their harvests. Such vagabonds seem to have been easily recognizable. Bede, for example, tells the story of how one aristocrat, wounded and taken prisoner, sought to win his freedom by declaring that he was a *rusticus pauper*, but his manners, his language, and his whole bearing gave him away, so that instead of being liberated he was sold into slavery. By the seventh century the typical pauper is no longer a slave (slaves had by this point become scarce) but a free peasant of humble status, looked down upon by others. This change was reinforced over a wide area by the ruralization of society that had taken place over the preceding two centuries.

Rusticus pauper: these are the words used by Bede. Even earlier, in the sixth century, Gregory of Tours provides authority for the assertion that the terms "pauper" and "toiler in the fields" had become synonymous. *Quidam pauper, quidam homonculus ex ruricolis,* this pauper, this nothing of a peasant: in such terms does Gregory describe four poor men. One of them gets up early in the morning to cut wood in the forest in the manner of the country people (*sicut mos rusticorum*). The other three depend for their livelihood mainly on a team of oxen. This is the only possession of one of them (*nec ei alia possessio*); for the two others it is an indispensable tool of their trade, which chiefly involves the hauling of manure.

Caesarius, for his part, sometimes shortens his sermons so as not to cause men with urgent work to do to lose too much time.[2] When he discusses the poor, he does not speak solely of those without food, clothing, and shelter. As an orator Caesarius was quite precise. His homilies deplore the indebtedness of the peasantry and the implacable mechanism of confiscation to which it leads.[3] The harshness in tax collection of the municipal magistrates, or *curiales*, was nothing compared with the selfishness of wealthy creditors who forced debtors, their backs to the wall, to sell off their land. "If someone says to you, Sell me your lands, you are gripped by fear and you consider it a curse. . . . How could you buy if someone else were not forced to sell?"

Coercion and malediction were the lot of the poor. The worst of all, Caesarius goes on to say, is the hypocrisy of the buyer who in expanding his estate passes himself off as a protector and benefactor: he pays cash and provides a service. But the seller, uprooted from the land, falls into a situation of dependency, if he is lucky enough to remain a free man.

Here we encounter what I earlier called structural poverty, poverty that was a consequence of social and economic organization. The pauper was a peasant, legally a free man and in some cases still the owner of a small plot. Yet, by the Merovingian era, lack of food and clothing, debt, and insecurity forced such peasants to submit to, and even to seek out, a powerful patron:

> Since it is well known to all that I have nothing with which to feed or clothe myself, I have begged of your pity, and by your will you have granted unto me, permission to deliver myself unto you or to entrust myself to your protection. Which I have done under the following conditions: you must help me and sustain me with both food and clothing so long as I am able to serve you and deserve your benefaction. So long as I shall live, I shall owe you service and obedience compatible with liberty and shall have no right to remove myself from your power and your protection.[4]

There is no better illustration of the forces that drove paupers around the middle of the eighth century to place themselves, by perpetual contract, under the protection of a powerful patron to whom they promised service and loyalty. The relationship changed color: what had been an economic relation became a social one.

The rural pauper was considered not only socially but also morally inferior to his powerful patron. The pauper was the recipient, the patron the donor. The poor man belonged to that *populus minor* of which Gregory of Tours had spoken and which was known in later centuries as the *menue gent*, the little people, the equivalent of what Moslem peoples referred to as *meskin*, a term that was taken over by the French in the word *mesquin* (mean, shabby), from which was derived *mechiné*, a term denoting a woman obliged to enter service for lack of the means to earn a living. Manual labor, however necessary, was held in low esteem for three historical reasons: the traditional disdain of the ancients for servile tasks, Germanic esteem for the military life, and the Judeo-Christian predilection for the contemplative life. This contempt for manual labor forms one aspect of the tripartite conception of the social order, in which manual labor occupies the bottom position, as expiatory punishment for sin. The identity between worker, peasant, and pauper thus naturally established itself in the manorial society of the High Middle Ages. Moreover, this identity took on an unfavorable cultural connotation. The *laborator* was not only poor and a worker, he was also an uncultivated person, a *paganus* (from which the word peasant is derived) and illiterate who, living far from the cities, had not yet received the enlightenment of the Gospels (which was why he was called pagan). The *illit-*

eratus was an uncouth rustic, hardly less stupid than his animals. Isidore of Seville scarcely distinguishes between rurality (*rusticitas*) and rusticity (*rusticatio*).

When a saint, like Siran in the seventh century, wished to live as a pauper among the poor, what did he do, and how did his eleventh-century biographer characterize his acts and companions? Living as itinerant a life as other vagabonds, he earned his living by helping peasants with the grape harvest, hauling building supplies, or fishing, or he joined the mendicants and the sick at Saint-Sernin in Toulouse. He participated in rustic labors (*rusticana opera*) because he wanted to be a man of no importance, without roots (*homunculus infimis, incola, peregrinus*).

THE OPPRESSION OF THE CAROLINGIAN ERA

Historians customarily use the contrast between the terms *pauper* and *potens* to characterize the social dialectic of the Carolingian era, although the terms themselves antedate that period. That is why juridical sources (such as conciliar canons and capitularies) and canonical and theological works are so useful for studying the development of poverty in the ninth and tenth centuries. For the restoration of royal power and the revival of ecclesiastical thought that mark the Carolingian renaissance made kings and prelates more keenly aware than ever before of their common duty to protect the poor.

The terminology reveals two aspects of poverty. The Second Council of Aix-la-Chapelle (836) referred to "paupers and all indigents."[5] Paupers were free men, not necessarily without land but dominated by the owners of large estates. These landowners, who to one degree or another wielded some public authority as well as the material force of arms, were known as magnates (*potentes*). The humble folk, the dependents of the magnates, were described by the adjective *pauperes* (the meaning of which was then just beginning to change).

The indigents, on the other hand, were the unfortunate, a subset of the group of paupers consisting of those who had somehow fallen beneath their station. This changing population comprised the victims of the imbalance in the rural economy: land was less abundant, while demographic pressures in some areas had increased. The level of technology remained low. Some peasants lacked even a hand mill and had to make do with mortar and pestle. Land clearing was inadequate and yields were stationary. Dividing up estates did not eliminate the need for labor. Young men whose fathers' plots no longer supported them found that the fallow land of the estates on which they had been born did not provide adequate work to keep them alive; there was no room for them on plots made available by the decline of slavery.[6] By the ninth century, as internal wars and new invasions by Scandinavians, Hungarians, and Saracens further heightened insecurity and as the dissolution of public authority aggravated the disorder, bands of men began to roam the countryside. At this point the potentes increased their pressure in order to reassert their control over the humble and downtrodden.

The sources indicate that there were degrees of power and poverty, for they refer to the strongest men as *potentiores,* to the less strong as *minus potentes,* and to the poorest of the poor as *pauperiores.* The word *potentes* was similar in meaning to *honorati viri,* whereas *pauperes* was close to *impotentes personae, privati homines,* and *minor populus.* Freedom was associated with *paupertas (pauper = liber),* so that poverty and servitude were incompatible. In the cultural sphere, the notions subsumed in the adjectives *doctus* and *cautus* also established a division between the pauper and the magnate: the pauper, by nature a simpler individual, was *minus doctus* and *minus cautus.* Finally, a distinction was made between the pauper and the person enrolled as a soldier or sailor *(matricularius).* The only word clearly equated with *pauper* was the term *humble.* To sum up, then, the Carolingian pauper was a free man; he was not indigent, given that he possessed, and could bequeath, some property. He was subject to a variety of obligations and forms of dependency. It was probably in this period that men of low status acquired the right to a permanent stake in their plot, or *allod.* Hincmar distinguished between various types of paupers: besides free peasants possessing meager property *(substantiolas)* he saw coloni oppressed by estate agents, the disabled, and even a provost locked in conflict with a powerful layman.

From the legal dispositions found in conciliar canons and capitularies we gain information as to the ways in which the potentes oppressed the pauperes. To begin with, legal dependencies stemming from the right of command (the *bannum*) provided many occasions for abuse: for example, unduly frequent convocations to comital assizes (in 816), centenaries (in 855), and the army (after 802 and in 811); repeated invocations of the right of lodging (in 850 and 876); and excessive taxes (already levied in 768 under Pippin) that ignored real values (829, council of Paris). Fraud in regard to prices was coupled with fraudulent measurement (also attacked by the council of Paris). As dispensers of justice, the potentes and their officals could refuse to hear the pauperes or could postpone judgment by various delaying tactics.[7] The pauper was increasingly without recourse against a denial of justice or an unjust sentence. Some were "illegally deprived of their patrimony" or "forced to sell or mortgage their property," according to capitularies of 805, 811, and 847.

Abuses were compounded by the use of force, which sometimes took the place of law. In the middle of the ninth century, some "magnates who, with their horses and other animals had devastated the meadows of the pauperes, did not forbear, in the following winter, to demand fodder for their horses."[8] A colonus of the church of Rheims saw his harvest and livestock confiscated by agents from a neighboring estate, but no judge would acknowledge that his rights had been violated. Hincmar was virtually alone in his day in insisting that the burden of proof should lie with the party making an accusation. The result was that the poor, in despair of human justice, placed their hope in divine intervention. Saint Rémi worked miracles far from his city. Some peasants of the Nivernais sought refuge in a chapel under his protection. When one of the grandees chasing them tried to kick in the door, his foot was caught in the wood, while his companions fled. Seized with fear, the guilty man broke down in tears, promised a horse to the saint, and confessed his sins. His foot was freed but he remained a cripple. Gangrene spread through his body and he died, repentant but chastised.[9]

For many pauperes, the scarcity of their own resources combined with the abuses of the powerful to render their condition precarious. It was difficult even for the wealthy to store enough food to survive the winter, and with the coming of spring many of the impoverished began roaming the countryside in a famished condition; the bishops were alerted. Price hikes in times of scarcity left many of the unfortunate in the hands of usurers. The Council of Paris (829) left a striking description of the situation:

> When in time of famine a pauper made weak by lack of all things goes in search of a usurer . . . he commonly hears this response: "If you want to buy, pay the price and take what you need."
>
> To which the pauper replies: "I cannot afford to pay the price, but I beg you to have pity on me and in whatever way you choose to lend me the money that I am asking, so that I won't die of hunger."

The usurer answers: "I can only sell you a *modius* of my corn for so many deniers. Or else you will pay me so many deniers at the next harvest, or make up the remainder of the price in corn, wine, or other goods."[10]

It was not uncommon for the lender to demand, in exchange for a single *modius* lent under such conditions, three or even four modii at harvest time; the same was true for a modius of wine.

‡ Speculation of this kind on future harvests and the needs of the poor foreshadows the pressures that a monetary economy would bring to bear on peasants in centuries to come. Though many pauperes owned a small piece of property, few had cash reserves. Some of the capitularies provided for relaxation of military service obligations for their benefit. Groups of six men were allowed to form, five of whom would bear the cost of providing the sixth with the necessary equipment for military service. In 866, those who earned less than a third of a denier per day were excused from military service. A third of a denier was the amount that the monks of Corbie distributed daily to their paupers at the beginning of the ninth century. In the early tenth century, Regino, abbot of Prüm, estimated that one denier of penitential alms was enough to sustain three paupers for a day. Thus it is tempting to suppose that a third of a denier per day was the minimum necessary for survival in the ninth century.

It became increasingly difficult for pauperes to count on the protection of the *missi* who theoretically assumed responsibility for their safety. In 829 Louis the Pious complained of the "culpable indifference" of some of the missi. Whether by negligence or incapacity they failed to carry out their duty at a time when domestic tranquility was threatened by innumerable wars and their aftermaths. How, then, are we to interpret the fact that kings gradually came to impose upon all their subjects the obligation to place themselves under the protection of a potens? From the pauper's point of view, such a confession of impotence on the part of the king could be interpreted as an expression of indifference to their fate as easily as a measure intended to enhance their security. In reality, the king shifted his obligation to protect the weak to the magnates.

This was the case not only in the northern portion of Carolingian France but also, in almost identical fashion, in the Mediterranean region and the rest of what had been the western empire. Sources from the south of France ascribe no more spiritual or evangelical significance to the term *pauper* than do their northern counterparts; the word referred to peasants owning modest plots of land, oppressed by powerful neighbors eager to annex their property. The most unfortunate became beggars and vagabonds (*mendici discurrentes*). In Catalonia all the poor were free men, but freedom had many degrees and the condition of the poor varied widely. While a few peasant families with ample good land and hired labor managed to rise above the rest, the bulk of the peasantry was extremely poor. Most suffered the humiliation of dependency and lived a precarious life at the mercy of the harvest. The last recourse against poverty was to seek help from others. Potentes gave, pauperes received. The social and economic structures thus interacted. One family head received a grant of land in Catalonia from Charlemagne in 795; as a dependent of the king, he and his children were entitled to royal protection as *pauperes liberi homines*. His descendants enjoyed the same privilege until 963, when, in return for a life annuity, they ceded their property to the church of Narbonne, which assumed responsibility for their protection. Not to stand alone was as much a psychological as it was a social and economic necessity for anyone who wished to escape oppression and impotence. Similar examples abound in the cartularies of northern Spain.

The situation in Italy seems to have been more diverse. While northern Italy conformed fairly well to the pattern sketched above, central Italy was somewhat different. The *incastellamento* of the tenth and eleventh centuries did not merely bring together formerly marginal members of society under the aegis of a lord; the role of vagabonds was minor, and it has been maintained that those subject to *incastellamenti* were quite the opposite of a subproletariat of tramps and beggars.

In England prior to the Norman invasion, there was until the eleventh century a considerable number of small property owners dependent on powerful lords; by the eleventh century, however, these had begun to disappear as poverty made inroads. Division of property and taxes led to pauperization, of which Ordericus Vitalis gives a stark portrait in his *Anglo-Saxon Chronicles*.

Thus a new world developed, in which power had changed its nature and violence its form. The potentes had disappeared and were replaced by land-rich aristocrats, among whom figured the *milites*. The pauperes too had disappeared, either by falling below the line of indigence or by being integrated into new forms of social organization.

Was the potens simply the brutal, greedy exploiter of men so often denounced in repressive but not very effective legislation? While this may have been the general case, the life of Gerald, count of Aurillac, who died in 909, offers a rare example of a magnate canonized by popular demand. Gerald did not renounce his social position, as did Saint Siran. He continued to manage his family property, retained the attributes of his rank, and never worked with his hands. Concerned about the lot of the peasants, or paupers, he saw to it that when food was distributed at the gates of his residence no one was excluded, and he gave over one ninth of his income to alms. When he saw a woman working with a swing-plow, he gave her the money to hire a laborer. His justice was strict but scrupulous: after sentencing a group of brigands to have their eyes put out, he felt remorse upon learning that one of them was an innocent peasant. What is noteworthy in all this is that a magnate was canonized for the way he played his social role and in spite of his powerful position. By way of comparison, the first peasant saint was not canonized until the twelfth century. In order to explain the delay we must examine the way society and in particular the Church viewed poverty and the poor up to the eleventh century, along with the uses to which the teaching of the doctors was put.

CHAPTER THREE ‡ THE DUTY TO GIVE ALMS: FROM REGISTRATION OF THE POOR TO MONASTIC HOSPITALITY

The obligation to be charitable antedated the Church, which made charity a condition of salvation. Theologians asserted that the property of the Church constituted the "patrimony of the poor." Islam made charity into one of its five pillars and assigned to the poor a portion of the revenue from the so-called *habous*.[1] Continuity as well as adaptation to social circumstances is evident when we compare the charitable practices of Latin Christendom with those of late antiquity or Byzantium. One example of this is the shift from the diaconia to registration of the poor. Subsequently, the need to adapt to changing conditions governed the evolution of the system of poor registration and ultimately led to the system of monastic hospitality. The primary role in dispensing benevolence was transferred from laymen to the monasteries, which acquired a kind of monopoly.

THE BISHOP, FATHER OF THE POOR

The first two centuries in the history of medieval charity, before Benedictine influence began to make itself felt, might well be called the "age of the bishops." The reference to "ancient canons" closest to the Merovingian period is a decretal of Simplicius (468–483) probably drafted by his secretary, Gelasius, who himself served as pope from 492 until 496. Under Clovis the council of Orléans (511) took its inspiration from this decretal, which enjoined bishops to assign one quarter of their revenues to the needs of the poor. The council decided that in rural parishes one third of all charitable gifts should be assigned to the poor. These rules were introduced in the eighth century in the new dioceses established in Germania by Boniface. The claim of the poor upon the income of the Church was so firmly established that the words of Saint Ambrose—"murderer of the poor" (*necator pauperum*)—were repeatedly used in reprimands directed at those who despoiled church property by the councils[2] and by bishops like Saint Caesarius.[3] Bishops were personally responsible for showing mercy to the unfortunate and for exhorting clerics and laymen alike to display their charity. Frankish, Visigothic, and Italian councils dealt repeatedly with these subjects. Around the year 500 no fewer than forty-one councils and synods, eighteen of them in France, concerned themselves with the poor. The bishop was the "father of the poor," and the bishop's residence became synonymous with the poorhouse.[4] At his gate the poor received food and clothing, sometimes from his own hands. Some bishops, such as Saint Dizier (Desiderius) of Verdun, went into debt to meet the needs of the poor. Gregory of Tours tells of as many bishops who were benefactors of the poor as he recounts magnates who oppressed them. Caesarius welcomed paupers at his table and ate with them, though it is true that the scantiness of his meals was notorious. Bishops were required to distinguish between what was church property and what was their own. This was the rule clearly laid down by conciliar legislation, as for example at Toledo. It was of course a grave offense to put church property to private use. The estates of the Church were to be managed with a strict and discerning eye in order to protect the poor. The rule that one quarter of the income from church property should go to the poor did not apply to the bishop's personal property, but the bishop was required to set a good example by making generous bequests. Some left all that they owned to the poor.

Besides setting a good example, the bishop was required to teach charity toward the poor. In this respect two men excelled all others, Saint Gregory in Rome with his *Pastoral Care* and Saint Caesarius in Arles with his *Homilies*. The substance of their teaching was traditional, derived straight from the Gospels: Christ is found in the poor; we possess earthly goods only to administer them; all excess belongs to the poor; alms wipe away sin, but God cannot be corrupted by charity; it is the duty of all Christians to give alms.

Turning to the practical side of things, poor assistance was, at least in the early stages of the poor registration system, a communal institution in both cities and rural villages. It is now fairly clear that the system derived originally from an eastern institution transplanted to the West. The agent of the transfer, as well as of the transfer of monasticism, was John Cassian. During a stay in Marseilles some time between 420 and 430 he described in his *Conferences* the diaconias of Egypt, which distributed to the poor one tenth of what was harvested by landowners in the vicinity. This institution also operated in Africa and Rome during the same period, under the name *brevis*. By the sixth century *matricula* had become the preferred term. But the meaning of both words was the same, referring to a list naming those paupers who were maintained at church expense. Pope Leo the Great (440–461) states that the system was run by lay managers (*praesides*). In the East the Council of Chalcedon (451) indicated that the official in charge of a *ptochotropheion* was a cleric.

The diaconia served as a public food supply agency and replaced the Roman Annona, which had been in decline and finally disappeared in the Ostrogothic period. From the early fifth century the diaconia seems to have operated under the auspices of the *ecclesiae regionum*, which were instituted at the end of the preceding century and which occupied the same premises as the old Annona. Registration lists of the poor in Ravenna are known to have been kept between 522 and 532. In Rome, Gregory the Great had a register used for the same purpose updated and placed for safekeeping in the pontifical palace. It contained the names of men and women of all occupations, from Rome and its environs, who received monthly distributions of wheat, wine, lard, fish, oil, vegetables, and cheese.

As for Gaul, it is known that the poor were registered before 470 in Rheims and around 520 in Laon. Gregory of Tours is quite familiar with the registration lists. He alludes to the list for Clermont for 556 and explicitly mentions one for his own city in 585. In the sixth century lists were kept in all major cities. In Metz in the middle of the seventh century the lists of the churches of the city and neighboring towns contained the names of 726 paupers.

The number of *matricularii* (from which derives the French word *marguilliers*, or churchwardens) was actually set at a fixed level and obviously did not correspond to the total number of indigents, which of course varied. During the Merovingian era the number ranged from a few to several dozen, depending on the church. The number twelve, symbolic of the apostles, was customary only in monastic registers of the Carolingian era, by which time charity had acquired a liturgical significance. The social function of charity predominated in earlier times, as can be seen from the identity of those who became church-wardens: a few women, mostly widows, but chiefly men, some disabled or ill, others able-bodied but empty-handed or victims of war, famine, or plague. These select few were chosen by the clerics of the church keeping the poor list. It is almost impossible to know the ratio between the number of churchwardens and the total number of paupers. It is certain, however, that the churchwardens represented only a small proportion of the total, a privileged few owing to the benefits that came with their position. It is not unreasonable to view them as prebendals in the modern sense.

The churchwardens, in exchange for their assistance in religious services and for their help in maintaining order in the sanctuary and protecting the right of asylum, were allowed to solicit outside the church. They enjoyed special protection and unparalleled security and were fed, clothed, and sheltered in the poorhouse (*mansio pauperum*) adjoining the church or (in episcopal cities) in the bishop's residence.

Increasingly, no distinction was made between the poor list and the residents of the poorhouse, which came to be regarded as a kind of hospital. The words *matricula*[5] and *xenodocheion* (imported from the East) were used interchangeably from the seventh century on to denote the same reality. Poor lists seem increasingly to have been associated with rural monasteries. Poverty moved from the declining cities into the countryside, and charitable services tended to move with it from the episcopal cities to the rural abbeys. In the monasteries, hostels were open to all comers, especially pilgrims, and these hostels assumed responsibility for the distributions of goods formerly associated with the poor lists.

The monasteries were too wealthy not to have suffered from the secularization of church property in the eighth century. Some of the most important and famous of the abbeys, like that of Saint Martin at Tours, became the property of laymen. Elsewhere, even when the transfer of ecclesiastical property was less scandalous in nature, the result was to transform the position of churchwarden into a sinecure granted as a kind of annuity not to a disabled or aged pauper but to a man in the prime of life and fit for work. In the eighth century, Saint Rigobert of Rheims and Saint Chrodegang of Metz attempted to revive the poor list on the model of the Roman diaconia, at that time still a living tradition. The Council of Aix in 816 reminded churchwardens of their duties and in particular of their obligation to be present on the church premises: it seems that some churchwardens behaved like rentiers. Some fifty years later Hincmar protested against the same abuses and attempted to revive the poor list in Rheims. The churchwarden had become a servant, almost an official, of the Church that maintained him. Poverty was elsewhere, and so were the real paupers. The poor were received in hospitals and religious sanctuaries. Many of these were founded at the instigation of bishops. Built near the bishop's or canons' residence, the descendants of these institutions are still found today near the old cathedrals: for example, the modern religious hospitals of Paris, Rheims, Laon, and Soissons. Others were founded by lay people such as the sanctuary of Saint Christopher established in Paris in 690 in a house donated by the mayor of the palace in Archambaud. Queen Brunhild was congratulated by Gregory the Great for her foundation of a *xenodocheion* in Autun. The old hospitals of Lyons owe their inception to the bishop as well as to the chapters of Saint-Jean, Saint-Paul, and Saint-Just. The list could be extended indefinitely and would pertain chiefly to the cities. But outside the walls, on the busiest roads, usually in the countryside and serving a rural clientele, the monastic hostels played an increasingly important role in the ninth century: other times, other paupers, other forms of charity.

CHARITY, A LINK BETWEEN HEAVEN AND EARTH

Between the irreversible decline of the poor list and the rise of the monastic hospices, the men of the ninth century cast about in search of some kind of equilibrium. This proved difficult to find, because the brutal reality of poverty and greed contradicted the ideal of the Sermon on the Mount. The ecclesiastic advisors of Louis the Pious dreamed of striking a balance "between Heaven and Earth."[6] A significant relationship was established during Louis's reign between decisions pertaining to the *pauperes*, which were promulgated by the councils (and especially by the 829 Council of Paris), and the reforms introduced in the Benedictine monasteries by Benedict of Aniane and Adalard of Corbie. An educational movement—preserved for us in a manual written by a woman named Dhuoda, said to be a great lady—sought to bring about the edification of a City of God in which the poor would have a place, protected by the ramparts of the Law.

The Carolingian renaissance involved nothing less than a search for the true roots of the moral order. In addition to documents whose authenticity has rightly been criticized, such as the False Decretals, the imposing volume of pastoral texts gives an indication of the amount of attention that was lavished on social conditions.

‡ The influence of Julianus Pomerius powerfully reasserted itself. In the eighth century Boniface, Chrodegang of Metz, and Paulinus of Aquileia all made use of his *De vita contemplativa*. In the first half of the ninth century various councils based measures for the defense of *pauperes* against the encroachments of the powerful upon a truncated version of his doctrine. Pomerius, not content merely to assert that church property serves two purposes, to maintain not only the clergy but also the poor, insisted that the clergy use the wealth of the Church

with moderation and manage it wisely so as not to injure the interests of the poor. The men of the ninth century did not fully appreciate the spiritual, social, and economic consequences of such thinking. Though opposed to the confiscation of land by the powerful, the most religious men of that era did not perceive the consequences of the resulting monopolization of society's resources. On the contrary, some of the finest clerical minds saw an advantage for the poor in the extension of resources intended for their benefit. In mid-century, Raoul, the bishop of Bourges, insisted simply that social relations should be imbued with charity and that the powerful should refrain from abusing their power over the poor: "Do not condemn them on some unjust pretext, do not oppress them, do not deprive them unjustly of their small belongings [substantiolas], and do not cruelly and pitilessly demand your due."[7] To which Raoul dared to add the following: "Know that [the poor] are your brothers and that they share the same Father to whom they say, 'Our Father, who art in Heaven,' and the same Mother, the Holy Church, which has given birth to them in the same sacred fount [baptism]."[8]

Raoul of Bourges may have expressed himself more plainly than some of his colleagues, but men like Theodulf and Jonas of Orléans shared his cast of mind. Their teaching was moral, if not moralistic. Jonas of Orléans does not appear to have been much concerned with the evangelical aspect of poverty. Provided that the rich man uses his property wisely and does not steal from his neighbor or the Church, he has fulfilled his moral duty. In De institutione regia Jonas is referring to the prince when he says that "it is part of his justice to rise in defense of the widow, the orphan, and the foreigner . . . [and] to nourish the poor with his alms." Hincmar of Rheims gave voice to the same thought when he said that one of the duties of the king is "to hear the plea of the poor and the weak against the abuses of which they are victims."

Thus the myth of the good king took shape: the good king was an equitable judge and protector of the poor and generously rewarded those who served him, while the tyrant lacked precisely these qualities. Anyone who wielded power was judged against the duties of his office or by comparison with idealized or sanctified representatives of his estate. Centuries of hagiography and folk tales contributed to this idealization of the good king, to whom the poor looked for peace and justice.

Better than anyone else, Hincmar of Rheims gave clear and voluminous expression to the ideal of a society in which moral and social equilibrium would coincide. During a conversation at Senlis in 869 or 870, Charles the Bald is supposed to have asked Hincmar to make a collection of texts pertaining to works of charity. In a letter addressed to Louis the German in 858, the archbishop had already taken the opportunity to set forth a social program in which hospitality for the poor played an important part. He had, according to Jean Devisse, previously annotated numbers of manuscripts, including in particular Salvian's writings on alms. Hincmar subscribed to the classical doctrine that the giving of alms has redemptive value and that avarice was to be vigorously condemned. He maintained that the poor were entitled to one quarter of the income from tithes and that the patrimony of the Church belonged to them. For Hincmar poverty meant not just insufficient income but encompassed any weakness, dependency, or want engendered or exploited by injustice and depredation. The proper remedy for injustice was charity. The pauper could choose one of three courses: he might choose servitude to avoid starvation, join with other free men in order to survive, or accept dependence on a powerful patron without giving up his freedom. The last case, typified by one Juan, a "Catalan" who lived in the eighth century, might be an example of a member of the group of *milites* acceding to the warrior aristocracy, thereby gaining both power and social consideration. In any event, Hincmar saw no more possibility of a change in the social order than did any of his contemporaries. He might well have subscribed to the following statement from the *Life of Saint Eligius:* "God could have made all men rich, but he wanted poor men in this world so that the rich might have an opportunity to redeem their sins."[9]

‡ The idea of benevolence seems to have been self-contradictory. On the one hand, the income and property of the Church, together with the charitable contributions of the faithful, were to be used to correct rather than eliminate social inequalities. The purpose of almsgiving was to insure the stability of the social order, that is, peace. On the other hand, Hincmar, an inventive thinker who based his ethics on intentions, points out that almsgiving has no spiritual value without charity.

Aging and discouraged by the upheavals of the late ninth century, which were especially hard on the poor, Hincmar was the last man of his day to hope that peace and justice could be achieved simultaneously. In the following century, however, his influence was revived in certain quarters, particularly among the imperial bishops. One figure particularly reminiscent of Hincmar was Ratherius, a native of Liège who served as bishop of Verona from 931 to 968. Though not really an original thinker, Ratherius once again spelled out the well-known categories of the poor during a time of particular hardship. For him, however, prisoners of war, pilgrims, and ruined nobles occupied a special place. He condemned mendicity as laziness and praised gifts of charity as the means of reestablishing the order willed by God. His citations from the New Testament are interesting: along with Luke and Matthew, John and especially Paul are frequently cited. In other words, charity was the essential ingredient for Ratherius as it had been for Hincmar. Thus distinct points of view were made to coincide: the insistence upon charity and the "economy of the gift" converged to "subsume in a common poverty the vast indigence" of a very harsh century, in which the strong were supposed to sustain the weak and the weak were supposed to serve the strong.

MONASTIC HOSPITALITY   There is a strong element of utopian thinking in the idea of a "society between Heaven and Earth." Hincmar saw matters clearly, however, when he reminded one of his suffragans, the bishop of Beauvais, of what he, Hincmar, regarded as one of the primary duties of a bishop: "To receive the poor or other guests in hospitals kept open for the purpose and staffed with the necessary personnel." He also believed that these hospitals must take the place of the poor lists, which had fallen into desuetude. But already the rural monasteries were better prepared to assume this role than were the slumbering episcopal cities.

Poverty in a spiritual sense is a component of asceticism in every religion: think of Hinduism, Islam, the Jewish ascetics of the Old Testament, and their Christian successors in the desert and the Celtic hermitages. The latter three traditions made their influence felt in the medieval West. Transmitted through a number of saints—Anthony, Pachomius, Basil, and Cassian, and, later, Colomban and Fructuosus—all of these traditions required the individual to renounce all personal property, to work, and to accept austerity in eating, clothing, and shelter. The monk who voluntarily became a pauper of Christ was drawn to the involuntary paupers (*pauperes inviti*) and gave them what he could. Because the disciples of Benedict of Nursia possessed large amounts of land in common, their poverty was a matter of controversy. Whether or not the Rule of Saint Benedict explicitly requires the monks to practice poverty has no bearing on the fact that, in the early days of the Benedictine Order, individual poverty was regarded as one means of ascetic self-denial. The disciple of Saint Benedict of course did not live in utter destitution, like an indigent. Monastic poverty was not a fiscal category but a means of asceticism, not a virtue in itself but a means of acquiring virtue. Thus the monk's predisposition to show understanding to the poor was reinforced by the rule and by custom and given the means to express itself in effective action. The Rule of the Master (circa 500–25), from which the Rule of Saint Benedict was derived, and the Regula Mixta both attempted to organize relations between the monks and the poor. Smaragdus of Verdun, Saint Benedict of Aniane (circa 816), Adalard of Corbie (circa 822), and Wala of Bobbio (circa 834–36), as well as the customaries kept by all the leading monasteries, all spelled out the traditions of Benedictine charity.

Saint Benedict of course attached great importance to hospitality. The pauper was a prime object of that hospitality, because the honor to be bestowed upon him (*congruus honor*) corresponded to the rank of the person of whom the pauper was the representative, namely, Christ. The reception of guests generally, and of paupers in particular, involved a specific liturgical ritual. Smaragdus's *Commentary on the Rule of Saint Benedict* classifies the works of mercy in much the same manner as subsequent generations. The poor must be comforted (*pauperes recreare*) with an open heart (*libente animo*) and even with gaiety (*cum hilaritate*) as well as generosity (*cum largitate*). A choice place was to be set aside for small children (*infantes*, under twelve years of age) and old people, who were divided into two revealing categories, the physically aged and the mentally senile, not to mention the mental defectives (*stulti*). Smaragdus was in some respects innovative. It was a break in monastic tradition—a new direction that some did not follow—for monks to extend hospitality to the disabled and to go out in search of paupers lest they sleep outside the monastery. Normally monks waited for the poor to come to them. On the other hand, Smaragdus is somewhat backward, although quite in keeping with the customs of his age, in interpreting the *congruus honor* as determined by the guest's rank in society: the powerful lord was to receive his respectful due (*obsequium*), whereas the pauper was to be greeted with friendly familiarity (*affectus*).

Benedictine benevolence was available to anyone for the asking.

Those who came to the gates of a monastery, we may imagine, felt that they were approaching the frontier between a world of penury and an island of abundance. They were also leaving a world of violence and entering a peaceful asylum, symbolized by the word *pax* inscribed in the pediment of the porch. Between life in the cloister and the work of charity there was no discordance. The liturgy of welcome began at the entry gate. It was there that various goods were handed out to the poor, and from there that guests were admitted to the monastery's hostel and even to certain aspects of the conventional life. Up to the ninth century the *porta* was the central service, the focus of hospitality and benevolence. Delegated by the abbot, first the cellarer and then the porter (*portarius*) took charge of the ritual. This job required the ability to mingle, and Benedict of Aniane therefore recommended that it be entrusted to a wise and elderly monk. We can gain a general idea of how the *porta* operated from his legislation of Aix-la-Chapelle, from Adalard in the statutes of Corbie, and from Wala's *Breve memorationis*. In the plan of the monastery of Saint Gall, the gatehouse appears in the entry vestibule, near the hostels and away from the buildings of the cloister itself. When there was more than one gate, the gatehouse was of course situated at the main entrance. The importance of the *portarius* depended on the number and diversity of his clients and on the amount of resources available relative to the total number of clients. At Corbie the porter was assisted by ten prebendals (*provendarii*).

One of the porter's jobs was to categorize those who came asking for shelter: prelates, canons, clerks, monks, traveling laymen, beggars and vagabonds, the sick and disabled. The Rule of the Master betrays some mistrust of gyrovagues and of lazy, disorderly vagabonds. Saint Benedict seems to have been more generous, but his recommendations for hospitality are not without subtleties: A person of rank knocks at the door, a pauper calls to be admitted. The porter may answer either with satisfaction (*Deo gratias*) or with a word of benediction (*Benedic*). The liturgy is then begun. Basically the same hospitality is offered to all comers, but with some differences depending on the status of the host: the feet are washed (*mandatum*), food is given, and shelter is offered. Concerning the period in question, some doubts remain as to the treatment of paupers. It may be that the *mandatum* of the poor was for reasons of hygiene already conducted daily. The poor were fed and sheltered in the *hospitale pauperum*, a building separate from the hostel where the wealthy were lodged. Those who were ill were treated by the porter himself and might be admitted to the monastery's infirmary. Those who took to the road again were provided with food.

The essential part of the ritual was the daily distribution made to all new arrivals (*pauperibus supervenientibus*). The ration at Corbie consisted of bread, beer, sometimes wine, vegetables, cheeses, lard, and sometimes meat. Shoes and clothing worn by the monks were also handed out, along with covers, wood for heating and cooking, and household utensils. From the ninth century on, gifts of cash were also made in some cases.

To meet the needs of so many guests, rich and poor, considerable resources were necessary. The porter accordingly had control of one tenth of all monastery revenues, including alms and gifts of all kinds, sometimes given in the form of cash but more often in kind (grain, wine, livestock, and so on). For obvious reasons, the rules drafted by Benedict of Aniane laid particular stress on the tithe for the poor. It is easy to imagine the gravity of the situation when lay lords confiscated the income from the tithe, and it is likewise easy to see the importance of the subsequent restoration of the tithe in the Gregorian era.

The extent of the porter's responsibilities and probably, too, the growing number of clients led in the second half of the tenth century to the replacement of this single position by two new ones. The *custos hospitum* had charge of accommodations for the wealthy, and the *eleemosynarius* (or almoner) was responsible for the poor. Distinct resources were assigned to each. The traditional tithe of the poor went to the almoner. For the maintenance of guests, a second tithe, known as *none*, was levied on the properties of the monastery in keeping with the Mosaic precept that one should give more than the Law requires. From this time forward, the importance of the position of almoner increased steadily. We can follow this development by referring to the customaries of the principal abbeys and their subsidiaries. Almost everywhere it led to the creation of a special office, the almonry (*eleemosynaria*). After the middle of the eleventh century we witness an increase in the number of almonries, which corresponds to a rise in the level of poverty.

From the customaries we know in detail the fundamentally liturgical character and the rhythm of Benedictine benevolence. The liturgy of the poor had both a temporal and a spiritual rhythm and consisted of both simple, everyday rites and more elaborate festive ceremonies. The number of people involved varied from a few to a vast multitude; some were permanent beneficiaries of monastic charity, others temporary. Care was taken of the body as well as the spirit. Some were maintained on permanent allotments of food and clothing, but most received temporary distributions. Benevolence took many forms. Some paupers were granted the permanent hospitality of the monastery. Meals were offered daily to a symbolic number of the poor: three at Saint Dunstan and La Trinité of Vendôme, twelve at Saint-Bénigne in Dijon, eighteen prebendals and seventy-two invited guests at Cluny. Weekly visits were made to the homes of the ailing poor (at Cluny and in England and Anjou, for example). Last but not least, the *mandatum* was celebrated daily in some abbeys, less frequently in others, but always with particular solemnity on Holy Thursday. The customaries allow us to imagine the serene gravity of the ritual, with its two contrasting cortèges.[10] The poor, selected by the almoner, were preceded and supported by monks. A monk came and stood in front of each pauper. Upon a signal from the abbot, all "bowed down, bent the knee, and adored Christ in His poor." Each monk then washed, dried, and kissed the feet of the pauper in front of him. Finally, the poor received the blessing and were given something to drink and a few deniers. A rite of purification preceded the ceremony, of course. The mass for the poor was celebrated earlier in the morning, and the feet of the poor received a preliminary washing in hot water intended to make them clean (*ut mundi sint*). The paupers were also fed to restore their strength. On important holidays such as Christmas, Easter, Pentecost, and All Saints', great quantities of wine and meat were handed out. Cluny distributed shoes at Christmas and clothing at Easter. Thus at regular intervals throughout the year charitable works were carried out by monks acting as proxies for their abbey's founder and benefactor. But to forget the fundamental connection between the alms of the convent, which like its wealth was a collective good, and the individual fasting of each monk, which was as personal a matter as the decision to abandon the world, would be to misunderstand the specific character of Benedictine charity. Each time a monk deprived himself of part of his ration, the remains were collected by the almoner and put aside for the poor.

‡ What can we say about the paupers themselves? The customaries tell us something about the poor in places like Cluny and Fleury-sur-Loire. Leaving to the *custos hospitii* and his assistant, the *stabularius*, responsibility for those who arrived at the monastery on horseback with their entourage, the almoner took charge of those who "came on foot."

He "restored" their strength and gave them something to take on their journey: the ration was a *livre* of bread per day and a measure (*justicia*) of wine as long as the guest remained in the hostel and half that amount for the journey. The clients of the almoner included the prebendals, who received a daily allowance which was increased on holidays; the ill, who were visited once a week; and finally, the rest of the poor—the children, widows, and aged, the blind and crippled, and all who were driven by poverty or disaster to seek help—in short, all the simple folk, or *minuti*, as the customary of Eynsham near Oxford calls them.

Only a constant outpouring of fresh spiritual energy could have prevented the liturgy of charity from hardening into formalistic ritual. The institutionalization of charity was made necessary by the urgency of the need. At Saint-Bertin in Saint-Omer, the function whose moral significance was summed up in the phrase *ministerium eleemosyne* became, from the eleventh century, an *officium* and acquired an administrative character, with stable revenues and prescribed attributions. It was thought that experience of real life outside the monastery might counter the tendency toward formalism. For example, the customary of Fleury-sur-Loire (circa 1020–30) specified that "hospitality be entrusted to a religious instructed in the spiritual customs . . . who, if possible, was not brought up in this place but [who is] rather a lay brother, delivered from the hazards of secular life and who, like an experienced navigator, has been able to skirt the cyclone of the world and cast anchor in the calm of a monastery; accordingly, he will feel more compassion and human sympathy for the poor and the pilgrims."[11]

‡A little flesh and blood is added to this idealized portrait by the following description, from the late eleventh century, of the almoner of the abbey of Saint Chaffre du Monestier in Velay, in the mountains of central France. The cartulary of this monastery describes the man in question thus:

> This office [i.e., that of almoner] has for the past thirty years been filled in service of the poor by a most religious man. . . . Before he assumed this post, the care of the poor and of pilgrims here seemed a relatively unimportant task, because there was no one to dispense succor to the poor and no succor to dispense, nor was there any place to receive those who came. After receiving the

order from his abbot, he set about distributing to the poor, with an open heart, what little he could find . . . and he restored and enlarged the house set aside for paupers and pilgrims. . . . From then on it often came to pass that a multitude of paupers, pilgrims, and people of all sorts without the strength to carry on came to this house from all over, and were given what they needed.

The text goes on to enumerate the resources assigned to the almonry and then adds this: "All of this the brother sought to collect on fixed terms to serve the almonry and not for other purposes, as sometimes happens in other cases. And he spent this money for the needs of this hospice for the poor, without prodigality or avarice, but with prudence, always considering the next day."[12]

THE DREAM OF PEACE The institutionalization of alms in the monasteries was symptomatic of changes that began to affect the condition of the poor in the latter part of the tenth century. The word *pauperes* continued to denote those who were indigent and/or in need of protection; it also applied to the *pauperes Christi,* those who chose destitution voluntarily for religious reasons. But as the numbers of people covered by the term increased dramatically, *pauper* took on new connotations.

The number of those receiving charity from the monasteries rose and fell with the cycles of climatic disasters, scarcity, and epidemic. Raoul Glaber hardly exaggerated the severity of the famine that struck Burgundy in 1032–33. William of Volpiano was frightened by what he saw there upon his return from Italy and admonished the monks of Saint-Bénigne of Dijon for their indolence in the face of misery. "What has become of charity?" he exclaimed. The reserves of the abbey must be distributed to the poor in order to relieve their suffering. The case was not unique. Raoul Glaber wrote that for the sake of the poor the churches must be stripped of their ornaments. In Rheims Abbot Richard was obliged to sell precious liturgical objects belonging to his monastery. Hoarding of such treasures (justified in this instance by the desire to exalt the glory of God) is of course a form of saving characteristic of a backward economy.

‡ The difficulties that the almoner faced in carrying out his duties are not difficult to imagine. This was a time when everyone was hungry.

When the archbishop of Trèves tried to hand out coins to the poor, he found that the price of food had risen so high that his gesture was met with scorn: "What good are your farthings to us?" the crowd protested. The archbishop had to sacrifice his own horses instead—a painful sacrifice indeed for a feudal magnate! They were quickly devoured by the famished mob.

More profound changes were also under way. The population was just beginning to grow again; plots of land were being subdivided and the number of young people was growing, signs of an impending imbalance between available arable land and the size of the labor force. Monastic estates, increased in size by donations, required many hands to work them. The use of the precarium, coupled with loans and aid from the monasteries, enabled some peasants to survive. Work at harvest time on church-owned land provided some with temporary employment or with a chance to earn additional income. Others lived permanently as farmers or artisans in the *familia* of some abbey: in 1075 the cartulary of La Trinité of Vendôme alludes to the "troop of servants" (*turba famulorum*). Before long, monks and peasants would set forth together, determined to bring virgin land under the plow.

‡ The nature of the protection required by the poor thus underwent a change. By the year 980 the oppressive dependency of the poor had been aggravated by the dispersal of what had been royal prerogatives (the so-called *regalia*) among a host of powerful lords. No longer was the principal division expressed by the opposition of *pauper* and *potens:* the new antagonism was between *pauper* and *miles*. The consequences of the change were twofold. In the first place, there arose a division between those who were armed and those who were not (*inermes*). The latter group included more than just the peasants: also without weapons and therefore weak were women, clerics, and, already by the eleventh century, a few merchants. Second, in countries like France, where royal authority reached a nadir around the year 1000, the bishops, determined to counter the excesses of the *milites*, took upon themselves what had been the royal mission to "restore the peace," a mission that the kings themselves had increasingly abandoned since the ninth century but that had never been forgotten.

Thus from the end of the tenth century we witness the emergence of a new aspect of the helplessness of the poor against armed might. New ways of protecting the weak were proposed with the so-called Peace of God and Truce of God. And the poor themselves made their voices heard in deciding what initiatives were to be taken in order to restore order. In 989 the Council of Charroux condemned "those who rob peasants or *other* paupers" and defined paupers as *agricultores* and serfs (*pauperes, id est agricultores*). The program for the restoration of peace proposed by the bishops who assembled in Poitiers in 1011–14 called for the defense not only of ecclesiastical institutions but also of the *inermes*, those who did not bear arms. Some time later, at Beauvais in 1023–25, a peace oath extended to the inermes the protection demanded for the poor. Thus the bishops and monks made common cause with the poor. Bishop Jordan of Limoges excommunicated milites responsible for unjustified acts of violence, and in 1038 his counterpart in Bourges, Aymo of Bourbon, led a "multitude of unarmed commoners" (*multitudio inermis vulgi*) against those who violated an oath to keep the peace. Was this insurrection one episode in a sporadic series of popular uprisings? If so, it may be worth recalling the existence of a conspiracy of serfs that came to light in 821 in the coastal regions of Flanders, as well as the existence of peasant guilds based on sworn oaths, which are denounced in a capitulary from western Francia dating from 884. Still later, at the end of the tenth century, Norman peasants rebelled during the reign of Richard II. But were these various popular movements connected with one another? And did the rebels share any sort of collective consciousness beyond a sense of outrage against the oppression of the moment?

Social tension was not the only form in which unrest manifested itself; anxieties were common to all strata of society and the exclusive province of none. People generally felt a need for moral purification. Such feelings manifested themselves in the towns (as at Arras in 1025) and the countryside (Champagne in 1030), as well as among monks and hermits almost everywhere, but especially in Italy with men like Romuald and Peter Damian, and in the East. The Gregorian reform, the popular Patarine movement in Milan, the eremitical movement, and the first Crusade created an atmosphere that enveloped rich and poor, laymen and clerics, voluntary and involuntary paupers alike. The times had changed: the pauper, still an object of scorn and neglect, was no longer quite as anonymous as he had been. Though he had yet to make his entry on stage as an actor, he was nevertheless the subject of much discussion.

PART TWO ‡ HUMBLE CHRISTIANS (LATE ELEVENTH TO EARLY THIRTEENTH CENTURY) ‡

‡Between the time of Peter the Hermit and that of Francis of Assisi, not only did the social position of the poor change considerably, but so did people's ideas about poverty and attitudes toward its victims. During this period of some 130 years, it is true that the meaning of the words *pauper* and *poverty* remained essentially spiritual. It is also true that we have no way of estimating the number of the unfortunate and can say only that it seems to have been large, at least at moments when natural disasters upset the precarious balance between the size of the harvest and the size of the population. Other factors came into play, however. Among the most important were population growth, the extension of the cash economy into the countryside, the weakening of the patriarchal family, the relaxation of hierarchical structures to permit peer associations, and the growth of the cities. Some men found that there was no longer a place for them in a rural society that had previously absorbed all hands without difficulty. Premonitory signs of the new era that historians now agree began in the 1180s can be detected as much as a hundred years earlier; the social and religious issues that came to the fore around the year 1200, and that exerted such tremendous influence on the fate of the poor, had in fact been brewing for more than a century. And much of the fermentation, it seems fair to say, was due to social and economic forces. People of course behaved in an infinite variety of ways. To men of wealth and power it seemed, particularly at the end of the twelfth century, that the temporal order was threatened. And even the most hardened of men feared that violence visited upon the poor might compromise their already doubtful salvation. In addition, the poor themselves began to act in ways which, if not exactly novel after the peace movements of the eleventh century, were in some respects rather worrisome. Without the escape valve provided by the First Crusade, the West might have experienced as early as the end of the eleventh century troubles similar to those that arose in the period 1180–1200. On the fringes of rural society, which remained stable, and even on the outskirts of the cities, which with their newfound vitality were more than hospitable to newcomers, groups of marginals and rebels lived beyond the pale and outside the faith.

The chronology of events reveals three phases in what was most assuredly a dramatic series of developments. The drama was played out against a background of sporadic scarcity and famine: the darkest times came at the end of the eleventh century and then again in 1125, 1144, 1161, and 1191–97. First came the roving bands of social outcasts, followed by the hordes that Peter the Hermit led off to the East: those racked by hunger were joined by others left to fend for themselves or unable to get on in society. These were people who had suffered a loss of social status. The problem was to get them back on their feet and reintegrate them into society. Much later was the coincidence, accidental or otherwise, of revolts in London and in central and southern France, together with the heretical movements of the Waldensians and Lombards. In one way or another these movements were composed of social rejects that the authorities felt compelled to suppress. The ruckus they raised was so great that it all but obscured the continuing obligation to aid the rest of the unfortunate, who remained as usual in their modest place.

Rehabilitation, repression, aid: the issues were thorny and full of contradictions. Various proposals for dealing with them were canvassed throughout the century, some disturbingly bold and innovative, others reassuringly traditional. Charity worked hard to keep up with proliferating injustice. Complacent cynicism and deliberate violence were countered by nothing less than a spirit of evangelical revivalism. Intellectuals enmeshed in theology and canon law could hardly ignore issues as fundamental to their concerns as poverty and charity. Around 1230, culminating a century-long development, a few theologians and canonists set forth the rights of the poor, animated by a spirit of justice warmed by the heat of charity. But this was a timid proposal compared with what was yet to come. And who was listening? Francis of Assisi had just died—he at least had caused a stir. Our examination of the twelfth century must be extended by a few years to take in his challenge to money, violence, and pride.

THE ASSAULTS OF MISERY

We do not lack for sources of information about the scope, persistence, and variety of poverty in the twelfth century. To be sure, quantitative data are hard to come by. But from the abundant records of cartularies, chronicles, hagiographies, correspondence, works of literature and iconography we can form a picture of what the typical pauper looked like, though few of the sources depict him directly.

When, some seventy-five years ago, Franz Curschmann compiled an anthology on famine, no lengthy commentary was needed: the misery of the twelfth century spoke for itself. Subsequent research has done nothing to contradict the picture he presented.

The Council of Clermont, which ended with the call to the Crusade, was held in 1095 in the midst of a period of severe economic distress. The chroniclers attribute to Pope Urban II arguments in favor of the Crusade that surely were not pure figments of their imagination: the population, they tell us, had increased to the point where "the land barely feeds those who cultivate it"; in the East lay treasures to alleviate the misery of the poor; and, finally, a Crusade would provide an opportunity for redemption and a diversion for the warlike pride of "oppressors of children, despoilers of widows, and trespassers on the rights of other men." Even though these words echo the sentiments of the earlier peace movements, it was not anachronistic to utter them in November of 1095. The harvest that year had generally been poor. In England, in Anjou, in northern and southern France, in Artois, and in the countryside around Tournai, Gembloux, and Liège (in present-day Belgium), monasteries found themselves unable to play their customary role as granaries for the poor. Anjou suffered a drought from March to September, followed by famine and disease. The catastrophe was not limited to Anjou alone. The most revealing incident took place in Tournai. The harvest had been so poor that the abbey lands and tithes yielded only a two months' supply of bread; the scarcity of food forced the monastery to make outside purchases. But the abbot, determined to preserve the serenity of the cloister from the anxieties of famine, continued to distribute food as usual to all the poor who asked for it, until one day, when all the monastery's reserves were depleted, he was forced to reveal to the assembled monks that a "great multitude of men and women" lacked the minimum necessary for survival. This intrusion of outside concerns causes stupefaction among the monks. The prior proposed reducing the amount distributed to the poor; the abbot refused. This story serves to introduce a classical topos. The abbot sends a monk to check on the contents of the grain hopper. Though it had been empty, it is now found to be full, and distributions of food to the poor resume with an inexhaustible supply. The story aptly captures the traditional predicament: in a time of unusual distress a horde of hungry people comes to the monastery begging alms; the monastery, situated in an isolated rural location far from the agitation of the world, has made a practice of distributing its surplus to the poor, and this is considered their rightful due (redditus pauperum); the crisis is resolved by Providence.

In reality, however, the difficulties multiplied. In Anjou in 1097, for example, spring floods rotted the wheat and brought an infestation of worms. Disasters struck a wide area in 1099. Once again the monasteries were unable to meet the needs of the starving populace. In some places poisonous herbs were mixed with the flour, killing many of the poor.

During this same period, some people were moved by the sight of such distressing poverty to go to the poor rather than wait for the poor to come to them. In 1095 Robert of Arbrissel founded a monastery at La Röé near the Breton border, and Peter the Hermit gathered a large following among the poor. Unfortunately, the East, which had absorbed a goodly number of the wretched, may have been the source of the resurgence of leprosy that now came to afflict the West.

Other signs of change accompany fresh misfortunes that began to arrive shortly after 1120. The first reports of trouble came from Portugal in 1122. Within two years there was difficulty in France as well: Anjou was hit by famine and disease. Then in Germany during the winter of 1124–25 the bishop of Bamberg was forced to feed thousands of indigents, who came to receive the handouts in such great throngs that they were likened to the merchants at an international fair. The allusion to the fairs is significant of economic changes which are further highlighted by an episode that occurred at Bruges in 1126. The *Chronicle* of Sigebert of Gembloux for that year mentions "a great famine in Flanders and many paupers dead of hunger." Sigebert goes on to say that "merchants from the South brought a large quantity of grain in a huge vessel. Upon hearing of this, a knight, Lambert of Straet, brother of the provost of Saint Donatian, and his son bought all this grain at a low price, along with all the tithes of the collegiate churches and monasteries of Saint Winnoc [at Bergues], Saint Bertin [at Saint-Omer], and Saint Peter and Saint Bavon [in Ghent]. Their storehouses were full of all sorts of grain; and yet they sold so dear that the poor could not afford to buy." Later, the chronicle goes on to tell how the count of Flanders, Charles the Good, sought to put an end to this state of affairs, which seems to have been utterly without precedent: human malice now magnified the harshness of nature. The developing cash economy and the rise of a commercial town provided an opportunity to speculate on the hunger of the poor. What might be called the "personalized" poverty of the rural parish, which monastic charity helped to alleviate, was now coupled with the "anonymous" poverty of an urban population more or less uprooted from its native soil.

Less than twenty years later the West was shaken by a new series of calamities. The first symptoms were reported by the *Annals of Lobbes* in 1142. A long rainy spell hampered the harvest, and scarcity of food led to high prices over a period of several years in the Low Countries, France, England, and Catalonia. In 1144–45 matters were not improved by severe wind, rain, and cold (even during the summer). In keeping with tradition the planet Saturn was blamed. Along the Rhine peasants were reduced to eating grass: "An innumerable multitude died of hunger." At Mormal those who were kept alive by the daily distribution of food were too numerous to count. In Anjou the famine continued into 1146. It subsided somewhat the following year, but the cycle of disasters continued as it often did with the outbreak of an epidemic. The "clamor of the poor" did not cease. Just before midcentury the author of the *Romance of Romances* expressed his pity for the "suffering people" in these terms: "For every villager there are a hundred paupers."[1]

The calamities of the twelfth century were less frequent but no less trying than those of the century before. Each generation suffered at least one major disaster. The *Acts* of Pope Alexander III indicate that in 1161–62 all of France trembled with fear: Aquitaine was in the grip of a severe famine; in Anjou mothers unable to feed their small children abandoned them at the gates of monasteries; northern and eastern France also suffered, and hard times persisted until 1166 in the Low Countries and Germany. The Iberian peninsula, which suffered a famine in 1160, experienced an even more serious recurrence in 1172; the *Annals* of Holy Cross in Coimbra speak of universal hunger and widespread mortality that spared neither man nor beast. Worst hit of all was again Anjou. According to a canon of Auxerre, the scourge afflicted all of France, forcing the monastic almonries to redouble their efforts.

After a respite of barely twenty years, the calamities resumed with still greater ferocity. Drought damaged the harvest in the Po valley in 1186. Four years later, unusually heavy rains spoiled the harvest everywhere and through erosion polluted the supplies of potable water. This heralded the beginning of a tragic series of heavy rains, floods, and lost harvests throughout Europe. From 1194 to 1196 fields went to seed before they could be harvested, and then only in late August, producing a very low yield. The winters, always difficult to survive, became catastrophic. The price of wheat increased tenfold, and prices of barley and salt also rose sharply in the Paris region and the north of France. Famine reached across Europe as far east as Austria and "from the Appenines to the [Atlantic] Ocean." As usual an epidemic made matters worse, especially in England. By 1197, after three years of crisis, not a single country seems to have been spared. The chroniclers are unanimous in bemoaning the situation, whose extent is indicated by the steps taken by kings and princes to limit the damage. A recurrent refrain in all the documents is the increase in the number of the poor (*excrescens multitudo pauperum*). In 1197 food supplies ran short as early as January. The winter was unusually long, and by June and July prices were so high in certain places that the famished poor, we are told, resorted to eating dead animals. When the harvest finally came, later than usual, it proved to be quite small. The abbey of La Vicogne had even less seed than the year before. In Champagne the grape harvest was poor. The abbeys could not make their usual distributions of food. Some sold their treasures to buy food at high prices: the monks of Saint-Benoît-sur-Loire sacrificed a magnificent silver crucifix in order to buy enough food to feed five hundred to seven hundred paupers daily. Many died of hunger at the gates of the monasteries. At Val-Saint-Pierre seventeen hundred were said to have died each day in 1197.

In vain, Philip Augustus sent urgent monitions to the bishops of France on behalf of the poor. In vain, Thibaud, count of Champagne, used his authority to organize poor relief and advised his barons to do the same. In vain, Count Baldwin IX of Flanders took steps against usurious speculation on food prices. The scarcity continued into 1198, a year of bad weather, floods, and late harvests. Food prices remained high throughout the year. Thus the twelfth century came to a catastrophic end, and the magnitude of the disaster concentrated the attention of contemporaries anxious about the future and solicitous of the needs of the poor.

THE PATHS OF MISFORTUNE   The people of the late twelfth century were aware that the brunt of the difficulty was borne by the growing numbers of the poor. Previously, in a time of chronic underdevelopment, it had been possible to single out the poorest of the poor for special help, and the immutability of the social order had made poverty seem a normal and permanent feature of the landscape. The ranks of the sick and beggars might be swelled in hard times by new recruits, but the social order remained unaltered. Thus we see the familiar, almost stereotypical features of the pauper or the handicapped person as depicted in the written and iconographic record.

The twelfth century with its growing numbers of charitable institutions has left an abundant literature of hagiographies, chronicles, and other sources that help us to diagnose the nature and extent of the physical suffering of the poor. That diseases were named for healing saints says a great deal about the state of medicine in this period: diseases were either chronic or fatal. Thus we have Saint Lupus's disease (epilepsy), Saint Lawrence's disease (eczema, shingles), and Saint Blaise's disease (affections of the throat). In the twelfth century Saint Anthony's fire (ergotism) and leprosy made unprecedented inroads in the West. Saint Anthony's fire was closely associated with poverty, since it stemmed from malnutrition and especially the use of cereal grains contaminated by ergot. Writing at the end of the eleventh century, Sigebert of Gembloux describes the horrible symptoms of the disease: a "holy fire" that consumed the body from within, burning limbs that turned black as coal and causing hands and feet to rot away. But it was not only the poorest men and women who suffered from diseases of scarcity; these ailments afflicted all strata of society, and contrary to what one might think, the indigent did not predominate among those benefiting from the miraculous cures recounted in the lives of the saints and miracle stories (from Saint-Benoît-sur-Loire, Conques, Rocamadour, and so on). Still, pilgrimages were "the meeting ground of the poor." Many texts describe how those too weak to walk on shriveled limbs were carried to the relics of miracle workers, besieged by throngs of sufferers who were treated rudely by the guardians.

Artists freely combined traits of infirmity and poverty in creating the iconography of the famished pauper, the beggar, the victim of disease, the prisoner, and the pilgrim. Their concern, essentially moral and religious in nature, was to exhort the faithful to acts of charity. The allegorical conflict between vice and virtue was not the only vehicle for this. Occasionally we encounter a work that reveals something of historical reality. The beggar who is helped by Saint Martin is shown in a miniature contained in a twelfth-century manuscript from Amiens as a cripple dressed in rags and supported by crutches. Somewhat better clad (the sheepskin was the poor man's fur coat) are the beggars who reach out for the alms offered by Saint Edmund in a miniature that dates from 1125–35. In a relief in the bronze door of Gniezno the almost-naked cripples shown passing beneath the shrine of Saint Adalbert are paupers as well as pilgrims. In the wasted, prostrate figure of Lazarus lying before the door of the rich man with a dog come to lick his wounds for his only consolation (from the celebrated Catalonian fresco of Tahull, circa 1123, inspired by Saint Sernin), we see an image of an authentic Toulousain pauper. Job, who is not a real pauper because he was wealthy before falling ill, evokes the distress of the man struck down by misfortune. He is depicted as such in the Souvigny Bible (late twelfth century) and on a capital of Saint-André-le-Bas in Vienne. Taken together, these examples suggest a portrait of the victim of misfortune: nudity signifies utter poverty; emaciation connotes hunger; sores, deformities, and crutches represent physical handicaps; and the dog suggests the absence of human companionship, whereas the large number of beggars represents the multitude of the poor. Broadly speaking, these iconographic details correlate with the expressions and terms used by the chroniclers, hagiographers, preachers, and charters in referring, however summarily, to the pauper and his miseries. The documents refer to the pauper as being either naked or clad in rags (*pannosus*) or a wretched cloak of hide. He is as hairy as a man of the forest. If he has any shelter at all, it is likely to be a hut (*domuncula*). His bed consists of a little straw on the ground and a miserable cover (*panniculus*). A small pot holds a meager pittance gleaned or begged here and there as it cooks over a fire that fills the hovel with smoke. The pauper always goes barefoot even though he is frequently on the move, either alone or in a group. But he never wanders far from the gate of the city, monastery, or castle that is the center of his existence.

This literary cliché and iconographic stereotype fairly accurately reflected the familiar and traditional pauper of the parish, known by name and assisted by the community of which he was a member. Beyond this lay a dissident world of outcasts: prostitutes, delinquents, vagabonds of all kinds, and rebels who had left their family or village because they had been thrown out or because they no longer had a place or felt restless in their traditional role. With nothing to hold on to or lose, they lived on the fringes of the forests with the *boisilleurs* whose portrait has been sketched by Marc Bloch: the forest edge was a place of ill repute that decent people avoided and that parents used to frighten children, whose elders feared that growing numbers of outcasts might upset the social equilibrium. In some cases it was but a short step from the life of a pauper integrated into the community to a life on the fringes of society.[2]

Economic factors were not the only determinant of poverty, nor was poverty the exclusive province of the rural laborer. Poverty was a complex phenomenon that drew recruits everywhere. The shortage of arable land, climatic disasters, the ravages of war, and the excessive birth rate left no group untouched. There was poverty among nobles as well as commoners, though admittedly the nature and extent of the phenomenon were different. The problems of the aristocratic *juvenes* are well known. Cut out of their father's inheritance, many young nobles made up the loss by participating in the Spanish *reconquista* or the Crusade or returned from the East in 1204 laden with Byzantine treasure, or, without going to quite such lengths, entered the service of the Plantagenets or the Capetians. Others suffered the misfortune of being taken prisoner; fortunes were bequeathed to the Church to buy their freedom, and the generosity of donors from the late eleventh century on is recorded in such places as the Green Book of the cathedral of Coimbra. Less unfortunate were those who, unable to maintain their social position, sought a rich marriage. Some men born nobles did not hesitate to grab the stilt of the plow. The sources mention others who stole sheep from property willed to a monastery by their ancestors. Peter the Chanter tells of one lay brother who set out for a fair with forty livres in cash to purchase various goods for his Carthusian convent. Along the way he fell into conversation with a "poor and decrepit old knight" and asked where this knight was headed. "I am buried under a mound of debt and am going to ask my creditor for a delay," said the knight. "I will go with you," replied the brother. Upon arriving, the lender threatens the poor knight and insults the lay brother who has interceded in the man's behalf, whereupon the religious hurls the forty livres at the creditor's feet in order to secure his companion's freedom.[3] This example from the writings of a moralist accords well with facts recorded in many charters. In the year 1200, for example, not far from Evreux in Normandy, a lord by the name of Geoffroy de la Bretesche announces that he is in great difficulty and in debt to a usurer for a large sum of money. War and the misfortunes of his time are responsible, he says, for his distress! And indeed, the armies of Philip Augustus and Richard the Lionhearted have for five years been locked in battle in the vicinity of Evreux, and the mercenaries of Mercadier and Cadoc have wreaked considerable havoc. Then there was the marriage of his daughter: leaving aside the ceremonies themselves, which could last as long as eight days, Norman custom demanded that the dowry be substantial enough to constitute a reasonable capital apart from any property of the spouse. And there are other reasons. The unfortunate lord continues his tale of woe: "I might well have lost all my land on account of the size of my debt and the amount of interest due, had I not received timely counsel and assistance." The counsel came from his family and friends, the assistance from the abbey of Lyre to which he ceded his share of the family estate in perpetual alms. He concludes his story in these terms: "I escaped the peril and anguish caused by the principal and interest that I owed."[4] For one such man helped over his difficulty by family and friends, how many were not so fortunate?

Commoners found it more difficult to escape adversity. A train of troubles led many into hardship. That there is a connection between a rising population and scarcity of land is hardly a novel discovery. It seems probable that scarcity itself, by encouraging the clearing of new land, helped many of the poor to survive. But not all land-clearing efforts proved successful, and many peasants could neither find new land to clear nor accept the hardships that went along with moving into the virgin plains of Germany or the valleys of Aragon. New monastic estates were not an unalloyed blessing: their establishment frequently involved curtailment of traditional usage rights and eviction of prior tenants. For example, the Cistercians of Maulbronn in Germany drove peasants from their land, though not from their homes, in 1159. Villagers resisted the establishment of a Carthusian monastery at Montrieux in Provence. It was only at a later stage, after the initial expulsions, that the Cistercians welcomed unemployed peasants onto their new lands. In addition, the fragmentation of farmland due to successive inheritances forced some peasant owners to hire themselves out as laborers on other men's land. It would be useful if we could determine what size farm was necessary to sustain a peasant at the poverty line (allowing, of course, for the variable quality of land). The problem is a difficult one and has yet to be adequately studied: still, it may be worth noting that in a number of regions the average size of a farm property tended to stabilize at between 1.5 and 3 hectares.

In reality, though, the determinant of viability was not the size of a farm but the means to work it: it was essential to own at least a few animals and a plow. Thus in the twelfth century we find one Etienne of Obazine in Limousin opposing the slaughter of animals, even in times of scarcity. His contemporary, Otto, bishop of Bamberg, distributed tools to peasants for use in the harvest. Before long, a minority of *laboureurs* (plowmen) would raise themselves above the mass of *manouvriers* who had only their hands and their courage with which to work (such as one family of peasants who, too exhausted to work their land, received assistance from William of Hirschau).

Debt is a traditional affliction of rural societies. A lucky few borrowed to buy livestock or tools or to build granaries and barns. Many more were forced to borrow, usually for a short term, in order to meet pressing family obligations or to pay the lord his invariable due. Originally the monasteries served as lending agencies, but they were eventually replaced by an assortment of promoters, money changers, seigneurial agents, Jews, and Lombards. Guibert of Nogent denounced the "frightful profits" of usurers, the "devourers of the poor." It was hardly by chance that mortgages were condemned by Pope Alexander III at the Lateran Council of 1179, just as their use was becoming widespread in the West. A mortgage then required cession to the mortgagee of all benefit and usufruct of the mortgaged property with no deduction from the principal of the loan, thus rendering illusory any hope of eventual reimbursement. The pope's condemnation had no immediate effect, and the disastrous consequences of peasant mortgages were evident in Normandy, the Chartres region, Picardy, and central Italy (to cite but a few of many examples) until at least the end of the twelfth century.[5]

In hard times the deleterious effects of indebtedness reached their peak. Peasants were caught in a vise: not only did they have to pay the traditional seigneurial dues and previously contracted debts, but now, in addition, they had to cope with rising prices and the demands of speculators. The charity of the parish no longer sufficed: creditors were relentless and the law permitted no delays. The peasant caught in such circumstances had no choice but to abandon his family, leave his land, and set out toward the unknown. Abandonment of one's land meant crossing the dividing line between poverty and indigence: this was the final break with the social order.

What had already occurred in the Cambrai region in 1144 and in the Loire Valley in 1161 affected a wider area in 1196 and 1197. The documents assembled by Curschmann show that in 1196 in the north of France between the Seine and the Escaut, famine reduced large numbers of peasants to begging and vagabondage. In the following year it was the turn of the grape growers of the regions around Rheims, Laon, Soissons, Beauvais, and Noyon. They had borrowed against the next year's grape harvest. The harvest was bad and they were forced to abandon their property.

A second stage in the inexorable decline into misery was marked by exclusion from society. The peasant who fled his property lived as an outlaw, almost a criminal. A man has to live, and to do so, many stole. This too was observed by the chroniclers. One, writing in northern France in 1197, mentions that "many people, reduced to such cruel necessity, chose to live contrary to custom, became thieves, and ended up in a noose."[6] Medieval society, intolerant of any violation of custom, showed no mercy because of extenuating circumstances. Peter of Blois speaks of unfortunate men condemned to death after resorting to theft or poaching in order to keep their families alive. The famine lasted from 1196 until 1198, but customary law was strict, and in England the Forest Assizes would brook no violation. Observations of the archdeacon of Bath are supported by testimony from other places as far away as the Ile-de-France and Champagne and by the archdeacon's colleague Peter the Chanter. Many were sent to the gallows or mutilated. It is hardly surprising, then, that the desperation of the poor was a frequent topic of moralists.

Fugitives from the plains took to the city as well as the forest. The number of urban poor was probably still relatively small in the twelfth century, and city paupers were not viewed with as much suspicion as the outlaws roaming the forests. They were, however, subject to new forms of misery that attended economic expansion. The butcher

Hagenel and his wife Hersent depicted in the *Chanson d'Aiol* must have been typical of many others. They had come to Orléans from Burgundy without a sou, "sickly, empty-handed, complaining, dead of hunger." Then, "by thrift they made so much lending out at usurious rates of interest that within five years they had amassed a fortune. They held two thirds of the city as collateral; they bought ovens and mills everywhere and did many free men out of their inheritances."[7] But for every pauper who became rich and turned to exploiting his fellows, many others remained mired in poverty. The poor often accepted work in the most despised trades: tanning, dying, and clothmaking. Before the invention of the fulling mill, fullers worked "naked and panting." According to John of Garland, dyers, with their nails stained red, black, yellow, and blue, were so ill regarded that "pretty women scorned them, except for those who received them warmly on account of their deniers."[8] It was also in the twelfth century, some time before 1173, that the spinners of Provins voiced a prophetic plaint that has been transmitted to us by Chrétien de Troyes in *Le Chevalier au Lion:* "We shall always be poor, we shall ever be hungry and thirsty. . . . Our employer grows wealthy on our earnings."[9]

In town as well as country, then, there was a direct relation between poverty and the absolute necessity to work day in and day out. As soon as work was lacking, the inexorable descent into indigence began, unless charity and justice took a hand. There was no dearth of opportunities.

CHAPTER FIVE ‡
CONTRASTS
AND SCANDALS

From the "pallors of hunger" shared by both the powerful and the poor during the great famine of 1032 (as recounted by Raoul Glaber) to the anxieties of indebtedness that the lord of La Bretesche shared with his peasants around the year 1200, poverty struck all levels of society. Its ravages were greater, to be sure, among commoners than among nobles. But the poor of the Middle Ages were not a homogeneous group. What all the unfortunate had in common was their humiliation and dependency, and it was only from the height of a spiritual vantage that the value in such a fate could be perceived. For, in yet another paradox of poverty, the poor formed what might be termed an "order" or estate in the economy of salvation.

CONTRASTS: HUMILIATION AND CONTEMPT

It became a literary cliché to identify the pauper with the peasant. While this image can hardly be said to have exhausted the actual variety of poverty, it did express the contempt that people felt for poverty—that antithesis of every positive value. The cripple and the leper were utterly devoid of beauty and grace. So was the hideous peasant Rigaut, who is described as follows in the *Geste de Garin le Lorrain:* "enormous arms, huge limbs, eyes a hand's breadth apart, broad shoulders, an enormous chest, bristling hair, and a face black as coal. He went six months without washing. The only water that ever touched his face was the rain." The villager in *Aucassin et Nicolette* is hardly more attractive. The poor cripples who frequented the pilgrims' sanctuaries were said to be repulsive and foul smelling and lacking not only beauty but also wealth: many, we are told, were misers and thieves. Incapable of virtue and generosity, the pauper also lacked all physical prowess: weak and penniless, his only weapons were cunning and mean tricks. He was also uneducated: "the peasant is like an ass."

Bad luck or illness could easily plunge a man into desperate poverty. It was much less common that a stroke of good fortune brought wealth and power to a pauper. And in any case most twelfth-century writers agreed that, while a man's status might change, his social nature (*natu-*

ra) remained immutable: "You can't make a falcon out of a buzzard." Let a peasant have all the gold in the world, he would remain what he was: a peasant. Thus convinced of the stability of society, all the rich and even many of the poor believed that poverty would always be with them. "Nature made (the pauper) empty-handed," we read in the *Speculum Stultorum* of Nigel of Longchamp. The rich, the powerful, the healthy, the poor, the weak, and the infirm all had their place in society, in which it was proper that they should remain. To justify this opinion men appealed to Scripture: "God," says a charter from the cartulary of the abbey of Saint-Laud in Angers, "has willed it that among men some are lords and others serfs." Consciences remained untroubled.

Poverty was an indignity if not a disability in the eyes of men with official responsibilities (*officium*). Poverty, we are told, made a man unfit for command, and it was thought indecent that those responsible for leading the Christian people should be poor. The Gregorian reformers themselves, determined to rescue the clergy from the control of laymen, paid particular attention to the benefices on which the clergy lived. Pope Innocent III made a point of the incompatibility between indigence (and a fortiori mendicity) and the clerical estate, and did so during the lifetime of Il Poverello of Assisi.

As a result of such attitudes, the victims of misfortune were advised to suffer in silence, their lot having been ordained by God. In addition, even though charity was recognized as a virtue and benevolence as a duty, both frequently coexisted with haughty disdain for the poor. Commiseration was not confused with compassion.

It is worth pointing out, however, that the sources may give a distorted impression. Most of them—treatises, sermons, literary works—were either addressed to the wealthy and powerful or composed by men who lived in that quarter of society. The writers had to tailor their examples to men not keenly attuned to the subtleties of charity and not easily aroused to deeds of benevolence. By all appearances knights gave alms frequently and often generously. But if the poor were the beneficiaries of those alms, they served more as means than ends. For the end, and to a certain extent the beneficiary, of knightly alms was the donor himself, and in this sense the pauper was at his service. Generosity was ostentatious by design, and pride and condescension were integral components of the act of giving. The point of almsgiving was to secure the donor's salvation by "extinguishing his sins." Human motives are of course always obscure and contradictory, and it would be presumptuous to say that knights gave alms solely out of self-interest. But what other form of charity could have been preached to, or expected of, men whose moral sensibilities were rudimentary at best? And if generosity, however egocentric, supplanted or at any rate compensated for brutality and oppression, was there not some progress? But even when great lords gave generously to the poor, their largesse rarely affected their subalterns, many of whom were crueler and haughtier than the lords themselves. A mixture of charity and largesse, noble alms were reparations for injustices committed, insurance for the hereafter, and attention-getting gifts. This was the opinion of Aiol and Erec.[1] But those who received these alms were required to make themselves "useful" and not presumptuous. When a cortege of indigents accompanied the body of Saint Alexis, a once-wealthy man who out of virtue chose a life of poverty, alms were handed out "to get rid of them." Erec gave money to clothe 169 of the unfortunate, but he makes no attempt to hide the fact that for him poverty is associated with shame and ugliness. Aucassin is bold enough to express scorn for a paradise encumbered with beggars and sick old men. Hell, he thinks, offers a better society. True charity was slow to make inroads in chivalrous circles: it occurred when a poor knight gave to help a still poorer one. But when a wealthy lord gave alms to mendicant peasants, his intentions were often utilitarian. Was the pauper loved or still secretly held in contempt?

‡ The foregoing observations are harsh; they are also incomplete, and I shall have more to say about the subject of aristocratic charity later on. Still more surprising than the giving of alms for self-interested reasons was the persistence of contempt for the poor in places where such contempt might have seemed a contradiction in terms. The Crusade, for example, was originally, and in its very essence, an affair of the poor. In principle it was a pilgrimage in which rich and poor mingled indiscriminately. But when we look closely at what it actually became, it is clear that the Crusade changed not so much in its object as in its very nature. The ambiguities of poverty manifested themselves in such a way as to cause great confusion. Just which paupers were involved in the Crusades, and what was the nature of their poverty? The chroniclers tell us relatively little about the identity of the paupers and pilgrims who took up the Cross. The *Gesta Dei per Francos* (Deeds of God through the Franks) describes a genuine poverty that

was shared by all, great and humble alike, and compounded of anxiety, anguish, fear, and privation. But the term *pauperes* is applied to the troops that followed Peter the Hermit and Peter Bartholomew, Gottschalk and Walter (whose surname was none other than "the Penniless"), or even that strange figure known as King Tafur, as well as to the multitudes of inoffensive paupers of both sexes and of all ages and social ranks. Albert of Aix saw the paupers as asocial men and women without resources. All the chronicles agree that paupers were useless militarily because their ranks were encumbered by invalids, unarmed, untrained, and unfit for combat. Anna Comnena declared that she was frightened by the hordes of the poor. Western knights were quick to despise their impoverished companions, and indeed to fear them and want them out of the way. The poor who traveled down the "highway of paupers" (as the land route to the East through central Europe was called) became the victims of the disastrous Anatolian expedition. Forty years later, the Second Crusade was marked by an equally tragic "purge" of the poor, who were abandoned to their cruel fate first upon reaching Iconium (Konya) and again at Adalia, where owing to the scarcity of ships only those ready for combat were allowed to board. By the Third Crusade there were no more paupers; but a short while earlier, in 1187, when all Latins in Jerusalem were considered prisoners of war after Saladin's conquest, the poor were again sacrificed. Fifteen thousand of them were sent into slavery in Muslim cities when the Christians could not muster sufficient unanimity to raise the necessary ransom.

Nor did the poor fare better at the time of the conquest of Constantinople. From the outset, the leaders of the expedition planned to send home all of the "disabled, poor, women, and other persons unfit for combat." After the capture of Zara the barons kept the spoils for themselves: "They gave nothing to the poor," who were sorely tried by hunger. The "high and mighty barons divided [the spoils of war] among themselves; the little people among their host received nothing, and so did the poor knights." In criticizing the selfish and contemptuous attitudes of the Latin lords, Robert of Clari interpreted the massacre of some of them by the Bulgars in 1205 as a judgment of God: "In such wise did the Lord God avenge himself for the bad faith shown toward the simple folk."[2]

In stating himself thus, Robert of Clari was indicating his agreement with various theologians of the late twelfth century. "It is the poor," wrote Peter of Blois, "the weakest of men, who will inherit the kingdom of God and the Holy Land: the two Jerusalems, terrestrial and celestial."[3] The poor themselves, after discovering that there was no place for them in the armed crusade, were quick to take up the tradition of pilgrimage. The tragic outcome of the Children's Crusade of 1212 is well known. Doomed to failure, the pitiful troop of young crusaders was abused and exploited, and its progress was halted in Sardinia. In the same year, Francis of Assisi himself set out for the East but was shipwrecked on the Dalmatian coast.

To the poor the New Testament held out hope of election, but even so poverty continued to bear the Old Testament taint of sin. Stephen of Fougères still saw it as a curse visited upon such people as the children of dishonest merchants as punishment for the sins of their parents. Others held that salvation was no more easily obtained by the pauper than by the rich man. The pauper, unable to sin by avarice, sinned instead by envy and rebelliousness. The blessings promised to the poor in spirit were never granted by law. The impossibility of redemption through alms compromised the redemption of the pauper. Before these attitudes could change, the purgative virtue of all suffering, including poverty, had to be recognized. This was the good news brought to the poor by the hermits of the late eleventh century who chose to share the pauper's life. In their trials we see a mixture of promotion and vocation.

PAUPER AND HERMIT MEET   Two quite different souvenirs have survived of the life of one of the most illustrious of the French hermits of the early twelfth century: Robert of Arbrissel. One of these, religiously preserved in the priory at Chemillé in Anjou, is a simple bronze-tipped walking stick bearing the cross of Saint Anthony the Hermit.[4] The second is the imposing monumental edifice of the abbey of Fontevraud, which grew over the centuries on the site of the original abbey founded by Robert. Apart from the church, it is doubtful that anything remains of the initial encampment, which included shelter for men and women, nobles and peasants, pious laymen and clerics, vagabonds and prostitutes. Robert's walking stick is quite unlike an abbatial cross; it was not a ceremonial object but simply a useful adjunct in his pastoral peregrinations. By contrast, the stone buildings of the abbey symbolize the gradual end of vagabondage and the solidification of much spiritual ferment. This contrast epitomizes the significance of the encounter between the suffering pauper and the religious hermit.

My purpose in what follows will be to analyze the nature of that encounter rather than to summarize the history of hermitism, which is well known. What were relations between hermits and paupers like? How and where did they meet? What came of their meeting?

There is an obvious geographical and chronological coincidence between the flourishing of hermitism (from Peter the Hermit to Eon de l'Etoile) and the recurrent tides of poverty from the famine of 1095 to that of 1144. The Gregorian reform provided a favorable climate for the growth of seeds sown earlier, in the time of Saints Romuald and Peter Damian. Natural disasters befell a population just beginning a long period of expansion. But neither reform nor disaster was a novelty, and their effects were not limited to any one region. The multitudes that followed Peter the Hermit came from all Christendom, but most hermits and their disciples never set out on the road to the East. Two facts are worth noting: first, the hermitical movement was especially influential among the masses of common people in certain regions, and, second, the development of the movement seems to have occurred simultaneously in a number of different areas. Italian hermitages were quickly joined by others in the area around Toulouse, in what had been Lotharingia, and especially in western France, in Normandy and Limousin. In central Europe the movement was strong in southern Germany, in the western parts of the Slavic countries (Poland and Bohemia), and Hungary. Signs of growing hermitical influence were evident in northern Spain and Portugal. And in England, finally, the flourishing of hermitism recalled the rise of the old monasticism of the ninth century.

Almost all the great figures of pastoral hermitism were contemporaries. More important than their birth dates are two other dates: when they retreated from the world and when they died. Saint Bruno, founder of the Carthusian order, held that the monks of that order should stand outside society as examples to other men. Shortly before and shortly after him (in 1076–78 and 1089), Stephen of Muret and Geoffroy of Chalard also showed the way to troops of itinerant preachers who left the "desert" to preach to multitudes. Between 1095 and 1110 several of the most famous hermits began their retreats from the world: Peter the Hermit, Vital of Mortain, Robert of Arbrissel, Bernard of Tiron, Raymond Gayrard, and, in England, Aldwine. By 1130–40 most of these men had died, but William of Vercelli (Italy) lived until 1142 and Stephen of Obazine until 1159; in England, where hermits seem to have been particularly long-lived, Godric of Finchal died in 1170 after more than seventy years of strenuous hermitic life.

The mutual attraction between itinerant hermit preachers and their clientele of paupers stemmed from many factors, the most important of which were probably a shared way of life, a similarity of attitudes toward society, and a profound convergence of aspirations (insofar as we know what their aspirations were).

The meeting of hermit and fugitive in the middle of the forest was not simply a literary cliché. The hard life led by Tristan and Isolde as social outcasts in the forest of Norrois was typical of the lot of aristocratic youths who had broken relations with their families. No more imaginary a figure than the two lovers themselves is the hermit Ogrin, who, leaning on his cane, delivers a sermon full of prophecy and biblical citation and who finally grants them pardon. There was no dearth of prototypes. Saint Haimrad, born in Swabia in the late eleventh century, was driven out of countless places by people of all sorts, even peasants, and chased by the dogs of a corrupt priest; he was a man careless of his dress and speech, of whom people asked, "Where does this devil come from?" But ultimately he settled on a wooded mountain in Hesse and won the sympathies of the lord and inhabitants of a nearby village. It was impossible to distinguish between the appearance of the hermit and that of a penitent, tramp, or vagabond: he wore rags, a sheepskin, a hooded tunic, and boots. The allusions made by the author of the *Liber de diversis ordinibus* (circa 1130) do not contradict the description given by Marbode, bishop of Rennes, of the appearance of Robert of Arbrissel, which was said to be indecent for a cleric: Robert, we are told, went about ragged (*pannosus*) as a beggar in a deliberate effort to model himself after Christ's precursor. Half naked (*seminudo crure*), he wore a "long beard." The description also fits the lay brothers of Grandmont. Some hermits were even more extreme, like the filthy and verminous Stephen of Obazine. One self-portrait of a hermit runs as follows:

> Leading a devout life
> In the high marshes
> In the depths of the leafy wood.

Toward the end of the century it was again the "rough and unkempt appearance, the stubbly hair and hairy beard" of the hermit that caught the attention of Peter the Chanter. Herrad of Lansberg depicted the hermit in similar terms on the Scales of Paradise in *Hortus deliciarum*. Peter the Chanter adds that the hermit openly proclaims his hatred of money and ostentatiously seeks the "outrageous and perverse."

Like Christ, who lacked even a rock on which to lay his head, the hermit slept on the ground and, if he settled anywhere, made do with only the most rudimentary shelter. Many hermits chose to live in "awful places." The hermit Girard built a cabin of tree limbs in Montreuil-Bellay. A cave was enough for the disciples of Bernard of Tiron who lived at Fontgombaud on the banks of the Creuse. Others built a rustic little chapel five meters wide and a cell surrounded by a garden, the vestiges of which remain at Butte Saint-Louis in the forest of Fontainebleau.

Hermits being vegetarians, they generally kept small gardens. Following their example, Tristan decides, along with Isolde, to lead a "beggar's life and live on herbs and nuts." Hermits rarely ate meat; the eating of fish was more common, as for example among the island-dwelling anchorites of Cordouan (in Gironde), Brittany, and England. The rest of the diet consisted of milk, eggs, bread, gruel, vegetables, wild fruits, and honey: a poor peasant's fare. The hermit also shared the peasant's manual labor, by which he earned his daily bread: the work consisted of tilling the earth and tending livestock, cutting wood, pottery-making, and basket-weaving, as with the Desert Fathers.

But for minor variations, this was the life led by hermits from such diverse areas as the forests of Limousin and the Craon area of lower Maine, Normandy and the Perche, England, the Ardennes, the Vosges, the Alps, and central Germany. The hermit was a pauper, a voluntary social outcast, and lived accordingly. "Pauper ego, mendicus ego," said the hermit Blandin, a swineherd. He was the son of a serf—as was Haimrad—but with canonical dispensation had been admitted to the priesthood. His case was an exception to the rule, however; most hermits deliberately chose poverty. The most common route to becoming a hermit, acknowledged by Yves of Chartres, involved spending some time first as a monk or cleric. For some the decisive factor in the decision to retreat into the desert was failure in the performance of some office (this was the case with Robert of Arbrissel and Bernard of Tiron). Others, like Christian of Alms or Hugo of Lacerta, were attracted by other hermits. Still others, such as Geoffroy of Chalard and Saint Bruno, felt an inner need for prayer and penitence; some, like

Haimrad and Bernard of Tiron, decided to withdraw from the world after a pilgrimage to Rome or the Holy Land. Retreat, whether temporary or permanent, might culminate with the decision to live as a cenobite in a traditional monastery. Historians have rightly emphasized the influence of the best educated of the clergy, and especially diocesan scholars, on the hermitic vocation. The scholars' deep knowledge of the sources of Christianity led them to place great value on the imitation of Christ and the Apostles as an ideal. In some places, as in Limousin, at Grandmont and L'Artige, the example of hermits from the East, encountered in Calabria or transmitted via Venice, may have served as models in ways that have gone unrecognized or been forgotten.

Not all hermits began as clerics or monks, however. Christian of Alms was a simple shepherd when he went into the desert, sometime before 1120. Hugo of Lacerta was a knight when he retired to Muret (circa 1109). Garnier of Montmorency was first a knight, then a monk, and he finally became a hermit in 1100. A plausible passage in the life of Bernard of Tiron states that many of his companions were of aristocratic birth, and there is little reason why those who went into the desert with Bernard should have been different from those who sought out other hermitages. Geoffroy of Chalard retired with two companions into a Limousin forest only after having studied as a layman at Troyes and Limoges (where he lived with a merchant) and subsequently entering the priesthood at Périgueux. Waderic, a man of noble birth, became a monk at the abbey of Saint Peter in Ghent. These examples show that, although the hermitical movement attracted the attention of large crowds, the initial impetus rarely came from the poor but generally from educated men (and women) of wealthy background, who, taking their inspiration from Saint Paul, set out to imitate Christ and to live a life of poverty. By doing so they drew nearer to the truly poor, a segment of the populace not firmly under the control of feudal and ecclesiastical institutions.

When hermits left their refuges, they did so in the manner of paupers: on foot, often unshod, or else mounted on an ass, the humble animal that carried Jesus into Jerusalem. Although some people went like Tristan into the woods to consult the man of God, the man of God also came out of the woods to meet the faithful. His clients were therefore of two sorts. Nearest and dearest to him were the poor. What was new was not that a Vital of Savigny, a Gayrard of Toulouse, a William of Hirschau, or the hermits of Montevergine in Italy, or Aldwine, Saint Caradoc, or Godric of Finchale in England should have come forward to help the poor, or that some of them, like the monks of Grandmont and Muret, should have set an example by helping others still poorer than themselves. Rather, what was unusual and disturbing to men like Geoffroy, abbot of Vendôme, and Marbode was the hermits' clientele: lepers and prostitutes flocked to hear the good news of a Christ who loved Lazarus and pardoned Mary Magdalen. The cult of the latter was popular in this period, which also witnessed a fashion for pilgrimages to Vézelay and Saintes-Maries-de-la-Mer. It was a novel idea to look upon the social outcast with an eye to restoring his or her dignity and reintegrating him or her into society. At Fontevraud lepers were not kept segregated, and repentant women were included in the life of the community. Robert of Arbrissel wished to die among his "dear patients and beloved lepers." A transition had been made from the *liberalitas erga pauperes* to the *conversatio inter pauperes:* the ideal was no longer to show solicitude to the less fortunate but to live as a pauper among the poor.

The crowds that flocked to hear the hermits included men and women from many walks of life: carpenters and metalworkers, goldsmiths, painters, and masons, farmers and vintners. To the dismay of the episcopal hierarchy, for whom Marbode may be taken as a spokesman, they abandoned the parish clergy, not so much out of love of religion (in Marbode's view) as out of curiosity and the attraction of novelty. The onlookers were not rich or powerful, but neither were they beggars: they reveal the true social dimensions of the hermitical movement. The popular preachers, men who moved about from place to place and enjoyed a good rapport with the crowd, were aware of the distress of the unfortunate and the aspirations of the majority. During the same period, the failure of the reform attempted by Pope Pascal II showed how difficult it was for the Church to appreciate fully the significance of the Gregorian movement and to strike a compromise between Christian sympathy for the poor and the need to find a place for the Church within the feudal system. An episode involving a monk by the name of Henri of Lausanne reveals, on a more modest scale, the nature of the limits that the hermitical movement confronted. Around 1100, it seems, while Bishop Hildebert of Lavardin, himself an admirer of the hermits and of Robert of Arbrissel in particular, was away in Rome, Henri caused a stir in the town of Le Mans. His impoverished appearance, his eloquence and the drama that accompanied it, and his success at converting the town's prostitutes had charmed the faithful, particularly those living in the suburbs, beyond the hopes of the prelate Hildebert. The trouble stemmed not so much from Henri's heretical preachings (later denounced) as from his vehement criticism of the rather unedifying behavior of members of yet-to-be-reformed cathedral chapter. The crowds were moved to enthusiasm by his calls for purification.

Here we touch on precisely what it was that established such a close connection between hermitism and poverty: the identification of poverty with purity. The Le Mans affair is not without analogy to the eleventh-century Patarine movement of Milan. It is not surprising that religious aspirations erupted with such turbulence in a city where spiritual ardor had been much in view since 1070, associated with the early stages of the communal movement in France. These religious aspirations expressed the hopes and fears of masses of people whose concerns about salvation had been awakened by the Gregorian reform movement. The popular protest against the wealth of the clergy was not economic in nature and was anti-clerical only by accident. Far from being anti-religious, the protest actually grew out of the identification of poverty with purity. Pushing the logic of the Gregorian program to its ultimate conclusion, the protesters demanded that the clergy live by an ideal of poverty exemplified by the poorest of the poor.

The enthusiasm with which the ideal of pure poverty was embraced does much to explain the character of the encounter between hermitism and poverty: the influence of each on the other, and the contrasting extremes to which that influence could lead. It was inevitable that hermitism, practiced as it was outside established institutions and customs, should lend itself to excess. Leaving aside those who professed opinions deemed heretical, like Henri of Lausanne, and eccentrics like Eon de l'Etoile, there were still other heretics who found it impossible to keep their behavior within bounds. Marbode had warned Robert of Arbrissel against allowing women whose vocation had not been put to the test to remain in the hermitages. At Grandmont and Fontevraud a reasonable place was found for women in the life of the community; in this the influence of Petronilla of Chemillé was decisive. Recklessness was tolerated at times. One of the best-known instances involved a man by the name of Hervé (who died in 1119). After leaving the abbey of Vendôme he shared an ascetic life with an English nun by the name of Eve, who waited on him as a servant and whose virtue won her the epithet "blessed" in a twelfth-century verse biography devoted to her memory.

In contrast to this is the prudence evident in the counsel given by Robert of Arbrissel to Countess Ermengarde of Brittany, who was under his religious tutelage. Robert praised the countess's desire for perfection but instructed her to bear with her unfaithful husband: "Your desire should be to leave the world. . . . However, you are bound, your bond cannot be broken. . . . Be merciful to the poor, especially to the poorest of them. . . . Be justly prudent in all things."[5]

The spread of hermitism has been likened to a conflagration. But the tenor of Robert's advice to Ermengarde, who was not a nun but a lay woman, should give us pause in understanding this term. My point is not to suggest that, leaving aside the Carthusians, the hermitic movement outlived its originators only by being absorbed within the existing monastic institution (in the form of cenobitism). For the conflagration did indeed rekindle the flame of charity toward the poor, to whom it drew the attention of society. To be attentive is, in the first instance, to see and to recognize. Men of the forest, the hermits did in a sense exorcise the woods in which they lived. In silence they meditated and found God. As a result, the myth of the forest lost something of its evil power. Poor, unordained, and alone, the hermits demonstrated to a society tormented by thoughts of the hereafter that, contrary to conventional wisdom, holiness can exist without noble birth, without the wealth to be generous, and without the cloister. The hermits attempted to alleviate poverty and to restore human dignity to society's rejects. They revealed in the poor a reflection of the suffering Jesus. By comforting the poor and admonishing the comfortable they proclaimed the possibility of salvation through poverty, by and for the poor. Quite obviously, the social and economic context in which the hermits lived was important; yet their work notably transcended that context. Their call was slow to be heard, however, and even then was only partially heeded.

DISILLUSIONMENT AND
UNREST AMONG THE POOR

On two occasions, in the middle and at the end of the twelfth century, the poor in various regions suffered bitter disillusionment. The Tafur affair[6] and the First Crusade had aroused in some minds the conviction that God preferred the poor to the impious and presumptuous. After Tanchelm led an anti-clerical rebellion in the Low Countries in 1110–15, an extraordinary young man, a Breton of aristocratic birth by the name of Eon de l'Etoile, became caught up in a movement that involved "vast multitudes of a rude populace" whose grievances, inspired by poverty, were tinged with heresy. Captured in 1148 after a series of violent incidents that led to drastic repression by the authorities, Eon, whose case was heard at Rheims in the presence of Eugenius III, defied his judges by claiming that he had been sent by God to "judge the living and the dead and the world and subject them to trial by fire." Eon himself may have lived quite high, or so rumor had it. But his movement was once again built upon a call for purification, which borrowed the voice of the poor. These examples should suffice to show that popular movements and heretical sects were in many respects intertwined. There can be no doubt that the poor paid a heavy price for this confusion. In their ignorance their hopes did not go beyond chiliastic anticipations sustained by a veritable eschatological mythology.

It seems rather anachronistic to attribute class consciousness or any notion of class struggle to the medieval poor and more useful instead to view the disappointed hopes of the poor in terms of messianic beliefs. It is true that the early twelfth century saw the renewal of sharp, short-lived peasant uprisings. In 1110 peasants of the Beauvaisis burned forests belonging to their bishop. In the Bray region peasants set fire to the suburbs of Poix in 1121. The peasants of Ponthieu invaded Saint-Riquier in 1125, and in Cambrésis a castellan was stoned to death in 1127. At the other end of Europe, in Galicia, the bishop of Sahagun had to confront an uprising of "field workers and little people" in 1110. Even without resorting to violence, peasants effectively opposed violations of "customary law," whose enforcement depended on their oral testimony. In addition, by fleeing, they could deprive an oppressive master of the manpower he needed to work his lands. That isolated conflicts did occur is undeniable. What is more, the coincidence of popular movements with periods of famine, in 1144 and especially in the 1180s and 1190s, shows that those movements were not unrelated to economic difficulty. But, while misery may have swelled the ranks of the roving peasant bands, their spiritual exaltation came from elsewhere. The hope of better times to come was heralded by the coming of "messiahs of the poor" who, it was believed, would reform the Church and change the face of the earth. One such was a Calabrian monk of the late twelfth century, Joachim of Floris, who prophesied the coming age of the Spirit.

After events in Italy in which Arnold of Brescia played a central role, other incidents in France (beginning in 1182) and in England (fourteen years later) give graphic illustration of the tragic disillusionment of the poor and of the aggravation of their problems by economic distress. In each case a prophet appeared and soon began to draw crowds of the unfortunate. The two prophets were men of the people, whose names are not without significance. A man with the very common name Durand led the French uprising of 1182. In 1196 it was William Longbeard, whose surname evokes both penitence and nonconformism. Durand was a shy and modest man, a carpenter by trade (like Saint Joseph), and "as pious as it is possible for a layman to be." He was a resident of the pilgrimage town of Le Puy, and the Virgin appeared to him in a vision. Prudently, Durand informed his bishop of this and with the bishop's authorization formed a confraternity whose insignia bore the inscription "Agnus Dei, dona nobis pacem" and whose members wore the commoner's cowl of undyed linen or wool (whence their name, the White Capes). In other words, this was a confraternity of honest penitents and posed no danger to public tranquility. There was apparently nothing at all unusual about the existence of such a group in a period that witnessed (in the wake of the earlier peace movements) the development of similar sects in many areas, for example, a few years earlier in Rodez. But the influence of Durand's White Capes spread rapidly, and "partisans of peace" were recruited from every walk of life and social order (although the lower orders were particularly strongly represented) and from every point of the compass: Berry, Burgundy, Aquitaine, and Provence. At this point things began to turn sour. The chroniclers, hitherto rather approving of what had seemed a pious and peaceful undertaking, begin to adopt a different attitude. What had been referred to as a confraternity now becomes a "confederation" of conspirators and a ruse of the devil, a travesty of what had been a mutual charity but has now become a "horrible, extraordinary, insane invention." Following the example of various communal conspiracies, the White Capes dared to demand that lords content themselves with collecting only what was due them. They challenged all hierarchy with an egalitarian ideal that threatened to undermine the social order. Given the prevailing climate in southern France in the late twelfth century, it was inevitable that the charge of heresy would be raised. The White Capes took part in several violent actions, and the authorities retaliated with brutal repression of the sect. The bishop of Auxerre showed some understanding of the White Capes' motives but reproached them for their failure to comprehend that servitude is the fruit of sin.

William Longbeard did not enjoy the same degree of initial approval as the White Capes. A more dynamic figure than Durand of Le Puy, William was the typical bad shepherd: though not well educated he had a way with words, was clever and a fine orator, and was a passionate though conceited man. The chronicle of William of Newburgh describes him as a dangerous demagogue. He arrogantly usurped the title of "provider to the poor" traditionally claimed by bishops. At the same time he flattered the poor and exhorted them to invade the dwellings of the rich:

> I am the savior of the poor. . . . You, the poor, who know the hard hands of the rich man, drink at my well the waters and the doctrine of salvation, and drink with joy. For the day is coming when you shall be visited. I will divide the humble and faithful from the proud and perfidious. I will divide the elect from the damned as the light from the darkness.[7]

The tone is revolutionary and aims even more to be prophetic, drawing as it does upon reminiscences of the Bible and especially of that most fiery of prophets, Isaiah. At least as important as economic grievances was a kind of frenzy of moral conversion. Longbeard failed: he was hanged, and the chronicle says that this was "for justice and piety." Many people ascribed miracles to him, and a popular cult nearly developed around his memory. The poor awaited the "saint of the last days." But Durand and William disappointed paupers in the end even more than Henri and Eon de l'Etoile before them.

Fickle, disillusioned, yet forever optimistic, crowds of the poor naturally followed whatever leader came to seek them out. Even before the twelfth century was over, the poor had turned to a new generation of hermits. It is true that Fulk, the curate of Neuilly-sur-Marne and famous primarily as the preacher of the Fourth Crusade, was not a hermit. He had nothing of the demagogue about him and won prestige by his asceticism and ardent style of speaking. A disciple of Peter the Chanter, he too became a model for the other preachers of Paris. He was invited to speak at Saint-Severin and Champeaux as well as in Germany. To all without exception he preached that no man should be harmed by violence. He often spoke out against usurers and speculators and, we are told, frequently shouted to his listeners, "Feed that man who is dying!" He enjoyed considerable popularity among the poorest of the poor, and his biography depicts him surrounded by people on stretchers who had been brought to him so that he might console them. Following in the footsteps of Robert of Arbrissel, he attempted to restore dignity to prostitutes, of whom there were many in the rapidly growing city of Paris. A centenarian might have believed that the time of the itinerant preachers had somehow returned! Fulk had emulators. In England the abbot of Flay in Kent also fought against usury and managed to have the markets closed on Sunday. The monk Herluin of Saint-Denis went to Brittany and in traveling up and down the coasts persuaded many people to take up the Cross and set forth on a penitential pilgrimage. Disciples of Fulk set off in many directions to preach repentance in his name. Unfortunately, the only one of these disciples whose memory has survived turned out badly, provoking yet another round of disillusionment among the poor. According to James of Vitry (whose record of this period is superb), Peter of Roissy grew rich by preaching perfection and by obtaining the position of chancellor in the church of Chartres in addition to the post of canon that he already held. Not even Fulk himself escaped criticism. People seem to have been disappointed that their idol did not couple his oratorical ardor with some spectacular ascetic practice or resounding miracle. James of Vitry's criticism goes still farther. He deplores the fact that Fulk, blinded, perhaps by personal success, to God's will, accepted too much money for himself. Despite the righteousness of his intentions, Fulk lost his ascendancy. This is an important observation, because it suggests that the one prerequisite for any sincere effort on behalf of the poor is to share their poverty.

Other disillusioning episodes include the misfortunes that befell many paupers at Zara and Constantinople in 1204 and the heart-rending Children's Crusade of 1212. The distress of the survivors is summed up in one sentence from the chronicles: "They returned home one by one, in silence."

Was it possible, then, for the poor to hope that one day they might be integrated into society? Scorn for them often turned to hatred. The affair of the White Capes and the London episode had left behind bitter memories of social subversion. Hostility to the poor is reflected in literature from around the year 1200 in the theme of the low-born upstart who seeks to force his way into the upper strata of society. Yet in a society where sacred and profane, spiritual and temporal were mixed, and where disorder was often confused with heresy, men did seek to understand, if not to resolve, the ambiguities of poverty. Toward the end of the twelfth century, for example, Saint Raymond, bishop of Piacenza, organized processions in which all manner of the poor were represented. The marchers shouted, "Help us, cruel Christians, for we are dying of hunger, while you live in plenty." The grievance was not new. More than a half century earlier, one author (at one time erroneously thought to have been Saint Bernard) wrote: "When the predator swoops down upon the poor man, we refuse to lend that man aid. . . . Christ is on the cross and we remain silent." Are we to conclude, then, that nothing was done, in word, or in deed, to make a place—even a very humble place—for the pauper within the Christian community?

CHAPTER SIX ‡
THE URGENCY
OF CHARITY

THE REVIVAL OF GOOD WORKS

In the twelfth century the Benedictine monasteries did not have as much of a monopoly on charitable assistance to the poor as they seem to have had in earlier years. The reason for this was not a loss of confidence on the part of donors, who were content to let the monks parcel out their alms and gifts. Nor was it some defect of organization. On the contrary, the importance of the almonry within the monastery increased. It was given a special building for its own use and assigned a portion of the abbey's regular income. In addition, the almoner collected from the monks leftover food and used garments. With these resources he was able to receive paupers into the monastery and to make regular distributions of food and clothing. By 1200 most Benedictine monasteries had adopted this system.

The burden of all this was heavy, even for a powerful abbey like Cluny, which devoted about one third of its income to assistance of the poor. When a general calamity struck, as at the end of the twelfth century, many almonries were overwhelmed by the influx of beggars. Some managed to continue operations but only by making sacrifices that threatened their financial well-being.

The growing disparity between income and expenditure was not the only reason for change, however. It is hard to escape the conclusion that monastic charity declined in part because the monasteries did not fully adapt to changing conditions. Not that war, famine, and natural disaster were previously unheard of. Nor can the spread of leprosy in the early twelfth century fully account for the increased demands made on the charity of the monasteries. Rather, the origins of the trouble lay in certain kinds of social change, as we have already had occasion to observe. Leaving aside the great calamities, the most distressing cases of poverty were likely to escape the attention of the monks altogether. Retired behind their cloister walls, surrounded by their own fields, monks rarely saw with their own eyes the most miserable of the poor: the social marginals and intransigents who lived in the forests or roamed the countryside and the tramps and prostitutes who inhabited the growing towns. Such paupers remained outside the existing system of relief. Admittedly, some monks, at Cluny for example, went out to visit the sick and indigent in their homes. But they went because the poor were unable to come to the monastery themselves. Still, the monks never ventured outside the monastery's *finage*, or administrative area, for the life of the monk was strictly governed, and alms had a place in the regular liturgy. Only a limited number of paupers were covered by the rites of the *mandatum*. In order to receive alms at the gate or hospitality in the abbey's hospice paupers had to appear in person. By the twelfth century, however, many people were no longer content simply to wait for the poor to come to them; increasingly, they went out in search of lost sheep. Hermits and itinerant preachers (*Wanderprediger*), for example, encountered the poor face-to-face, and they were not alone. More durable and widespread than the brief enthusiasm for hermitism was the revival of charity based on gospel teachings. All of this required finding new sources of alms, new techniques of distribution, and new ideas about the nature of poverty and charity.

It would be of great importance if we could somehow learn more about the way in which the doctrine contained in the Sermon on the Mount was presented to ordinary Christians. Already evident in a ninth-century pastoral letter written by Hincmar, the influence of the sermon helped to shape the medieval peace movements and contributed to the extraordinary awakening of popular spirituality that took place in the eleventh century (and about which modern historical research has uncovered a great deal of information). The *Elucidarium*, which was just coming into use as a confessor's manual in the eleventh century, has nothing explicit to say on the subject. We must therefore turn to other sources, such as one pamphlet typical of the sort of teaching aid that would have been available in 1093 in the cartulary of Mas-d'Azil, which sets forth the duties of the Christian man and woman. The text of the pamphlet consists of eight articles, five of which concern charity toward one's fellow man. The first two articles prescribe love and obedience to God, and the last exhorts the believer to keep the image of his death always before his eyes. The five middle articles list the works of mercy:

> Keep charity always in thy heart.
> Admonish those who quarrel to restore brotherly peace.
> Relieve the poor.

Visit the sick.
Bury the dead.[1]

These five precepts would later be expanded to seven, but the essential points are already covered. The second point, which touches on the hope for peace (a hope with particular resonance for the poor, who bore the brunt of wartime devastation), expresses one of the most widely shared aspirations of the period that runs from the time of the peace oaths to the age of Saint Francis. The third point, vague as it is, anticipates future developments in feeding the hungry, clothing the naked, and easing the lot of those held in prison. The program of charity here outlined was designed to win salvation. It is worth noting that it was intended for an audience of laymen as well as clerics, and at a time (the late eleventh century) when towns were beginning to challenge the supremacy of the countryside.

The invitation to laymen to join the clergy in works of charity met with a number of unusual responses. The Gregorian reform movement and the revival of the cities both had an impact on these new forms of charity. In keeping with the new Christian ideal that men should cleave as closely as possible to the message of the Gospels and the way of life of the early Church, some members of the secular clergy created a new kind of ministry, in which charity work was combined with a rigorous ascetic life similar to that of a cloistered monk. Stimulated by the hermitical movement, this new concept of the pastoral mission first developed in the early eleventh century in the Mediterranean region, where the influence of Carolingian institutions was less powerful and the need for reform greater than in the north. Later on, in northern Europe, in the area between the Seine and the Rhine for example, some of the clergy outdid their southern colleagues by adopting the stricter of the two rules attributed to Saint Augustine; to men seeking perfection and the charity of the Gospels they prescribed a new way of life (*mos nova*) more rigorous than the old (*mos antiqua*). These regular canons (that is, canons living according to the rule of Saint Augustine) differed from monks in that the canons, who became the nuclei of spiritual life in the cities and rural towns, went out into the world to work each day as pastors. Their preaching was made more credible by the fact that they abided by a strict rule of personal poverty. They demonstrated their charity directly rather than by adhering, as the monks did, to a contemplative ideal. The monks of Cîteaux and the canons of Prémontré both attached positive significance to poverty, though in different ways, symbolized by their white habits of undyed raw wool.

Religious poverty took a variety of forms: individual or communal, spiritual or material. Hermits, monks, and canons were said to belong to one of two *ordines*, the *antiquus* or the *novus*, depending on the nature of their poverty. The two orders were also distinguished by their different approaches to charity. When a chapter of canons chose to live by a rule, it often laid down regulations governing its charitable endeavors, regulations similar to those in force in the monasteries. The *provisio pauperum* was guaranteed by income from the common canonical property, which was used to build hospices for the sick and for pilgrims as well as to support the activities of a chapter officer specially charged with distributing alms to the poor; this officer was known as an almoner, just as in the abbeys.

Where charity work had been neglected, the chapters revived the canonical rule specifying that one quarter of the revenue from tithes should be assigned to the poor (the so-called *quarta*). The *Decretum* of Gratian most appropriately reaffirmed this principle. It would be interesting to know how often concern for the poor is mentioned in the sources as one of the reasons for restoring the tithe (from the time of the Gregorian reform onward). As early as the eleventh century, Fulk Nerra, count of Anjou, reinstated the rights of the almonry of Ronceray for the benefit of "the poor women's charity." In 1122 similar actions were taken in the dioceses of Rheims and Soissons. Unfortunately, detailed information of this kind is rare, possibly because the legal status of the dues in question was not affected, or because the quarta was understood to belong to the poor and needed no explicit mention. By the same token, when the right of the poor to a portion of the tithe is mentioned explicitly, this may be because it was felt necessary to remind Christians of their duty to give alms.

Another kind of traditional charitable institution was also restored as a result of the canonical movement. Gerhoh of Reichersberg advocated the restoration of the *xenodocheia* in episcopal cities and of the *ptocheia* in rural parishes. The *ordo novus* was also instrumental in the founding of new institutions, which supplemented those already in existence. Various evidence suggests that the canons were influential in the hospitals: for example, the fact that hospitals in various places were placed under the patronage of the same saints, each with his or her own special virtue: Christopher, Giles, James, John, Julian, Mary Magdalen, and Nicholas. The internal organization of all these hospitals was similar, with a provost or archpriest at the head. We can also see the influence exerted over the customary practices of hospital congregations by certain chapters of canons regular, such as Saint-Victor of Paris, whose *Liber ordinis* (composed at the end of the eleventh century) was widely known. Other influential chapters included Prémontré, Saint-Jean-des-Vignes in Soissons, Herival in the diocese of Toul, Murbach, Santa-Croce of Mortara, and Saint-Ruf, which was recognized in a papal bull of 1154 as the chief chapter of 108 affiliated communities from Porto to Coïmbra.

In some places the canons distinguished themselves by providing specialized forms of charity. It may be that because the chapters developed and had roots in the cities, they tried to adapt their efforts to the needs of the time. There is reason to believe that their intellectual influence extended to the realm of medicine. Can it be mere coincidence that a considerable number of surviving medical manuscripts come to us from the libraries of chapters associated with fairly large hospitals? This is true of Chartres, Saint-Victor of Paris, Lyons, Ivrea, Salzburg, and Bamberg, among others. It is more certain that some chapter hospitals specialized in the treatment of specific diseases in specific geographic locations. It may also be that because canons were recruited in an urban milieu and knew the dangers of the open road, they had a better idea than most monks of the sort of assistance required by poor vagabonds and other travelers and pilgrims who were often lumped together with itinerant paupers.

It had long been the practice to locate hospices on routes followed by pilgrims, who were classed along with other paupers as Christ's poor. Older institutions dotted the roads to Rome and Santiago of Compostella. The hospice of Roncevaux on the road to Compostella was not the only hospice on the *camino frances*, though it was one of the best known. Besides the roads normally followed by the Jacquotins, as pilgrims to Compostella were called, there were other hospices across the Iberian peninsula all the way to Portugal, at Braga, Santa-Cruz of Coïmbra, and Alcobaca. The *romieux*, or pilgrims to Rome, were equally well served: the *via francigena* included well-known stopping places at Mont-Cenis, in the hills that bear the name of Saint Bernard of Menthon (or of Montjou), in the val d'Aosta, and all along the roads leading to Rome and the Monte Gargano. In Tuscany, the hospital of Altopascio became the center of a veritable hospital complex.

The improvement of travelers' accommodations in the second half of the twelfth century is obviously related to the growth in traffic associated with the revival of trade. Not all travelers were poor, but all faced the same dangers in crossing the mountains. It is worth noting that among the travelers who crossed the Alps by the via francigena on their way to the fairs of Champagne was one Bernardone of Assisi, the father of Saint Francis. Pilgrims were people who had chosen temporary poverty out of a spirit of repentance. The number of itinerants increased dramatically. The roads through the mountains and forests were served by several well-known monasteries. In the twelfth century the Benedictine abbey of Chalais operated thirteen alpine outposts. In France's Massif Central the hospital of Aubrac offered travelers shelter and safety. Charitable institutions operated in the forests as well as the mountains. For the woods, even though sanctified by men of religion and idealized in courtly literature, remained places of terror and danger. Forests covered the plateaus and plains and formed the boundaries not only between seigneuries and kingdoms but also between security and danger. Hence, from the late eleventh century on, the forests of the old Lotharingian territory between the Scheldt and the Rhine witnessed the arrival of monks, canons, and even laymen, who gathered in places like Afflingen, Flone, Arrouaise, Vicogne, and Saint-Inglevert to help the poor and other travelers. The same is true of Burgundy, Limousin, and Maine.

Rivers were another natural obstacle. Even with the patronage of Saint Christopher, charity alone could not cope with their unpredictable and capricious behavior. So in that progressive age, the twelfth century, charity was married to technology in the building of stone bridges. Bridge building demanded men, money, and time. Laymen established confraternities and, later, congregations, not unlike monastic or canonical orders, for the purpose of building bridges. These prospered in the mid-twelfth century in the south of France, where the waters are especially violent and capricious. Still unforgotten even today is the work of San Domingo of La Calzada (who died early in the twelfth century) in constructing the bridge over the Aragon. The work of the "bridge-building brothers" on the Rhône has become legendary. The saga of the shepherd Bénézet begins with a vision: this boy of twelve then harangues the crowd during an eclipse of the sun, arouses the suspicion of his bishop, and finally performs a miracle by hurling a massive boulder into the Rhône: the first stone of the famous "pont d'Avignon" and the founding act of the "charity house on the Rhône" that was built in eleven years by a brotherhood of men and women. This pious work, granted indulgences by both the bishop and the pope, was the result of a poor man's initiative. It attracted alms, sustained beggars, and later made a hospital of what had been a mere shelter next to the bridge for paupers, pilgrims, and other travelers. The men and women who built the bridge at Avignon truly deserved that their memory be immortalized in a popular song.

Avignon was not the only site of a bridge across the Rhône. Lay confraternities began building other bridges at about the same time, for example, at Lyons in 1180. In 1189 a bridge across the Durance was begun at a place which was once known as Maupas (for *mauvais passage*, bad crossing) but which changed, significantly, to Bonpas (*bon passage*, or good crossing). This enterprise served as a model for the work undertaken by the residents of Saint-Saturnin-du-Port (between Avignon and Lyon), who changed the name of their town to Pont-Saint-Esprit (Holy Spirit bridge).

Thus the second half of the twelfth century was a time of change and enterprise in charitable as in other endeavors. Although some older canonical chapters ceased to look upon assistance to the poor as an essential part of their spiritual activities, and some hospitals, like the one at Vercelli in 1175, became prebendal institutions, charitable fraternities were founded on lay initiative in the cities, and some of these were eventually transformed into permanent congregations. One of the best known of these was the fraternity founded by Gui of Montpellier around 1160. This was a hospital society dedicated to the care of the poor, the sick, and abandoned children. Governed by the rule of Saint Augustine and approved by the bishop of Maguelonne, the new order spread rapidly, extending its influence as far as Rome, where by the end of the century it maintained two houses, one of which was associated with Santa Maria of Trastevere. In 1198 Innocent III commended this congregation, dedicated to the Holy Spirit, to all his bishops, and named the house of Montpellier the head of the order. Six years later the pope donated the old and unused *schola* of the Saxons near the Vatican for use as a shelter for abandoned children, many of whom were thrown into the Tiber by women who had themselves been abandoned. This hospital is still in existence today. Coming at about the same time as the ministry of Fulk of Neuilly, this episode tells us a great deal about the extent of misery around the year 1200.

All Europe seemed to reap the harvest of poverty simultaneously. Contemporaries saw a mixture of wheat and chaff: catharism was part of the chaff, voluntary poverty and good works were part of the wheat, though for us it is probably best to treat the motives of the heretics as distinct from the motives of almsgivers and hermits. Yet the fact that there was a close relationship between the practice of poverty and the quest for purity surely suggests that the motives of a heretic like Waldo drew upon the same sources as other movements deemed orthodox. However that may be, the order of the Holy Spirit was not alone in performing its good works; its members worked alongside the members of other orders, such as the Antonines and the Hospitallers.

The history of the Antonines—or Antonites, as they are sometimes called to distinguish them from their homonymous counterparts in the East—is shot through with contradictions and legends. What is certain is that on a pilgrimage route in Viennois, at a place known as La-Motte-Saint-Didier, an almshouse, staffed by laymen, was founded in 1150 to serve the victims of Saint Anthony's disease. The word *pauper* appeared in the seal of the house (*sigillum pauperum*) in 1198. Abuses by the alms collectors of Saint Anthony's were severely reprimanded by Innocent III in 1210. But the saint's reputation as a miracle worker attracted sufferers from great distances. The story of the pilgrimage of Hugh the Carthusian, bishop of Lincoln, in 1200 includes a horrifying portrait that is worthy of note despite the critics' doubts about this particular text.[2] By the second half of the twelfth century the house's renown was attracting many men and women, and by 1200 they were being sent out to many other hospices from Lons-le-Saunier and Lyons to Forez and Gap. In Dauphiné alone there were eight or nine affiliated almshouses.

In the same period the order of Saint John of Jerusalem assumed a dual role, to wage war and heal the sick. Such a dual role was not easy to play, however: Alexander III was obliged to warn the order not to forget the service of the poor on the pretext of going off to do battle in the Holy Land. The statutes of the order, revised in 1182, contain a solemn and minutely detailed reminder of the "utility of the suffering poor." The order devoted most of its efforts to the holy war in the East, but its influence in the West led to the adoption of its statutes by many hospitals, including those of the Order of the Holy Spirit. The phrase "our lords, the afflicted," first coined by the brothers of Saint John, became the motto of nearly all the charity hospitals.

The need for hospitals became so pressing that another order, the Order of the Holy Sepulchre of Jerusalem, was quick to extend its original vocation by establishing a mission to shelter ailing paupers and pilgrims, for which it received many donations throughout the West, but particularly along the pilgrimage routes.

‡Even a superficial survey of the charitable congregations would be incomplete if it failed to mention the orders whose specialty it was to redeem prisoners of war. The prisoner issue was not a new one, particularly in those parts of southern Europe that bordered on Muslim territory. It is worth noting that prisoners were among the most frequent recipients of gifts and legacies recorded in the *Black Book* of the Coïmbra cathedral at the end of the eleventh century. In the twelfth century these gifts were entrusted to the confraternities and military orders, to the hospital and the Holy Sepulchre. More specialized congregations were organized at the end of the twelfth century. The legend that attached to the name of Saint Felix of Valois is of little importance. The honor of establishing a knightly order (under the patronage of the Trinity), whose members were supposed to devote their lives to the care of the ailing poor and to the redemption of prisoners from the Saracens, belongs to a Provençal, Saint John of Matha (whence the name given to his disciples, the Mathurins). To accomplish their ends they collected alms throughout Christendom and did not hesitate to go to infidel territory for the purpose of negotiating ransoms; in keeping with a fourth vow added to the three usual ones, they sometimes gave themselves over as hostages in exchange for the freedom of other prisoners whose ransoms they had been unable to negotiate. Innocent III approved their rule in 1198. In Spain a similar initiative by King Alfonso II, approved by Alexander III, led to the founding, in 1180, of the Orden del Santo Redentor, a prelude to the creation—some forty years later by another Aragonese monarch in conjunction with the Languedocian Saint Pierre Nolasque—of a partly clerical, partly knightly order whose name is suggestive of its mission: the Order of Mercy.

Laymen were no longer content to rely on clerics and monks to perform works of charity on their behalf. From the middle of the twelfth century they began to take this responsibility upon themselves, giving directly to the poor. The growth of a cash economy enabled increasing numbers of laymen, and especially members of that new social group, the merchants, to rival the generosity of feudal lords and monasteries. But economic considerations alone do not suffice to explain changes in the pattern of charitable giving. Had lay givers lost confidence in the monasteries to fulfill their duties toward the poor? Were they looking for a more direct and effective means to insure their own salvation? If so, the change in attitude may have resulted from the lay community's increasing awareness of the moral and spiritual function of the poor within the larger society. For some time there had been a growing tendency to establish a more personal relationship between benefactor and recipient, even within the context of monastically administered charity. At Cluny, for example, the monks assigned specific paupers to certain donors, whose gifts were used to clothe, feed, and provide shoes for the designated recipients.[3]

It was not so much the forms of lay benevolence as the identity of the benefactors that underwent a change. Straightforward almsgiving, both individual and collective, remained the most common form of charity. Charity through bequests does not appear to have been common, though this may be due only to a dearth of surviving documents, despite the growing role of magistrates in the northern cities and the importance of notaries in the south. With the increasing influence of Roman law in practical affairs we learn a great deal about the charitable intentions of those who made wills. The term *eleemosyna* of course refers to gifts made for religious purposes, but the rather selfish concern of donors for their own salvation led them to designate specific categories of recipients: paupers begging their daily bread, marriageable girls without dowries, invalids, lepers, and captives. Charitable gifts were catalogued, and with help from all strata of society the number of hospitals and other institutions increased enormously.

Almsgivers ranged from the top to the bottom of the social hierarchy. The charity of kings and princes rivaled the benevolence of the Church. Power, particularly consecrated power, carried with it obligations of justice and charity. The generosity of kings like Louis VII and Philip Augustus was part of a tradition that runs from the piety of King Robert (the Pious) to the saintliness of Louis IX (Saint Louis). In 1152 Louis VII instituted annual distributions to three hundred paupers at the monastery of Argenteuil to honor the memory of Suger. Louis's son Philip took such an active interest in leper hospitals that we have almost as many documents pertaining to them as we have for various other hospitals belonging to the royal estates in Meaux, Noyon, and Senlis. These institutions were ultimately combined in a department of state known as the royal almonry, which appears to have been established around 1190. In response to severe economic distress at the end of the century the king took unprecedented measures. In 1195, according to Rigord, the royal historiographer, he gave generous alms from his own revenues and ordered his prelates and subjects to do likewise. At about the same time, Philip of Alsace, count of Flanders, followed the example set by his predecessor Charles the Good, who owed his epithet to steps he had taken to relieve victims of the famine of 1126. Similarly, in 1199, an Escelini, lord of Ferrara, made generous bequests to eighteen charitable institutions in his city. Alfonso IX (the Noble), in gratitude for his victory at Alarcos in 1195, established the King's Hospital at Burgos.

Chronicles and hagiographies tell the same tale, with a bit of legend mixed in. Ordericus Vitalis celebrated the Empress Matilda as the "consoler of the poor." Popular legend has it that her first husband, the emperor Henry V, died an edifying death among the poor in the hospital of Angers. In fact he died in 1125, and the *hôpital* Saint-Jean was founded in 1180 by King Henry II, a product of Matilda's second marriage. Henry II carried on the charitable traditions begun by his father Geoffroy Plantagenet, renowned as a founder of leprosariums, by establishing poorhouses not only in Angers but also in Le Mans (Coeffort), La Flèche, Saumur, Bauge, and Fontevraud. Yet, at his funeral in 1190, four thousand paupers waited for alms near the Fontevraud bridge; William the Marshall says that an order had to be given to turn them away, for lack of money.

High on the list of noble families who made a name for themselves as charitable donors was the house of Blois-Champagne, which established hospitals at Les Montils, near Blois, and in the fair towns of Provins and Bar-sur-Seine. Another prominent family was the house of Burgundy, which established the Charity Hospital in Dijon. The house of Lorraine and the counts of Toul and Verdun also distinguished themselves. In their concern for the poor the lords of Lorraine did not simply establish hospitals but also saw to it that their ministers took steps to protect the helpless.

Lesser lords matched the generosity of princes, albeit on a smaller scale. If charity was widespread, however, there were nevertheless important differences from donor to donor. Chivalric literature exalted almsgiving as a kind of prowess, and the pauper who received alms served to magnify his benefactor's ostentatious glory. Similar ostentation is found in the terms of wills: men wished to maintain their rank, even in death. But the size of the gift, the number of people helped, could measure a man's guilt as well as his rank. Forcible seizure of property belonging to the Church and therefore to the poor could place a man's soul in jeopardy, and many who felt guilt over such acts made restitution, gave alms, and erected crosses of safeguard which the poor could embrace to claim their right of asylum. Declarations made prior to the preparation of wills are even more revealing. If on the brink of the grave it was rather late to regret "the violence that knights are in the habit of visiting upon the poor," it was never too late to acknowledge death, the great equalizer, "which overturns the towers of kings and the huts of paupers with equal abandon."

‡ Laymen of other estates also participated in this general effort to supplement the charitable work of the monasteries. The number of charitable institutions increased considerably in the twelfth century. Rural communities developed new forms of assistance beyond the traditional alms available to needy parishioners. Many villages acquired their first infirmaries and leprosariums. The spread of leprosy raised serious administrative and public health issues for those who wielded the power of the ban; hence most of the leper hospitals were founded by lords. Infirmaries, on the other hand, were often founded by commoners, and in both France and England around the year 1200 the care of the sick seems to have been entrusted quite commonly to confraternities and other early forms of mutual aid societies. From the early twelfth century, for example, three parishes affiliated with Saint-Père of Chartres boasted peace fraternities that maintained buildings (the so-called *domus fraternitatis*) for religious and charitable purposes. We know from records of a conflict between the monks of Bergues-Saint-Winnoc and the fishermen of Mardyck that in 1209 the residents of this tiny Flemish fishing village collected the tithe themselves and distributed a third of what they collected to the poor. In the hilly Tarentaise region, from 1175 until the French Revolution the "bread of May" was distributed to the poor to tide them over that difficult month. Similar examples could be multiplied at will. But it was in the cities that new forms of lay charity, individual as well as collective, were most strikingly in evidence.

It stands to reason that small hospitals were frequently built in the cities or on roads leading to them, for that is where the poor were found. New types of charitable institutions were of course quite common in the most highly urbanized areas, around the Mediterranean and in the Low Countries. The edifying story of Werimbold, who died in 1150, was held up as an example. Made wealthy by usury, he had led a sumptuous life in a beautiful house built of stone and wood and surrounded by considerable land. His wife gave food to the poor. When she died, Werimbold retired to a monastery with his four children. He gave gift after gift, maintaining twenty-five paupers at the abbey of Saint-Hubert, paying for the upkeep of a bridge and the equipment of a hospital. So much giving finally left him a poor man, and he ended his days among the poor as their servant. A half century before Saint Francis of Assisi, Werimbold had sought identification with the poor: this was not a course that everyone was willing to take. Some attempted to rival the generosity of the aristocracy, ending their lives with charity that accomplished the dual goal of consolidating the social gains of a lifetime and crowning business success with moral justification. But most bourgeois giving was neither sublime divestiture nor calculated gift. For example, Alard of Chimay and his wife founded a hospital at Rheims which was dedicated to Saint Mary Magdalen and devoted to the poor. Also dedicated to Mary Magdalen was the oldest of the fifteen leper hospitals known to have existed in Artois in the twelfth century. Still more discreet forms of charity included the adoption of young children, provision of dowries for poor girls, or simply willing a sum of money to a charitable institution. Unfortunately, few bourgeois wills from this period have survived, but some that have, from Nivelles, Brussels, Angers, Toulouse, and Arles, indicate the purposes to which bequests were to be put.

Women played an important role in lay charity. We have previously encountered the case of Ermengarde, the countess of Brittany and devotee of Robert of Arbrissel. Robert's advice to her, to "be merciful to the poor, especially the poorest of them," might equally well have been given to Ermengarde's contemporary, the *matrona* Richilde, a bourgeoise of Brussels who founded a *domus hospitalitatis* attached to Sainte-Gudule.

Charity took collective as well as individual forms. Charitable confraternities first appear in the twelfth century in the role of mutual aid societies offering their members spiritual as well as material assistance. Some confraternities assisted only their own members or gave only modest annual alms to the poor of their city. Others were more generous (examples are known from Anjou). The members of the confraternity of Château-Gontier kept an almshouse, and those of Angers and La Flèche maintained leper hospitals. In Béthune the confraternity of the Charitables of Saint Eligius, founded in 1187, is still active today, continuing its original purpose of providing burial for members and paupers. Southern France took no back seat to the north in this regard: confraternities in the cities of Languedoc and Provence were stimulated by the rapid development of similar organizations in Italy. Consider, for example, the confraternity of Saint Nicholas in Millau, which began semiannual distributions to the poor in 1182. In

Zamora, Spain, merchants built a shelter near a bridge for the use of the poor, and their bishop authorized the building of a church next to this shelter in 1167.

Besides these collective forms of charitable assistance, communal authorities were forced by the increasing numbers of paupers to take a hand in dealing with the problems of poverty. As early as the twelfth century we find these authorities establishing controls over the foundation and administration of charitable institutions. These applied first to the leper hospitals, for obvious reasons of public health. It is only logical that such controls should be observed first in the areas where urban life developed earliest. A few examples chosen at random: the residents of Huy in the region of Liège, as always in the forefront of urban history, helped to administer the property of the leper house known as the Grands Malades. In Metz in 1179 the bishop reminded the city authorities of their duty in the following terms: "The aldermen will leave intact the rights of orphans and widows, poor as well as rich."

In Germany the *Bürgerliche Spital* first appears in the second half of the twelfth century. The charter of Châteaudun, inspired by that of Lorris, provides that paupers who felt they had suffered some injury might appeal for damages to a council of bourgeois. At Narbonne a council of *probi homines* was given responsibility in 1177 for approving relief measures and overseeing the recruitment of personnel to minister to the sick. Municipal authorities thus moved decisively to assume responsibility for the supervision of charitable institutions.

‡ It is impossible to give an exhaustive list of all the different charitable institutions that developed throughout Europe in this period. At best one can offer a representative sampling. If the locations of charitable institutions were marked on a map of Europe, a few empty spaces would stand out. Their density was of course greatest in the areas where the population was most concentrated, but even in hard-to-reach mountainous areas hospitals were found along major roads, as we saw earlier. The Pyrenees and Alps possessed important hospices. In Anjou charitable institutions developed quite early. In Paris, in addition to the ancient Hôtel-Dieu, which has occupied its present location ever since the early Middle Ages, the Saint-Gervais hospital was built in 1171, the maison Sainte-Catherine opened its doors to young women in 1186, and the Hospital of the Trinity on the rue Saint Denis was built by the bourgeois of the city and opened to pilgrims en

route to Compostella in 1202. The city was ringed by leper hospitals, and there were important hospitals in all the major cities of the royal domain: Pontoise, Compiègne, Soissons, Beauvais, Laon, Rheims, and Noyon. In Chartres the Notre-Dame almshouse was supplemented by an old synagogue that was transformed into a hospital in 1179 and by a leper hospital dedicated, as was so often the case, to Mary Magdalen. The area that is now eastern France could boast of major hospices at Nancy, Metz, Toul, and Verdun.

In the south there were several major centers, about which a great deal is now known. Hospitals were founded with increasing frequency in Toulouse starting in 1184, and by the early thirteenth century the city counted twelve hospitals and seven leprosariums. In Narbonne three new establishments were added to five others dating from the twelfth century and divided between the city and the burg, not counting the so-called Charité des Blancs and the Oeuvre des suaires des pauvres de la cité (which saw to the burial of the poor). Though relatively unpopulated, the Rouergue was the site of a host of new foundations at the end of the twelfth century: between 1179 and 1200 five new hospitals were added to five others that had been established since 1100, including those at Aubrac (1120), Saint-Antonin (1163), and Millau (1164). New hospitals were established with each new catastrophe, sometimes in the very places where the catastrophe occurred: in Rodez, Sainte-Marie-du-Las following the peace treaty of 1170, and especially Millau (site of the *hôpitaux* Saint-Esprit, Saint-Antoine, and Saint-Jacques).

Throughout Christendom there were hospitals both new and old in episcopal and imperial cities, as for example at Rochester (1194) and Winchester (1215) in England; Barcelona, Tarragon, and Burgos in Spain; and Coïmbra in Portugal.

A glance at Italy shows that the development of hospitals there came early, as did the growth of the cities, and that Italian hospitals attained a degree of specialization rarely equaled elsewhere. As early as 1168 the hospital of the Brolo in Milan was devoted especially to foundlings. The same was true of the hospital of Borgo San Spirito in Rome. By way of comparison, it is worth noting that a region that appears relatively ill equipped in the years before 1220, Lazio, actually boasted any number of *xenodocheia* attached to churches, cathedrals, and collegiate churches, as well as communities of lay men and women receiving assistance and a number of leper hospitals, including eight in the southern part of the province alone.

The picture painted by James of Vitry in his *Historia Occidentalis* (circa 1223–25) thus takes on a special significance.[4] James, first a canon at Oignies near Liège, then a legate in the East, bishop of Acre, and finally cardinal, had acquired a vast experience of the world. With the familiarity of one who had seen the clients of many hospitals, he enumerated them as follows: paupers, invalids, "pusillanimous" individuals, the feeble-minded, the miserable, those who cry and those who are hungry, and lepers—all *pauperes Christi*. Although his praise of those who care for all these sufferers is not unmixed with criticism, James says that one must have "the courage of a martyr to overcome one's repugnance at the unbearable filth and stench of the patients." The poor and the sick are everywhere. The hospitals he cites are chosen deliberately from Constantinople (then Latin) to Spain, from Liège to Paris to Rome. James of Vitry might have borrowed the words that his colleague Eudes of Châteauroux used to describe Notre-Dame of Paris and said of many hospices for the poor that they were built largely with the "farthings of old women." In Paris, James had heard the lessons of Peter the Chanter, who paid close attention to the poor. He had witnessed the devastation of the last six years of the twelfth century and had heard Fulk of Neuilly give heart to prostitutes through his preaching. The misery of the poor was for James and some others— but not for all his contemporaries—a matter of experience as well as reflection.

A POOR MAN'S THEOLOGY   James's experience was that of a generation forced to face the problem of the pauper's place in society. It was no longer enough merely to revive old charities and develop new ones. To an unprecedented degree the poor had made their voices heard. Men had seen the White Capes in action and heard the demands of William Longbeard. The number of the poor had increased just as relaxation of old ties of dependency made them bolder and as the cities provided opportunities for a new way of life. What is more, their cause met with new encouragement, not to say active support. The Goliards, rebel clerics who with the disdain of city dwellers looked upon peasants as "rustics, liars, and detestable good-for-nothings," objected to the social order and, if the word is not too strong, demanded higher status for the humble of this world. There was a certain similarity between the cause of the poor and the essentially religious movements led by Waldo, Durand of Huesca, and the Humiliati. It was while listening to a jongleur recite the life of Saint Alexis that Waldo discovered his vocation. Ordinary vagabonds were indistinguishable from members of the poverty sects sketched by Walter Map: "Barefoot, wool-clad, and without baggage." As for occupation, many of the poor militants of Lyons, Aragon, and Lombardy chose the humblest sort of work and became weavers, so that contemporaries often made no distinction between workers in this trade and members of the movement. For some people poverty and heresy were virtually identical. The time had come—or, rather, had come once more—when society found it necessary to reflect upon the status of the poor.

With the rise of the merchant in a society previously dominated by knights, avarice and charity came to occupy the same rank as pride and humility: concepts overlapped and clashed in dialectical disputations that left nothing simple and clear-cut. Such matters were most naturally discussed in the urban schools. Robert of Arbrissel had studied in Paris and taught in Angers; Odo of Tournai studied in Orléans and taught at Toul; Alan of Lille taught in Paris, as did Peter the Chanter, whose influence helped to shape the thinking of Fulk of Neuilly, James of Vitry, and Raoul Ardent. The name of Abelard is too well known to belabor. His contemporary Gerhoh of Reichersberg taught at Augsburg. There were major schools in Bologna and Chartres. It was also in the cities that Arnold of Brescia, Waldo, Francis of Assisi, and Dominic began their careers. The new culture of the cities, shaped in part by Roman law, provided the critical tools; traditional theology and canon law provided the principles; and experience provided not only raw facts but also an avenue to the outside world.

In the twelfth century ecclesiastics keen to remedy society's ills brought church doctrine to bear on what they saw happening in the cities where they were established. One approach was to establish a casuistry of poverty and almsgiving. Another was to remind men, through forceful preaching, of their pressing duties. We shall here be concerned only superficially with speculation on the nature of spiritual poverty as experienced, individually as well as collectively, by monks and other religious; our main interest, rather, will be in what church thinkers had to say about paupers who did not choose their poverty voluntarily—those who either resigned themselves to their fate, endured it unwillingly, or rebelled against it. Distinctions formulated by church authors lead us straight into the subject. Gerhoh of Reichersberg distinguished between involuntary paupers such as Lazarus (*pauperes cum Lazaro*) and voluntary paupers like the Apostles (*pauperes cum Petro*). Raoul Ardent referred to the first group, the involuntary paupers, simply as *pauperes*. In the twelfth century the Cistercian lay brother combined in one life both the apostolic and involuntary forms of poverty: his lot was a humble one, a life of manual labor but also a life of ascetic silence and prayer—as poor and contemptible in his way as the peasant, the lay brother was nevertheless as religious as the monk.

Although reflection on poverty was fostered by the conditions of life in the cities, the exponents of the new urban culture were neither the first nor the only thinkers to treat the subject of the poor. Discussions of poverty had spiritual and emotional as well as intellectual ramifications and transcended questions of economic causality. Christian ideas about poverty had deep roots, and in the twelfth century old— sometimes very old—traditions and currents of thought again rose to prominence. Just as the men of the eleventh century believed that they were reinventing the *vita vere apostolica* after a lapse of nearly a millennium, so the men of the twelfth century rediscovered—either on their own or with the help of such *auctoritates* as Augustine, Ambrose, Jerome, Isidore, Bede, and Gregory the Great—unambiguous Christian teachings concerning the duties of the rich and the rights of the poor. Moreover, the Greek Fathers regained their rightful place among the sources of the Christian tradition: not only Basil but also John Chrysostom. Also new—and rather rare in the Middle Ages— was the use of the Epistle of James: the willingness to allude to a text that evinces a particularly harsh attitude toward abuses of wealth is not without significance. Twelfth-century writers appealed not only to Christian sources and to the Bible but also to such pagan moralists as Cicero, Seneca, Horace, Apuleius and even to the *Lex Rhodia* to excuse and justify cases of exceptional need.

Over the course of the century the writers in question, influenced by the traditions of either canon law or theology, justice or charity, hammered out the church position on the duties of the rich and the rights of the poor and carved out a place for the pauper in medieval society.

There is little point in reproducing here the traditional and oft-cited teachings of the Fathers concerning the duty to give alms and the spiritual value of charity. Gratian, drawing heavily on the work of his predecessors, brought order and clarity to the patristic heritage. Burchard of Worms was no less strict than Hincmar when it came to the restoration of the tithe, the patrimony of the poor, and of property stolen from the Church to the detriment of the poor: "These paupers," he said to the rich, "are your neighbors and cannot defend themselves." Yves of Chartres showed himself to be equally severe toward those who speculated on the harvest. In contrast to condemnations of this kind, positive arguments were put forward to justify almsgiving on grounds of justice; such arguments can be found in the *Sentences* of Peter Lombard as well as in the work of men as different as Abelard[5] and Saint Bernard.

The poor, or at any rate a particular class of the poor, were afforded a place in society, a place in both the natural economy of the world and the spiritual economy of salvation. As early as the eleventh century Adalbero, bishop of Laon, recognized the usefulness of the nonfree in his *Carmen ad Robertum regem:* "Through them food and clothing are provided to all, for no man is capable of living without them." This sentiment was echoed by Abbo of Fleury, who asserted that through their work "the multitude of the entire Church is sustained." What had been a mere commonplace took on new substance in the concept of mankind developed by the twelfth-century masters. By listing labors once termed "servile" among the mechanical arts—the cogs of that great machine, the world—these writers made room for such despised groups as field hands and wool, stone, wood, and metal workers in their picture of society, which they saw as an organism regulated by moral and customary laws. Hugh of St. Victor rehabilitated the manual trades by including them, in his *Didascalion,* among the factors favorable to technological progress and social development. The social body was, like the human body, a unified, harmonious whole that stood on its "feet," the class of manual laborers. "The *res publica* goes barefoot, so to speak," said John of Salisbury, "when laborers and artisans are subject to injustice." In Chartres, analysis of the theory of society according to which men are divided among different *ordines* yielded such new notions as *conditio* and *status* designed to take greater account of sociological realities. Such work paved the way for a change in the traditional concept of worldly estates. In virtue of their function, a place, although admittedly an inferior one, was found in the social hierarchy for laborers and artisans.

A distinction was made between estate and status or condition. According to James of Vitry, the status of the poor was such that "they earn their daily bread by working with their hands, and when they have eaten nothing remains on their plates." Poverty, like illness, might strike any member of society without depriving that person of membership in the social order into which he or she was born. It was the misfortune of peasants that their position was a precarious one and that they could easily fall into indigence. This is the view taken, for example, by Stephen of Fougères, bishop of Rennes, in his *Book of Manners*, written in 1175–80; he shows compassion for the poor and recognizes the usefulness of their labor but has little esteem for the peasant.

In keeping with the logic of this conception of society, those who had no social function had no place in society. Some had withdrawn voluntarily from social life, others had been expelled. What placed these people outside the community was not poverty but marginality. Their only salvation was to reenter ordinary society. Given the context, however, it is not difficult to understand why, a century earlier, efforts to rehabilitate such people by men like Robert of Arbrissel and Fulk of Neuilly were considered by many to be aberrations as outrageous as the asocial or rebellious behavior of those whom they sought to save.

From the spiritual standpoint, however, things looked somewhat different. Poverty, like any form of suffering, had potential spiritual value. Through this spiritual function poverty recouped its standing and indeed found some justification: it could be useful to the pauper as well as to the rich man, for whom it served as a means of sanctification. In some respects the sharing of poverty in the broad sense of the term grouped its victims into a sort of spiritual *ordo*, an *ordo* with no existence outside the economy of salvation, the communion of saints. The poor thus acquired a new social standing, and it is here, I think, that one finds the key to twelfth-century thinking and attitudes toward poverty and the poor.

Most authors apparently conceived of the poor man in terms of his relation to the rich man. The pauper would seem to have been created and placed in the world for the sake of the rich man's salvation. Men never tired of pointing out the reason why: it was more difficult for a rich man to enter the kingdom of heaven than for a camel to pass through the eye of a needle. The giving of alms became the subject of countless treatises, letters, and sermons. The primary function of the pauper was to receive, because it was a duty for the rich man to give. In theory as well as practice the twelfth-century reaffirmed the teaching of the ages, further analyzing, articulating, and extending the tradition in keeping with the twin principles of charity and justice.

‡ One fundamental fact, pointed to by every writer on the subject of poverty, is that by nature the rich man and the poor man are the same,

"made by God from the same mud and borne up by the same earth" (in the words of Yves of Chartres). This in no way contradicted the belief in a hierarchy of functions, though it did lend support to the following idea, which, though derived from patristic and even classical pagan authors, was more original: that all earthly goods are held in common—"by natural law, everything is [owned in] common," ran the axiom in the form in which it was commented upon by Uguccio, who was following Gratian. The frequent use of words like *communicare, communicatio, communis,* and *communicandus* in speaking of the obligation to share is characteristic of twelfth-century habits of thought. At the same time, the old tradition of family-based claims to land was being supplemented by such new forms of association as communes, confraternities, craft guilds, and universities. Furthermore, the theory of the natural community of property, coupled with the principle of the pauper's right to the rich man's excess, was not incompatible with the feudal concept of the divided domain. From the distinction between eminent and useful domain, which implied that one and the same object could be the property of more than one rightful owner, jurists readily derived the idea that property could be owned both individually and in common. Possession thus became a matter of usufruct, and the owner was no longer seen as a *dominus* with the right to use and abuse but rather as a *dispensator:* this was the term that had long been applied to the bishop in his capacity as administrator of Church property and advocate of the poor, whose patrimony that property was. Thus the position of the pauper was one of waiting for others to discharge their duty toward him; this gave him a claim upon others, in exchange for which he incurred the obligation to pray for their souls. Twelfth-century authors are noteworthy for having clearly defined the nature, modalities, conditions, and extent of the work of charity and for having set forth the reciprocal rights and obligations of both rich and poor.

Thinking on these subjects was particularly vigorous toward the end of the century. Late in life, Hilduin, the chancellor of Paris (d. 1193), Peter of Blois, the archdeacon of Bath (d. 1196), Peter the Chanter (d. 1197), Peter Comestor, also a canon of Paris (d. 1198), Raoul Ardent (d. circa 1200), Alan of Lille (d. 1210), and Uguccio, one of the leading luminaries of the Bologna school (d. 1210), experienced the difficult final years of the twelfth century and witnessed the rise of the Waldensian heresy and the exploits of Durand of Huesca. The existence of poverty was for these men a pastoral problem.

The requirement to give alms was such a general obligation that even the poor were required to help one another. Saint Bernard exhorted a group of peasants to whom he was preaching to share what they had and help their neighbors. "No office, no sex, no condition, no age is exempt from the duty of charity," wrote Peter the Chanter, who castigated prelates and clerics of every rank whose abuses, he said, "are digging the grave of the poor."[6] Still harsher by virtue of the specificity of its allegations was a letter addressed by Peter of Blois to the bishop of Lisieux, Raoul of Wanneville, chancellor to the king of England. The great crisis of 1194 had not yet begun, but the harvest was late; the poor were hungry. After opening his letter with the customary greetings to a bishop, the archdeacon addresses himself to Raoul personally, in the following terms:

> The Lord erected you bishop to be the salt of the earth; beware of becoming the insipid salt that people throw on doorsteps to be crushed underfoot. . . . You leave the service of Christ vulnerable to opprobrium and scorn. . . . The Lord has shown you the straight way to salvation. A horrible famine is working its ravages on the poor. . . . *Pauper Christi vicarius est.* . . . Therefore open your heart and your storehouses, so as not to risk the judgment of damnation. . . . Already thousands of paupers are dead of hunger and misery and you have yet to touch a single one of them with the hand of mercy. . . . Already the harvest is turning yellow in the fields, and you have yet to comfort a single pauper. You are thinking of opening your storehouses not to alleviate the suffering of the afflicted but to sell more dear. . . . Other bishops have here and there borrowed to help the poor. But you are content to pocket your cash.[7]

In other words, the pauper was a favored creditor. Everyone was obliged to give according to his means and his estate.

Raoul Ardent lent his unique subtlety and profundity to thinking about the problems of poverty. Earlier in the century, a text attributed to Rupert of Deutz had described with monastic unction the symbolic gift of oneself to the poor: "The ewe gives her flesh to those who are strong, her milk to those who are weak; she covers with her fleece those who are naked and gives her skin to warm those who are cold."[8] Raoul's style was more vigorous. His hard-to-translate phrase *eleemosyna negotialis* has been interpreted to mean "pledged alms," in the sense that the donor pledges his whole person to the recipient of his charity; for Raoul, almsgiving was supposed to create a close personal bond between benefactor and recipient. The implication, of course, was that the Christian sacrifices himself in the service of others. Raoul listed the ways in which this could be done; he also proves that charity is an obligation incumbent upon all and explains what attitude a Christian should in conscience take toward the pauper. The rich man, the man with money, should use that money to help the indigent, widows, orphans, and marriageable girls. He should also grant postponements of debt to those who owe him money. The rich man, the man with influence, eloquence, and power, the officer, prosecutor, judge, or lord, should treat the pauper justly and refrain from exploiting him. The rich man, the man with physical strength and the strength of arms, should use that strength to aid and defend the weak. The rich man, the man who knows and practices a manual trade, should follow the example of the shoemaker who devoted one day a week to serving the poor for free. The rich man, the man who has knowledge, should put that knowledge to use on behalf of the ignorant and offer them his advice. Was there anything new in all this? Certainly not. Raoul took his inspiration from the parable of the talents in the Gospels and from the teachings of Saint Paul. Was Raoul anachronistic? No. He was simply asking that the poor of his time be given their due, a place in society that would answer the demands for purity, charity, and justice formulated in diverse ways by Waldensians, Humiliati, and other movements of popular protest such as those led by Fulk of Neuilly and his emulators. For Raoul Ardent the pauper was an object of love.

Was it necessary, however, for all the poor to receive an equal share of alms, without distinctions? A man like Gerhoh of Reichersberg was quite sensitive to the distress of the "crowd" of "paupers who lie with Lazarus before the door" as well as to the suffering of victims of feudal violence (which he firmly deplores in a letter to Henry the Lion) and of homeless invalids. As for Peter the Chanter, even though he says "do not consider the person of the pauper," still he holds that discrimination is essential (*Vidi cui des*). It is sacrilege, according to Peter, to give what belongs to the poor to those who are not poor. False paupers are usurping the place that rightfully belongs to the truly unfortunate: actors, disreputable persons, and men disguised as beggars, of whom he gives a portrait whose vividness cannot survive translation: "claimitant per plateas sub specie pauperum. . . . trivaliter se influentes, tremulosi et varias figuras aegrotantium induentes."[9] Along with these impostors he ranks the pseudo-preachers, half mountebank, half magician, with their false relics and fake bulls. James of Vitry also fulminated against this group. The warning issued by Peter of Blois is less clear-cut. The indigent person's vice or virtue matters little, he says; no limitation should be placed on charity. In another era Saint Ambrose had suggested an order in charity: *parentes, socii, fratres*, and then others. Peter, ostensibly reporting on a dialogue between himself and King Henry II at the abbey of Bonneval, states that the king observes a hierarchy in his almsgiving: the bulk of his charity goes to the liberation of the land where the Lord once lived; the next largest part goes to the poor; and the rest to orphans and other needy individuals.

Finally, it was deemed essential that the pauper's share be pure in origin. A gift of property acquired by evil means was wicked and thus unacceptable. This opinion, unanimously shared, was expressed in the following terms by John of Salisbury: "He who gives what he has stolen from the poor is like a son who would immolate his brother."

As for the amount of alms, it was generally held that the rich man should give whatever he held in excess, beyond his needs; this was difficult to pinpoint precisely, because it depended on so many things. Raoul Ardent went somewhat beyond this common opinion, however, maintaining that almsgiving should result in some measure of privation.

Twelfth-century thinking on the subject of poverty derived from traditional patristic writings about justice as well as charity. Writers did not limit themselves to reaffirming the right of the poor to the rich man's excess or to a quarter or third of the income from tithes and church property. Nor were they content merely to remind princes and bishops of their duty to protect the poor. Had they done no more than this, they would never have gone beyond viewing poverty from the standpoint of the rich, that is, exclusively in terms of the rich man's duty. But the question arose whether the poor could legitimately insist that their rights be observed. Traditionally paupers had been allowed to protest to their bishop by way of the so-called evangelical denunciation if they felt they were the victims of undue exactions or violence. Yet their right to the rich man's excess was not a legal but merely a moral claim, hence the appeal to the bishop was not truly a legal action. It was therefore up to the bishop to take action on his own in defense of the poor, in keeping with a tradition that Saint Bernard was pleased to see embodied in his own time by Saint Malachy in Ireland. During the period when the peace institutions were in operation, various self-defense movements were organized, the best known being the one that was involved in the Bourges affair in the eleventh century.

The end of the twelfth century saw a number of revolts that ended, as we know, unhappily.

The problem of theft by the needy was a difficult one to resolve. Gerhoh of Reichersberg tolerated no justification for theft and condemned the intention to appropriate another person's property. At most he was willing to make allowance for extenuating circumstances, which might reduce the gravity of the sin and justify a reduction in punishment. The law shared this viewpoint. In the *Miracles of Saint Benedict* we read an indulgent account of a theft committed by a needy man more out of indigence than out of malice. Gerhoh's position was shared by Peter Lombard, Peter of Poitiers, and Uguccio. However, Peter the Chanter maintained that the authorities have the power to force the wealthy to give alms. Charles the Good did as much in the case of the Bruges merchants who speculated on food stocks during the famine of 1126. At some point between 1194 and 1197, Richard the Englishman was persuaded by the theory of need to invoke the *Lex Rhodia* in order to absolve a starving man of guilt for a theft he had committed: Richard compares a society in the grip of famine to the crew of a ship in distress, in which case he says all property is held in common and available to all without exception. From there it was but a short step to the exoneration, and indeed the justification, of the starving thief. This step was taken by Uguccio and his disciples. As seen by the Bolognese master, the right of the poor man to appeal to his bishop against the rich man was little more than a legalistic device to legitimize his action in taking the law into his own hands. By the beginning of the thirteenth century it was generally accepted that the starving thief was innocent of any crime. Culminating these developments, the bishop of Paris, William of Auxerre (d. 1231), dealt with alms in the opening chapter of his treatise on justice, in which he states in no uncertain terms that a pauper in need and in a situation where all property is deemed to be held in common may without sin appropriate the bread he needs in order to survive.

Make no mistake about it, however: it was not esteem of the poor thief or his estate that justified his behavior and authorized his reacceptance into society. If poverty was not a vice, it was nevertheless a misfortune, and mendicity was a disorder. Both were opportunities for sin. Before he acceded to the papacy as Innocent III, Lothar of Segni, writing on the misery of the human condition, lucidly described the suffering of the poor man, his oaths, and even his rebellion against God; his concluding words are "O miserabilis conditio mendicantis."

The pauper was not automatically a saint, not even the voluntary pauper, much less the involuntary one. "Blessed are the poor in spirit, but not all of them," shouted Peter of Blois while preaching the Sermon on the Mount on All Saints' Day. The same sources that speak with contempt of the poor mention the urgent need for conversion. When Rigord, writing about Fulk of Neuilly, says that the poor were evangelized, he is to be understood in the pastoral rather than the gospel sense. In the year 1200 most men did not just despise the pauper, they feared him. They were afraid of his rage; his presence was a living reproach. This, in part, is the significance of the theme of the pauper Lazarus in the iconography of the period.

An attitude that was learned as well as experienced, fear of the pauper, like esteem, was not simply a reaction to the pauper as an individual. The role assigned to the poor was not a purely individual one. This was still another sign of the pauper's humiliation. For the pauper symbolized Christ, and as the representative of God the Judge, that familiar figure of the Romanesque era, he was to be feared. Peter Lombard stressed the function of alms as the atonement that "wipes away sin." The pauper was regarded as a kind of natural-born intercessor, a guardian of heaven's gate. Whether Christ was totally or only partially impoverished had become a matter of controversy, but in any case Christ was again made flesh in the poor. In dedicating the church of Saint-Martin-aux-Jumeaux, bishop Thierry of Amiens pointed out that Saint Martin had clothed Christ in the guise of a pauper: a traditional but ever-popular tale, as well as a point of theology, reminding the learned that to imitate Christ was to accept poverty. The old refrain, *Nudus nudum Christum sequi,* recurs many times in the works of the writers I have been examining. It occurs with particular urgency in a sermon delivered by Prévostin, canon-chancellor of Paris, shortly after Innocent III's bull of 1198 concerning the crusade: "How do you imitate me? You are afraid to be poor, and I was poorer than you, wherever I lived." Not only was the pauper the image of Christ the Judge and Christ the Redeemer, he was also Christ Living and Present. This is the meaning of the Hospitallers' motto, "The poor are our lords." To a large crowd in 1189 Alan of Lille explained the vocation of "simple folk" in these terms:

> Christ cannot make his dwelling place the house of the prelate, where simony resides. Shelter is denied him in the dwelling of the knight, where pillage finds safety. There is no lodging for him

among the bourgeois, for there usury lives. He is turned out by the merchants, who are governed by falsehood. Among the common people he has no place, because theft reigns supreme. Where, then, will Christ live? Only among the paupers of Christ, of whom it is said, Blessed are the poor in spirit.[10]

Four centuries before Bossuet, Raoul Ardent spoke of the *dignitas pauperum Christi* and referred to the poor as the "judges and gatekeepers of Heaven." *Pauperes Christi:* imperceptibly the phrase was extended from cloistered monks to all the poor—the poor with whom Robert of Arbrissel and Stephen of Muret had lived, the poor among whom Peter of Blois thought one should live in order to acquire sanctifying virtue ("Locum eligisti ubi posses inter multos pauperes unus esse"), and last but not least, the poor with whom Saint Francis of Assisi would soon merge his identity.

Is it accurate, then, to say that the place of the pauper was already among the elect? Hildegard of Bingen, in her *Visions* (circa 1141–51), saw "the whole Church much honored by its miserable [*egeni*]," and the poor ranked high on the Scale of Perfection proposed by Herrad of Landsberg. Doubtless there was much ambiguity. A moment ago the word *vocation* was used; but vocation suggests predisposition and choice. The reality was different. The position of the pauper did indeed rise over the course of one century, the twelfth, during which everything there was to say on the subject of poverty seems to have been said—but that rise was a mystical matter, a theoretical construct. Even when sublimated as a representative of Christ, the pauper in himself remained a forgotten figure: he was seen as the means by which his wealthy benefactor could earn salvation. He disappeared behind the image of Christ the Judge and Savior, or else his torment was portrayed in the features of the suffering Christ. The pauper continued to sleep beneath the porches of churches alongside the penitent. He was overshadowed by the rich, and indeed by God himself, whom others wished to see in him. Looked at realistically rather than symbolically, the poor, so numerous at the beginning of the thirteenth century, remained as humble as ever. Although they lived in humility with all its spiritual, redemptive connotations, they also lived in humiliation, bearing the weight of society's contempt.

PART THREE ‡
THE DESTITUTE
CONFRONT
THE RICH (FROM
SAINT FRANCIS TO
THE GREAT PLAGUE) ‡

‡ The "illustrious thirteenth century" did not last very long. For some historians the thirteenth century really begins in the years 1212–15, that brief period during which a Christendom that spanned East and West witnessed the remarkable coincidence of Las Navas of Tolosa, Bouvines, the Fourth Lateran Council, the awakening of the universities, the rise of Paris as a world capital, the flourishing of the Champagne fairs, and the power of Venice. For others the century does not really begin until 1229–30 with the end of the Albigensian war, the growth of the mendicant orders, and the effective beginning of the reign of Saint Louis. By contrast, historians are generally agreed that the end of the period of glory came as the final third of the century was about to begin. For it was then, even before the death of Louis IX, that stability and prosperity, patchy as they may have been, were shaken by symptoms of new social and economic difficulties. Thus the period of relatively good times lasted scarcely more than a generation. Still, the memory of that period lingered even among the poor: in France as "the good times of King Saint Louis," in Spain as the reign of the "wise" Alfonso X, in Italy and indeed throughout Christendom as the time of the Poverello of Assisi. This nostalgia for a period of relative peace and justice suggests that the collapse was rude and yet not so brutal as to destroy all hope or quell the anger of the poor.

CHAPTER SEVEN ‡
A FRESH LOOK
AT THE POOR

What was new about the way in which Saint Francis and Saint Dominic looked at the poor? Only the poor themselves can tell us for certain. But as usual they remain silent, stunned perhaps at having been understood and recognized at last. They remain, as always, humble and humiliated. But now at least they are held up as a contrast to the pride, violence, and avarice of the rich and powerful and declared to be not only images of the suffering Christ but as such, and such as they are, capable of playing a role in society (which is not the same thing as being used by society). For Francis and Dominic the pauper was a living human being, and poverty was a concrete reality. Rather than subscribe to some theoretical notion of what poverty was, they wanted to share the life of the poor. And they went looking for genuine poverty where it had recently found fertile soil in which to grow: in the cities.

My purpose in this chapter is not to discuss the life and works of the founders of the two principal mendicant orders but to discover the secret of the influence that they and their disciples were able to exert over the fate of the unfortunate.

TRADITION AND NOVELTY IN SAINT DOMINIC AND SAINT FRANCIS

The work of Dominic and Francis on behalf of the poor proved more successful than that of any of their predecessors; the Poverello succeeded where Waldo failed. My point is not to draw a contrast between the founders of the mendicant orders and their forerunners but to suggest that these two saints represent something new in the history of poverty. The work of Dominic, canon of Osma, gave new life to the old aims of the twelfth-century canonical movement, whose influence on works of charity we discussed earlier. Francis was not the first layman to comfort the downtrodden with his friendship and with the good words of the Sermon on the Mount. In their desire to live as paupers lived, with the poor, Dominic and Francis put into practice the recommendation of Peter of Blois, to live as a pauper among the poor. The idea was not original with them. Nor were they the originators of the doctrine of alms or of the idea of combining justice with charity; it was not they who formalized the rights of the poor. The hermits pioneered the practice of withdrawing from the world and then returning to preach the good word to the disinherited. Francis and Dominic had none of the privileges of the lay confraternities. Nothing that they did was without roots in a millennium-old tradition of charity. Like their predecessors they drew inspiration directly from the Gospels and the Acts of the Apostles.

What was new about the approach of Dominic and Francis no doubt came from their attentiveness to what we would nowadays call "signs of the times," which they called the will of God and the needs of their contemporaries. They did not shun the world or hold it in contempt, except to reject sin. They did not shun the countryside, where the emancipation of the serf was negated by the development of new forms of dependency. They did not shun the cities, where the rise of a cash economy made money more alluring than ever. Francis rejected the rules of monastic life proposed by the Curia in order to avoid isolating himself like the black and white monks and the Carthusians. Dominic continued to operate within the bounds of the canonical institution but as a pastor with a straightforward and adaptable style all his own, systematically attuned to the problems of the day. Rather than retreat from the world, Francis and Dominic raised their voices in protest against the arbitrariness of lords, the iniquity of judges, the asperity of merchants and speculators, and the animosities that divided families, cities, and nations. The evils that they fought were avarice, pride, and violence, not the world: for the world, after all, was the work of God, a work whose beauty and harmony inspired Saint Francis to lyrical heights.

Underlying the attitudes of both Franciscans and Dominicans was a single, universal theology and anthropology. Following different routes, the learned canon who founded an order of preaching intellectuals and the *idiota* (meaning one with little or no formal education, a term that Saint Francis humorously applied to himself) somehow arrived at identical ways of looking at men and the world. Dominic's vision derived from twelfth-century philosophy, whereas Francis's was the fruit of direct spiritual intuition; yet both men saw Nature as a marvelous creation designed to serve the needs of all mankind. All men were in essence equal, and all were equally redeemed by Christ; hence all enjoyed equal claims upon a patrimony originally held in common. Because both Dominic and Francis saw God as a savior and man as a redeemed sinner, they shared the same intimate understanding of the real problems of poverty.

Because Dominic was willing to share the uncertainty, the suffering, the disillusionment, and the hopes of the poor, he was credible as an opponent of the Catharist heretics and their stringent way of life. Both Dominic and Francis were irresistibly drawn to the humiliated Christ, on whom they modeled their lives. In a society where money tended to augment the power of those who had it and to diminish the status of those who did not, their role was to preach that the poor have value as human beings, and indeed that they are sacred images of Christ. They started from Christ and reached out to the poor. We shall do the same, in the hope of discovering what poverty was really like. The most significant and hence best-known episode in the life of Saint Francis is the kissing of the leper: before the kiss could be given, Francis had to overcome his own repugnance. This was something new: the poor and the afflicted were valued for their intrinsic human and spiritual worth and not as mere instruments for the salvation of the wealthy. In the late twelfth century the phrase *vicarius Christi* had been applied to the pauper; also significant was the extension to all the afflicted of the phrase *pauperes Christi*, previously reserved for monks alone.

The early thirteenth century saw an increase in the number and variety of the poor to whom Francis brought "a message of triumph over poverty."[1] Francis would not have been pleased had he known that artists would repeatedly depict him bowing down to the poor, for he always believed that he was lifting himself up to their level. Neither he nor Dominic was condescending or paternalistic.

Francis was still a young man and Dominic only a little older when great calamities swept the world at the end of the twelfth century. As a student at Valencia Dominic had had the opportunity to aid the victims of famine. Shortages of food, compounded by a growing population, forced many people without work, particularly the young, to take to the roads. In Italy, Francis, who had once dreamed of going on a crusade, surely must have been aware of the sad fate of the paupers abandoned at Zara. The "children" who in 1212 were left to fend for themselves in Sardinia when Genoese shipmasters found it expedient not to give them passage to the East were not much younger than Francis himself. It was then that Francis decided to marry Lady Poverty and formed his first group of disciples. In the countryside, according to one English prelate, many peasants had "nothing but a stomach and, what is worse, nothing to put in it." Elsewhere, landless laborers reverted to a kind of second serfdom by swearing servile homage to a lord. On two occasions, first in Castille and later in Languedoc, Dominic attempted to experience this form of dependency. For him, "the pauper is essentially a man whose weakness leaves him at the mercy of everyone in society."[2] The cities especially—cities that the merchant of Assisi knew well—were rife with the two scourges of usury and prostitution. The spectacle of usury inspired in Francis such a horror of money that his almsgiving nearly ruined his father, just as his free-spending ways as a young man had nearly ruined has father once before. And the sight of rampant prostitution in Toulouse inspired Dominic to open the doors of the hospice Arnaud-Bernard to the poor girls of that city.

Tendentious—and contradictory—exaggerations make it difficult to know what the real Saint Francis was like. But no matter how much the anecdotes have been retouched, there is no doubt that the Poverello was ready to experience poverty of every kind and degree. The life of Saint Dominic, though less obscured by legend, is scarcely less abundant than the life of Francis in charitable acts toward the poor of all estates. Dominic helps peasants with the harvest and shares the work of masons and other artisans. And Francis helps a poor priest by selling a package of fabric and a horse without his father's knowledge. Even the impoverished nobility is not left untouched: aristocratic girls in Toulouse are received into a school at Prouille founded by Dominic as an alternative to education by the Cathars, this being the only possibility previously available to their impecunious parents. Also noble is the poor knight to whom Francis gives the brand new armor and equipment of which he had been so proud. Similar in some ways to the episode involving Saint Martin at Amiens, the story of Francis and the knight is set in a totally different economic context: in the impoverished society of the late Empire, Martin gives only half of his cloak; in a society of relative abundance Francis gives everything he has.

This willingness to give away everything, expressed in another way by the episode in which Francis causes a scandal by stripping off all his clothes in the center of Assisi, expresses not just spiritual detachment but a determination to live a life of true poverty. Francis and Dominic did not adopt the Carthusian hermitic style or the Cistercian cenobitic style because they wanted to know the poor better, and to be better known by them, than they could have done had they lived apart from the world. Contemporary memoirs recount the facts. It was Francis's wretched clothing that shocked the English chronicler Matthew Paris, along with the absence of shoes, the lack of "sure" lodging, the manual labor to earn his daily bread coupled with the humiliating reliance on alms when necessary, and the renunciation of learning as a form of wealth—in short, the repudiation of ownership in any form whatsoever. Saint Dominic regarded learning as a form of service: the calling of the man of learning was to convey his knowledge to others. It was easy for him to combine this idea of his calling with a life of poverty similar to that led by people who had not chosen their lot voluntarily. In his rare writings Dominic almost always uses the noun *pauper* to mean the involuntary pauper. Since food, clothing, and housing are mere necessities, says Dominic, they should be "base" or "mediocre." Their absence is reason for joy.

Francis had to endure not only forms of poverty that he chose deliberately but also physical suffering that he never sought: problems with digestion and vision and even his stigmata (for we are entitled to believe that these were symptoms of some sort and not merely emblems of Christ's Passion). Thus Francis, perhaps even more than Dominic, was apt to include all the afflicted in his sweeping view of mankind, as the final words of the rule of 1221 suggest: "All babies and small children, poor and rich, kings and princes, artisans, farmers, serfs and masters, all virgins, widows, and married women, all children and adolescents, the young and the old, the healthy and the sick, all peoples, races, tribes of all tongues, all nations, and all men of every region of the earth."

THE MENDICANT ORDERS SEEK OUT THE POOR

In naming the order he founded, Francis deliberately chose a word commonly used in his day to refer to the lower strata of society: *Minores* (or Friars Minor, Minorites), which carried pejorative connotations of dependency and legal incapacity. The impoverishment of the mendicant friar extended even to the loss of his name: Franciscans and Dominicans both used the names of their heavenly patrons and were identifiable only by the additional mention of their native towns. The friar lost himself in the anonymous crowd of the poor. To insure that his friars would be even more available (one is tempted to write: even more malleable), Francis would have preferred not to found an order at all. Saint Dominic had a quite different conception of hierarchical institutions, whose rigid framework he thought left a good deal of room for maneuver.

The rapidity with which the mendicant orders spread proves that their goals were well attuned to the concerns of the day. The Dominicans and Franciscans shared their success with other, less important mendicant orders, such as the hermits of Saint Augustine, the Carmelites, and the Brothers of the Penitence of Jesus Christ, who were known as "Bags" because of the shape of their habit. In France in 1270 the Minorites maintained more than two hundred convents in five provinces, and the Preachers (that is, the Dominicans) ninety in two provinces. Among the first to call upon the services of the mendicants were certain bishops, starting with Fulk, the bishop of Toulouse. In Metz another bishop proclaimed "the presence of the Preachers profitable to laymen and clerics alike." James of Vitry stated as early as 1216 that "the Minorite order was truly the religion of the poor of Christ." Nevertheless, the mendicants did not immediately establish themselves within the cities. To do so was not the intention of either Dominic or Francis. Both men, and especially Francis, were afraid that settling in a fixed location would be incompatible with the life of the poor, whose uncertain living conditions and mobility they wished to share. When the early Dominicans and Franciscans came to the city, they stayed with friends in modest houses or even hovels. When they began to settle in the towns, they did so at some distance from the center of things, away from luxury and the worldly life in some barely incorporated suburb where the poorest of the poor resided: this happened when the Minorites came to Bologna in the third decade of the thirteenth century, as well as when the Dominicans moved into the Saint-Jacques area of Paris and into the poor Clos-Saint-Marc district in Rouen.

What changes permitted the mendicants finally to move into the cities? For one thing, the mendicants themselves came to see the cities, where poverty bred amidst plenty, as the promised land of their ministry. For another, the inhabitants of the towns, with varying degrees of clarity, came to see the mendicants as the answer to their moral anxieties. In a turn of events that may at first seem paradoxical, monks—individually poor but collectively wealthy—ceased to shun the cities as "sinkholes of iniquity," and mendicant friars—communally as well as individually impoverished—flocked to the cities in search of the rich and the poor, with a particular predilection for the latter. The more important, populous, and wealthy the cities became, the more paupers they sheltered, and hence the more mendicant friars. Cities seem to have been ranked by the number of mendicant convents they contained: Jacques Le Goff has suggested that the leading cities could boast of as many as four, while the least important had only one.

Was there a direct causal relationship between urban growth with its social consequences and the influence of the mendicant orders on poverty? Yes, in the sense that the mendicants became an integral part of the social fabric of the cities. They went to the cities in search of the most acute forms of poverty, so as to hold out hope of social rehabilitation to the most abject of outcasts. Still, it is a general truth that the causes of any historical phenomenon must be of the same order as the effect produced. Since the rise of the mendicant orders was a religious phenomenon, its causes must also have been religious. Economic growth in the cities offered the mendicants a field of action but did not engender that action. Nor did urban institutions shape the organization of the mendicant orders, which developed within an ecclesiastical framework. If the mendicant orders helped to transform the cities in which they worked, they did so not by wielding authority but through the credible witness that they were able to provide owing to their impoverished yet fraternal way of life.

One significant new feature of the mendicant orders was that the principle of fraternity so essential to their definition accorded well with the horizontal forms of solidarity prevalent in the cities and particularly respected by the poor. The traditional ecclesiastical model was vertical and hierarchical: the preaching of the prelate filtered down to his flock. This was now supplanted by a model of reciprocity, of charitable sharing. This tendency first began to develop a century earlier in the communes and confraternities. It is also evident in thirteenth-century community movements that brought together, in unprecedented new ways, laymen and clerics, rich and poor, to work in a common cause on which the mendicant spirit left its mark.

Associated with the rise of the mendicant orders in northern Italy in 1233–34 was a unique instance of such a movement: the "great devotion," or *Alleluia*, of which Fra Salimbene has left an eyewitness account. A wave of popular enthusiasm spread from city to city. It was hoped that this would result in the purification and regeneration of urban life. In many ways similar to the peace movements of two centuries earlier, the Alleluia was encouraged in Romagna primarily by the Dominicans and in Lombardy primarily by the Franciscans. Floods coupled with an infestation of grasshoppers had damaged the harvest and produced shortages of food, arousing the anger of the poor against speculators. The masses, in the grip of millenarian hopes, were receptive to the prophetic ardor of popular preachers like the Dominican Giovanni of Vicenza and the Franciscan Girardo of Modena. The former was assigned the task of reforming the communal statutes of Bologna and Verona; the latter received a similar mission in Parma, and others were assigned the same task in various other cities. These men, imbued with the spirit of their respective orders, incorporated provisions favorable to the poor in the new statutes. In Bologna and Vercelli laws allowing usurers to hold debtors legally at their mercy were abolished. While Giovanni of Vicenza was preaching in Bologna, it is said that a mob pillaged the house of one usurer and demanded that its owner be put to death. In Parma the Commune decided to remunerate attorneys who represented widows, orphans, and paupers. Throughout the region the mendicants helped to restore peace between warring factions and in troubled cities—a peace fervently desired by the poor, who bore the brunt of civil unrest. Popular ferment of this sort, in which sentimentality and utopia mingled with politics, occurred only in Italy, where its results proved ephemeral. Elsewhere, mendicant friars who became counselors, confessors, and chaplains to princes and kings were able to guide and in some cases to correct the conduct of these rulers toward the poor. Much is known about the role as advisers to Saint Louis of mendicants such as Gilbert of Tournai and Eudes Rigaud, a Minorite who eventually became archbishop of Rouen. Saint Louis assigned mendicant friars to investigate the actions of bailiffs on the royal estates and to redress any wrongs that they might have committed. Both the king and his subjects believed that because the friars practiced poverty for themselves and displayed concern to protect the poor, they were worthy of confidence. Those friars who were dispatched in search of injustice discovered the poor along the way. The complaints that they noted came mainly from widows, old people, and peasants who had suffered from heavy taxation, wicked judges, and armed violence: a common and monotonous litany of grievances, similar to those heard by other investigators, also mendicants, dispatched by Saint Louis's brother, Alphonse of Poitiers. The mendicants knew where to find the poor and, once they were found, how to talk to them and make them talk.

It was an important part of the mendicants' pastoral role to seek out the poor and bring them into closer contact with other laymen. Unfortunately it is difficult to find out a great deal about what they actually did, even if complaints from the secular clergy give us some idea of the extent of their operations. The Fourth Lateran Council placed great emphasis on the pastoral mission of the church, involving both supervision of confessions and exhortations to be just and to give alms; in this the mendicants were expert technicians, envied by the rest of the clergy. Few parish priests could move a crowd as skillfully as a Dominican preacher. A person might confess the most egregious sins to a traveling confessor with near certainty of never seeing him again, and many were willing to accept as penance from such confessors the obligation to give considerable sums as alms. On a more regular basis, the chapel of a nearby convent might become the meeting place of a local confraternity, a sort of consensual parish through which a good portion of what was collected in alms made its way to the poor. Confraternities commonly maintained local hospitals as well. The mendicant chapel held services that were less routinized than those of the parish church, attendance at which offered the additional pleasure of thumbing one's nose at the curate. People also derived satisfaction from being able to work out their bequests to the Church with the advice of a friar rather than at the dictate of the priest.

The mendicants did not escape criticism, however. Among other things, they were accused of supplanting the genuine paupers and taking what was given as alms for themselves. At a later date, this charge may have acquired some basis in reality. In any case, mendicant convents frequently played the role of intermediary between the poor and the rest of the faithful, a role previously held exclusively by the monasteries of the Benedictines. The Benedictines did not altogether relinquish that role in the thirteenth century, but the "charge of souls" assigned to the mendicants by the papacy insured that a very considerable proportion of Christian good works was carried out, if not by the mendicants themselves, then at least under their influence.

The charitable work of the mendicants was supplemented by such lay organizations as Third Orders and *béguinages*. From the first rule governing a tertiary order, the *Memoriale*, and the life of, say, Saint Angela of Foligno, one might conclude that the tertiary orders emphasized purely spiritual pursuits. In practice, however, they were deeply involved in charitable endeavors. Without evolving like the tertiary orders toward a common rule, the *béguinages* retained full autonomy in carrying out their role, which made some of them all the more effective in meeting local needs. They were particularly numerous in the territory between the Seine and the Rhine, with some sixty-odd houses in the Strasbourg region alone. Suspect as their autonomy may have been in the spiritual realm, it was quite otherwise in the realm of charity. This explains why the Council of Vienne (1311) showed itself less harsh toward those *béguinages* whose good works were manifest.

It is hardly surprising that little information has survived about the charitable activities of the mendicant orders and the movements they inspired. Themselves poor, the mendicants kept no records of the alms they received, and what evidence we have is mostly indirect. There is no corresponding dearth of information, however, when it comes to the mendicants' other mission, that of teaching laymen to show charity toward the poor, a lesson that was tirelessly repeated in confession, in sermons, and in edifying biographies.

EDUCATING CONSCIENCES   Mendicant friars were most zealous in carrying out the mission of educating consciences called for by the Fourth Lateran Council. The confessors' manuals, most of them written by mendicants, reflect an effort by the Church to adapt itself to the needs of urban society. One of the first manuals, that of Thomas of Chobham, looks upon indigence as an estate and begging as an occupation. Other manuals, frequently copied and glossed, such as those by Raymond of Peñafort (circa 1220–21), Alexander of Hales, John of Freiburg, William Peyrault, and, in the early fourteenth century, Jean André, depict poverty as both a state of mind and an existential reality. Poverty as a state of mind was a common obligation of all Christians, even the wealthy. Poverty as an existential reality lent itself to casuistic discussion. As we saw earlier, need could excuse the theft of food or clothing. It was also accepted as justification for nonpayment of debts and for failure to observe Sunday meals and fast days. These discussions led to further identification of the pauper with the person in need. Conversely, the need of the indigent was the basis for the duty to give alms. The confessors' manual repeated the traditional nostrums according to which almsgiving "wipes away sin" and the pauper provides his benefactor with the means of salvation.

In a sign of social change, the confessors' manuals begin to distinguish one kind of pauper from another in the final decades of the thirteenth century. Diverging from Raymond of Peñafort, John of Freiburg invokes the moral law of labor to reprove "false paupers"— the able-bodied, slackers, vagabonds—and harks back, by way of the *Decretum* of Gratian, to the repressive legislation of the early Middle Ages.[3] Jean André deems it necessary to point out that "poverty is not a vice" (*paupertas non est de genere malorum*) and to react against the age-old view that it is the result of a sin and a sinful state. The mendicants faced a difficult task in their attempt to rehabilitate the pauper, for circumstances conspired against them.

The moral and spiritual teaching of charity was encouraged by measures taken by the Fourth Lateran Council to promote preaching, especially by Dominicans. Unfortunately, theory and reality did not coincide. Many of the Preaching Friars were academics, more theologians and specialists in canon law than preachers. Some others had as their goal the collection of alms for their convents, for which purpose they contrived to produce relics, some more authentic than others, as well as to sell indulgences that proved attractive to many who liked to count the days, months, and years they could expect to spend in Purgatory. Still, of the thousands of sermons that have survived, many were inspired by what seems to have been genuine sensitivity to the suffering of the poor and made use of powerful techniques for arousing compassion.

Mendicants traveled assigned preaching itineraries, and the sermons they gave along the way provided ideal opportunities to instruct large numbers of people in the nature of poverty. To some extent tailored to the status and background of the audience, such sermons often incorporated vividly detailed moralistic tales, or exempla. So common was the use of exempla in preaching that anthologies of them were prepared by mendicant preachers or admirers of the mendicant orders. The best known anthologizers include Gossouin, John of Chatillon, John of Metz, Jacques of Provins, Guy of the Temple, Guibert of Tournai, the Pole Peregrine of Oppeln, a master general of the Dominicans known as Humbert of Romans, and, at the end of the century, Nicholas of Byard; the most prolific of all was Stephen of Bourbon.

From these sermons we gain some idea what sort of image of the pauper preachers believed most likely to move their audiences. The features of that image are conventional: the pauper is thin, blind, covered with sores, often lame, hairy, and dressed in rags. He begs from door to door, at church entrances, and on public roads. He has scarcely anything that can be called a shelter and lacks money even for a decent burial. For Peregrine of Oppeln, the poor can be divided into categories according to various physical and moral afflictions: there are the starving, the blind, the lame, the infirm, the leprous, the orphans, and the aged, as well as the dependent, the ignoble, and the contemptible.

‡ Such traditional views on rare occasions give way to more ample conceptions of poverty. An anonymous thirteenth-century Franciscan has left a rudimentary social theory in one *Tabula exemplorum*. The cause of poverty, he says, is human selfishness. The Creator has given humankind all that it needs. It is now incumbent upon men, who live in that structured body, society, to distribute the goods that God has given in an equitable manner. The destitution of the poor is a consequence of the superabundance of these goods in the hands of the wealthy. Peregrine of Oppeln, for his part, compares human society with the Red Sea: just as in the sea the big fish eat the small, in society the poor are devoured by the rich and powerful. The devil having sown the seeds of selfishness and rebellion among men, truth and charity have gone by the boards, the world is governed by "an eye for an eye," and it is therefore as red as the sea with the blood of victims.

Preachers rarely went so far as to demand reform. Only a few preached subversion, and even then at a rather late date. Some preachers addressed themselves directly to the poor, but only to recommend patience in tribulation and to persuade their listeners of the spiritual advantages of their situation and of the dignity that attached, in the eyes of God, to the function of the poor in the communion of saints, that of prayer. Almsgiving, the most common theme of the exempla, could be presented in a variety of ways. Thus as trade assumed a greater importance in the economic life of society, alms were often compared to the payment of a toll that opened the way to heaven.

Mendicant teaching on poverty, though not innovative, did emphasize certain aspects of the Christian tradition of charity over others and gave additional impetus to the movement to aid the poor. Never before had the message of charity been broadcast so widely or enjoyed so elaborate a doctrinal foundation. What is so interesting about Peregrine of Oppeln's sermons from the late thirteenth and early fourteenth century is that they were preached in the easternmost part of Roman Christendom, where the Dominicans maintained thirty-two convents and the Minorites some forty or more. Nearly two hundred of the Polish Dominican's manuscripts survive in twenty-five libraries throughout Europe. Peregrine left his native Poland only once, in 1311, to participate as a provincial in a Dominican chapter general at Carcassonne and at the council of Vienne. It is therefore all the more noteworthy that we find him adding to the patristic *auctoritates* not only Hugh of St. Victor but also the *Summa theologica* of Thomas Aquinas, whose writings had yet to receive the unhesitating approval of the Church or even of his own order. Clearly, then, contemporary philosophy did have an influence on mendicant teachings in regard to poverty and charity.

This is not the place to delve into the dispute between the mendicant orders and the secular clergy. In any case I fully subscribe to the view that, had Saint Francis still been alive, "he would probably have disqualified the antagonists and consulted those who were truly poor,"[4] who often seem to have been forgotten in the debate. In mitigation, can it be said that by 1250–60 the problem of poverty was no longer as acute as it had been at the beginning of the century? That Saint Bonaventure could have written in 1255 in his *Quod renunciationem* that famine was a thing of the past (*manifeste colligitur ex omnibus temporibus retroactis*) and take pride in his own generation's improved diet makes it somewhat less surprising that academics could have engaged in such interminable discussions about the problems of poverty.

Both sides in the debate looked upon charity toward the poor as a goal, but their arguments in favor of charity differed. For the seculars, service to the poor was one of the traditional justifications for the Church's ownership of property, the "patrimony of the poor." This was the view of men like Gérard of Abbéville and William of Saint-Amour. On the basis of his own and his family's experience of poverty, the latter included among the poor the large numbers of clerics without benefices, many of whom lived from hand to mouth. Was this in fact poverty? Service to the poor was also a matter of concern to mendicant academics, but for them the question was whether such service required absolute destitution. The proponents of the notion of "poor usage" and "moderate" ownership held that the possession of some resources, and even of some reserves, was indispensable for the charitable mission. Saint Bonaventure (*De paupertate*) was close to Saint Thomas (*Contra Gentiles*) in this regard. Thomas, while naturally repudiating any superfluous income, regarded the complete absence of material resources as an impediment to mystical contemplation and an obstacle to charitable endeavor. Giovanni Olivi, on the other hand, held that assisting the poor, however important, must take second place to spiritual purposes.

Besides the possibility of charity, another concern of the academics was to know who received alms, what they were receiving, and how they received it. Earlier thinkers had laid the groundwork for this aspect of the debate. William of Auvergne, writing on good and evil (*De bono et malo*) in the first half of the thirteenth century, did not limit himself to considering theft by needy persons. He analyzed the various forms of poverty in some detail. For him, gnawing, animal hunger could easily be distinguished from natural, healthy hunger, the former being characterized by extreme voracity without concern for the quality of the food. A man suffering from such hunger might well throw himself headlong, like a dog or a pig, upon any object whatsoever, even filth. Such hunger was ravenous, insatiable. A good observer of the behavior of the undernourished, William of Auvergne seems to have been more clearsighted than Gérard of Abbéville, who was quite willing to condemn the gluttonous behavior of a pauper who flung himself upon some vile dish (*foedissima gule flamma*): in Gérard's opinion, the man was not a true pauper. Besides hunger there was thirst, which the suffering victim might try to slake by drinking brackish water that only increased his suffering. There was also nakedness, which bared shameful deformities and sores that the pauper might attempt to hide beneath wretched rags. Cold left men shriveled, bent, and stiff. The pauper had no shelter from bad weather: anyone without home or hearth was truly an indigent, and William of Auvergne observed that the lack of a fire for cooking and warmth was "the very sign of poverty." On top of all this was the ultimate misery: indebtedness, which through the inexorable accumulation of loan upon loan led straight to servitude.

We should be careful, then, not to exaggerate the abstract character of scholastic theorizing, whose dry, disembodied form can easily conceal prior observation of actual facts. Awareness of the miseries of involuntary poverty is not lacking in Saint Thomas. He knows that there are men who cannot manage to eat the one indispensable meal each day. He sees the injustice in an excessive inequality of wealth: the opulence of one entails the indigence of another, and waste benefits no one. Thomas looks upon need as a great evil, because it endangers man's equilibrium in his spiritual and physical unity. Privation of such severity must be combatted, and in Thomist thought the exigencies of physical life are held to be even more imperious than the exigencies of spiritual well-being.

In the thirteenth century it was unthinkable that such principles should give rise to a program of social reform. There is no point looking for answers to our questions in treatises intended to help the clergy of another era apply their religious doctrine. Scattered in various places in the *Summa theologica* (especially II, 2), Thomas's ideas about poverty also emerge, perhaps even more clearly, in consultations that he held with confessors and princes as well as in his sermons and occasional works.[5]

A part of the economic thought of the scholastics was concerned, at least in a negative sense, with protecting the poorest of the poor: for example, scholastic ideas about usury, hoarding, speculation, abuses of taxation and the courts, and the just wage. In a more positive vein, the duties of all Christians toward the poor were an explicit part of scholastic teaching. In this respect the scholastics were for the most part content to adapt and elaborate the positions of their predecessors.

Because the manner of giving is more important than what one gives, one must give courteously and with respect for others, wrote William Peyrault. Giovanni Olivi's statement of the conditions under which alms should be given might well have commanded universal assent: true alms, he said, should be given promptly, joyously, abundantly, and reasonably. Only the last of these conditions might have aroused controversy. How much should one give? Where did superfluity begin? Since superfluity was a relative matter, Saint Thomas and Saint Bonaventure sought to pin it down precisely. One definition of superfluity, acceptable for laymen at least, was that too much is what remains once one's own needs and the needs of one's family and dependents have been taken care of. In a hierarchical society of orders, it goes without saying that such needs included whatever expenditures were necessary to maintain one's social rank. The amount therefore varied according to one's status. Still, if a neighbor was in difficulty, it was a duty to help him out by sacrificing some part of what one did not absolutely need. Contemporaries said, along with Eudes of Châteauroux, that ordinary alms should come out of what was superfluous and extraordinary alms out of what was necessary, with one proviso: alms must come from legitimate property and income. Stolen goods did not qualify, whether they came from larceny, misappropriation of an inheritance or dowry, violence, injustice, illicit speculation, or usury. The usurer's gift was the "substance" of the poor. Justice must precede the giving of alms. A bishop of Angers around 1220 recorded in his synodal statutes that "almsgiving is not always the ideal means of repairing sin, because before generosity is possible justice must be done." Posthumous restitution of ill-gotten gains (by means of a will) does no good because it comes too late, said William Peyrault.

As for the recipient of alms, few agreed with Saint Francis that wicked people might share in the benefits. The general opinion of the scholastics was that alms must not encourage idleness. Begging was not looked upon with favor. William of Saint-Amour, for example, used the generic Latin term *trutannus* to describe able-bodied persons who made a career of begging, as well as young *béguines* and members of bands and sects like the neo-Messalians of Paris who pretended to live a life of prayer while maintaining themselves at other people's expense. William, a very traditional advocate of the seculars, limited the right to receive alms to the sick, children, old people, the involuntarily unemployed, and others in exceptional circumstances. Charity must not, he argued, become a pretext for indiscriminate handouts. In each case the right of the prospective recipient to receive alms should be carefully scrutinized, and he should be advised to find work to support himself. William's narrow-mindedness was not merely the result of inflexibility; he anticipated by several centuries certain authoritarian forms of charity. It would not be long before charitable initiatives by laymen coupled with renewed economic difficulties would put both generosity and ingenuity to the test.

CHAPTER EIGHT ‡ THE FLOURISHING OF CHARITABLE INSTITUTIONS

COLLECTIVE CHARITIES

The "revolution in charity"[1] that began in the twelfth century really came into its own in the thirteenth. There was little change in the nature of charitable endeavors, but the proliferating services and institutions settled into more stable organizational forms, better adapted to the social conditions of urban life and a cash economy. In addition to charitable contributions by individuals, there were new collective and even administrative initiatives, indicating that in a society where money played an important role, concern for the indigent was mandatory.

No longer was nearly all charity administered by monks. But monastic almonries were far from a thing of the past: monasteries that had had no almonry in the twelfth century established one in the thirteenth, and among monastic offices the almoner's was one of the most richly supplied in rents, dues, and services. This was not without drawbacks: the almoner who controlled a regular source of income was all too likely to look upon his position as a benefice. The survival of traditional almonries was also threatened by the new orders, which began to attract gifts and clients. To be sure, the liturgical ritual of distribution of food and *mandatum* to a selected group of paupers was scrupulously maintained. But at monasteries such as Cluny, Corbie, Tournai, Mont-Saint-Michel, Saint-Ouen in Rouen, and Saint-Denis charity no longer seemed to serve as important a social function as before. The demands of the poor were no longer so great as to force the monks to slaughter their livestock, and the leading abbeys devoted no more than two to five percent of their income to distributions and hospitality. Records of pastoral visits attest to this decline of the monastery's traditional charitable role. Eudes Rigaud, visiting the province of Rouen, blamed the situation on a decline in almsgiving and even more on mismanagement. No doubt the shift of indigence away from the countryside and into the cities also played a part. In Florence, for example, by the fourteenth century the Benedictines of La Badia and the monks of Vallombrosa had been maintaining hospitals for more than two hundred years.

Monastic charity was supplanted initially by the work of newer orders: the Templars, who according to court documents made distributions three times a week, the Hospitallers, who according to investigations of their activities in 1338 and 1373 engaged in similar practices, and the mendicant orders to the extent that the friars, themselves poor, were able to distribute alms.

The charitable activities of bishops and canons were also institutionalized through the establishment of episcopal and canonical almonries. To help distribute alms during pastoral visits, Simon of Beaulieu, archbishop of Bourges from 1281 to 1294, appointed an almoner, a position that did not exist twenty years earlier when Eudes Rigaud visited Rouen or when Nicolas Gellent visited Angers. Permanent, fixed almonries were established in a number of episcopal sees. In Barcelona a reorganization of canonical revenues in 1226 was behind the institution of the *Pia Almona de la Seo*, which distributed daily meals to 50 paupers on the average but which in the famine year of 1317 provided 1,920 meals to 178 individuals. In 1288 the bishop of Valencia set up a permanent almonry to distribute food on Saturdays and major holidays as well as to maintain a hospital. In taking similar steps in 1311 the archbishop of Bologna ordered his suffragans to appoint a number of *uomini da bene* each year in each district of their episcopal cities to take charge of the collection and distribution of alms. Elsewhere, provincial councils and synodal statutes encouraged and regulated charitable gifts. This was true of France, for instance, particularly in the western provinces, most notably Angers, and of Spain, at Valladolid (1322) and Tortosa (1343). Curates were reminded of their duty to give lodging to travelers and paupers.

Somewhat slower to act than lesser bishops, the pope finally created an official department of paupers in the papal curia at Avignon. Almsgiving by princes, even princes of the Church, was a personal matter. Popes and cardinals had always been attentive to this duty, but a permanent department was ill suited to nomadic character of the papal court. Once the court had settled in Avignon, however, a specialized department financed by direct payments and bills of credit drawn against papal collectors administered papal alms under the supervision of the chamberlain. The papal almonry came to be known as the Pignotte, doubtless from the *pignotta*, or small loaf of bread that used to be distributed to the poor, who also received other food, clothing, and shoes as circumstances required. Because the papal bureaucracy was in the habit of keeping careful accounts, we know the receipts and expenditures of the Pignotte over a considerable period of time, with few gaps. Unfortunately, its gifts did not go only to the genuine poor. Paupers themselves do not appear in the documents—we see only an indistinct mass. All we know is the relatively constant amount that was spent ostensibly on their behalf. Papal alms also went to charitable institutions, particularly hospitals, scattered throughout Christendom.

Pope Benedict XII showed himself particularly generous in 1340. To aid the inhabitants of northern France (Cambrésis, Vermandois, Thierarché), then suffering from the first skirmishes of the Hundred Years' War, the pope sent one of his chaplains, a man with the prophetic name of Bertrand Carit, to distribute to the poorest victims of the war a sum of 6,000 florins in gold (or 8,900 *livres tournois*) transferred by the bank of the Buonaccorsi in Florence. This gift was augmented by further contributions from the bishop of Laon and the king of France, Philip VI.

The Pignotte is an intermediate case, resembling both the ecclesiastical almonries and the princely ones. The latter were established in the courts of almost all European princes in the thirteenth and fourteenth centuries. Generosity, like justice, was a princely affair, and for a Saint Louis "administration was a supreme form of serving one's neighbor."[2] To turn this formula around, one might equally well say that, for Saint Louis, serving one's neighbor was what was best in the exercise of power. So much is stated explicitly in the king's *Instructions* to his son. The royal almonry did not begin with Louis IX, however. Philip Augustus had granted charters of privilege and safeguard as well as gifts and foundations to leprosariums, infirmaries, and hospitals, in some cases renewing previous grants. The role of the royal almonry should not be confused with the king's personal charity. Think of the edifying anecdotes told by Joinville about Saint Louis or by William of Saint-Palthus, the confessor of Queen Marguerite, or about the detailed information contained in the canonization proceedings. Louis IX was the founder of the Quinze-Vingts and other homes for the blind such as the one in Caen; among the miracles ascribed to him, many involve curing blindness. The episode with the leper of Royaumont recalls the kissing of the leper by Saint Francis, who was a model for Saint Louis. Concerned, like Francis, about the scourge of prostitution, Louis IX founded the Maison des Filles-Dieu in Paris. The sick were aided by the establishment or renovation of hospitals in Vernon, Pontoise, and Compiègne, to say nothing of the favors granted to the Hôtel-Dieu in Paris. In the mind of Louis IX and his contemporaries, the poor were first and foremost invalids and beggars. It was for their benefit that the king staged public meals, some of which, we are told, were attended by as many as two hundred guests. He also launched administrative inquiries into confiscations of property and other injustices committed against the poor. Thus there were two Saints Louis: the legendary figure of hagiography who unbeknownst to the members of his own retinue would leave his bed at night and go to lie among the poor at the Vernon infirmary, where he is said to have slept in a bed which was subsequently kept empty and maintained as the "bed of the blessed Louis," and the politician who ordered the investigation of allegations of injustice and saw to it that strict accounts were kept of his gifts of alms.

No other king of France can compare to Louis IX for his personal involvement in charitable activities. After him, however, the royal almonry would continue to operate as a regular department of the royal household responsible for supervising the work of all royal infirmaries and hospitals: its supervisory duties included appointment and inspection of personnel, distribution of subsidies, auditing of accounts, and judging matters of litigation.

The royal almonry of France was not unusual. Alphonse of Poitiers shared the charitable concerns of his brother Louis. Besides looking into allegations of injustice, he established an almonry and appointed a gentleman by the name of Peter the Treasurer who seems to have played an important role in many gifts and charitable foundations attributable to the count. Outside France, Saint Louis had emulators among his Castilian cousins: in 1216 Ferdinand declared his wish that his gifts of alms should benefit everyone (*tam bono homini quam malo*). Other emulators include his English brother-in-law and nephew, Henry III, and Edward I, during whose reign there was apparently a royal almoner at court, to whom allusion is made in a document dating from 1277.

We can gain some idea of what princely charity was like from the records of the almonry of the countess of Artois, Mahaut of Burgundy: her accounts reveal a meticulous attention to such details as sources of income, type and frequency of gifts, recipients, and means of distribution, including bailiffs and hospitals such as those founded by the countess at Hesdin and Salins. Mahaut inquired about the needs of the poor wherever she went. In Calais during the severe winter of 1306 she had alms distributed to the neediest following a preliminary inquiry.

In 1321 eleven thousand people received the benefit of her generosity at Saint-Omer. What was done by a princess who was rightly or wrongly reviled in her own time was even more surely done by others of more saintly reputation. In the thirteenth century the daughter of the king of Hungary, Elizabeth of Thuringia, who died in 1231 and was canonized four years later, was famous for her charity. A hundred years later, in 1336, Elizabeth of Aragon, the wife of Diniz I of Portugal, established an almonry to serve the victims of the disasters of 1333, prisoners of war, abandoned children, and victims of venereal disease. At her behest a hospital was founded at Coïmbra and placed, significantly, under the patronage of Saint Elizabeth of Hungary. In this same period the Aragonese court maintained an almonry first established by Pedro the Ceremonious as well as a *procurador dels miserables* whose responsibilities included bringing food and clothing to prisoners and sending a doctor to visit the prison each week. The *padre de los Huerfanos* saw to the needs of abandoned children and provided dowries to young girls and work for apprentices.

The princely almonries were as much a part of tradition as their ecclesiastical counterparts, which they resembled. Both dispensed charity to the masses in a hierarchical and providential manner. The princely almonries are distinguished for having been one of the first secular charitable institutions, though, to be sure, in the Middle Ages it was scarcely possible to differentiate lay from ecclesiastical, spiritual from secular. The thirteenth century also saw the development of secular charitable initiatives at the parish level and in the confraternities. Originally intended to provide mutual assistance, these local institutions were encouraged by the influence of the mendicant orders to broaden their efforts. Few records of charitable institutions at the parish level have survived, but we have enough to have some idea of what they did. Though the names of the institutions vary from place to place, their goals were similar and they seem to have functioned in similar ways. In the absence of an adequate comprehensive account, we must settle for a few comparative remarks.

In the phrase *common alms*, the adjective refers to the parish and lends a significant new twist to a banal noun. Sometimes the terminology used was even more concrete: the word *purse* was sometimes substituted for *alms*. In the Low Countries and the Empire the expression *the Poor Table* referred to a table placed next to the church door for the purpose of making distributions to the poor. The expression is not unrelated to the phrases used to describe the first credit institutions or banks (*moneychanger's table* or *exchange table*). Combining the concrete with the spiritual, some poor tables bore the name of the Holy Spirit. In southern Europe local charity funds were named for the receptacle in which alms were deposited: in Rouergue the poor fund was called the *pauper's bowl*, in Spain the *pauper's plate*, and in Italy the *pauper's trunk* (*ceppo*).

As early as the thirteenth century there were poor tables in rural parishes in what is now northern France and Belgium. At Prisches in Hainault we know that the Poor Table owned land and had regular sources of income because in 1330 it leased to the count of Avesnes a half-interest in a windmill for an annual rent of twenty *sous parisis*. But for the period prior to 1350 we know a good deal more about urban poor tables, which were much the same everywhere, than we do about rural ones. We know of the Poor Table of Saint-Omer because the aldermen of that town assigned certain revenues to the Poor Table and arranged for food to be distributed in two parishes. "Tablekeepers" appointed by the curate managed the property and income from gifts, bequests, rents, and alms, records of which were kept by the "collector." This system of management by prominent laymen under the supervision of the parish clergy was in wide use: for example, in Brussels and Dinant in the mid-thirteenth century, in Calais, where Countess Mahaut institutionalized the system in three parishes, and in Compiègne, where the position of poor table administrator was looked upon as apprenticeship for work in the town government. Sometimes, a single poor table was left intact even after a town was divided into two parishes, as at Douai and Mons, whereas in Louvain the Common Table of the Great Holy Spirit supervised the work of separate poor tables in the new parishes.

Much is known about the Common Alms of Mons. It was preceded by the so-called Good Houses, which assisted the poor in the twelfth century. In the following century the city appointed administrators of the poor fund. That their responsibilities were important is clear from a document dating from 1290 indicating the amount of property amassed through gifts, bequests, and annual collections for the poor. Recipients of assistance were divided into two categories. The first was made up of paupers inscribed on a list kept by the almoners and aldermen and updated annually; those on the list carried a token authorizing them to receive regular assistance. The second group consisted of others entitled to public assistance from time to time. Assistance was in the form of money (particularly after 1308) as well as in kind (bread, salt pork, especially at Christmas and Easter, and clothing). The Common Alms also saw to the burial of the poor and, what is particularly noteworthy, provided for the upkeep of "poor pupils in the school" of Mons (1286). Unfortunately, we do not know the schedule of distributions for this period. Many other examples might be cited from Holland, Germany, and England. Common alms seem to have been collected almost everywhere in France. The bishop of Grenoble, during his visit to Vif-outre-Drac in 1340, pointed to the absence of charity distributions as contrary to custom (*antiquitus constituta*). In the diocese of Angers fines payed by blasphemers went into the "poor purse." Penitential alms prescribed by confessors were also frequently paid into these parish funds.

It is clear that parish institutions in the north were similar to those in the south. For example, in Rouergue in the late thirteenth century there were "poor bowls" in both the episcopal city of Rodez and its suburbs. "Poor collectors" made regular rounds and administered funds obtained through confiscations and fines imposed by the consuls, who were actually in charge of local charity. The same is true of Millau, where the consuls supervised annual collections and in the thirteenth century added three new distributions to the two that existed previously. Municipal participation in charitable assistance came early to the south of France.

Spain provides two additional examples of charity at the parish level. In the diocese of Valencia in 1288, a "father of the poor" was elected in each parish and given the task of handing out sums of money every Saturday. In addition to money, meat and rice were handed out on holidays, and on All Saints' Day winter clothing and blankets were also distributed. The father of the poor also made home visits and saw to it that a doctor regularly examined the poor. Those receiving assistance were listed in a poor book. From the late thirteenth century Barcelona possessed a system of charitable institutions appropriate to a city of some forty thousand inhabitants. In addition to the Pious Alms of the Cathedral, there were "poor plates" (*plats dels pobres*) in the four parishes—Santa Maria del Pi, Sant Pere de les Puelles, Sant Jaume Apostol, and Sant Miquel y Sant Cugat del Reco del Forn. In the maritime district of Santa Maria del Mar, a poor plate was first established in 1275 at a time of economic distress. Quite popular to judge by the bequests that contributed to its holdings, the work of this organization was supervised by *probi homines* who were elected annually.

The work of the poor tables in the Low Countries and of the poor plates in Spain was carried on in northern and central Italy, in the *contado* as well as the city, by organizations like the *ceppo* of Carmignano, which owned property in land, and the Society to Feed Christ's Poor of San Godenzo in the Mugello. But in Italy the confraternities seem to have played a more important role.

Since the charitable endeavors of the confraternities are so well known, I shall here cite only a few examples emphasizing the most important aspects of their work. Charity was not the raison d'être of most confraternities but rather a natural extension of their original objectives. This observation is true even of the confraternities of piety and penitence, whose primary aim was to promote the spiritual progress of their members. It is even more true of the trade confraternities that developed in conjunction with, or in some cases as forerunners of, the craft guilds. Originally the purpose of such groups was to promote mutual aid among members, and this aid was eventually extended to the poor and sick. Confraternities were common in the Low Countries, particularly among weavers, fullers, shearers, dyers, and ironsmiths. One of the oldest was the Charity of Saint Eligius at Béthune, whose original purpose was to provide its member ironsmiths with a decent burial and prayers for the departed soul; subsequently it assumed responsibility for a hospice that sheltered a dozen paupers in 1332. Many confraternities saved the leftovers from their common meals for the poor and required members to leave a bequest and to pay a portion of their earnings into a poor fund known as "God's denier."

Distributions were made both on major religious holidays and on special occasions such as funerals, when assistance would be handed out to paupers in the cortege. The number of recipients was in some cases quite high. The confraternity of the Holy Spirit in the small town of Montbrison, for example, aided as many as three thousand indigents.

The name of the Holy Spirit was associated with quite a number of charitable confraternities. We encounter it in such places as Lyons, Geneva, Freiburg, Payerne (Peterlingen), Sion, Zurich, Cologne, and Brussels. Even more frequent was the patronage of the Virgin, examples of which were common in Normandy.

We have an unusually large amount of information about the role of confraternities in Florence.[3] Mendicants there could choose among various sources of assistance and even combine several different ones, for in addition to handouts from the parishes and the convents distributions were also made by the *arti* and confraternities. The most important confraternities were maintained by the Franciscan Tertiaries, who since 1229 had operated the hospital San Paolo dei Convalescenti, and by the powerful company of Or San Michele, a good example of a devotional confraternity that was transformed only three years after its foundation (in 1291) into a charitable organization. These two institutions were endowed with sufficient resources to be active in several different kinds of charitable endeavor. The poor had to be fed, clothed, and housed. In time of war or famine they flocked to the city from the *contado*. To the shelter provided by hospitals, convents, and private palaces, Or San Michele added its Monlupe hospital and Florence poorhouse. Its regular work involved distribution of food and clothing several times a week at its headquarters in Or San Michele. In addition, the brothers toured the contado every two months, at which time they distributed alms to the poor in the countryside. Surviving records of Or San Michele tell us a great deal about the methods of almsgiving and distribution in the first half of the fourteenth century.

Like other charitable organizations, the company had a dual system of distributions: one for all who came begging, the other for a regular group of indigents. Each beggar received a few deniers and, depending on the season and the vagaries of supply, clothing and bread. In 1324 nearly a thousand paupers were served on three occasions between 13 and 31 October. In 1347, we are told, six to seven thousand indigents received assistance three to four times a week, and in the then rural district of Santa Maria Novella alone eighteen thousand gifts of alms were handed out. In that year the confraternity devoted one quarter of its revenue to the manufacture and distribution of bread.

Unlike the larger number of anonymous beggars, the few hundred indigents whose names appeared on the list of regular clients of the confraternity enjoyed special privileges. These regulars were chosen after consideration of their family and occupational situation, and next to each name the camerlingo's reason for selection is noted. The amount of aid received by the regulars ranged from four to twenty times the amount given to other beggars. In 1324 the average gift was five sous. In addition they received regular handouts of food (especially bread), clothing (tunics), and shoes. Regulars carried a ticket known as the *polizza* entitling them to receive their due and for this reason were said to be registered *in polizzis*. The company of Or San Michele, with its highly developed organization and its concern to tailor its efforts to the needs of the time and the circumstances of each individual, typifies the kind of charitable institution that flourished so widely in the thirteenth century.

Collective charity was not limited to the distribution of aid. Some almonries and confraternities maintained hospitals. Furthermore, confraternities and communities of tertiaries like that of San Paolo in Florence were associated with *béguinages* whose occupants often educated the children of the poor and staffed the infirmaries in addition to distributing alms.

Charity found many other occasions in the thirteenth century to bridge the widening chasm between the rich and the poor. In the Iberian kingdoms, still locked in combat with Islamic forces on their own territory as well as in Africa and on the Mediterranean, paupers who fell victim to a razzia or boarding party would have been in dire straits indeed but for the work of the redeeming orders, which had been founded in the previous century and which, with the assistance of various confraternities and gifts of alms, organized prisoner exchanges and paid ransoms. Although their success was on the whole limited, in some cases their work proved remarkably effective.

By contrast, the abominable treatment of the poor by the courts was an almost daily scandal. Saint Louis was fully aware of this when he launched his inquires and wrote his *Instructions* to his son. A similar indignation against wicked judges may be found in Philippe de Beaumanoir's *Coutumes du Beauvaisis* and in the sermons of many preachers. In order for the poor to receive decent justice they needed competent defense. William Peyrault sketched out a legal ethics and defined the responsibilities of the legal profession toward the poor. Some years later, the Church, by canonizing Saint Yves of Tréguier, held him up as a model for judges and lawyers. In popular iconography the saint is often shown flanked by his clients, the widow and the orphan—a sign of the times. Another was the appointment of "poor-lawyers" in several areas. The courts of Senlis, studied by Bernard Guénée,[4] were not the only ones in which paupers found it difficult to meet the costs of justice. At the Council of Vienne in 1311 a memorandum of the bishop of Angers, Guillaume Le Maire, vigorously protested the abuse of the poor in the courts. Subsequently the tradition of the bishop as defender of the poor was invoked in defense of the claim that clerics should not argue any case in court except on behalf of paupers. In the fourteenth century the count of Savoy, Amadaeus VI, established the position of poor-lawyer. In a similar vein, Alfonso XI of Castille in 1337 established an official scale of legal fees and ordered the *alcaldes* to provide a lawyer to the poor. In mid-century the city of Valencia had an *advocat dels miserables* on its payroll, and Lyons employed a similar official. Poor-lawyers were common in Spain and Italy in the fifteenth century.

Even in death charity worked to repair inequalities. Many confraternities took care of burying paupers as well as their own members. For was burial not the seventh of the works of mercy, and necessary to insure that the bodies of paupers—Christian bodies—would not be buried indecently and without prayers, like the remains of animals? Usually the role of the poor in funerals was strictly symbolic: they followed the bier of a wealthy or powerful personage and prayed for his soul. For reward they were given alms after the services. We would know next to nothing about how the poor died were it not for the records of the confraternities and hospitals and rare documents concerning life in the parishes. To die in a hospital was almost a privilege for a pauper, for the chaplain would offer his spiritual assistance while the brothers and sisters would do their best to alleviate the dying person's final sufferings. The hospital books record expenditures for winding sheets and for the wages of the grave diggers who buried the body in the hospital cemetery (when the canonical regulations governing the confraternity permitted it to maintain one—if they did not, the body would be buried in the pauper's section of the parish cemetery, in which case members of the confraternity paid to insure that the dead would receive the prayers of the church and a tombstone). The Charitables of Béthune were not without imitators. In Narbonne a "fund for winding sheets for dead paupers" was in operation in 1227. Documents pertaining to the Common Alms of Mons prove that, contrary to common opinion, in the fourteenth century it was not true that all the poor were simply wrapped in winding sheets or even left completely naked and buried in shallow graves: the Common Alms paid for paupers' caskets. The confraternities paid the customary funeral fees to priests who officiated at the funerals of the poor. Bishops were sometimes forced to take sanctions against curates too intent on collecting their parish fees at the expense of the poor: an exemplum relates the story of one bishop who, upon learning that a curate had neglected his duties in connection with the burial of a pauper, performed the rites himself and then insisted that the curate pay him the sum to which he, the bishop, would have been entitled had he been the curate's vicar.

Until quite recently the poor were
almost the only clients of hospitals,
places in which they felt truly at
home. When the twelfth-century Hospitallers popularized the expression "our lords, the poor, our lords, the sick," they were not just
giving vent to pious sentimentality. Hospitals both small and large
proliferated throughout Europe in the thirteenth century, and though
their spread has been extensively studied in historical monographs the
record is still not complete.

I shall not dwell here on the rather special case of the leprosariums,
which segregated rich as well as poor lepers from the rest of society.
According to the English chronicler Matthew Paris there may have
been nineteen thousand leprosariums in western Christendom by the
middle of the thirteenth century. Hardly any town was too small to
warrant a leper house, and many were crowded around the outskirts of
large cities. England and Scotland are said to have had more than two
hundred. A century later, the diocese of Paris alone boasted some fifty-
odd leper houses, more than half of which were run by rural parishes
and confraternities. Only fifteen of these housed sick patients. In 1321
a frightful massacre followed rumors that lepers had poisoned the
wells. It is clear, however, that leprosy declined from the end of the
twelfth century to the middle of the fourteenth, and the number of
new foundations of leper houses diminished. But this did nothing to
improve the lot of victims of the disease. Treated as if they were the
living dead, lepers were outcasts and even more feared than vagabonds;
the greater the attention paid to them, the more keenly they must have
felt their humiliation.

The best we can do at present is to give a rough estimate of the
number of hospitals of all sizes available to the poor and the ill for a
night's lodging, for temporary or permanent shelter, or for treatment of
specific diseases. Other questions are almost impossible to answer:
How were hospitals distributed geographically? What was the hospi-
tal-to-population ratio, given that the size of the population itself remains difficult to estimate? How many patients could the hospitals
and hospices serve? From a great deal of research, of uneven quality, it
is possible to draw certain limited conclusions. In the highly urbanized
and in some sense industrialized regions of northern France, the
Netherlands, and Italy, hospitals were established by bourgeois benefactors as well as by the Church and the aristocracy. In Lille a prominent citizen established the Gantois Hospital, not far from the Count-

ess Hospital founded by Jeanne of Flanders. The situation was similar in Douai, Bruges, Ghent, and Brussels. The city of Saint-Quentin was particularly well endowed, with seven hospitals, two infirmaries, a *béguinage,* and an orphanage. In Italy even modest cities were well supplied with hospitals, and economic centers such as Milan, Genoa, Venice, and Florence were particularly well off. Florence, according to Giovanni Villani, was served by more than thirty hospitals. Certain hospital-based confraternities spread to large numbers of towns: for example, the Disciplinati of Saint Thomas, founded in 1316, were well known in Venezia, Friulia, and Trentino.

The fair towns of Champagne required sufficient hospitals to serve the needy retinue of the great merchants. In Provins, contributions by the bourgeois of the town as well as the counts in both the upper and lower cities made possible the completion of construction work on the existing hospital and the renovation of the hospice of the Holy Spirit. Hospitals of equal importance were found in Lagny, Bar-sur-Seine, and Meaux.

As for Paris, a capital city in many senses of the word, some sixty hospitals were barely enough for a population estimated at more than two hundred thousand in 1328. The size of these hospitals varied widely, from the old Hôtel-Dieu down to the tiny maisons-Dieu. Hospitals were located in the City, the populous Right Bank area, and in the outskirts along the main roads, while the abbatial almonries of the Left Bank, at Saint-Victor, Sainte-Geneviève, and Saint-Germain-des-Prés, continued to make their customary distributions of alms. The early fourteenth century saw the establishment of additional hospitals, chiefly at the instigation of laymen: these included the hospice of Saint-Julien-des-Ménétriers and especially the hospital of the confraternity Saint-Jacques-aux-Pélerins, which was destined to play an important role in the life of the capital.

Urban hospitals were no less important in the major cities of the Empire, but there the period of growth came later. In Hungary and Poland, too, hospitals developed later than in western Europe. In the thirteenth century (circa 1220) bishops assigned the brothers of the Holy Spirit and the Crusaders to serve the hospitals of Cracow and Breslau. In England only a few cathedral towns (Winchester, Canterbury, and Oxford) had hospitals comparable to those of the major cities on the continent; the development of hospitals came later there.

In southern France and on the Iberian peninsula the growth of the cities bolstered old traditions in the care of the poor and sick, but development of hospitals there remained, with a few exceptions, relatively modest in scale. The large number of hospitals should not, however, mislead us into thinking that the needs of a correspondingly large number of clients were served. Toulouse and Narbonne had a dozen hospitals each at the beginning of the fourteenth century. In the Iberian peninsula, besides the hospital centers of Barcelona, Valencia, and Seville, there was also Cordoba with some fifteen hospitals, eight of which were built prior to the fourteenth century. In reconquered Andalusia, Christian charity merely had to breathe new life into old Muslim institutions still in operation in the kingdom of Grenada. Finally, in Porto (Portugal), at that time a relatively large city, there were no fewer than three hospitals, which it is worth noting were dedicated to Santa Clara, the Holy Spirit, and Our Lady of Rocamadour.

As for rural hospitals, it is impossible to give a comprehensive account. There are few archives, and often only the chance survival of a document reveals the existence of a particular hospital at a particular moment. It is to be hoped that the inventories and maps of charitable institutions now available for Poitou and Anjou will soon be supplemented by similar guides for other regions.[5] In those regions hospitals were referred to as almonries; typically these were small hospices or infirmaries of a type not uncommon even today in the larger rural towns. Population growth and the settlement of new communities were apparently responsible for the increase in the number of such establishments in the vicinity of cities like Nantes, Poitiers, Bressuire, Thouars, Pouzauges, and Saumur. These were modest facilities: the almonry of Saint John in Craon consisted of "an enclosure, a small chapel, and a house in which paupers were lodged in a hall on the ground floor while the almoner climbed a ladder to the garret that served as his room."[6] Organizational structure varied according to the size of the almonry. In the thirteenth and fourteenth century laymen generally played a part in the selection of personnel, also recruited among the laity. Rural hospitals similar in form to these almonries but known by various other names were found throughout Christendom, though more densely in some areas than in others. Examples are known from the Netherlands, Germany, and England. In Italy the small hospitals maintained by the Disciplinati in the Venetian hinterland have been studied. A small town by the name of Torres-Novas in Portugal was the center of a group of ten small hospitals maintained by the members of a confraternity. Although the few examples cited are hardly sufficient to draw any comprehensive conclusions, it is worth noting that these rural hospitals were widespread. They must have played an important part in the lives of very humble people, about whom it is difficult to learn a great deal.

An essential piece of information about a hospital is the number of patients it can accommodate, and it is unfortunate that the documents rarely provide such figures. Estimates can be arrived at in various ways. It is logical to assume that the size of a hospital is roughly proportional to the size of its endowment. Inventory and accounting records reveal the amounts of furnishing, bedsheets, blankets, kitchen implements, and food supplies purchased to feed and care for patients. From records of purchases of winding sheets and coffins and payments of grave diggers' wages it is cometimes possible to calculate the number of deaths in a particular hospital. Sometimes the founder of a hospital will specify that the establishment should serve a certain number of patients or have a certain number of beds: the two figures are not the same, for until quite recently each hospital bed served more than one patient. New construction of course expanded a hospital's capacity, and from the number of square feet devoted to patient wards (assuming that this number is known) it is possible to estimate the number of beds.

In major hospitals, wards as large as forty meters long by fifteen to twenty meters wide were not uncommon. The space was divided into two or three bays, separated by columns. This plan was followed, for example, at Provins, Tonnerre, Valenciennes, Tournai (Saint-André), Seclin, Lille (Countess Hospital), Angers, and Le Mans (Coeffort). The paupers' hospital of the city of Narbonne included one large ward, a women's ward, and a paupers' ward. The ward at Tonnerre contained forty separate alcoves. The number of patients accommodated varied widely from one hospital to the next. Some founders set a figure of thirteen patients in honor of the apostles (just as the *mandatum*): this was the case, for instance, at Saint-Michel in Angers in 1314, which served nine paupers and four blind patients. Smaller hospitals had an even smaller number of beds, sometimes fewer than six. Rural almonries usually had from twelve to fifteen beds, while those located on the outskirts of cities were somewhat larger (La Fôret near Angers had twenty beds). As for city hospitals, the average size seems to have been established at somewhere around twenty-five or thirty beds (for example, Narbonne, Annonay, Millau, Rodez, Genoa, Lisbon).

A few very large hospitals were exceptions to this general rule. The Hôtel-Dieu in Paris could accommodate 406 patients. In Florence in 1339 thirty hospitals of various sizes provided a total of 1,000 beds.

The Roman hospital in Borgo Santo Spirito had 300 beds. The hospitals at Nüremberg and Regensburg had between 200 and 250 apiece. Joinville's estimate that Saint-Nicolas in Compiègne could accommodate 130 paupers would seem dubious were it not for an inventory of 1264, which speaks of 200 patients: which is exaggerating? What are we to make of the fact that the hospital of Tonnerre had 40 alcoves (and therefore at least 80 patients) whereas the annual number of deaths, based on records of "expenditures for digging graves," stood between 100 and 150? Was the death rate higher here than it was elsewhere? The cemetery was enlarged in 1306. At Hesdin in one year there were 12 deaths. There are too many variables and too many unknowns to permit any firm conclusions to be drawn.

The size of the staff should in principle have been proportional to the number of patients. Thus, assuming we know the staff size, we should be able to deduce the number of patients—were it not impossible to determine what the staff-to-patient ratio was. But since a larger staff meant a larger patient population, we can rank hospitals comparatively according to the size of their staffs. The smallest hospitals were staffed by a single individual: a prior or prioress, master or mistress, or rector. In larger hospitals the head of the staff was assisted by others. The number of chaplains was also variable. In 1220 the Hôtel-Dieu in Paris counted 38 brothers (30 of them laymen) and 25 sisters. At Amiens there were 7 brothers and 8 sisters, at Brussels 3 brothers and 6 sisters, at Rodez 6 brothers and 6 sisters, and at Tonnerre 13 brothers and 7 sisters. Eudes Rigaud, who visited Normandy between 1261 and 1267, found 10 priests, 20 sisters, and 12 serving women in Rouen, 5 priests and 10 sisters in Caen, and 4 brothers and 12 sisters in Pontoise. Still puzzling, however, is the size of the staff of the Aubrac hospital in 1310: it employed 120 brothers, assisted by a number of sisters and oblates.

The legal status of the various charitable institutions is another indicator of their relative size. For example, some hospitals were permitted under canon law to maintain a church, a bell, or a cemetery: in other words, they enjoyed some of the privileges of a parish. From the beginning of the thirteenth century on, we find a fairly haphazard pattern of growth in the number of foundations, reflecting increased lay interest in the poor. Because the growth process was so arbitrary, however, the ecclesiastical, and before long also the civil, authorities felt the need to impose some order.

Concern for the poor was not the only motive for the ecclesiastical authorities' intervention. A certain distrust attached to groups of pious individuals engaged in charity work without official sanction or canonical supervision. The response of the Church was to promote the adoption of official hospital statutes incorporating prescriptions set forth by the councils of Paris (1212) and Rouen (1214) and above all by the Fourth Lateran Council (1215): these statutes give us some idea of the growing popularity of charity work and of the spirit that animated it. What the councils did was to prescribe vows to be taken by those oblates who gave themselves to the tasks of caring for the sick and poor. As a result, it became increasingly common for such tasks to be confided to established orders, congregations, and fraternities. Thus the spiritual life of hospital communities was generally governed by the rule of Saint Augustine; the communities took their spiritual inspiration from the practices of Cîteaux, Saint-Victor, or the mendicant orders. The internal organization of the hospital, however, was still based on principles established by the Hospitallers of St. John, the Antonines, the brothers of the Holy Spirit, and the Domerie of Aubrac.

Concern for competence, which in its spiritual aspect required increased reliance on religious to run the hospitals, began to manifest itself in the medical side of things as well, though of course medical competence in this period was still quite limited: the hospitals provided more shelter than treatment. Patients were fed an ill-balanced diet of salted meats, bread, and wine on the grounds that this was necessary to make up for the undernourishment endemic among the poor. For similar reasons it was felt that patients should receive the comforts of which poverty had deprived them—whatever their hearts desired. Hospital statutes rarely made distinctions among patients. Sometimes certain maladies were singled out at the behest of a founder: for example, the Narbonne statutes mention *contracti*, or patients suffering from advanced rheumatism. More commonly, a ward was set aside for women in labor (as at Narbonne, Saint-Mâlo, and Saint-Pol). Occasionally, abandoned children would be singled out for special attention (as at Bruges from 1231, Rheims from the early fourteenth century, and Provins). Such practices became common in 1330–40: the hospital of Tonnerre purchased one hundred baby bottles in a single transaction; in Venice, a *fraticello* by the name of Petruccio of Assisi shouted "Pietà! Pietà!" while begging alms for a hospital that eventually took the name Pietà—an indication of the large number of children abandoned or exposed in this period. At Bar-sur-Seine, however, the hospital staff refused to accept foundlings brought to the gate by the mayor of the town for fear of encouraging mothers to abandon their offspring. The blind were the beneficiaries of the first specialized hospitals: the homes for the blind founded by Saint Louis were soon joined by others in Chartres (founded in 1291) and London (St. Mary's, founded in 1331). As for madness, it seems that people were still reluctant to regard the mad as truly ill rather than possessed or criminally inclined. The first asylums appear in the second half of the fourteenth century, as we shall see, but a Bible with moralistic commentary said to date from 1250 for the first time includes help for the mad among the works of charity.

In the absence of adequate technical knowledge, specialization followed mainly professional lines and respected the tendency toward ever finer social classification and compartmentalization. Guild confraternities maintained hospitals for their members: for example, weavers, fullers, and shearers in Brussels, Ghent, and Venice and ironsmiths in the Liège region. Sailors, traditionally viewed as potential disease carriers, were early to benefit from specialized hospitals and lazar houses. The name of the shipfitter Auffredy has been associated with the sailor's hospital of La Rochelle since the beginning of the thirteenth century. In Venice, a surgeon by the name of Gualtieri, who was appointed in 1300 by the Signoria to take care of the sick and wounded on the galleys, in 1318 became governor of St. Anthony's Hospital for poor, aged, and invalid sailors. Some hospitals were reserved for the members of particular social groups. St. Mary's in London and St. Giles's in Norwich (1340) were restricted to aged and ailing priests. Homes for "good children," as they were known, were established in many places not only as schools for penniless children but also to treat those who were ill. St. Nicholas's Hospital in Brussels, previously open to all, was restricted to poor patricians in 1306. This development is noteworthy not only because it suggests growing social exclusiveness but also because it reflects the development of a new category of paupers: the victims of a financial setback leading to a loss of social status.

The secular authorities, charged with keeping the peace, were also concerned that charitable institutions should function in an orderly manner. The merchants who administered the cities were of course concerned with maintaining their profits, and it was therefore logical that they should wish to see the growing numbers of hospitals, which commanded more resources and patients than ever before, under sure and steady management and staffed by reliable people. Municipal magistrates were not yet interested in supplanting the ecclesiastical authorities but rather wished to cooperate with them.

There was constant crossing of the divide between the spiritual and the temporal powers: first we find urban authorities and lay founders calling upon religious to staff their charitable institutions, while later we find bishops (as in Poitiers in 1305) recommending that laymen be appointed to head almonries owing to absenteeism on the part of clerics. Areas of cooperation—and potential conflict—involved the appointment of administrators and supervision of their management. Various solutions were tried, but the trend was toward granting supervisory authority to the municipal magistrates. The ecclesiastical authorities, which had tolerated the patronage of churches, allowed hospital rectors to be nominated by their founders. The Mézières hospital was a lay institution from its inception in 1214–15. In Brussels the bishop appointed the lay supervisors of St. John's Hospital upon recommendation by the aldermen. In Douai the mistress of the *béguines* herself placed the hospital maintained by her house under the control of the aldermen. At the beginning of the fourteenth century the hospitals, infirmaries, and Common Alms in Mons were all administered by a municipal commission. The consuls of Narbonne were regarded as "lords and patrons" of the city's hospitals in the middle of the thirteenth century. Hospital administrators, some of them laymen, swore an oath to the councils upon assuming office. Even rural almonries allowed aldermen and mayors to supervise their operations. On the other hand, confraternities that maintained hospitals retained their freedom of action. They enjoyed the best of both worlds, being secular in origin, secular and clerical in composition, and religious in their statutes. They became a part of the urban power structure.

Communal authorities were thus not lacking for motives to expand their role in the operation of charitable institutions. The need to support growing numbers of beggars, to finance hospitals, to maintain orphans, and to preserve the health of the city were all problems of concern to both the authorities and the institutions. The deterioration of the economic and social situation that began at the end of the thirteenth century called for bold new measures.

THE MEANING OF PERSONAL CHARITY   At the root of all forms of benevolence lay the generosity and charity of individuals, not only those who personally gave alms but also those who built collective institutions and spurred the authorities to help the poor. But different individuals made their contributions in different ways. True alms are by nature spontaneous, free, disinterested, discreet, and habitual. Not all gifts of alms fitted this description, however. The thirteenth century was no different from any other period in history: some people gave simply because it was customary or obligatory to do so. Customary contributions included parish collections and confraternal dues, Lenten offerings, contributions in return for a dispensation to marry despite a spiritual or blood relationship, penitential alms imposed by a confessor, and fines levied for some infraction, for example, on a sailor who was late to join his ship or who became drunk and fell asleep while on watch. Nor was the thirteenth century unique in the ostentation that sometimes surrounded large donations. What was new, however, was that for the first time the merchant, with his condescending generosity, began to rival the lord, with his proud largesse. That some contributions were made with ulterior motives is certain, since a good reputation is often conducive to success. Ulterior motives could even be spiritual: the man who could claim his own paupers as he might claim his own peasants and lackeys was inclined to view them as his intercessors, who would pray for the remission of his sins and the granting of his salvation. Yet none of this should blind us to the importance of compassion for the poor and infirm as a motive for charity. It should be clear, therefore, that if personal charity was the basis of all charity, interpreting the meaning of personal charity within the context of social life in general is a delicate matter.

The individualization of charitable giving in the thirteenth century was linked to efforts to educate the consciences of individual Christians. Almsgiving by city merchants was one result. Another was an adaptation of the forms of charity to the requirements of a cash economy. Still another was a vogue for charitable bequests.

Charitable giving was common to all social groups. It was common for families to make a single contribution. One Bordeaux couple, for instance, founded a hospital on the Dax road for pilgrims and for the poor of the surrounding region. Another example of a family contribution gave rise to a legend: the story is that the trunk (*ceppo*) of a felled tree produced flowers in the middle of winter, thus indicating the site chosen by God for a paupers' hospice pledged by a family from Pistoia, the forerunner of the present-day Ospedale del Ceppo. That bequests for charitable purposes were widespread in England is attested by the granting of licenses for donations by mortmain. William of Saint-Amour distinguished between the indigent and the voluntarily poor in making a bequest to the former on condition that they were "honest and not lazy." Historians have analyzed hundreds of bourgeois wills from Douai, Provins, Toulouse, Narbonne, Rouergue, Provence, Forez, the Lyonnais, Anjou, Normandy, the Netherlands, and Spain. In the thirteenth century church synods and councils exhorted the faithful to remember the poor in their wills. The wealthiest donors left money to build hospitals, while the poor themselves left a few sous or a blanket or sheets. All Christians arranged for food and other goods to be handed out on the day of their funeral to a number of paupers that varied according to the means of the deceased. Those who could afford it arranged for similar distributions in subsequent years on the occasion of the mass marking the anniversary of their death. The vogue for charitable bequests spread even to the peasantry. Some charitable institutions were more popular than others: parish almonries, confraternities, and hospitals (which received more than 25 percent of all bequests). As the popularity of donations by will continued to grow, the size of bequests in the cities tended to increase. In Paris in 1334, Jean Roussel and his wife left a sum of money for the construction of tile-covered dwellings on the rue des Poulies (today the rue des Francs-Bourgeois) intended to house "good people," two to a room, on condition that they agree to say a Paternoster and an Ave Maria each day for the repose of their benefactors' souls. Their fellow citizen Nicolas Flamel of the parish of Saint-Jacques-de-la-Boucherie made a name for himself by establishing a similar home for workers on the same terms.

Much fun has been made of such posthumous donations and handouts, which spared donors the need to make any sacrifices while they were still alive. Some contributions by Flemish and Italian merchants were paltry compared to the amount of business they did. The *conto di Messer Dommeddio* must be tracked down in the discreet pages of their "secret books." One of the merits of the mendicant orders was to have shown the way to salvation through alms to merchants whose occupation was the object of formal reproof. The mendicants set forth the idea of sanctification through expenditure of cash, much as the older orders had sanctified the use of the sword—the one for the sake of the indigent, the other for the sake of the weak: weak or indigent, paupers all.[7]

The charitable use of new practices associated with the cash economy was another novel feature of charity in the thirteenth century. In the books of some merchants an account was opened for the benefit of God and the poor, and sums accrued therein were paid out to confraternities and hospitals. Management of the funds was carried out by the merchants, the same ones who administered episcopal and confraternal resources. In Florence, Or San Michele bore the name and employed the methods of a company. The *polizze* held by its regular clients have been compared to financial instruments issued by a bank. Elsewhere in Europe, especially in the Netherlands, tokens of lead or copper stamped with the insignia of the issuing institution served the poor in lieu of regular money. These tokens replaced the small coins that constituted the bulk of alms and alleviated the hardship for the poor that shortages of these coins always caused.

‡ The monetization of alms marks a new stage not only in the economic development of charity but also in its moral and social aspects. Was a gift of money more degrading than a gift in kind? If so, money alms had a compensating advantage. The indigent were free to spend their tokens as they pleased, thus affording them a limited yet real freedom of choice. This helped to preserve the personal dignity of the poor, which was all the more important as economic difficulty increased the number of "shamefaced paupers." As a result, it was easier to provide the discreet assistance required by the "secret poor" who did not beg and continued to live in their own homes, hiding the shame of their distress. Mutual aid also helped. In the Netherlands as well as the Italian communes the social elites automatically defended their own members against adversity.[8] Among those assisted in this way in overcoming their difficulties were bankrupt bourgeois, artisans or peasants suffering from partial or total unemployment, dowryless girls on the point of marrying beneath their station or becoming prostitutes, and orphans unable to enter a trade. Many bequests, contributions, and foundations were intended to remedy such ills. The issue was stated in especially clear terms by the archbishop of Ravenna in 1311. He distinguished between, on the one hand, paupers who publicly received alms and accepted distributions of goods and, on the other, those to whom he referred as *poveri vergognosi*. Such a distinction is reminiscent of the Or San Michele's practice of distinguishing between those paupers to whom it granted *polizze*, whose names were listed in the company's books, and the anonymous mass of indigents and vagabonds. Members of confraternities made home visits to needy people whom they knew by name and by sight. This, too, was new.

Thus some of the poor received more than just assistance; they received a modicum of dignity as well. This was no longer simply the spiritual dignity of the "pauper of Christ." The new question of the shame of the poor obscured an issue of human dignity. Francis of Assisi and those who followed him saw that the tragic dimensions of this question stemmed from the fact that attitudes toward poverty had always been ambiguous, and they realized that the most important thing was to reach out to the pauper directly, as to another person. Elizabeth of Hungary, for example, went beyond the usual forms of assistance and formed close relationships with poor people, thus personalizing the act of charity through actual involvement in the physical and moral suffering of labor. Thirty years later, in order to demonstrate his intimacy with distress, Facio of Cremona bestowed the significant name Consortium Spiritus Sancti upon the institution that he created to alleviate the suffering of all the unfortunate, and especially of "paupers who from a fortunate state had fallen into indigence." Facio died in 1272. As conditions worsened, growing hardships revealed which institutions were robust enough to survive and which were not up to their assigned tasks.

CHAPTER NINE ‡
REALITIES AND DISAPPOINTMENTS

STRUCTURES AND CONJUNCTURES: THE WORKING POOR

Signs of Crisis The development of a regular system of alms and of a network of hospitals involved more than just a revival of old institutions. The mendicant orders saw the charitable institutions as a retort to the inequalities associated with the growing cash economy. As we saw earlier, Saint Bonaventure in 1255 believed that famine was a thing of the past. Three years later, Matthew Paris, who generally pays only fleeting attention to the poor because he finds the subject banal, assures us that famine has just killed fifteen thousand people in England. Never mind the accuracy of the figure, for Matthew uses numbers pretty much as he pleases. It is the juxtaposition of these two contradictory assertions that is worthy of note. Hardship had never been fully eradicated. As we shall see shortly, there were warnings of impending trouble, such as the episode involving a heretical sect known as the Pastoureaux (shepherds) in France or the Alleluia enthusiasm in Italy in 1233. Once again the cities of the Italian peninsula were affected by food shortages, high prices, and riots: Piacenza in 1250, Parma in 1255, Bologna in 1256, Milan in 1258, Siena in 1262, Florence in 1266, and Venice in 1268. In Flanders discontent had been brewing since 1245. The poor in the Liège region made trouble on several occasions between 1251 and 1255, demanding that rich and poor be treated equally in the eyes of the law and that the burden of taxation be equitably distributed. Similar demands aroused the city of Cahors in 1268–70. Such incidents were symptomatic of new difficulties. Natural disasters and storms were not the only problems, although these invariably led to scarcity and famine. Historians of climate tell us that between 1250 and 1350 there were sixteen unusually cold winters, seven of them extremely so. But even seven severe winters do not by themselves account for all the difficulties. Still, research in Forez has shown that between 1277 and 1343 there were thirty-four years of scarcity, that is, one out of every two years in which food supplies fell short of demand.

Man's wickedness probably did more than nature's caprices to aggravate the distress caused by steady economic decline. Compounding the scarcity of food, rising prices and rents, monetary instability, increasing taxes, and the exploitation of manual labor created new forms of poverty and raised anew the question of how best to help the poor. This was the price of economic growth.[1] Before we consider the effects of growth upon the poor, it is worth pausing a moment to take our bearings.

So-called popular uprisings were hardly the work of the poor themselves. "Middling" men who challenged the magnates for control of urban affairs did not make the cause of the poor their own, but they did play a role in furthering that cause. Indeed, the unrest that marked the ninth decade of the thirteenth century in many towns between the Seine and the Rhine, including Rouen, Cologne, Arras, Douai, Tournai, Ghent, Ypres, and Bruges, as well as in central Italy and Barcelona, can be traced to economic difficulties of which the poor were the primary victims. Less than twenty years later, in 1300–1302, it was again in Flanders that humble folk led by the Brugeois Pierre Le Roy (known in Flemish as De Coninc) displayed their dissatisfaction with the urban patriciate, the lords, and even the king of France. There were similar disturbances at about the same time in Brabant.

In the Low Countries the problems were as much political as they were social, and opposition leaders belonged to the bourgeoisie. But famine affected a much broader area. The famine that struck the Iberian peninsula in 1302 prefigured the famine of 1315–17, which affected all of Europe. According to the *Chronicle* of Ferdinand IV of Castille, "men were dying in the squares and streets; so deadly was the famine that a quarter of the population died, and people ate bread made from weeds. Never before had humankind experienced a famine as murderous and severe."[2] One wonders what words the chronicler would have found had he lived to see the Great Plague five decades later. Between 1315 and 1317 the entire Atlantic coast of Europe was affected by a series of storms and floods followed by speculation and price increases. The English had to buy corn in France during the winter of 1315–16, and in the following summer workers rioted in Provins owing to "the public famine and the dearness of bread." In Flanders shortages became calamities when grain was exported to regions where it was in even shorter supply. Prices rose to twenty times their normal level. The poor "let themselves die in the streets," and city accounts record the amounts of money spent to bury them. Workers in the textile industry in Ypres were particularly hard hit.

Monetary fluctuations had for years encouraged speculation on grain shortages, and not only in Flanders. By 1262 inflation and black-market trading of food had come to Venice. Somewhat later France experienced even worse problems. In 1306 Philip the Fair decided to devalue French currency by approximately 39 percent, a decision that was unfortunately announced in advance and immediately sent all prices skyrocketing. In Paris rents tripled, with disastrous results. Creditors insisted on being repaid in hard currencies. In January of 1307 artisans pillaged the home of the master of the mint, Etienne Barbette. Severe repression followed, and those unhappy about subsequent further alterations in the value of money were reduced to composing broadsides such as the following, in which the king is compared to a magician who bilks the laborer and the pauper:

> The king, it seems, works wonders.
> First twenty sous became sixty,
> Then twenty, four, and ten, thirty.
> Of gold and silver all is lost
> And never will the needy see
> Either heads or tails again
>
> . . . .
> From the wheat we've been left the straw.
> The wheat's for the king, the straw's for us.

A combination of negative economic factors finally led to a crisis in the middle of the fourteenth century. Let us briefly recall some of the significant and well-known incidents of this crisis. In Flanders, for example at Douai in 1322, food shortages aggravated a situation caused by competition between the rural and urban textile industries, which had already resulted in widespread unemployment. The harvests were no better in the two following years: dry, stormy summers followed by heavy rains at sowing time and then by deep winter freezes were responsible for the crop failures. By July of 1324 there were so many paupers in the streets that the count ordered the monasteries of Ghent to distribute at once all the grain collected from the tithe and stored in warehouses. This wise measure was compromised by an inopportune tax increase. The result was an uprising throughout maritime Flanders that lasted until 1328 and that drew part of its support from urban and rural workers who had nothing to lose and everything to gain.

From one end of Europe to the other similar difficulties erupted one after another. Florence had to endure food shortages and high prices several times between 1321 and 1330. In 1329 crowds of the poor assembled at churches and almshouses to await handouts. Many had come to the city from the *contado*. According to Villani it was impossible to put a price on any bread in the shops. The poor who needed to eat had no money, and the rich who had money also had stores put aside and did not need to buy.

A crucial point had been reached in the aggravation of poverty. A flood in 1333 prolonged Florence's misery. Distress seems to have been constant for a period of ten years in southern France, particularly in Rouergue. Champagne was also hit: Provins, in difficulty owing to the decline of the fairs and the crisis in textiles, suffered from unemployment and food shortages in 1316, 1330, and 1348. Bad harvests in 1333–34 caused much suffering in Spain and Portugal. By Christmas bread was a rare and priceless commodity in Barcelona, and the shortage lasted until April. The ensuing riot ended in summary executions of some of the rioters. Famine reigned in Castille, Galicia, and Portugal. People ate dead animals and filth. The dead were buried several to a grave, sometimes even in the fields.

In upper Provence in 1340 and 1347 storms and bad harvests forced many peasants burdened by heavy debts to take to the roads as beggars and vagabonds. Some debtors were condemned by default in the Castellane courts. The economic difficulties in Provence were compounded by the unrest (in the area of Brignoles, for example) that followed the death of King Robert of Anjou in 1343.

Italy was hit by a plague in 1340. Disease was indeed persistent, for as Sanudo tells us, "war, plague, and scarcity reigned almost constantly" in the years leading up to the Great Plague of 1348–49. The same chronicler reports that the years 1343–54 were among the most tragic in the history of Venice. Add to this the frequent homicide that grew out of disputes over scarce food, especially in 1347. The *Camera del Frumento* was overwhelmed. To end this sad litany let us turn to central Italy. Florence, which in 1338 had found it difficult to feed the "multitude of paupers from various regions" who, according to one anonymous chronicler, had flocked to the city, had to endure the combined effects of plague and scarcity in 1340 and further shortages of food in 1344 and 1346. Paupers were numerous in the humble neighborhoods around Santa Croce and Santo Spirito, and the hopes that the poor had entertained in 1343 during the rule of Walter of Brienne had been reduced to nothing.

The year 1347, which culminated a "decade of misfortune,"[3] was a terrible one for all of Italy. Horror was added to horror: civil war, famine, and epidemic combined with economic and monetary difficulties (in Venice the rate of inflation was 1200 percent). Sanudo's account accords with that of Giovanni Villani. Everywhere there were earthquakes and floods. In Orvieto there was speculation on wheat while the poor went hungry. In Bologna starving peasants raced about the city. In Siena a crowd gathered in the streets at the cry, "Death to the dogs who are starving us!" In Florence, in the wake of the bankruptcy of the Bardi and the Peruzzi in 1346—a sign of economic crisis—the famine was so severe, according to Villani, that six thousand people died of hunger and the commune had to aid 60–80 percent of the population (which numbered between eighty and ninety thousand). The fate of the poorest of the poor can only be imagined. A moratorium on the payment of debts was a useful measure but not a panacea.

So much for the situation on the eve of the Great Plague. What services were offered by the large number of charitable institutions? And to whom were those services available? Before we attempt to answer these questions, let us take a moment to consider the victims of misfortune.

The Poor in the Cities   The variation in the number of the poor with the cycles of the economy surprised contemporaries, who tried to cope as best they could. The brothers of San Paolo and Or San Michele in Florence may not have been able to grasp the structural causes of poverty, but they did show a certain perspicacity. By distinguishing as they did between, on the one hand, the total destitution of professional beggars and other anonymous paupers and, on the other, the permanent indigence of those who scraped by on very little, they show their apparent awareness of *working poverty,* by which I mean the condition of those whose toil and effort did not assure them food, happiness, or independence. The working poor knew and perhaps even worked at a trade and sometimes owned a small amount of property, but the scantiness of their resources and their dependency on an employer left them vulnerable to accidents and economic circumstances. There were people of this sort everywhere, not just in Florence, and the recession uncovered new forms of poverty in rural areas as well as in the cities.

In Italy and more particularly in Florence the working poor formed only a part of the *popolo minuto* and did not constitute a group apart. These poor workers were for the most part *sottoposti,* that is, lower-level craftsmen belonging to one of the city's *arti* or guilds. Workers at this level formed relations with one another only occasionally, but they were still bound by fairly strong ties to patrons (usually prominent families or clans) who afforded them protection and sometimes food in exchange for their support. These ties of patronage created factions, but one should take care not to confuse the factions of a medieval Italian city with modern political parties or social movements. The *sottoposti* were viewed with suspicion by the wealthy merchants who dominated the *arti*. In 1335 the silk *arte* forbade coalitions. The wool *arte* kept an eye on the numerous and restive dye workers, who were important because the quality of the fabric depended on their work. Walter of Brienne's decision in 1343 to create two new *arti* of dyers and carders did not survive the opposition that it immediately aroused among the *popolo grasso* of the major guilds. Also short-lived in their effects were his decisions to limit the arbitary power of weavers to set wages and to remedy inequalities in the courts.

Details of the life of a *sottoposto* may be gleaned from various pieces of direct evidence. "I live by the work of my hands . . . to feed my four children, all very young. I am a poor *popolano* forced to earn my living with my hands, and I am not strong enough to stand up to him," declared one Florentine artisan caught up in a dispute with a member of the powerful Bardi family. Chronic indebtedness was so common among the poor that Giovanni Villani takes note of the view, current in Florence in 1340, that usury is not a mortal sin. It is interesting to find him using the obsolete word *impotenti* to describe paupers incapable of freeing themselves from debt. Two masons accused of harboring admiring sentiments toward Walter of Brienne after his departure voice the opinion that "Florence is a bad city for artisans and simple people."

Dyers, wool carders, masons, laborers: the economic crisis did not spare even the *popolo grasso*, whose possible fall into the clutches of poverty is covered in the statutes of the *arti*. Among the indigents helped by Or San Michele in 1324, for example, we find two notaries alongside a ragpicker, a pit-sawyer, two cobblers, a handkerchief manufacturer, three ironsmiths, and three brokers. Recent work has shown that if all these occupations were vulnerable, then ordinary wage workers were even more so.

To judge from the records of the Santa Maria Nuova hospital for the eight years preceding the Black Plague, the situation had become critical for farm workers, gardeners, and construction workers, particularly those with families. If we translate their nominal wages into calories, we see that workers with families must have been teetering on the edge of survival. The daily wage was equivalent to less than 1,000 calories, far below the 3,500 required for a normal existence. By 1326 many workers found themselves in desperate straits, and many more followed them in the years after 1340.

The case of Florence, for which we have particularly good evidence, illustrates the way in which a new category of paupers developed. Traditionally, poverty was the consequence of inability to earn a living, whether as a result of incapacity (due to age or infirmity), unemployment, ruin, or loss of capital. Now for the first time we see a large number of people who have regular employment but still cannot make a decent life for themselves or their families. This new group of paupers had its place in the life of the city; the poor shared in their city's battles and festivals as well as its misfortunes. To be sure, they did not enjoy the full rights and privileges of citizenship. There are signs of segregation in housing, as in the Santa Croce and Santo Spirito sections of Florence and the Ovile section of Siena as well as in Orvieto and Pisa, along both Genoese "rivers," and in Venice, where vestiges still remain in certain *contade* of the Giudecca. In most cases, however, newcomers, who were suspect precisely because they were new, were forced to reside on the outskirts. In the central city the poor rubbed elbows with the rich and lived in close proximity to their patron's "clan." Such paupers were not outcasts but dependents— useful dependents. The new poor could be treated with contempt but not ignored.

‡ The new urban poverty also developed outside of Italy, with some differences owing to occupational and regional characteristics. In the ports, for example—Venice and Genoa, Marseilles and Barcelona, Bordeaux and Nantes, Rouen and London, Bruges and Lübeck—large numbers of workers depended on the good will of merchants and shipfitters: carpenters and caulkers, sailmakers, longshoremen, sailors (some specialized, some not), fishermen, fishmongers, and carters. This was a self-sufficient world of hot-tempered men and women: that temper flared into the open in Calais in 1298 and again in Saint Mâlo and Genoa in 1306, when sailors mutinied against shipowners.

Further inland the range of occupations varied little from city to city. In Rouen, for example, the textile industry relied on wage labor from the middle of the thirteenth century; the best-paid workers were concentrated in the outlying parishes of Saint-Vivien and Saint-Nicaise and in nearby towns like Darnetal. In Toulouse, dyers, woodworkers, ragpickers, candlemakers, and fishermen were concentrated in the isle of Tounis, while other workers mingled with the wealthy in the episcopal city and burg of Saint-Sernin. In Besançon the poor lived in the Chamars district on the right bank of the Doubs. In Paris, working poverty, already perceptible in Etienne Boileau's *Livre des métiers* (book of trades), emerges even more clearly from an examination of the tax rolls (for the tax known as the *taille*) under the last Capetians. Many of the observations above concerning the place of the poor in the Italian clans can be carried over to poor dependents of English families, the *paraiges* of Metz, and clients of the bourgeoisie in the imperial cities.

Once again the Low Countries present a situation strikingly similar to that in Tuscany. The textile workers who went on strike in Douai in 1245, the members of the *gueudes* or guilds declared illegal in Arras in 1233, the Flemish workers thrown out of work by the interruption of wool imports from England between 1270 and 1274, the textile workers who rose in revolt at Bruges, Ypres, and Ghent, and the city workers, especially in Douai, who had to compete with the rural textile industry—all of these are examples of the working poor. We know something about the condition of Flemish workers, though there is far less information available about their situation than about their Florentine counterparts. Much is known about the employees of Sir John Boinebroke in Douai thanks to the records of judicial proceedings that followed his death in 1285 or 1286, which have been studied by Georges Espinas. An importer of English wool, Boinebroke put out work to local artisans, sold them raw materials, and bought their finished goods. When he sold raw materials he put bad wool in the bottom of the sack under the good and insisted on high prices. He questioned the amount of work done and the number of hours required and refused to pay what his workers claimed they were due. In debt to a woman who worked for him and who asked to be repaid, he answered thus: "Out of my sight, you busybody, get yourself a job plucking skins. The sight of you appalls me." When he lent money he insisted on repayment in labor rather than cash, thus leaving the debtor bound to him without hope of escape, particularly since there was no authority to which the person in debt might appeal. The *eswardeurs* or guild officials could not find against a powerful entrepreneur who on several occasions served as alderman of his city. The technical nature of the work, which required ten to fifteen different operations to turn raw wool into finished product, weakened the position of the worker relative to that of an employer who controlled the entire chain of production. This example, apparently typical of prevailing labor practices, sheds much light on the dependent status and precarious position of the worker who might at any moment be thrown into poverty. Clearly, people in the late thirteenth century had to cope with problems of labor, wages, and prices that are often thought to have originated with the industrial revolution.

The Rural Poor The nature of working poverty changed in the countryside as well as the city. In the words of Georges Duby, "growing inequalities in wealth were the clearest form of structural change in peasant society during the final phase of agricultural expansion, which covers the thirteenth century." The new poverty in rural areas reflected a decline in the position of large numbers of peasants relative to their lords and to a minority of wealthy farmers who had had the wit and wherewithal to profit from economic growth. Among the various factors responsible for this aggravation of the peasant's situation some were more important than others: inadequate size of the peasants' plots, uncertainty of employment, heightened dependency, and indebtedness.

When all due allowance is made for variations in terrain, climate, and crop, it remains true that most peasant families were short of land. The reduction in size of the average holding, due in part to population growth and in part to the fragmentation of the patriarchal family, came to a head just as clearing of new land began to slow. One English peasant in three possessed a plot of approximately six hectares. But one third of this land lay fallow every year, and assuming a yield of five quintals of grain per hectare the remainder produced only twenty quintals annually, half of which went in dues to lord, king, and Church. Now, a plot of six hectares is considered to have been the minimum that could support an English family of five up to the time of the Black Plague. But 46 percent of all tenants in 1280 had only three hectares at their disposal.

This figure, confirmed for this period by records of lands dependent on the Ewelme hospital, was reversed in the second half of the fourteenth century. Across the English Channel, on an estate belonging to the abbey of Saint-Bertin, 70 percent of the tenants farmed fewer than four hectares in 1305, and 30 percent farmed fewer than two hectares.

In nearby Flanders, in the year 1328 during which the battle of Cassel put an end to a local peasant uprising, of the 3,185 persons killed who were natives of the Furnès region, 1,222 were rural artisans who owned houses with no land and 891 owned nothing at all. Documents pertaining to prosecutions of those involved in this insurrection reveal that of the 193 persons whose property was confiscated by the court, 95 farmed plots whose size ranged from two to two-and-a-half hectares and seventeen had no land at all. Although we find plots of between four and six hectares in Brabant, in Hainault, where the terrain is more varied, the minimum plot required to maintain a family at the poverty threshold varied from thirty to forty ares (1 are = 100 square meters) up to five hectares.[4] Around 1300 in Cambrésis, 45 percent of the peasants found themselves in difficult straits: 33 percent had plots that were too small and 12 percent were beggars. By contrast, the deep topsoil of Picardy enabled 36 percent of peasants to live in relative security with plots of only two to three hectares in size. Still, another 33 percent with plots of less than one hectare found it difficult to make ends meet, and a further 12 percent without land lived in utter poverty, begging and wandering from place to place, emerging from obscurity only to lend a hand in the work of harvest and threshing.[5] As for southern Champagne, information pertaining to Rumilly-les-Vaudes in 1345 yields a similar picture, with a good third of the peasants living on very meager resources.

The Ile-de-France seems to have been somewhat better off. Its soil was very rich but still there was not enough to go around, as the population density was always quite high. But the well-balanced terrain, the variety of uses to which the soil could be put, and the proximity of the Paris market made the years around 1300 "a high point of sorts."[6] New techniques such as crop rotation were used even by peasants on their own plots, improving yields and reducing the number of paupers in comparison with other areas, at least until the last thirty years of the fourteenth century. Only a minority of peasants lived on plots of less than one hectare, and two thirds of all plots were prosperous enough to afford their cultivators some measure of autonomy. Even areas at some distance from the capital, in Brie, the Vexin, and the region around Chartres, were relatively well off.

Examination of other regions would reveal still other examples, but the basic picture is the same throughout the great plains of Europe in which grain-growing was the dominant activity, whether in Germany, Poland, or the Po valley. If a peasant possessed a plot large enough to permit an adequate mix of crops, he lived in relative comfort; if not, he lived in misery.

Outside the grain-growing regions the situation was somewhat different, but we lack sufficient data on which to base any judgment. What was the poverty threshold in wine-producing areas, for instance? Or in forested regions? Or in areas specializing in the production of poultry and cattle? Mountainous terrain was different from flat terrain, and climate also made a difference. Was there a "Mediterranean type" of rural poverty? Or were there perhaps several Mediterranean types? Here it may be that it was not so much the crop mix as the possibility of irrigation that made the difference. There was considerable variation from region to region. In Catalonia, 20–25 percent of peasants lived in poverty, as was also true in the county of Foix—at Montaillou for example—in Languedoc, and in Provence. But in San Gimignano owners of small plots accounted for 65 percent of all peasants, and some peasants living near Orvieto farmed plots as small as a few dozen square meters.

In any case, inadequate resources meant finding some way to acquire what one could not produce alone. The simplest solution was for two to four peasants with small plots to join forces: this was common in Lyonnais and Forez, for example. Peasants frequently accepted work as artisans, as in Flanders, where peasant labor aided the growth of the rural textile industry. The most common ploy, however, was for the peasant to hire himself out as a day laborer, either on a permanent or seasonal basis. Thus a rural proletariat developed throughout Europe, composed of French *brassiers, manoeuvres, bergers,* and *valets,* English *cottiers,* and German *Sörtner* and *Gärtner.* It has been estimated that in 1300 one half of all peasant households in England survived thanks to outside wages earned by the family head. In the same period between 33 and 72 percent of the inhabitants of certain villages in the Namur region were forced to hire themselves out. Such a situation had never before been seen on so broad a scale, although several decades earlier Guillaume Le Clerc painted the following still valid if not very flattering portrait of the landless peasant with little appetite for labor:

> When to dig or thresh
> A man must accept three or four deniers
> He won't do much but lay himself down.[7]

To the estate of Thiery d'Hireçon—as to farms throughout the Ile-de-France, to the lands of the Hospitallers, to the vineyards of Burgundy, and to estates of the abbey of Ramsey or in the German or Lombard plains—veritable armies of workers came at harvest time. There was competition for the services of harvest laborers, and that, coupled with rising food prices, led to a doubling of wages for agricultural day laborers between 1300 and 1325. But the rise in the cost of food during the same period nullified this increase. Although many peasant wage-earners managed to avoid poverty, the poor tables in some parishes in northern France were obliged to assist as many as one quarter of all parish residents.

Uncertainty of employment and tightened ties of dependency were two other major factors in the development of the new rural poverty. Even though rural life in many ways changed very little, agricultural work was always uncertain, varying with the season and at the whim of the employer. The need for agricultural workers to sell their labor made their situation in some respects comparable to that of urban laborers. When Giovanni Villani discusses the uprising in maritime Flanders, a comparison with the *popolo* of Florence comes naturally to his mind. Workers were employed not only by traditional lords but also by wealthy peasants who had somehow amassed a fortune and risen above the rest. One such was Jehan Inglevert, who owned forty hectares near Saint-Omer and employed a dozen servants.

If selling one's labor was a precarious business, so was contracting for the use of land on a short-term basis. Tenant farming and share-cropping originated in Germany and the Low Countries and spread to England, France, and Italy (where sharecropping was known as *mezzadria*). Sharecropping arrangements enabled the lessor of land to readjust his rents as prices rose and fell. The peasant sacrificed all stability and security. In the first half of the fourteenth century, for example, rents due the abbey of Ely were fixed by short-term contract at 57 percent of production, and the value of these rents tripled. For the peasant the rent increase was a part of his precarious tenure and in no way lessened his dependence. In fact it may have had the opposite effect, since the tenant could no longer make the case that he had a hereditary right to work the land.

New forms of servitude also developed. Servile homage was common in southern France. In England judicial archives record repeated attempts by lords to maintain their peasants in villenage and even to extend that status to free peasants. Villenage left the peasant subject to unlimited demands by the lord. It was tempting for a lord's steward to require for his own benefit personal services beyond the customary level, as the steward of the prior of Christ's Church in Canterbury did on the Bocking Hall estate in Essex in 1330; on this occasion justice was done.

There is no doubt that the concern for profit was responsible for many new aspects of poverty. Landowners were encouraged to seek the best possible return on the smallest possible outlay, so that, for example, English landowners naturally responded to the Flemish demand for wool by turning to the profitable practice of raising sheep. Those who did so lent a helping hand to the likes of Sir John Boine-broke. But it is only fair to point out, too, that the same sensitivity to profit also led to the introduction of technical innovations on farms in the Ile-de-France (70–150 hectares in size) and that these innovations benefited the entire region.

‡ Indebtedness is always a serious problem in the countryside. By 1300 the sale of ground rents was a universal practice whose disadvantages to peasants far outweighed its advantages. The system provided a means of obtaining cash without recourse to usurers. But an increase of five to eight percent in the *censive* or ground rent, often paid in kind, added to annual costs and burdened the land for a long time to come—often for the lifetime of the owner or even longer. Ground rents were purchased by neighbors, sometimes peasants themselves, by the bourgeois of nearby towns, by religious establishments, and by lords, sometimes the same lord whose land the tenant cultivated; the practice increased peasant indebtedness and dependency.

The evil of usury continued to spread. In the late thirteenth and early fourteenth century Lombards and Jews moved into the countryside. Loans at 30–40 percent and more were not uncommon as short-term advances for the purchase of seeds, an animal, or commodities for immediate consumption; such loans were often payable in kind within the year, say after the harvest, at the time when seigneurial dues were paid. One moneylender, Lippo di Fede del Seca, patiently amassed a *podere* of twenty-five hectares at Pontanico near Florence by waiting until the peasants got into trouble, presenting himself as a lender, then forcing the debtor to sell and go to work for him as a tenant farmer or hired laborer. After moving to France, Lippo became one of the thirty of forty Lombards who engaged in moneychanging activities in Auxerre and Rouen and in the Paris area around 1325. The moneylenders' shops were similar to the *casane* that their compatriots maintained in the small towns of Savoy. Jews lent money in Normandy, Burgundy, and Roussillon. Christian notaries went to some trouble to conceal the sources of loans in the documents. In one hamlet in upper Provence, two brothers loaned out four livres and eighteen sous in 1335 for the purpose of buying seed and paying for plowing; in exchange they took possession of the entire harvest in advance.

To judge by court records, the path from the moneylender's shop to the courts was short and well-trodden: first came the loan, then the delay in repayment, followed by default, seizure of the property, flight, vagabondage, delinquency (burglary, theft, violation of the salt laws), and crime. Evidence of this in Provence (Castellane) is available in the records of the *baillie* of Moustiers-Sainte-Marie. The exodus from the countryside of peasants in distress reached such proportions in 1317 that the abbey of Saint Victor in Marseilles resorted to confiscation to prevent peasants from deserting their villages.

Peasants were not the only inhabitants of the countryside to fall into debt. Even at this early date some noble families had already begun to feel the first effects of a shaky feudal economy. The various classes of country people rubbed elbows in poverty. In the Albigeois, for example, the disposition of debts held by heretics condemned by the Inquisition between 1308 and 1323 turned up one Bertrand III of Lautrec, a noble unable to pay for repairs to his castle, along with a crowd of peasants (who accounted for some 53 percent of the debtors). Most of the debts were quite small, suggesting just how short of cash borrowers were.

New faces appeared in the traditional portrait gallery of rural poverty. Saint Louis's investigators had discovered in their travels the widow, the orphan, the ailing old man, the peasant complaining of an unjust exaction of a wicked judgment, and that perpetrator of unmotivated mischief, the village idiot: a banal family portrait! But now we find growing numbers of ordinary villagers among the poor, and we find them everywhere. At Montaillou, for example, in the Ariège region: who was poorer, the cobbler or his customers, who could not pay the cobbler for his work on their husbands' shoes until they had sold their chickens at Pentecost? Ten families of woodcutters lived as nomads without steady income in the wake of a brawl and a miscarriage of justice. "A blue overcoat on top of a tunic, with an axe and some birch faggots slung over his shoulder": the description of a man who has neither the means nor the need to buy anything for cash. The village weaver raised sheep tended by his children. In this village the shepherd was distinguished for being a Catharist saint by the name of

Pierre Maurin, but in general the shepherd was the stereotype of rural poverty, whether he kept his animals in the mountains or the valleys or followed them from pasture to pasture. The occupation of shepherd had yet to be rehabilitated as it was by Jean de Brie in the fourteenth century or transformed into a pastoral idyll as it was in the fifteenth. At the beginning of the fourteenth century the shepherd was no more highly thought of than his animals. Paid by the lord or by his villagers, the shepherd lived a life that allowed him to remain aloof from other people and from the authorities, which was both an advantage and a disadvantage. Turning now to another region, Flanders, we find the same poverty. Consider the Flemish peasants condemned in 1328: many of them owned only rude huts, indeed, in some cases, only a half or even a quarter of a hut, along with a few ares of land subject to heavy rents. Lankin Wekins, for example, had only "a share in a rude hut and four measures of land lying in Ychtenghiem and in Cokelarde owing, for the one, nine deniers parisis per year to Jehan Drussatre and, for the other, twelve deniers parisis per year to Kasin of Coukelare." These possessions were confiscated. To be one of the new poor was not a good thing. It was better to have been poor for a long time (*pauper*) than to have been recently impoverished (*depauperatus*). The neologism is noteworthy. One ruined noble in Montaillou said, "I am held up to general scorn on account of my poverty."

A curious anthology, of interest to ethnographers, could be compiled from literary and popular sources concerning the condition of the rural poor at the beginning of the fourteenth century. Here are three examples. One comes from England. A canon of Leicester writes of the impossibility of escaping villenage:

> Peasant William, I pray you tell me about your case.
> . . . .
> I do not advise you to plead against your lord.
> Peasant, you will be vanquished, you who want to vanquish
>   your lord.
> You must endure what the custom of the earth has given you.

The second example, the Poem of Alfonso XI, comes from Spain. Its author describes a peasant who has fallen victim to arbitrariness and misery:

> Our fields become deserts
> For want of justice.

We are toilers
Left to the mercy of the world.
They take our property
And do us harm.[8]

Our third example, a song (*Kerelslied*) from the time of the uprising in maritime Flanders, is contemptuous of the peasant who dares to make his voice heard:

> All the Karls have long beards. They wear torn clothes. Their hats sit bizarrely on their heads, and their shoes are in tatters.
> *Refrain:* Curdled milk, bread, and cheese, that's what Karl eats every day, and if he ate any more would his wits would be dulled.
> A thick slice of rye bread is all he needs: he holds it in his hand as he heads for his plow, followed by his ragged wife, who with her mouth full of fibers works her distaff until it is time to prepare the supper porridge.
> *Refrain:* Curdled milk, etc.
> We will punish the Karls. They must be subdued.

This was not merely a literary theme. Villani had earlier used similar language to characterize the peasant victors of the battle of the Gold Spurs (1302): "The vilest people in the world . . . because of their baseness known to all nations as butter-filled rabbits." William in England, Karl in Flanders, tomorrow Jacques in Ile-de-France: distress lay in wait for field hands as well as city laborers. How many paupers were there all together?

The Number of Paupers Without tax records we would have little to go on. The idea of classifying by wealth for fiscal purposes first appeared in the second half of the thirteenth century in response to the financial needs of cities and states as well as to moral and social concerns. The latter occasionally found vigorous forms of expression, as at Arras in 1275, where Adam de la Halle displayed his satirical wit by issuing a naked warning to the patrician speculators, embezzlers, and tax cheats who ruled the city—"for now," as Adam said. Before long the tables would be turned as the wheel of fortune, spun by a "deaf, dumb, blind" woman, turned full circle. It was thought wrong that the weak should bear the burden of the strong; in addition, there was a need to determine which citizens were eligible for the post of city magistrate. Accordingly, it was decided that estimates should be made of wealth and income so that a minimum taxable level could be determined. Above that, minimum taxes were to be proportional to wealth. Below it were the poor, but the cutoff was variable and hence so was the definition of "fiscal pauper." Furthermore, those not subject to taxation were not normally listed on the tax rolls. Finally, taxes were generally apportioned by "hearth," that is, by household. But historians have had enormous difficulty determining how many individuals or even how many families corresponded to a single household. The answer varies from period to period and location to location. In other words, the sources are not easy to interpret.

The Italian cities were the first to employ the new methods of taxation. By the late twelfth century Pistoia had adopted a system of taxation that "balanced poverty and wealth, wealth and poverty." The system was subsequently adopted in Siena, Florence, Pisa, Lucca, Genoa, Venice, and in the end almost everywhere in Italy. It spread to southern France. In 1263 Alphonse of Poitiers ordered each locality to prepare an estimate of the wealth of all inhabitants. Not confined to Languedoc (which serves here as a convenient example), the practice was widely employed throughout France in the fourteenth century.

In order to understand the condition of the poor it is essential to discover whether the use of such methods achieved a minimum of social justice. Indigents and beggars were exempt from taxation, for good reason. But what about the working poor in the cities and in the countryside, whose lives were not so much penurious as precarious? Few tax lists have survived from periods earlier than the fifteenth century. The cadastral survey (*catasto*) of Orvieto for 1292 concerns the city and its *contado*. The poorest people, that is, indigents and beggars receiving public assistance, accounted for about ten percent of the population. Those who lived solely by what they earned and who owned no land accounted for approximately 20 percent. If we add to these two groups the owners of very small plots, who, though subject to taxation, actually had very little and teetered on the edge of survival, we arrive at a figure of 35–40 percent of the population that can be classified as poor, which correlates well with observations made in a number of other European cities.

It is a pity that the records of the Florentine *estimo* date back no earlier than 1365. As for Florence's previous tax system, there is a law of 1342 that specifies which *miserabiles* and *pauperes* were exempt from taxation: those owning no land in excess of one hundred lire in value and who are neither craftsmen nor wage-earners (in other words, they must be unemployed). Also included in this group were insolvent debtors and those with insufficient means to survive in the face of increases in the price of food. Although exempt from taxation the names of such people were to be kept in a special register identifying them as *nihil habentes*. This phrase did not imply total indigence, however; it was simply an administrative designation applied to those who in such-and-such a year owned no property subject to taxation. People on this list were not beggars. Ignored by the tax authorities, they were not obliged to declare their property or submit to inspection by tax collectors. How many paupers would have escaped our notice altogether were it not for the records kept by the confraternities and a few other scattered bits of evidence? For instance, Giovanni Villani tells us about one will from the time of the 1333 flood that provided for 6 deniers to be distributed to every pauper in the city; all were locked up simultaneously in Florence's numerous churches and then, as each person was let out, the 6 deniers were handed over. Since the total disbursed came to 430 lire, there must have been 17,900 recipients, and that figure does not include the "shamefaced poor" who did not claim their share.

Figures from other cities and countries are not too far out of line with these. In 1295 at Lunel in Languedoc 18 percent of the population was classified as exempt from taxation on the grounds of poverty. At Carcassonne nine years later 33 percent of the population was "too poor to pay taxes." The estimes of Toulouse provide better data. Unfortunately, of the declarations of wealth for tax assessment purposes prior to 1348 only one for 1335 has survived, and that concerns only the records for the built-up area north of the episcopal city and says nothing about the segment of the population too poor to pay taxes. Still, we know that half of those who made declarations, some 476 out of a total of 936, fell below the minimum taxable level (ten *livres toulousaines*). Their total wealth accounted for less than 6 percent of the total for all declarers. As in the case of Florence we must be careful not to be misled by the term *nihil habens*. But allowing for the total omission of laborers, journeymen, servants, and beggars, the overall impression is one of a society in which wealth was very unevenly distributed and in which the number of people living in a modest, vulnerable, insecure, or indigent condition exceeded the number who were comfortable or wealthy. It should be pointed out that the Toulouse census was conducted at the beginning of a depression.

What was true in the south was true also in the north, as is revealed by records of the *tailles* for Paris and even more clearly for Rheims. The term *menus* (small) in the northern system of classification was roughly the equivalent of *nichils* (nothing) in the Toulouse system. In Paris the *menus* accounted for 42 percent of all taxpayers in 1297 and 47 percent in 1298. For the six parishes of Rheims in 1328 the figures ranged from 40 to 60 percent. As in Toulouse, mendicants were not included in the Rheims lists, for they were not considered citizens (*bourgeois*) of Rheims. In Paris the menus contributed 5 percent of the total collected in taxes, and in Rheims from 2 to 5 percent. Wealthy citizens of Rheims lived in all six parishes, and there seems to have been no segregation or absolute predominance of any social group in any of the parishes.[9] In Rheims as well as Toulouse, then, the small taxpayers, who were in fact poor and in some cases nearly indigent, were poorly paid craftsmen and workers whose jobs did not require significant skills; the fact that the names on the tax rolls change over time suggests that there was some social mobility.

We also possess good quantitative data for Provence thanks to a fine collection of comital court records.[10] Some of these records pertain to the late thirteenth century and to the first half of the following century. In the *baillie* of Sisteron as many as 53 percent of all cases heard involved prosecution for debt; in Castellane the figure was 58 percent. Most of these cases involved loans made for current consumption, and using the information contained in the court documents we can form a rough idea of the numbers of the poor. Between 1303 and 1316 in Castellane, 250 families out of a total of 1,000–1,200 hearths had judgments of the court handed down against them. Of these, 150 were occasional debtors while 60 were persistently before the courts. Of these, 19 had 4 judgments against them, and 13 others had 7 adverse judgments. Comparison of these figures with records pertaining to the hearth tax, which was first imposed in 1303, shows that of the 60 hearths repeatedly in court for debt, one third was not taxed in 1303 and another third was taxed at the minimum level, that is, at a level corresponding to that applied elsewhere to *nichils* and *menus*.

Another line of research has been to compare debtors' lists with lists of corvées (obligatory labor services) compiled during an inquiry held in 1297. Such a comparison yields conclusions similar to the foregoing. Of 120 tenants, 73 owed labor services to their landlords. Of these, 26 were able to satisfy their obligation simply by supplying an animal, but 91 who had no team and plow had to provide personal labor services. From the same documents we know that, in 1304, Easter assessments on herds of more than ten head could be paid in one locality, Courchon, by only 17 of the 35 individuals subject to corvée. The 18 others had no oxen, only sheep. In 1312 this assessment applied to only 7 people and in 1316 to only 8 people.

Records of the head tax in some rural areas also provide evidence of the number of indigent. When a seigneurial scribe in the Low Countries noted that "many a pauper" could not pay the burgher's tax he was not mistaken: the poor accounted for 29 percent of the population, and the reason for their inability to pay seems to be that they possessed no plow gear.[11]

Though scattered and diverse, the quantitative data take on significance from comparative evaluation and correlation with other observations. Closer examination of the sources will probably yield a more accurate idea of the numbers of the working poor in both urban and rural areas. At the same time, economic historians are attacking the fundamental problem, which is to determine the standard of living—or, in practical terms, the purchasing power—of the poor. It is not enough simply to emphasize the effects of climate and weather, availability of arable land, agricultural technique, tax levels, or fluctuations in the grain markets. Ultimately, a sure understanding of late medieval poverty in all its geographical and social detail can only come from a comparison of wages with prices, particularly bread prices, over a long period. That the social meaning of indigence changed in the early fourteenth century makes it all the more important to understand how wages and prices varied. For it was in this period that the traditional poor were joined by working men and women whose wages were not adequate to avoid economic hardship. As needs changed, so did aspirations.

THE HOPES AND DISAPPOINT-
MENTS OF THE POOR

The Needs of the Poor Even the unlettered understood their own needs. The artisan I cited earlier, a father of four and a *minuto* upset about losing his job because the Bardi were above the law, was not the only person in Florence, or elsewhere for that matter, who understood that his entire fortune lay in the strength of his arms. Or—to shift attention to another region entirely, far from Florence—consider the following words, said to have been spoken by the heretic Jacques Authier, commenting on Satan's inciting the angels to rebellion. Reflecting the aspirations of his audience of shepherds, Authier has Satan say: "I will lead you into my world and give you oxen and cows and wealth and a wife for companion and you will own your own houses and have children." Note the implicit hierarchy of goods: first livestock, then money, then a wife, then a home, and finally, in fifth place, children.

It may not be out of place here to mention the theme of the "land of Cockaigne" (never-never land), to recall the importance of festivals and banquets in the life of the common people,[12] and to call attention to the significance of the carnival.[13] What is this never-never land about which men dream?

> The name of this land is Cockaigne,
> Where the more you sleep, the more you earn.
> . . . .
> And I tell you, no matter which way you go,
> By whichever path or high road,
> You find people seated at table,
> With white napkins under their chins,
> And they can eat and drink
> All they want without danger.[14]

The starving pauper dreamed of finding food and pleasures aplenty in this wonderland: fables often reflect the frustrations and obsessions of real life.

A similar interpretation applies to the fabliaux. The animal world that figures in the *Roman de Renart* is of course an allegory of a peasant society, and to understand the nostalgia of the poor it is enough to invert the terms used for afflictions. In this work we find an ex-villein who has grown wealthy and is served by other peasants, and another man who, having fallen into poverty and villenage, is mistreated by his master. He has nothing to sell and nothing to buy, his children cry for hunger, his wife is pregnant, he goes into debt, cannot pay it back, takes flight, wanders aimlessly, steals in order to eat, is offered shelter by peasants or in a castle. He is served the pauper's meal. He eats until he can eat no more, falls asleep, and dreams that he is still eating. Hungry because he has no money, the pauper is conscious of his inferiority: "Poor man who has nothing, [you] were made of the devil's excrement."[15]

The poor also desired security and justice. But isn't there also evidence of pride—a sin common to all levels of society—in the following two verses of a poem about "the rook who shrewdly drank":

> Shrewdly and subtly
> One escapes from scarcity and poverty.

The poor knew that hunger was their lot; unlike the rich they lacked reserves of grain and allies to escape its racking tortures. The feelings of the poor were a compound of bitterness and impotence, injustice and insecurity, and in the circumstances it is hardly surprising that their aggressive instincts did not always remain in check. Indeed, as we shall see, the restraints on the poor weakened as the Middle Ages waned.

As we noted earlier, some of the poor were referred to as "shame-faced": in other words, they were ashamed of their condition, too proud or too modest to make a show of their situation. But others expected help, whether out of fatigue, indifference, or habit. Or did they have a sense that they were entitled to alms? We shall probably never know, given the difficulty of finding out what the poor thought about their situation and how they saw themselves.

There is evidence that the poor also helped themselves. Specific instances of this are so far rare but nonetheless significant. Certain aspects of the work of confraternities can be interpreted as examples of self-help by the poor. In the Torres-Novas region of Portugal the poor helped one another not only in exceptional circumstances, for example, after a fire, but also by lending a hand or a day's work to assist in routine agricultural chores. Similar objectives were part of the reason for the existence of the previously mentioned *Consortium pauperum verecundorum* in Ravenna (1311). Even more unusual were the confraternities of the blind that by the early fourteenth century had existed for some time in Barcelona and Valencia. The statutes of these confraternities, evidence of which dates from 1329, provided for the sharing of a guide (*lazarillo*) as well as of alms received and for visits to sick members. It seems probable that such instances of mutual aid grew out of a desire on the part of the poor to help one another. No doubt they also wished to assert that lively sense of dignity and independence that is so common among the blind and to show their annoyance with widespread indifference to the perennial woes of others.

The Limits and Failures of Benevolence   It is reasonable to ask how effective charitable institutions were in dealing with poverty and in meeting the true needs of the poor. Giovanni Villani held that the teachings of the clergy and of the mendicant orders had borne real fruit; charity, according to him, was widely practiced by individuals as well as organizations and was not just a pious wish. Was he exaggerating? And does his view hold good outside of Florence?

In Florence we find a particular concern with working poverty (as distinct from mendicant poverty) on the part of the Tertiaries of San Paolo and the brothers of Or San Michele. It may be that, because the lay brothers of the confraternities were closer to the ordinary life of the poor, they had a better idea than the clergy of the pauper's needs. The regular clients of the confraternities, those written in the registers, were artisans (tanners, curriers, wood-sellers, locksmiths, butchers), including probably many *sottoposti*. Merely because charity was adjusted to the social group does not in itself prove that it met the needs of the recipients. Charles de La Roncière has calculated that the sum of five sous, which in 1324 became the customary amount of alms, was in that year the equivalent of a day and a half of manual labor or six or seven kilograms of wheat. In 1347, allowing for interim changes in wages and prices, the same sum equaled two days' work but only two kilograms of wheat. Six kilograms of wheat is the equivalent of fifteen thousand calories. This was an appreciable amount for a bachelor, who (allowing for the frequency of distributions) thus received about five hundred calories per day as a supplement to his wages. But each member of a family of five would have received a supplement of only one hundred calories per day. These are the figures for 1324; by 1347, however, five sous amounted to only five thousand calories. On the eve of the plague and in the midst of economic crisis, this difference might well account for many dietary deficiencies, particularly among children. Charity is by nature only a supplement to other means of subsistence, and there are limits beyond which survival is impossible. Or San Michele did its best to alleviate the poverty of which it was aware, but its assistance could not have been sufficient. Was this also true elsewhere? Other examples are known where aid was adjusted to the recipient. In Pisa, for instance, in 1335, steps were taken to improve the lot of galley slaves and sottoposti. In order to put an end to the injustices from which sailors suffered when their contracts were broken, an official known as the *scrivano per parte de marinari* (sailors' secretary) was placed on board each ship along with the owner's secretary. In general, however, the recipients and forms of charity remained what they had been in the past, and aid to the working poor was not yet a regular part of the work of most charitable institutions.

There were also other limits to charity. Without delving once more into the distinction between the good poor and the bad, between those who deserved charity and those who did not, it behooves us to remember those whom the charitable overlooked. In 1264, for example, the Council of Vernon prohibited Jews from entering hospitals under its jurisdiction, and in the same region in the time of Eudes Rigaud access was also denied to travelers in good health. Perhaps the space was needed for the sick and the poor!

By the early fourteenth century inappropriate use of resources and out-and-out abuses threatened to compromise the otherwise laudable effort to expand the number of hospital beds. Abuses denounced even earlier by James of Vitry remained in spite of persistent efforts to root them out. The requirement placed on all hospitals without formal rules and regulations to adopt a statute forthwith did not accomplish the desired goal, nor did the transformation of many hospitals into convent-hospitals and closer supervision of hospital management by civic authorities. New abuses came to light. Some *béguinages*, even those attached to hospitals, were suspected of harboring heresy, as we have seen. Other, smaller *béguinages* were turned into little more than retirement homes for wealthy old women. Hospitals were commonly regarded as benefices. Clerics had themselves assigned to hospital posts but never took up residence, and laymen were named to positions of responsibility for which they lacked the requisite skills. Some hospitals were not kept up, their revenues were diverted to private ends, and either by negligence or by design the number of admissions declined. Voices were raised in protest against such abuses. We have already encountered one such protest, by the bishop of Poitiers around 1300. His colleague in Angers, Guillaume Le Maire, voiced similar complaints. Charges of abuse were the subject of a council held in Ravenna in 1311 and in the following year were treated in the canon *Quia contigit* by the council of Vienne.

In order to insure that hospitals would persist in the purposes laid down by their founders and benefactors, the awarding of hospital posts as benefices to the secular clergy was henceforth prohibited; instead, these positions were to go to "knowledgable, competent men of good reputation," who were to swear an oath to discharge their duties faithfully. A report on the operations of the hospital was to be prepared annually, and parish priests were prohibited from interfering with chaplains in the discharge of their ministry to the poor. The council chose, however, to exempt from these rules hospitals maintained by monastic orders, as well as certain *béguinages* engaged in assisting the poor.

There is no doubt that the decisions of the council of Vienne were put into practice. The effects of these reforms will become apparent in subsequent chapters. But it may be worth pausing here to cite just two examples. In Brussels in 1311 the Terarkem infirmary, which had served *béguines* exclusively, was transformed into a hospital for sick and poor women. The *béguinage* of Notre-Dame-de-la-Vigne was closed and its pensioners scattered throughout the city.[16] In Angers in 1327 Bishop Fulk of Monthefelon announced two synodal decisions that echoed the decisions of the council of Vienne: curates and rectors were given a year to provide detailed accounts for hospitals operating within their areas of responsibility so that reforms might be undertaken. In fact, however, the authorities had to wait fifteen years before all the reports were in hand!

Reform was necessary, but it came at a price. Increased institutionalization carried with it the danger of forcing innovation to fit the mold of the existing system, and precisely at a time when society was undergoing rapid change. In many ways time eroded the improvements that Dominicans and Franciscans had brought to the lives of the poor. Reform came to a standstill, it seemed, just when innovation was most sorely needed.

Theory Lags behind Reality Earlier I asked whether the mendicant orders were successful in their efforts to rehabilitate labor and the poor. Some say that the answer is yes in England, where some of the poor received better treatment in the thirteenth century than ever before, but no in Germany, where attitudes of contempt toward the peasantry seem to have been accentuated, in literature at any rate.[17] Be that as it may, it is certain that the dispute within the mendicant orders over the signifiance of poverty served to inhibit innovation with respect to charity. The Spirituals, obsessed as they were with the idea of voluntary poverty, succeeded in putting poverty first and charity second, with the paradoxical result that they were less closely in touch with the poor than the companions of Saint Francis had been. Their intellectual fixation on the concept of poverty left them cut off from social reality. And their rhetoric, by this point nearly two hundred years old, stood as a screen between the mendicant friars and the poor. The Spirituals were not solely responsible for this, however.

This aspect of the question of poverty in the case of Florence has been exhaustively studied by Charles de La Roncière, using sermons, moral treatises, and lives of saints. In a sermon preached by the Dominican Giordano da Rivalto at the beginning of Lent in the year 1304

we find nothing new in the way in which poverty and alms are conceived: poverty is a necessary evil, an opportunity for salvation both
for the poor, through patience, and for the rich, through alms. The
pauper remains, as always, an object of pity. This was the common
teaching, and it is repeated in French sermons of the early fourteenth
century, in moral treatises, and in literary works such as one anonymous poem that exhorts the rich to aid the poor during the famine of
1316. In this there is nothing surprising. Ever since the compilation of
the *Legenda major* around 1260 all the great exemplars, including
Saint Francis, had been presented in attenuated versions. The picture
of the pauper that emerges from these is a vague abstraction, a generalized portrait without precise details of the sort we find in the stories
of the indigent father or the man persecuted by his employer. Poverty
was still captured in traditional images, which reflected some aspects
of reality but not others. Troubling as it may be to us, it is not really
surprising that preaching based on these images should have enjoyed a
brief period of popularity, for men are always slow to change their
traditional ways of thinking. Large numbers of people flocked to Florence to hear the sermons of Giordano da Rivalto, Simone da Cascia,
and Giovanni da San Gimignano. Seldom was preaching so popular in
Florence as it was between 1320 and 1348.

Yet the everyday reality of working poverty was completely absent
from that preaching, because no one who earned even a modest wage
was looked upon as poor: an examination of these sermons with an eye
to finding concrete moral counsel concerning work and wages turns up
nothing. At most there are a few general observations, textbook formulas. These sermons may have kept up the spirits of those who hoped
to alleviate the suffering of the poor, but they did nothing to encourage
people to think about how that goal might be achieved.

One man dared to break the silence: a Dominican by the name of
Taddeo Dini. He was unusual in many ways, not least for his allusions,
remarkable at that time, to the Epistle of Saint James. He was unique,
too, in the way he understood and presented the problems of the poor.
The poor, he maintained, are not passive creatures but active individuals whose grievances are heard by God and who deserve justice
and a decent wage. The working poor had a place in Taddeo's view of
poverty, and he held out hope not just of eternal happiness but also of a
change in the earthly lot of the poor. If others held such views, they
rarely expressed them in public.

A few other men are also distinguished for their perceptive views of poverty, different from Dini's but no less bold. One pioneering thinker was Walter of Coincy, who as early as the first half of the thirteenth century classed as poor those artisans who worked to satisfy the needs of other men while earning little for themselves:

> The smith, the laborer,
> The tailor and polisher
> Fatten us with their sweat. . . .
> They are tired and dull and worn out
> And to us seem rugged and gay.[18]

Turning next from light literature to the administrative archives, we come upon an opinion quite unexpectedly turned up by the sheriff of Caen, who in 1297 made inquires in connection with a prosaic matter of dike improvement. Among the people he consults is the viscount of Montgommeri, whose insight into the problems of his day is reminiscent of a royal *intendant* of the eighteenth century. According to Montgommeri, elimination of dams for mills and fisheries would increase agricultural production and decrease the number of paupers. There were, he said, some seven thousand of them who traveled as much as five leagues to receive alms at the abbey of Troarn.

Next, turning back to literature and shifting our attention to the Mediterranean, we find Raymond Lull, as usual straddling the dividing line between lucidity and utopianism. He remains faithful to the theological view that the existence of the poor is necessary to the economy of salvation, but still he is obsessed by the idea that wealth could be distributed in a more equitable manner, obviously by way of alms. "O Queen!" he cries out to the Virgin in his *Libre de Sancta Maria*, "How ill-apportioned are the riches of this world!"

Finally, we have brother Bernat Puig, lector of the Carmelites of Barcelona. Had he read his compatriot Raymond Lull, and did he perhaps feel called to play the role of "canon of mercy" that Lull describes in his *Blanquerna?* Brother Bernat caused a scandal with the sermon he preached in the cathedral for Christmas of 1333. The harvest had been bad and the winter harsh. The preacher launched a violent and overt attack on the city councilors, who wrote to the prior of the Spanish Carmelites to have this "sower of discord" removed from their city. Rather than exhort the people to endure high grain prices patiently and to beg the assistance of the Lord, said the councilors, Bernat stirred up the populace. Here the lines were clearly drawn between two opposing

conceptions of poverty, and it is interesting that we find battling together on the same side and in similar circumstances the Florentine
Dominican Taddeo Dini and the Catalonian Carmelite Bernat Puig.

The Illusions of the Poor   Not every-
one who acted as or declared himself to be a defender of the poor
equaled the men mentioned above in lucidity or disinterestedness.
One of William of Saint-Amour's complaints about the mendicant
orders was that their preaching in the vulgar tongue encouraged heresy—popular movements with eschatological overtones.[19] And whatever else we can say about William, he did not lack diligence in arguing
his case. His charge that Joachimism was a breeding ground for messianic heresies was probably not without foundation. Still worse in his
eyes were preachers who led the unfortunate to believe in an imminent heaven on earth rather than in ultimate salvation. For him the
problem was that simple folk seriously misunderstood the meaning of
the prophets who preached in the late thirteenth and early fourteenth
century. They were deluded. Hugh of Digne's *De finibus paupertatis*
surely bore little direct relationship to the visceral problems of involuntary poverty, but the Joachimism of which he made himself the
preacher and of which the Spirituals made themselves propagandists
seemingly responded to the hope of the poor for a better world. One
should, of course, distinguish between the Franciscan Spirituals and
the Dominican Spirituals and acknowledge frankly that some of these
prophets were truly concerned about the distress of the poor. So were
some of the Béguines and Cathari, Pierre Maury being an example of a
Cathar whose care for the poor was genuine. Not all heretics were
"fanatics of the Apocalypse," and even those for whom this description is apt were not all fanatical to the same degree.

There has been much discussion recently about the social implications of the sect known as the Apostolici, led by Segnarelli and Fra
Dolcino. Some writers have argued that the sect's questioning of the
social order was responsible for its suppression.[20] Others argue that
the development of the movement among the peasants did not have
the significance that has been assumed, because the level of social
tension in early fourteenth-century Valsesia was not particularly
high.[21] Both sides in this debate agree that social motives did play a
part in determining the behavior of those peasants who suffered under
seigneurial demands. Accordingly, we are told, some genuine paupers

did play a role in a movement that held out to them hopes of a better life.[22] In any case, paupers who took part in Fra Dolcino's movement were misled into espousing a cause that was not directly their own. A half century later in Rome, the poor were again misled, in quite another manner, by the blandishments of a Cola di Rienzo. But those astonishing illusions are another story.

In the interim, other men pondered various strategies for attacking poverty. Intelligent and ambitious, these strategies were unfortunately also utopian. We find an account of one of them in the *Dialogue* of Arnaud of Villeneuve (1309). Arnaud believed he had found in Frederick II of Sicily, a protector of the Spirituals, a prince willing to give him a hearing. He therefore proposed a plan based on the idea, worthy of a Saint Louis, that royalty is a divine ministry: a king's first concern should be with the poor, victims not only of oppression by the rich but also of wicked constitutions and of legal violence committed by royal officials. The prince, Arnaud maintained, should grant a weekly audience to the poor and travel frequently to different parts of his realm in order to hear grievances. Frederick II seems to have been inspired by his counsel. Constantly on the go, Frederick was a visible figure to his people. In 1310 he took measures favorable to slaves, especially Greeks deported by Almugavar pirates, and during his lifetime he showed great generosity to the indigent. In his will he founded a hospice at Messina for vagabonds and with great foresight envisioned the merger of small hospitals. But his policies did not survive him and in the end the ambitions of Arnaud of Villeneuve remained a generous but unfulfilled dream.

This was even more true of the cogitations of Raymond Lull, interesting as they are. In *Evast et aloma* and above all in *Blanquerna* Lull dreamed of a Church that would truly stand up for the poor and lead them into battle against the rich. Blanquerna himself takes to the streets to rally the poor gathered at the gate of the canons' residence; some of the canons themselves become defenders of the unfortunate. The "canon of poverty" leads the procession, shouting "Justice! Justice!" first in front of the archdeacon's residence and then in front of the bishop's. The "canon of mercy" then plays the role of advocate, denouncing injustice and dishonesty—the cloth merchants are his primary target—and threatening to move from words to action. Finally, a third figure arrives on the scene, the "canon of persecution." Raymond Lull seems to speak in favor of rebellion when in reality he is calling for social harmony in the most traditional terms, urging that the wealthy save their own souls by making their obligatory gifts of alms.

Exploiters of the Wrath of the Poor

Like Fra Bernat Puig, Raymond Lull's canons were not being insincere when they justified, aroused, directed, or defended the wrath of the poor. For had they not found in the work of scholastics like Henry of Ghent grounds on which rebellion could be justified? Henry, after establishing the principle of obligatory obedience to the sovereign, goes on to say that the subjects have the right to present their grievances and, if those grievances are not received, to disobey.[23]

By contrast, strikes and coalitions were condemned and suppressed. That judicious jurist Philippe de Beaumanoir is categorical in this regard in his *Coutumes de Beauvaisis.* Of course this book dates from a period when northern France was prey to social unrest. From the late thirteenth century on, the poor city dweller or peasant refused to resign himself any longer to a passive role. Unfortunately, however, every time the poor tried to make their voices heard, their efforts were coopted, distorted, or exploited by others and ultimately stifled or suppressed. As so often happens in history, the poor were used as shock troops in the service of causes that demagogues had persuaded them were their own.

Care should be taken not to confuse the rebellions of the poor with urban unrest. The most representative instances of rebellion were the two movements that have come to be associated with the name Shepherds (*pastoureaux*). In both cases, first in 1251 and then again in 1320, the humble and the young paid the price, just as in the Children's Crusade of 1212. In 1251, "leaving animals in their pastures they set out without bidding farewell to either mother or father" and entrusted their messianic hopes to the ministerings of outlaw priests who styled themselves bishops. Their guide, the Master of Hungary, looked like a prophet, with his "great beard like that of a penitent" and his "pale and meager face." These descriptions are taken from the chronicles of Primat and Saint-Denis. Archibishop Eudes Rigaud watched as the rebels invaded the Rouen cathedral on the day of a synodal meeting. In 1320 it was "a horde of peasants and common people" including "even sixteen-year-old youths, without money and all their belongings in a double sack carried over the shoulder with a stick." They were organized in groups of tens, hundreds, and thousands, with "masters and banners." Only God knew what they were up to. Bloody repression ensued in both instances, leaving the poor disillusioned once more.

‡ This is not the place to describe or analyze urban unrest. Urban uprisings probably stemmed initially from tax grievances in which the poor must have had a part. But in the early stages of urban troubles, prior to the middle of the fourteenth century, the real objective of these uprisings was to enable men of middling status to gain access to municipal power, and in this the poor were not directly concerned. In the area between the Seine and the Rhine, in the 1280s, again in 1302, and yet again from 1323 to 1328, especially in Flanders, as well as in the period 1333–48 in Barcelona and Florence, large numbers of the poor took to the streets and bore the brunt of the ensuing repression without winning any major gains for their children. In some cases the poor were victims of their confidence in awkward or incompetent leaders, while in other cases they were the dupes of ambitious demagogues. This was what happened in 1280 in Rouen and also in Flanders, where the Kokerulle of Ypres and the two Moorlemayes of Bruges left behind memories of abortive rebellions whose failure was paid for by the common people. A short time later, in 1285, a man who is described as being of "base condition," one Beranguer Oller, somehow managed to persuade most of the poor of Barcelona to swear an oath that they would follow his orders. Although the poor joined Oller's movement, it represented not their interests but those of an upstart petty bourgeoisie that had achieved sufficient status to desire more. In Bruges in 1300, Peter de Coninc, the son of a poor family, who lived on what he earned as a weaver and never possessed more than ten livres of his own, "had so many words and spoke so well that it was a fine miracle, for which the weavers, fullers, and shearers believed in him and loved him so much that he could say or order nothing that they did not do." Similarly, the poor participated in an uprising in coastal Flanders that lasted five years and ended in repression, even though the cause at issue was not really their own. The movement was led by landowners who enjoyed a fairly comfortable position, the uncultivated, hardworking descendants of the men who had built the polders. The pioneering spirit of independence that they inherited from their forebears made them intolerant of certain burdens placed upon them by various lords, the count of Flanders, and the Church. They deemed themselves victims of misfortune, though they hardly were so to the

same degree as the smallholders and laborers from whom they themselves demanded much toil and whom they led in a lost cause.

These disturbances were not limited to northern France and the Low Countries. The Empire had troubles of its own, which increased after 1330. There were uprisings in Strasbourg in 1332 and in Zurich in 1336. In each case artisans went to battle solely to obtain a place on the municipal council for their guild leaders. Italy also provides interesting examples. Earlier we saw how the *minuti* placed their hopes in Walter of Brienne. His fall was the occasion of a major fracas (1343). Villani tells the story of how Andrea Strozzi attempted to stir up the *sottoposti* of the San Lorenzo district, the wool carders and combers, calling them a "starving rabble" whose apathy had permitted the fall of the man who had brought them grain at ten sous per measure instead of twenty. The poor who went to court with their leader admitted to having been persuaded that "the poor would become rich."

The same illusion befell the poor of Siena a short while later. Led by members of the aristocratic Tolomei family, a mob gathered in the city in a time of famine. Thirty-two people were sentenced to death in the ensuing repression, including five wool carders, six hosiers, and two tailors, along with assorted cutlers, basket and saddle makers, and other craftsmen.

When Andrea Strozzi branded his common followers a "rabble," he was only continuing a long-standing attitude of contempt for the poor. Caffo degli Agli spoke of artisans in the following terms: *Questi artifici! de la merda!* Francesco Sacchetti called them "lechers." But the *minuti* seem to have gotten in a few licks of their own against the "wolves and hawks who want to rule the people."

It is not necessary to go back very far to find evidence of a tradition of contempt toward the poor, a tradition whose ancient origins we discussed earlier. For example, the moral limitations of the *Romance of Sidrach*, one of the most widely read romances in thirteenth-century France, are striking. It advocates almsgiving, admits that rich and poor are by nature equal, and yet finds it normal that the poor should work harder than the rich because hard work gives them a stronger constitution. The poor must not mix with the wealthy, moreover, because the pauper's lot is like that of "sheep who jostle one another in a pond, or frogs who crush one another's feet because they are so small." Furthermore, the poor must make way for the rich everywhere "except in battle": was this unconscious cynicism?

The middle of the fourteenth century marks the close of more than a hundred years of economic boom and bust, a period of unprecedented social change much influenced by the preaching of the mendicant orders. Poverty now extended to new categories of urban and rural workers who could no longer make ends meet. Charitable institutions proliferated, but there seems to have been no awareness that their clientele had changed. Poverty was still looked upon by everyone as an evil, but the pauper remained a pauper and the working poor were all too often neglected. Most unfortunate of all, perhaps, was that those who saw men as fundamentally good and naturally equal were harder on the poor than anyone had ever been before. Here is the way in which the *Roman de la Rose* depicts Dame Poverty in the allegorical frescoes of the Walled Orchard:

> All she had on was a thin sack crudely sewn together, which served her as both overcoat and tunic and was her only wrap, so that she often shivered. Remaining somewhat apart from the others, she crouched and huddled like a poor dog, for the poor are miserable and ashamed wherever they find themselves. Cursed be the hour when the pauper was conceived, for he will never be well fed, well clothed, or well shod. Nor will he ever be loved or exalted.

On the eve of history's greatest plague, were the views of Saint Francis and Saint Dominic forgotten? Yes and no. It is time now to see how subsequent generations responded to the problem of poverty.

PART FOUR ‡ PAUPERS AND BEGGARS: ALARMING PRESENCES (MID-FOURTEENTH TO EARLY SIXTEENTH CENTURY) ‡

CHAPTER TEN ‡
THE BLACK PLAGUE AND SOCIAL UNREST IN THE LATE FOURTEENTH CENTURY

THE PLAGUE AND THE POOR

The Black Plague ravaged the poor. It did not eliminate poverty. Who could have felt safe from the scourge? The plague, brought from Caffa by Genoese ships, spread in the port cities, which had no sanitary safeguards to protect them. The first attempt to impose a quarantine did not come until 1377, in Ragusa.[1] From the first ports to be affected on the Adriatic, the plague spread to the Mediterranean in the spring of 1348 and then to the Atlantic Ocean and the English Channel before finally spending itself in the Baltic in 1350. The disease spread inland along the continent's major avenues of communication, inexplicably sparing a few pockets such as Béarn, Flanders, Hungary, and Bohemia. The contamination spread to England from two directions, via Calais as well as the Atlantic, while Germany imported the contagion first from Italy via the Tyrol and a short while later via the North Sea and the rivers that emptied into it. People of all ages fell ill, and perhaps a third of the population of Europe died of the disease.

Although the plague spared no one, the poor, who had been racked by a prolonged series of famines, were extraordinarily susceptible: "après la famine, la peste domine" (after the famine, the plague rules), as a popular rhyme had it. Although the chroniclers, like artists given to depicting *danses macabres*, emphasized the equal vulnerability of the rich and the poor, much evidence mournfully attests to the predominance of the indigent among victims of the disease. The plague first attacked poor sections, as at Rimini, Orvieto (where the rich were spared for three months), and Narbonne (where dyers living along the banks of the Aude were the first to fall). Elsewhere the disease was at its worst among the poor. Prominent residents of Lincoln were all but spared. In Lübeck the mortality rate of 25 percent among property owners was only half the 50-percent average for all German cities. As for northern France, it seems that the poor were twice as likely to die as the rich. Thus the plague has been called the "proletarian epidemic."

Some contemporaries were aware of the selective mortality of the plague. Guy de Chauliac, the most famous physician of his day, who witnessed not only the Black Plague but also the recurrence of the disease in 1361, noted this difference between the two pandemics: "In the first more of the common people died, and in [the second] more of the rich and noble." His colleague Simon de Couvin, who took part in discussions concerning the plague held at the Faculty of Medicine in Paris, showed rare perspicacity as well as an awareness of social psychology: "The person whose diet was poor and insubstantial fell at the first scent of the disease. The extremely poor fellow of the common sort (*pauperrima turba*) willingly accepted death because for him to live was to die. But cruel Fate respected princes, knights, and judges: few of them succumbed, because they had been granted a comfortable life in this world." Was this a mere literary flourish? La Fontaine of course used the plague as a literary theme in *La Mort et le bûcheron*, long after the events. While the epidemic raged, however, there was no time for idle jest. To be sure, the *Decameron* is composed of speeches that Boccaccio attributes to young aristocrats eager to divert themselves and forget the plague. But a learned physician could hardly amuse himself by observing the agony of the poor. Each of his words strikes home.

The physicians of the fourteenth century believed literally that a "scent of disease" was enough to strike down a pauper. It was then thought that the infection, in both its bubonic and pneumonic forms, could be transmitted by inhalation, indeed by a mere glance. The appearance of purulent black sores (whence the name Black Plague) was followed by the development of buboes in the groin or armpit accompanied by an extremely high fever (up to 107 degrees), delirium, and hemorrhage. The progress of the disease depended on the condition of the victim. Death from septicemia could occur in two to three days.

In October of 1348, the Faculty of Medicine of Paris, in a formal *Compendium de epidemia*, declared that weakness, along with fear and obesity, was the principal predisposing factor for the disease. But Simon de Couvin was right to lay the blame primarily on malnutrition. The diet of the poor (for which we have evidence in the case of Florence, for example) was seriously deficient not only in calories but also in proteins, lipids, and calcium, as well as vitamins A and C (which prevent scurvy) and D (which prevents rickets). In the period 1340–47 it was difficult if not impossible for an artisan to obtain enough meat, cheese, milk, and vegetables to add to the staple "gray bread" (which consisted essentially of a mixture of barley and spelt).

Florence was not, it seems, an isolated instance; the diet of the poor in nearby Orvieto was apparently similar. Evidence from other European cities is consistent with these observations. In rural areas malnutrition was more important than undernourishment: grains were of poor quality, too much salted meat was eaten instead of fresh meat, starch consumption was excessive (in peas, broad beans, and porridges), and drink too often consisted of vinegary wines and contaminated water. No one, and certainly not the poor, came close to meeting the sophisticated dietary prescriptions laid down by the Faculty of Medicine for escaping the plague: good wheat bread, white meat, and young lamb should be eaten, said the doctors, vegetable consumption should be limited, and leeks, onions, and turnips, "which engender flatulence," should be avoided along with other "light and subtle" foods. Most resistant to the plague were those of "dry and healthy" constitution.

Not only the diet but also the prophylactic measures recommended by the Faculty of Medicine were beyond the reach of the poor. Though pompously formulated, these hygienic recommendations were mainly commonsensical, often inappropriate, and for the most part ineffective. Only the wealthy could afford to live in warm, dry rooms. A wool spinner like the one described in the *Ménagier de Paris* would have lived in a tiny, dark, unheated room on an upper story of one of the tall buildings that had grown up on the right bank of the Seine as the population of the city increased, or else at ground level in an attached shed. In any case, the animal that carried the disease, the black rat (*Rattus rattus*), actually thrived in warm, dry places. Rats rarely strayed more than two hundred yards from the warmth of dwellings, and the poor might have fared better if their homes had been still colder and damper than they were. The wood and straw used for construction and roofing were perfect for the rat, which also thrived—and traveled—in ships' bilges. Rural dwellings were healthier. But whether these were built of stone, as at Dracy in Burgundy or Rougiers in Provence (where archeologists have been able to reconstruct houses of the plague period), or of wood or cob as in Normandy, Flanders, and England, rats were attracted by the nearby silo and stable and by the warm hearth around which family life revolved. Recurrent epidemics demonstrated the futility of the customary English practice of building a new family house with each new generation.

The real plague vector was the flea that lived in symbiosis with the rat, and to have eliminated the flea would have required such elementary hygienic practices as washing skin and clothing. Only the wealthy could afford such fashionable novelties in the 1340s. How many peasants and city workers wore (and, more importantly, changed) linen shirts under their outer garments of coarse wool, often obtained second hand, or of common furs such as rabbit, cat, fox, or sheepskin? Although skins were worn with the fur on the outside, parasites were not thereby eliminated. People washed infrequently, so that the medical advice not to bathe was superfluous for many. At best the advice to stay away from the bathhouses would have reduced opportunities for contagion. But peasants never went to bathhouses anyway. The Faculty's other recommendations were of no use to the poor: to work less, to engage only in moderate exercise, to sleep with the head raised on "good, fine-smelling sheets," to use costly aromatic disinfectants, incense, myrrh, and aloes of Socotora, and to sprinkle one's room with rose water.

The poor may have been fortunate in their ignorance, for trusting to nature may have saved many of them. To be fair, though, physicians did treat the poor, and some of them could not be prevented from accompanying Minorite friars to the homes of the sick, where they contracted the disease while caring for its victims. Pope Clement VI recruited several doctors to treat the poor of Avignon for free. In Venice a special confraternity was formed to bury the poor.

Can it be said that the poor suffered more than other social groups in the Black Plague? The high mortality rate among urban workers may distort the picture. The plague also ravaged the countryside, and even today deserted villages in some parts of Europe stand as reminders of the extent of damage. Despite malnutrition among the peasantry, however, some rural villages, especially those far from the great cities and major roads, were spared. The physical resistance of peasants living in the hills of upper Provence is attested by a letter written by a Dutch canon in April of 1348. When victims of the plague who had been abandoned by their families died, the authorities enlisted "sturdy country folk from the mountains of Provence, miserably poor men of strong constitution who are known as *gavots* [that is, natives of the Gap region—*Trans.*], to carry them to their graves, in exchange for a hefty sum." But later he expresses his surprise: "Even some of these miserable *gavots* [to whom he refers elsewhere as "lechers"] die after a short time, infected by the disease as much as they are worn down by poverty, just as all the other paupers of the Pignotte have died who used to serve at the funerals of the wealthy."

Wages aside, what were the feelings of these despised but useful *gavot* undertakers? We will never know. Nor is it easy to make out the reactions of the poor themselves to the plague. No doubt the poor were neither more nor less afraid than the wealthy, although Simon de Couvin was shrewd enough to detect a measure of resignation, not to say fatalism, in the attitude of those who lived constantly on the verge of starvation. Ethnology, liturgy, religious practice, and hagiography can all shed light on the behavior of the common people. For example, there were special processions held in Florence, Orvieto, Barcelona, and Bath in 1348 and 1349. The poor participated in special masses for times of plague according to a ritual established by Clement VI in 1348. They made devotional offerings and appealed to the saints for aid, especially to Anthony, Adrian, and Sebastian (later, Saint Rock, a contemporary of the plague epidemics, would be added to this list of healing saints). During the epidemic a statue of Saint Sebastian pierced with arrows was placed on display for public veneration, and Gilles Le Muisit drew large crowds when he said two prayers in the saint's honor. In Norway, a legend dating from the fourteenth century explains that the family name Rype (meaning wild bird) was first given to the survivor of a family wiped out by the plague, who had taken refuge in a forest near Bergen.

Just as lepers had once been accused of poisoning the wells, now the poor were accused. A report of the *viguier* (provost) of Narbonne dated 17 April 1348 took note of the confessions of "paupers and mendicants of all nations" accused by public hue and cry of having "thrown into the waters, houses, churches, and food supplies, with the purpose of killing," powdered potions received from unknown persons who had also given them sums of money. Nine such miscreants had already been drawn and quartered. Where there were no convenient paupers to blame, popular anger was directed primarily at Jews, as in Catalonia and in the Rhine Valley. Popular wrath was also aimed at lenders, usurers, and the rich.

AFTER THE CALAMITY:
RESPITE AND RELAPSE

After the dead of the plague were buried, Europe experienced a period of scarce manpower. The pandemic had brutally resolved the population problem by eliminating the surplus mouths to be fed. People asked only for a better life, the poor along with everyone else. In a memorable passage Matteo Villani traced the social and moral consequences of the plague:

> The little people, men and women, owing to the excessive abundance of things, were no longer willing to work in their usual

occupations. They demanded the most expensive and delicate food. . . . It was assumed that there would be an abundance of all the products of the earth, but on the contrary, because of the ingratitude of men, there was scarcity of all things. . . . Most things cost twice as much as before the plague, if not more. The number of workers and products of each craft and trade rose in a disorderly fashion. . . . Grievances, lawsuits, disputes, and fights broke out on all sides over wills and inheritances.

What was left by the plague victims scarcely improved the well-being of the surviving poor. A sheet, a bed, a few personal belongings, a corn bin, a goat: that is what one indigent might have left to another. The advantages of a concentration of property accrued only to those already well off. As Yves Renouard has written, "death made the rich richer and left the poor as poor as ever." The opportunity that did present itself to peasants and workers stemmed from the need for manpower and the rising price of scarce labor. Contemporary observers make up for the silence of the archives. For example, Jean de Venette observed that "when the plague was over, it was as though a vacuum had settled upon many towns and cities." And Gilles Le Muisit, nostalgic as he was for the old times, carried his lucid analysis still further: "The widespread mortality of 1349 killed so many farmers and vintners, so many workers of every trade . . . that there was a great lack. All the workers and their families demanded exorbitant wages." The word *demanded* here takes on new meaning. As though commenting upon it, Agnolo di Tura of Siena echoed the sentiments of Matteo Villani: "After the great pestilence of the previous year, everyone lived just as he pleased."

Confusion reigned everywhere. In one place harvests were not gathered for want of manpower. In another peasants left their plots to claim better land nearby. Serfs took advantage of the confusion to escape from their dependent status, attracted by the cities and the hope of earning high wages as craftsmen. The law of supply and demand ruled the market, as Matteo Villani observed. But the scarcity of labor may not have been the sole cause of rising wages. Emigration from the countryside into the cities preceded the plague, and the influx of newcomers to the labor market might have lowered wages, at least in relatively unskilled occupations. Then, too, rising wages were accompanied by a rising cost of living, the cause of which, again, may not have been that food was in short supply. For money was also in short supply, adding still further to the economic disequilibrium.

For the poor, the rising wages were a stroke of good fortune (with increases, according to some authorities, ranging up to 100 percent in the countryside and 150 percent in the cities). Workers were in great demand. In Toulouse master craftsmen enticed apprentices and helpers from their rivals. In rural areas, especially in England, where the persistence of slavery in the form of villenage had been particularly oppressive, landlords vied with one another to keep tenants on their plots. Change was rapid. After the plague the number of manorial estates worked entirely by compulsory labor decreased by half, while the number partially worked by such means doubled and obligatory labor services were converted into money rents on forty-four manors (compared with six in the previous period). Emancipation, reduction of dues, and short-term contracts were the procedures most commonly employed, and wages paid to agricultural day laborers increased.

In the cities, higher wages benefited all laborers, both younger workers and skilled journeymen. This assertion is supported by evidence from places as widely separated as Paris and Florence. In Paris the day's wage for mason's and roofer's helpers working on the *hôpital* Saint-Jacques rose by 100 percent between 1348 and 1353. In the same period the price of wheat, which in 1350 rose briefly to three times its level of the year before, fell in 1352–53 to a level equal to or slightly below that of 1349. In Florence the wage index for four occupational categories has been calculated as 200 (at least) for 1350–56 (based on an index of 100 for the period 1326–47). The sharpest increase was in wages for laborers and journeymen in the weaving trade, a group particularly hard hit by the plague. Here, as in Paris, wheat prices rose until 1353, after which a period of low prices lasted for fourteen years. In England, journeyman mason's wages rose at least 20 percent after the plague. Agricultural day laborers were paid an estimated 2.35 times as much in the period 1340–60 as at the beginning of the century. Similar increases have been found in the years after 1350 in Navarre, the Tyrol, and Cracow.

Poor people who did not benefit from the increase in wages—the needy, the ragged, the ashamed who hid their poverty at home—benefited from another kind of good fortune: the growing number of charitable bequests. Their brush with death reminded people of injustices they had committed and sent many to see their notaries as well as their priests. Bequests were not typically as large as they had been a century earlier, but we can gain some idea of the desire to make amends through alms by studying the increase in the number of wills in different areas, an increase that parallels the progress of the plague. Bequests went mainly to hospitals and confraternities. Large amounts of money were involved. In Florence, the company of Or San Michele received 350,000 florins in charitable bequests for the poor. Since many of the poor had died, however, a part of this amount was allocated for the execution, by Andrea Orcagna, of the highly ornamented altar table still visible today in the sanctuary that served as the company's chapel. This use of alms for purposes other than poor relief is revealing of the way in which members of the confraternity conceived of poverty. It is certainly true, in any case, that the working poor were now less impecunious than they had been before the plague. Although I do not go so far as those who maintain that the plague inaugurated a golden age for workers, it does seem that in Florence workers enjoyed a "miraculous decade" in the period 1350–60.

In Italian cities where the patrician class was in power, governments felt the need to control wages. The government of Orvieto set strict maximum wages in 1350 for all categories of workers from masons to wet-nurses. Wage supplements in the form of food and lodging, which could add substantially to nominal wages, posed a problem for the regulators. In Florence the Signoria issued several edicts concerning wages and prices, the most important of which dates from 1355; price levels were of course of great concern to the needy.

The state of the economy tended to favor wage-earners, and even people in modest occupations discovered that their wages were on the rise. A typical construction laborer, who earned an average of two solidi seven deniers per day in the period 1340–46, earned nine solidi two deniers in the period 1350–56, nine solidi six deniers in 1363–69, and as much as nine solidi nine deniers on the eve of the Ciompi rebellion. Things were more difficult for families with children than for single workers, but humble families were helped appreciably by the earnings of women in this period of improved employment prospects. Children born in Florence between 1355 and 1360 had the unusual good fortune of belonging to the only generation of the century whose crucial early development was not hampered in some way. There was no rent problem during this period. As for food and clothing, the facts happily support the righteous indignation of Matteo Villani against the presumptuousness of the *minuti* bold enough to take advantage of "the excessive abundance of things." Humble folk easily managed to find clothing to wear. Consumption of poor-quality grains declined as that of white bread increased. The poor, it was said, were "starved for meat" and consumed large amounts of pork and poultry. They also began to drink better-quality wines. Improvements in the diet of the poor have also been noted in Provence, Languedoc, Germany, and England. People became accustomed to dietary changes first introduced in the years after the plague. As a result, the economic downturn that occurred around 1370 proved all the more unpleasant and helped to create the atmosphere characteristic of the era of the Ciompi.

One should be careful, however, not to overstate the improvements that occurred in the life of the poor in Florence in the decade that followed the Great Plague. Prosperity, even here, remained tenuous at best. Wages for textile workers began to decline as early as 1360, and by 1366 there were signs of recession in the wool and dying trades. But at least the poor had enjoyed a period of respite.

‡ Elsewhere the poor also enjoyed a period of respite, though to a lesser degree than in Florence owing either to adverse legislation or to military and political conditions. Municipal and national governments and representative assemblies such as the English Parliament, the Spanish Cortes, and the French provincial Estates to one degree or another regulated wages, prices, guilds, labor mobility, unemployment, and begging—all matters of concern to the poor. Municipal authorities in other countries were less powerful than in Italy, where the Signoria was sovereign. Still, in Toulouse, for example, we find the *capitularii* (or city magistrates) controlling the wages of tanners. In Amiens the city council set a maximum wage in 1359. The magistrates of Metz not only fixed the maximum wage but moved to control hiring in 1355. In the cities of Flanders rising wages seem to have been offset by higher food prices. The weavers of Ghent took their revenge on one group of workers, the fullers, who had won a victory in 1349. In 1359 the fullers were reduced to the status of second-zone citizens. Wages limits were set in Hainault in 1354. Simultaneous intervention by the state in the social life of all countries was both a novelty and a sign of the times. In the Iberian kingdoms and in England the state's role began as early as the middle of 1349, while the epidemic was still raging.

From the point of view of the poor, government intervention had both positive and negative aspects. In Aragon, for example, in July of 1349, maximum wages were set for tailors, tanners, blacksmiths, carpenters, quarrymen, plowmen, shepherds, and domestic servants, some of whom were asking for wages four to five times higher than they had earned before the plague. Whether this edict was effective is open to doubt, since it was reissued two more times in the following year. The king of Castille asked for and obtained similar legislation from the Cortes at Valladolid in 1351. Alfonso IV of Portugal went even further: not content merely to limit wages, as he did in 1349, the king tried to stem the tide of vagabondage and begging of which the cities complained and to keep people from leaving their jobs. He ordered that vagabonds be expelled from the cities and refused admission to hospices. More liberal measures were adopted in Aragon, where certain categories of peasants were granted reductions of dues, exemptions from the tithe, and moratoriums on debt repayment. In Valencia, the fishermen of Albufera were granted dispensation from services due the crown. The results do not seem to have corresponded to expectations. Labor problems continued throughout the peninsula, compounded by further episodes of plague and famine. The Cortes in Lisbon heard complaints in 1371 of fields being deserted, workers demanding high wages, and cities being overrun by tramps and beggars. In 1375 it issued the so-called Sesmarias law, intended to restore agricultural production by regulating wages and services and compelling all unemployed but able-bodied tramps and beggars to go to work. Navarre and the territories ruled by the kingdom of Aragon were also faced with the problem of restoring agricultural production. The *remensas*, the Catalonian counterpart of the Portuguese *Sesmarias*, was animated by a seigneurial reaction that had dramatic consequences at the end of the fourteenth century. But the peasants, and even the serfs, emerged the winners.

Beginning in June of 1349 England took similar steps, with similar consequences. There, however, the system was more complete and methodical, as a result of which it helped to establish principles that influenced the life of the poor for a long time to come. In England as elsewhere the poor were quick to seize the advantage offered by the plague. But the attitude of "some who are unwilling to work unless they receive exorbitant wages and others who prefer to remain idle and beg rather than earn their living by working" led to a wage freeze, enforced by fines imposed upon workers and employers who violated the regulations. Men who were able to work were prohibited from begging and receiving alms, and wage limitations were bolstered by a prohibition against changing jobs. These were the essential points of the Statute of Laborers that formed the basis of English law up to at least the Elizabethan period. Enforcement of this statute, especially strict so far as workers were concerned, gave rise to a large number of court cases and stirred resentment that eventuated in the rebellion of 1381.

In France, necessity, and perhaps also the English example, inspired two ordinances. The fact that in 1354 it proved necessary to reissue the wage schedule of 1351 shows how difficult it was for the authorities to control the actual movement of prices. The schedule provided for salaries a third higher than they had been before the plague, so that a mason's assistant should have received 20 deniers per day during the summer, but in fact he received between 36 and 42 deniers per day in 1354. Partially offsetting this toleration of higher wages, the law prohibited piecework rates, obliged the unemployed to find work, and denied vagabonds access to hospitals and alms. The authorities were in fact greatly concerned with vagabonds. The 1351 ordinance is noteworthy as the first official document in the French language to give an official list of the categories of people living on the fringes of society. It concerns primarily the *prévôté* of Paris, where the influx of vagrants was considerable. The king was greatly concerned about the public order.[2]

The first requirement for protecting the interest of the poor (understood broadly to include all the needy) was to provide security. Their purchasing power was reduced not just by wage controls but also by repeated devaluations, rising prices, and taxes assessed to finance foreign wars. As for the peasants, reduction of seigneurial dues mattered less than security of tenure and protection against requisitions—seizures—effected either in due form or by force, rightly or wrongly, by armed men of all sorts, including ordinary bandits. In the interlude between the first phase of the Hundred Years' War, marked by the defeat at Crécy (1346), and the second phase, marked by the defeat at Poitiers (1356), there occurred not only the episode of the plague but also an obscure civil war between King John and his son-in-law Charles the Bad, king of Navarre, as rival coteries intrigued around the throne.

In such circumstances, it is hardly surprising that the poor, like everyone else, turned to those who claimed to offer help against both the king's scheming entourage and the nobility which had shown itself incapable of discharging its function—to defend the people—on the field of battle. The eloquence of the demagogues did the rest. The poor followed those whose promises conformed to their hopes. In Paris, to which many laborers and vagabonds fled in the wake of the plague, a mob led by Etienne Marcel upheld the cause of the Estates. Didn't the

Great Ordinance of 1357 reflect the wishes of poor people with its prohibition of extortion and its authorization of self-defense for purposes of "revenge"? After Marcel, provost of the Paris merchants, exhorted the artisans of Paris to quit their work and follow him, power lay in the streets, where it remained for the next two years. The worst came on 28 February 1358, when three thousand artisans invaded the palace inhabited by Prince Charles, regent for his imprisoned father. Within six months, however, the people realized that the provost's cause was not their own but rather that of the king's rebel son-in-law and of a segment of the Paris bourgeoisie. The mob "murmured greatly" and stood by when Etienne Marcel was assassinated. Marcel had counted on the support of other cities such as Toulon, Montbrison (where tax collectors were attacked in the so-called Cépage insurrection), Rouen (where the supporters of the king of Navarre had seized the castle), Troyes (which was in turmoil because of a conflict over working hours in the textile industry), Amiens (where the furriers were leading a tax revolt), the episcopal city of Laon (where Robert the Cock, an associate of Marcel and prosecutor of the city, "plotted the death of the great"), and Arras (where the "little people" took the fore by assassinating seventeen nobles in 1356).

The provost of merchants had also hoped to take advantage of the Jacquerie [the peasant uprising of 1358—*Trans.*]. This was another affair, a "terror" whose suddenness and violence led contemporary observers into impassioned exaggeration. According to their accounts, the Jacquerie was a widespread insurrection. It is true that disorders were reported in the Bray and Amiens regions, in Artois and Ponthieu, in Champagne and Perthois. But in fact, if we leave aside the Longjumeau area south of Paris, the center of the revolt lay to the north, in the plain of France and Beauvaisis. It was there, at Saint-Leu-d'Esserent, not far from Creil, that the first turmoil erupted on 29 May 1358, when, according to Jean le Bel and Froissart, peasants armed with "iron rods and knives" vanquished a troop of armed men. The Jacquerie was limited not only in geographical extent but also in numbers: it involved only five or six thousand men, according to Jean de Venette, who was inclined to exaggerate. Why, then, did this brief furor (which lasted only fifteen days) arouse such widespread interest? The answer is that people were afraid of its violent nature and remembered it with great emotion. The causes of the Jacquerie were also emotional, like the Great Fear [during the French Revolution—*Trans.*] to which it bears a strange resemblance. And it took on a deep emotional significance: in French the word *jacques* has come to mean a poor, rebellious peasant. It is interesting to note that the word *grève*, or strike, dates from the same period as *jacquerie.*

Although the great majority of participants in the Jacquerie were undoubtedly peasants, the *Great Chronicles of France* tell us that the "working folk" were joined by "rich men, bourgeois, and others," and even more certainly by renegade soldiers. Carle was chosen as leader because he "spoke well and thought well." He may have developed a sense of organization and command through military service.

A rebellion is not a revolution, and the Jacquerie was no revolution. Some who were forcibly conscripted or who became caught up in the enthusiasm of the moment claimed that when they saw the banners "decorated with fleurs de lis" they thought they were serving the king. Although the Jacques were surely anti-noble and joined in the general condemnation of the cavalry that fared so poorly in the battle of Poitiers, they were more opposed to the abuses of the seigneurial system than to the system itself. One of them is supposed to have said, "Let's let anything go and all be masters." More commonly, however, lords were criticized for staying away from their estates in service of the king. Simply because there was a rebellion, does it follow that it was caused by severe poverty? Jean de Venette wrote that "the blackest poverty prevailed everywhere, especially among the peasants, whose suffering the lords increased by seizing their goods and taking control of their miserable lives." Some of the Jacques were no doubt laborers whose hopes of earning higher wages had been disappointed. And the "unimportant poor seller of poultry, cheese, eggs, and other trifling commodities" from Acy-en-Multien who somehow found himself caught up in the Jacquerie and wound up in prison must not have been the only one of his kind. It may seem paradoxical, however, that the cantons involved in the rebellion were the wealthiest in the Ile-de-France, in which only "a handful of serfs" remained. Explanations for all this may follow the lines laid down by Guy Fourquin, who cites the disparity between agricultural and industrial prices, higher taxes, and pillaging mercenaries as precipitating factors. The rebellion grew out of impatience with such abuses. Humble people vested their hopes in the uprising. It is certain that they suffered in consequence, and it also seems plausible that they were used as pawns by ambitious leaders, of whom Etienne Marcel was not the only one. Once again the poor paid the price.

Some twenty years separated the aftermath of the Black Plague from the major disturbances of the late fourteenth century. During this period the condition of the poor in Europe remained stagnant, continuing at the same mediocre level. There were variations from region to region, however, and between cities and countryside.

Plague, famine, and war—the usual triumvirate—continued to afflict those who were already poor and added new paupers to the ranks. Quantitative estimates of the effects of various disasters are impossible to come by. Plague was virtually always present, with particularly severe outbreaks in 1360–62 and 1374–75. The first of these was as selective as the 1348 plague had been, affecting children and young men. The chroniclers were struck by the number of widows, clad in black from head to toe, who were seen wandering the streets of Paris. Hospitals in many places proved inadequate to cope with the second major outbreak of plague. In 1363 the bishop of Paris complained of the inadequacy of the Hôtel-Dieu. The five buildings of Santa Maria Nuova in Florence proved too small, and the hospital's expenditures increased fivefold. In Mons the Common Alms ran out of funds in 1371. For the poor, misfortune was compounded by misfortune as the plague combined with famine, especially in southern Europe, from Aquitaine to Provence and Portugal to Italy. Those who dwelt in the countryside had two advantages over their brothers in the cities: reduced risk of contagion and ready access to food. The cities faced major problems in requisitioning foodstuffs and controlling food prices and in some cases were forced to import grain over long distances. The English authorities in Aquitaine and local officials in Provence somehow managed to cope, though not without difficulty, but in Languedoc poor administration by the duke of Anjou sowed discontent whose extent became manifest some years later with the Tuchin insurrection. Cities such as Draguignan, Montpellier, Béziers, and Toulouse had great difficulty getting hold of stores "maliciously" held back by certain individuals. In central Italy attempts by the papal administration to count heads and distribute food came to nought. The poor went hungry.

Taxes were increased without regard to the circumstances, further aggravating the difficulties. By plunging Languedoc into poverty Louis of Anjou succeeded in making himself universally unpopular. Hearth taxes imposed by Charles V were a heavy burden; even though he had the resumption of war with the English as an excuse, these taxes were resented because they came on the heels of another heavy imposition to pay the ransom of King John and on top of sums extorted by companies of mercenaries. Taxes were in any case a lesser evil than the ravages wrought by mercenaries in Italy, Provence, Burgundy, Champagne, and Aquitaine. Froissart has described the wretchedness of "the poor toilers . . . who cursed the mercenaries . . . singing between clenched teeth, 'Get away, you filthy toads.'" And, while a Merigot Marches candidly admitted his crimes prior to sentencing, investigations in Gâtinais and Quercy revealed similar instances of extortion, murder, and arson, which reduced families to poverty and forced them to leave their homes. For the sake of objectivity I should add that the pillagers were themselves poor, after a fashion: many were younger or bastard sons, in some cases of noble families but without inheritance, while others were unemployed mercenaries and outcasts of every stripe.

Plague, famine, and war, disastrous as they were, were only stations of the cross in the passion of the pauper. Social and economic problems were endemic, and the worst was yet to come. Rural France seemed untroubled except for heavy taxes and the disruption of war. But in England, the legislation of 1349–51 had gradually been strengthened with the apparent objective of reducing wages to their pre-plague levels; trials were frequent. Similarly, Czech historians have uncovered the social roots of the Hussite affair in an aggravation of rural poverty in Bohemia during the second half of the fourteenth century. Even Scandinavia was shaken by disturbances among the peasants, the most serious of which was crushed in 1361 by the Danes at Visby. Finally, one of the poorest and most despised of all occupational groups, the salt makers, began to attract notice. Between 1360 and 1370 Venice had to cope with attempts by its salt makers to move to other mines in the hope of avoiding Venetian taxes and securing better living conditions.

In the meantime, certain problems came slowly to a head in the cities. A tendency toward increased occupational compartmentalization, characteristic of the fourteenth century, combined with problems arising from the recession to limit access to master craftsman status and to impose prerequisites that poor journeymen could not meet: in order to become a master craftsman, journeymen were sometimes required to execute an expensive masterpiece or at least to pass an examination and were almost always obliged to pay entrance fees. Masters did not scruple to increase the number of their apprentices in order to secure cheap help. The provost of Paris even authorized this practice, as in the case of the curriers in 1371. The textile industry was particularly prone to social problems. Because of the many technical operations involved in the manufacture of textiles, control of the entire process, from manufacturing to financing and sales, could be concentrated in a few hands. This led to the development of a hierarchy of positions and wage levels in the industry. Given the conditions that prevailed in the fourteenth century, particularly the latter half, social conflict was inevitable, especially since the guilds and city governments were in the hands of what Hans Van Werveke, speaking of Flanders, referred to as a "clique." Lesser men had no choice but to obey their betters.

The use of bells to regulate the course of the working day became increasingly common in the fourteenth century. This practice reflected a new awareness of the connection between time and money, with time itself now measured by the clock, the use of which also spread widely during the same period. City charters and guild regulations record these innovations, whose geographic distribution follows that of the industrial centers. An episode that occurred in York some time between 1352 and 1370 takes on symbolic value: two clocks were installed at the site of the cathedral then being built, one to call the faithful to services, the other to call workers to the job. The time of prayer and the time of work: the first belonged to God, the second to the merchant. A bell tower was put into service at Aire-sur-la-Lys in 1355, another in Ghent in 1358, and yet another in Thérouanne in 1367. At Comines a law of 1361 provided for fines in case workers should seize the bell tower to signal a rebellion. The symbol of alienated time, the bell also became a symbol of rebellion.

Tension between the rich and the poor existed in most European textile centers. In the Holy Roman Empire there was a spectacular uprising in Augsburg in 1368. In Prague poor textile workers were pitted against their employers. In Leyden the fullers went on strike in 1372 and temporarily left the city. It goes without saying that Italy and the Low Countries provide choice examples of the conditions in which poor artisans lived.

Admittedly, observations made of conditions in the textile industry in a few selected cities cannot be generalized to other trades in other places. We have seen, and we shall see again, what measures were taken to alleviate the suffering of the poor in these same textile centers. Still, it is worth stressing that the fullers of Ghent, for example, could never forget what that city's weavers had done to them in 1359, when the fullers were denied the right to speak in chapter meetings, to refuse work, and to quit their jobs, while their wages remained stagnant. Unrest continued, and when the town government was reorganized in 1372 the fullers were again kept at arm's length. In Brussels there were riots in 1360 and 1364 and a fire nearly destroyed the Grand-Place, but here the patriciate was forced to give in.

In Florence and Siena the situation began to deteriorate in 1368. Unemployment persisted for nearly ten years and led, as usual, to emigration. In the Florentine construction industry the wages of a single worker declined by one third between 1370 and 1377 to pre-1360 levels. For the father of a family the decline reached 40–45 percent. The "miracle years" faded to a memory. Problems cropped up in all areas, sometimes in acute forms. Grain stores were pillaged in 1368 in a riot that was followed by sixteen executions. In a strike two years later dyers demanded higher wages and forced the Signoria to grant them the right of association. The exodus of the unemployed and growing indebtedness were the leading issues of the day. The attitude of the *minuti* became threatening. In 1367 their support enabled the Ricci clan to win out over the newly rich and the Guelphs. Afterward, a secret society was formed by the proponents of a people's policy. One of its members was Salvestro de' Medici, destined to play a leading role in the future. But was the purpose of this group really to defend the poor, or was it to exploit them for the benefit of a particular family?

Was Florence influenced by the example of Siena? The latter city had been the scene of much unrest. In the episodes of 1355 and 1368 the interests of the poor had not counted for much, but things were different in 1378: the situation had taken a marked turn for the worse. The statutes of the wool guild left the *sottoposti* in a position of abject dependence. Upon entering the guild they were obliged, in exchange for a cash advance, to swear never to do anything to harm either their profession or their master. The word of the master was to carry *contra il lavorante infimo*. Poorly paid and subject to a strict schedule of fines for various offenses, the Ciompi of Siena were, according to the chronicle of Donato di Neri, "the most contemptible of the plebs." In 1370 food prices rose in the wake of a shortage and unemployment reached worrisome proportions. In the hope of obtaining better wages, three hundred Ciompi illegally formed the Compagnia del Bruco in 1371. The name was an almost totemic symbol of their neighborhood (*bruco* is Italian for caterpillar). Their march on the Signoria ended in failure. "Although they made a great deal of noise," Donato continued, "they who wanted to slay the masters of the city were the victims of an inhuman repression." Other disturbances, smaller in scope but similar in significance, took place in Bologna and Cremona: "The artisans of the wool guild," Donato concludes, "had let their voices be heard." Seven years later, in Florence, they were to raise their voices still higher.

CHAPTER ELEVEN ‡ THE RISE OF PAUPERISM

THE ANGRY POOR

A hermit and prophet by the name of Calixtus, one of many who preached the impending end of time, is said to have predicted that between 1378 and 1420 the world would endure great tribulations. If this was indeed his prediction, he could hardly have done better. Co-incident with the Schism in the Church, the period from 1378 to 1383 saw Europe shaken by an un-precedented series of disturbances. Hardly had these subsided when fresh troubles arose: the *remensas* agitation in Catalonia and, around 1420, the beginning of the Hussite uprising. The poor had their role to play in all these events, which had important implications for the future.

Another prediction attributed to a Minorite Friar made the rounds of Florence in 1378, the year of the Ciompi rebellion: the rebellion, it was said, was a warning that in ten years' time the "simple folk" would wipe out the powerful, the "vermin of the earth." Which sorts of paupers were called to play the role of God's avenging angels? Certainly not the traditional poor, who remained inhibited by their indigence, their humble condition, their weakness, and their infirmity. Though beggars were present at the scene of some riots, they were not the instigators. It was different with the new poor—able-bodied workers who suffered from low and uncertain wages and yet retained a sense of their dignity and worth. When calamity struck these people were recognized as paupers, but charity did not resolve all their problems. And times had changed. The brief period of higher wages that followed the plague had stimulated certain desires. The working poor insisted upon a better life. How? And why at this precise moment?

The fact that disturbances occurred at about the same time in widely separated places suggests that, allowing for local variations, the issues involved were similar. But the fundamental motives of the rebels were not monetary, social, or moral in nature. Nor were the poor the only actors in the rebellions. Still, the disturbances did bring poverty-related issues into the open and even resolved a few of them, while avoiding others. But the concerns of the poor were never entirely absent.

Mere coincidence does not imply coordination. There are no evident direct links among the various disturbances that mark the period 1378–83 and no connection between those disturbances and the uprisings of 1420. The earlier troubles erupted in various cities with the suddenness of an explosion, except in Flanders, where the difficulties were longer-lived. Later came peasant revolts that lasted for a considerable length of time and covered a wide area. In the first phase (1378–83), rebellion may have been contagious. In any case, it is worth looking for similarities among uprisings in different places. In the later peasant rebellions, the grievances of the peasants were at times similar to those of the urban rebels who preceded them, but mere similarity is no warrant for assuming that the urban uprisings somehow inspired the rural revolts.

The paupers involved in all of these disturbances did share one trait in common. Some of those who lived through the troubles of the 1380s had also endured the era of the plague, but many had not, and their memories therefore extended back no farther than the comparatively prosperous period that followed the epidemic. People almost never come to regard a situation as intolerable unless they have something else to compare it with. Some rebels harbored memories of other bitter experiences in the past: the fullers of Ghent, for example, recalled their humiliation in 1359. Nostalgia for a better time, rancor, and misery combined to produce something like a festering abcess: all it took was an accident to puncture the abcess and release the built-up poisons. A minor episode, something that may have had little to do with the underlying issues, was all that was needed to provoke a crisis: a dispute between a master craftsman and one of his workers, for example, or between a landlord and one of his tenants, or an incident with a tax collector. In any case, it would be misleading to try to pinpoint the role of the poor in these disturbances by looking for some typical underlying process.

‡ The events of the period 1378–83 were preceded by troubles that had been smoldering for years in southern France, in the mountains of Auvergne. In the region of Saint-Flour various outcasts, craftsmen, and peasants had formed a sort of guerrilla troop in the bush which, since 1363, had come to be known as the Tuchins. The same name was attached subsequently to those who participated in a widespread insurrection in Languedoc, which lasted until 1384. After the famine of 1375 a new tax aroused opposition in the cities: in an atmosphere of

social strife the rebellion spread, in April of 1378, first to Le Puy, Nîmes, and Pont-Saint-Esprit, then to Aubenas, Alès, Montpellier, Clermont-l'Hérault, Béziers, Carcassonne, Albi, and finally to Toulouse, where 1382 was the "year of tribulation."

The only connection between the Ciompi rebellion and the insurrection in Languedoc is that both occurred in the same period. But the violence that reigned in southern France for six years spent itself in a single summer in Florence. In the six weeks between May 1 and June 18 Salvestro de' Medici, who had been named gonfalonier and president of the college of Priors, succeeded in arousing enough popular support to thwart the Guelph faction's practice of banishing its enemies. In two separate series of riots the Ciompi managed to seize power and install a council (balia) dominated by the figure of Michele di Lando, a wool-carder foreman. Before August was over, an intransigent faction of the Ciompi that claimed to express the will of the *Popolo di Dio* quarreled with Michele di Lando and Salvestro de' Medici. But the latter were swept away by the forces of reaction, which on the bloody day of August 31 began the lengthy process of reestablishing the dominance of the *popolo grasso* and the *arte maggiore,* a process not completed until 1382.

In the same year reaction also triumphed in other parts of the continent. In Flanders troops sent by the king of France helped the count of Flanders defeat the rebel communes at Roosebeke on 27 November 1382. Contemporaries saw only the political aspects of the insurrection. To be sure, textile workers and other paupers seem to have had little direct concern with the incident that instigated the rebellion: the digging of a canal that bypassed Ghent in favor of Bruges. Nor were the ambition of Philip Van Artevelde and the control exercised by Ghent over other cities in the region matters that greatly interested the poor, any more than did Flemish involvement in the Anglo-French conflict or the Schism in the Church. Still, the hostility between the fullers and weavers of Ghent had not yet died out. Everyone in the textile trade had an interest in keeping the trade alive in the face of the interruption in English wool imports. Business rivalries notwithstanding, the alliance of masters in the textile trade had objectives beyond mere political opposition to Count Louis de Mâle. The bourgeois were determined to maintain their own social privileges as well as the freedom of the communes. "Long live Ghent" was more than a rallying cry: it became a symbol. It was shouted at Malines and Liège, where rebellion also broke out in 1380, as well as in Saint-Quentin in 1381 and in

Rouen, Amiens, and Paris in the following year. The cry signified opposition to an onerous tax system that weighed most heavily on the poor.

In 1382 the workers' rebellion in England was finally put down and urban uprisings in France came to an end. In both cases tax policies were the source of widespread discontent, but the poor had particular grievances of their own. In England they were the victims of the "poll tax" established in 1377 to replenish a treasury depleted by military adventures undertaken by Edward III during his long reign. The tax was assessed first by community and then by hearth; it probably spared the indigent but fell heavily on villeins, who had to pay a sum equivalent to three days of a laborer's wage. In addition, the gains made by artisans and peasants after the plague were jeopardized by the new tax.

Resistance to the poll tax took various forms. At first it was mainly passive, involving underestimation of the number of taxpayers and obstruction of royal officials in their efforts to monitor the assessments. A confrontation between one tax official and a group of peasants on 30 May 1381 led to an armed uprising which in less than two weeks engulfed the counties around London and even the capital itself. The events are well known. So are the personalities who took part in them, such as Wat Tyler, a veteran of the French wars, and John Ball, an itinerant preacher. The insurgent peasants were in communication with various people in London, including some of the city's aldermen, one of whom opened a bridge across the Thames to the rebels. Froissart claims that thirty thousand rebels invaded London: the figure seems improbable. Be that as it may, once the rebels had entered the city there were enough of them to pillage the homes of the wealthy, in particular the Savoy, the palace of the unpopular John of Ghent, uncle of Richard II. They also backed Wat Tyler in the demands he presented to the young king. These demands amounted to a political program whose scope exceeded the requirements of the humble. We do not know who inspired it. It was in fact of little importance to the poor whether "true" communes should be allowed the right to ratify the king's actions without regard for the rights of Parliament, or whether the number of bishoprics should be reduced to one. The poor were more interested in division of church lands among the faithful. Above all they wanted to see villenage abolished and the worker's statute rescinded. These observations explain why the crowd enthusiastically welcomed the concessions that Tyler won from the king in their meeting at Mile End on June 14 and why it fell prey to disillusionment on the following day when its idol was assassinated during a second meeting at Smithfield. Legend has it that the people wanted to avenge Tyler but that Richard II turned them aside by declaring, "I am your leader, follow me." Trusting in the promise of the king, whose legitimacy no one doubted, most of the rebels withdrew. By the feast of Saint John the last holdouts had been crushed, and repression proceeded so rapidly that Richard II was able to grant an amnesty before Christmas. The whole affair was dispatched more quickly than in Florence. The authorities henceforth concentrated their attention exclusively on some two hundred fugitives, who were accused of heresy. Indeed, owing to the religious implications of the rebellion, those whom Froissart refers to as "mad priests"—passionate propagandists who had been imprudent enough to praise poverty unduly—became the objects of an extended witch-hunt.

With "devilishness" (to borrow once more from Froissart) barely suppressed in one place it broke out again in another. As calm returned to London trouble again loomed in Ghent and Languedoc, and before the winter of 1381–82 was over rebellion had broken out in several French cities. As in England, new taxes aroused anger. The reestablishment of the *aides* (customs duties) by the dukes who governed in the name of Charles VI proved as clumsy as their abolition in the first place by Charles V, overcome by scruples on his deathbed. The hated tax stirred Rouen to rebellion on 24 February and Paris on 1 March. The movement spread to Normandy (to Caen, for example) and Picardy (especially Amiens) and through Orléans to Sens and eventually as far as Lyons. Simple folk, who were especially hard hit by the heavy new tax and who tended to express their grievances more spontaneously than others, were frequently instigators of the troubles. In Rouen it was the "mechanical workers" in the textile trade who assembled in the Old Market and, choosing one of their number as a stand-in for the king, had him sign acts abolishing the *aides*. In Paris all it took was a threat by tax collectors to seize a greengrocer's stall in one populous street on the Right Bank to bring together a large crowd, which shouted "Down with taxes!" and took off in pursuit of the tax collectors. But these episodes in Rouen and Paris were just opening rounds: violent insurrection was still to come. In Rouen mobs opened the prisons and pillaged convents and the homes of the wealthy. In Paris a violent mob broke into an arms depot and made off with three thousand lead mallets [*maillets*]; thus the rioters came to be known as Maillotins. Despite thirty deaths the authorities continued to evade the issue. But time was of the essence. Negotiations were held in both Rouen and Paris. In Rouen and certain other cities such as Amiens, some bourgeois made common cause with the rebels. The Rouennais, with their Norman legalism, succeeded in extracting from the monks of Saint-Ouen a number of duly sealed charters and forced the king's representatives to ratify the ancient privileges of the Norman Charter by raising the traditional hue and cry [*clameur de haro*], from which this episode derives its name: the Harelle rebellion. The attitudes of the Parisian bourgeoisie were also divided, but for the time being fear of the riotous populace seems to have dominated. In a quandary, the king's uncles blew hot and cold. They faced two major problems, one fiscal, the other political, both with implications for the government's ability to maintain order. The dukes decided that they could afford to give in on the tax question, which won over the common folk. They promised a return to the tax system in use during the reign of Saint Louis, a system that remained popular. But retreat on the political front was impossible. This was of scant interest to the humble, who nevertheless had a share—perhaps more than their share—of the quick and pitiless repression that followed the uprising.

It proved necessary on two occasions for the authorities to take further repressive measures. The king entered Rouen as a conquered city on March 29. In a symbolic act the bells that had been used to call the people to riot were taken down from their belfries. A royal proclamation abolished the commune, to the dismay of the bourgeoisie, and a special tax affected all residents of the city but hit the poor with particular severity. Paris had to wait a while longer to learn its punishment, which was no less harsh for the delay. Conspiracies persisted: certain conspirators met at the Pré-aux-Clercs on the pretext of playing bowls or skittles or "flying the dragon" (that is, flying kites) while in reality they plotted. With the autumn over and the Flemish revolt crushed at Roosebeke, the king moved to punish Paris just as he had punished Rouen. As always in the aftermath of an insurrection, the city lost its autonomy, the post of provost of merchants was eliminated, and justice was meted out to a former confederate of Etienne Marcel who had hitherto been spared. The repression was harsh, and so were the punitive taxes imposed.

Contemporaries were struck by the fact that troubles erupted simultaneously in Italy, France, Flanders, and England. The agitation in the cities of France was not unrelated to the agitation in the cities of the

Low Countries. Chroniclers noted the presence of Flemish visitors in Florence in June 1378 and in London in June 1381. These visitors seem to have been textile workers driven into exile by unemployment. There is no reason, however, to blame them for the troubles. Five of them were hanged by members of the butchers' confraternity in Florence, and several were murdered by the London workers. Xenophobia, competition, and jealousy won out. There was also a charge that the Flemish rebels and especially their leader Philip Van Artevelde harbored sympathies for the heretical Lollards. As for the Parisian insurgents, Buonaccorso Pitti, a visitor from Florence who was present in Paris at the time of the uprising and who has left an impartial eyewitness account, found the rebels quite similar to the Ciompi though he was unable to detect any connection between them. The author of the *Chronicle of Saint-Denis* did suspect ties among the various troublemakers, however: "Almost all the people of France rose in rebellion . . . and according to rumor they were aroused by messengers from the Flemish, themselves in the throes of a similar rebellion, and also stimulated by the example of the English." He does not mention Florence. But what would he have said had he thought to link the events in France to the change of dynasty in Portugal, with its accompanying social upheaval, or to the first signs of serious social difficulties in Barcelona, or to the persistent unrest in the cities of the Empire?

High taxes, coupled with the fact that the guilds and city governments were controlled by a small number of patrician families, were the main causes of difficulty in the German cities. Brunswick and Lübeck experienced unrest as early as 1374, and agitation persisted in Brunswick until 1380 and in Lübeck until 1385. In Lübeck there were major tests of strength between craftsmen and patricians. But hostility wavered in these cities, and lower- and middle-level craftsmen, including journeymen and poor workers, sometimes allied themselves with factions of the patriciate, whose internal squabbles set the tone of urban life. There were disorders in Hamburg and Stade in 1375 and 1376 and in Gdansk in 1378. In Stralsund, Karnsten Sarnow failed, despite support from the guilds, in his attempt to oust the wealthy Wulflam family from the city (1391). By contrast, the guilds of Cologne, undeterred by prior failures (especially in 1370), overthrew the domination of the powerful clans that made up the *Richerzeche*. But this rather late episode was an exception to the rule: in the Empire, too, the spread of rebellion was followed by repression, with various cities agreeing to help one another punish those responsible for the troubles.

‡During the fifteenth century the wrath of the poor manifested itself in two major episodes: the *remensas* movement in Catalonia and the Hussite war. Other scattered instances of rural and urban unrest were but minor commotions compared with these.

The remensa was the sum paid by a peasant to be excused from the obligation to perform certain servile tasks, pejoratively known as *malos usos;* it was added to the usual ground rents. In Aragon at the end of the fourteenth century, between a quarter and a third of all peasants were subject to this system of payments (*pagenses de remensa*). As in England in the time of Edward III, landlords attempted to withdraw concessions made at the time of the plague in order to keep labor on their estates. This attempt was rather badly received, all the more so because some peasants, having improved their position in the interim, hoped to free themselves from their subjection and abolish the malos usos altogether. The "first revolutionary remensa generation," to borrow a phrase from Jaïme Vicens Vivès, spontaneously manifested its opposition to the practice around 1390. In addition to the malos usos, the issue of how abandoned land should be settled and farmed was a further bone of contention. By 1410 incipient rebellion against the landlords had developed into open disobedience, burning of harvests and dwellings, and death threats; crosses were erected and trenches dug. Subsequently the organization of the movement was improved. Peasants held assemblies, organized themselves in groups, and chose representatives to defend their interests. Renowned jurists such as Tomas Mieres affirmed the justice of their cause, and the royal bureaucracy supported the peasants against their lords. Legal wrangling complemented direct action. The issue was further complicated by the political struggles in which the crown of Aragon was involved. The remensa movement does not appear to have forged ties with the Busca, a democratic party that came to power in Barcelona in 1453. The civil war that occurred in the early years of the reign of King Juan II delayed resolution of the rural issue. It was not until 1486 that Ferdinand the Catholic decided to abolish the malos usos, the chief source of so many woes.

Hussitism had from the first found considerable support among the rural poor and urban artisans in distress. Indigents, according to F. Graus, accounted for at least 40 percent of Prague's thirty-five thousand inhabitants. Low wages led to unrest in Prague in the years 1380–85. In the countryside John Huss found poorly paid workers laboring alongside serfs. Early in the insurrection, around 1419, the audiences that were inflamed by the eloquence of the Premonstratensian John of Zeliv consisted of indigent inhabitants of the new city of Prague. The processions he staged were the first major demonstrations of the uprising. The "Mount Thabor volunteers," though not all miserably poor, dreamed of a classless society and lived a life of shared poverty inspired by the Bible and the apostles. From its rigorous ideal and tight organization the movement acquired discipline and exalting strength. Otherwise it could never have survived five crusades or endured until the death of its second leader, Procop the Great, in 1434. The Hussites attempted to found a communal society on the basis of an idealized poverty. In so doing they not only harked back to earlier attempts but anticipated things to come.

Compared with the desperate and interminable battle of the Hussites—a war with social and national as well as religious dimensions—other fifteenth-century conflicts involving the poor pale into insignificance. The Bohemian struggle may have found an echo in Velay and Forez under Charles VII. A few castles were attacked by wretched peasants, whipped up to fanatical enthusiasm by popular preachers who taught them that all men are born equal. Were they descendants of Tuchins who had experienced the influence of the Hussites or Lollards? And while we are at it, it is worth mentioning the proto-socialist agitation of the Lollards in England at the beginning of the fifteenth century.

Two quite different rural social movements in France are worthy of note. In 1393 the vintners of Auxerre went on strike for better working conditions. Then, in 1451, the salt makers of lower Poitou rose in rebellion. But unrest among the poor was mainly evident in the cities, generally in connection with events that did not concern the poor specifically. The simple folk of Paris took part in riots led by Caboche in 1413 and again in 1418 in the time of Capeluche. The presence of the poor can be detected in every tense period between 1411 and 1449 (as recorded by the Bourgeois de Paris). The poor were also involved in all the Lyonnaise *rebeynes,* in 1423, 1424, 1430, 1435, and especially 1436, as well as in sporadic urban disorders during the reign of Louis XI, for example, in Dijon. These examples are all from France, but mention might also be made of the brief rebellion led by Jack Cade in England in 1450. Similar episodes occurred in other countries. At its peak the wrath of the poor was significant enough to have inspired some writers to attempt to determine what role the poor had played in these events.

Most of the surviving testimony of
contemporaries seems to reflect
stupefaction, disarray, outrage, and
anger in the face of this social unrest. The sources are almost wholly
one-sided. The administrative records take a sharply disapproving
line, as do court documents. Notarial papers are more objective. As for
letters and chronicles, few share the open sympathy for the Ciompi
that we find in the so-called Squittinatore Chronicle by an anonymous
author or in the journal of the shearer Palo di Guido. Foissart, though
an enemy of all who threatened the established order, wished to be
well informed and sought to understand events, in particular the rebellion of the English workers, which to him seemed an aberration.
Sermon writers and moralists were generally hostile to disorder, but
some were not without sympathy or pity for those victims of misfortune who became caught up in popular movements of one kind or
another.

If we hope to make out the fleeting silhouette of the poor, if we wish
to find out who they were and pursue their anonymous activities, we
must pay close attention to the sources and resist the temptation to
give Manichaean explanations. The poor were not simply black or
white, good or evil.

Those who lived through the periods of social unrest, particularly
the years around 1380, seem to have felt that a huge wave of troubles
had arisen suddenly out of nowhere and broken over them with fierce
violence. The numbers they sometimes cite to prove their point are to
be treated cautiously, but the general impressions of contemporary
observers are worth taking seriously. Is it possible that the number of
paupers was so great? Were the poor recognized for what they were?
Whether or not there were exactly five thousand paupers in St. Mark's
Square in Florence on 25 August 1378 is not the point. What matters is
that those who were there shouted, "We have nothing to eat!" When
the Religious of Saint-Denis speaks of a "multitude of men known as
Tuchins," it is the context that is most important for our purposes: the
Tuchins, we are told, are "abject because of their secret practices" and
"arose as unexpectedly as worms that have wriggled their way to the
surface of the earth." It is probably true that the ranks of the Ghent
rebels had swollen from a few hundred in 1379 to a few thousand in
1382, since the king was obliged in that year to send an army against
them, but we can hardly agree with Philip Van Artevelde that "thirty
thousand people had gone without bread for two weeks." There was a

call for price controls on bread so that people of modest means could afford to eat; to make up for the shortage, it was urged that the Collace, or bourgeois assembly, be opened "to the poor as well as the rich." A short while later came the remarkable episode of the "twelve thousand soldiers and other people who had nothing to live on and who already bore the marks of famine." Having set out from Ghent, they found the gates of Brussels closed when they arrived, because "no one knew what they had in mind." From there they headed for Louvain, whose gates were also closed, and finally to Liège, where they found "six hundred [!] wagon loads of grain and flour." That, at any rate, is the way Froissart tells the story.

In Rouen, a riot began with two hundred textile workers, which is not implausible, but before long it seems that "all the people" had risen in rebellion, just as they would do in Paris eight days later. There is no point asking how many English workers participated in the rebellion in London or in the countryside—swarms, according to the mayor of London. If they could be surprised in their sleep, he feels, "they could be killed like flies." In Catalonia we know that one out of every three peasants paid the remensa, and in Bohemia the Hussite insurrection assumed a national character. In London it was said of the Hospitallers of Saint John of Jerusalem, who had inherited the hospital of the Templars, that "even the oldest and most crippled flee with the agility of rats or evil spirits." In France it was said of the Tuchins that their battle cry was "Kill, kill all the rich." But the same cry was imputed to all rebellious paupers. Even so thoughtful and charitable a man as Phillipe de Mézières attributed the following words to a peasant in his *Dream of the Old Pilgrim:* "If the nobles had resisted our cruelty, we would have taken their lives and seized the government of the kingdom." An inhabitant of Orléans is supposed to have said, at about the same time, that "we have no king but God" and, after complaining that all he earned with his needle and thread was confiscated by the government, added that he "would rather see . . . all the kings dead and buried than see [his] son with a pain in his little finger." It is dangerous to generalize, but it does seem clear that the poor were always in the forefront of the struggle, whether in their own behalf or in behalf of some other cause.

Rebellion was potentially a powerful weapon, not because the poor themselves were powerful but because the threat of an uprising could arouse such powerful fears. But the poor were unable to take advantage of this weapon, for a number of reasons. As Bernard Guénée has observed, "the ideas of the rebels, when they had any, were for a long time as timid as their passions were violent." This was particularly true when the rebels were in fact genuine paupers. Their goals were necessarily basic and immediate: to escape the predicament in which they found themselves, to reduce their burden of rent and taxes, to restore the better times they had enjoyed in the past. Scarcity and high prices were everywhere the rebels' targets. In France they attacked the *aides,* in England the poll tax, in Florence and Flanders low wages and restricted access to the position of master craftsmen, and in Spain, England, and Bohemia the perpetuation of servile labor obligations. The health regulations established in the wake of the Plague were another universal complaint. The nostalgia for times past, as scourge-ridden as those times may have been, was not lost on Froissart: "For the great comfort and abundance of goods which the people then enjoyed, this rebellion came to life and arose from nothing." He is speaking here of the English rebellion, but his remark is also applicable elsewhere.

The rebels, besides being handicapped by their short-term view, lacked the imagination to conceive a new way of life. The poorest looked forward only to sharing the wealth of, and the most violent only to supplanting, the rich. The triumphant Ciompi dubbed sixty men "knights of the people." In England, rebellious workers allegedly believed that Richard II was going to make Wat Tyler a knight when they met at Smithfield. Knighthood would have afforded Tyler legitimacy of two kinds: that of arms and that which flowed from the hand of the king. For to simple folk the king remained the king (notwithstanding the disparaging remark of one Orléanais, cited earlier); it was the monarch's advisers and officers who bore the brunt of popular protest. In France, for example, Saint Louis's heir continued to be surrounded by the halo of justice even as a young child and, later, after he had become a lunatic. Of all the rebels only the Hussites were true revolutionaries, bent on changing society from top to bottom.

The rebels, then, were ruled by passion and aimed to achieve short-term results. This explains the suddenness of popular uprisings, the susceptibility of simple men and women to wild rumors, and the ease with which they could be swayed by a variety of influences, particularly oratory. Down to the nineteenth century and even beyond, Europe continued to experience sudden outbreaks of violence whenever food supplies ran short. The riot that occurred in Paris on 1 March 1382 was typical of many subsequent riots: it all began with a rumor. According to a letter of remission granted to the lord of Clermont in 1380, "the populace of the place imitated the example of the Montpellierians." The news spread quickly from Ghent to Amiens and Rouen and from Rouen to Paris, as well as throughout England and Flanders. The Religious of Saint-Denis, who refers to the *fama publica*, was one of the keenest observers of the situation.

When poor rebels were left to their own devices and not coopted for other causes, their methods of action were as elementary and disorganized as their motives were simple and basic. Vandalism, arson, brutality, and sometimes murder were the general rule. The chroniclers, who were hostile to the rebels, may have exaggerated their crimes, but they did not invent the violence. An important question is the degree to which the poor were conscious of any solidarity among them. If so, what kind of solidarity was it? Some became caught up in the agitation through contagious enthusiasm, as in the case of one Parisian youth of nineteen who at first "mused and watched" the riot of the Maillotins along with others and then decided to join in: the old story of an onlooker becoming caught up in a fracas almost unwittingly. More aware of solidarity with a particular group was a "poor laborer" (in this case an artisan) from Amiens, who repeated "what the people of his camp had told him and urged him to say." The tallow merchants of Paris rejected the tax of 1382 "with a single voice," thereby demonstrating the unanimity of a modern trade association or union. There is evidence that solidarity existed among villeins in England, among the members of guilds, among the various guilds in a particular city, and among similar guilds from different cities. We see this at times in the Ciompi rebellion. We also see it in the rebellion of the weavers of Bruges, Ghent, and Ypres: the Ghent weavers were welcomed in Bruges on 3 May 1382 with the cry, "All for one!" And John Ball said, "If we march together, all manner of men who are serfs will follow."

Solidarity between villeins and artisans was less common. With Froissart we may mention the alliance of the poor of London with the poor of the open country: "These are our people," it was said in London of the rural workers, "and what they do, they do for us." The Londoners then let the rural workers know that "they would find London open and the common people on their side." But these ties of solidarity came undone as readily as they were made, for they lacked the solidity of the traditional and time-honored vertical social ties. Poverty by itself could only forge temporary bonds, the product of shared adversity. But even though poverty recruited its victims from all walks of life, people experienced the same ordeal in very different ways. The servile status of the English villein, for example, might have had something in common with the dependent status of the journeyman craftsman, but the two were hardly identical. Poverty was not enough to constitute a class. It could engender groups, but traces of class consciousness are hard to find even among the Ciompi, since each individual remained the client of a particular clan. The potential force of a paupers' rebellion came from the number of paupers and the possibility of concerted action, not from internal, conscious cohesiveness of the paupers as a group. Each action required external coordination. Collective action by the poor had one great weakness: the restive poor were tempting prey for violent, irresponsible, and demagogic leaders.

With these remarks in mind one can, without being systematic, distinguish three aspects (corresponding to three phases) of popular unrest involving poverty-related issues. The poor were actors or figureheads in rebellion (though often manipulated); they were also, in some cases, beneficiaries; and they were always victims.

With the help of contemporary observers we can follow the changing cast of characters in the theater of social unrest. Initially the working poor occupied center stage, even if they were not always in control of the action. The chroniclers of the Ciompi rebellion have little to say about the mendicant poverty of the *poveri, deboli,* and *miserabili.* They do, however, record the self-serving interest that both parties showed in the plight of beggars: palaces were sacked on 20 June, we are told, so that "the poor could have their share," whereas the forces of reaction, before they regained the upper hand, attempted to quiet the beggars by handing out free grain on 30 August. In the interim, the burning of the granary of Or San Michele on 22 July was hardly in the interest of the indigent. Broadly speaking, begging is presented as a consequence of the disturbances. This was the case with the starving multitude led by Francis Ackerman from town to town along the road from Ghent to Liège.

Even those contemporaries least disposed to favor the troublemakers clearly indicate the importance of the simple folk. Stefani tells us who the Ciompi were by listing the different departments of the wood guild. The dyers, combers, and carders, who chafed under the leadership of the *lanaioli,* spearheaded the rebellion, and Michele di Lando emerged from their ranks to become a leader. It is worth noting, however, how diverse the *sottoposti* were. Some were themselves employers of hired labor and had the same attitudes toward their workers as they accused the rich of having toward them. They were motivated more by envy and resentment than by need. The ciompi were denounced by their enemies as "coarse, filthy, and badly dressed" and as "ruffians, criminals, thieves . . . base, worthless men." Yet Stefani himself acknowledges their integrity, even in the midst of riot. "So that no one might say that they had stolen, they set fire to the houses of the rich." One of their sympathizers adds the following detail: "Woe unto him who tried to keep anything. If they found him out, they would seize him and his booty and throw it into the fire. Some were beaten and injured because they had stolen." The chronicler most favorable to the Ciompi found a moral justification for the pillage of Guelph palaces and convents where, as rumor had it, the wealthy had stored their treasure in the hope that it would remain safe: destruction by fire, this chronicler says, was an act of purification. Already we encounter the prophetic side of the rebellion of the poor.

In Flanders, the Blue Thumbs did not start the rebellion of 1379, but they were quick to join in. Everywhere the textile industry suffered from the "hampering and damaging conditions" deplored by inspectors of the textile guild in Arras in 1377. Production was slowed by competition from Brabant, England, and Normandy. Stagnant wages, heavy sanctions (fines, redoing of shoddy work, imprisonment, eviction from the profession, and banishment), and the closing off of opportunities for advancement stirred resentment among carders, dyers, and fullers. It is hardly surprising that they should have joined the demonstrators. In Ypres, of fifty-five rioters punished by the courts, sixteen were fullers, five weavers, two cobblers, one a wooden shoe maker, one a glove maker, one a blacksmith, and two were archers; some twenty others were peasants or unskilled artisans.

Similarly, those who participated in 1382 in the first urban disturbances in France were described in neutral, sometimes sympathetic terms, appropriate to modest artisans, to "men of small estate," "servants" (*juvenes famuli et pauperes humiles*), simple people (*infimi*), "coppersmiths, textile makers, and people of poor stock." Letters of remission granted when punishments were meted out indicate the occupations of the accused, showing that all were minor artisans or merchants. The list is too long to give in full. The best brief characterization is found in a document that pertains to Sens: a "great quantity of common people," *populaires*, the equivalent of the *minuti* in Florence. We have already encountered Buonaccorso Pitti's observation that the Maillotins (*Maghietti*) were like the Ciompi in Florence. They were not beggars. As much can be said of rebels in England, Catalonia, and Czechoslovakia, as well as of the guildsmen who participated in the rebeyne of 1436.

With the infiltration of beggars into the ranks of the poor we come to the second phase of the disturbances. In Florence the "confused and unarmed mob" (*gens stolida et inermis*) was overwhelmed by released prisoners (let out of jail by the rioters themselves, as is customary in all subversive movements) and by hard-core elements that joined the insurrection in August. "We will turn the city upside down," said one of these militants, "we will kill and rob the rich who scorned us. We will become the masters of the city. We will govern it to suit ourselves, and we will become rich." As the same thing happened in Paris and Rouen, we find a change in the tone of the chroniclers. Their benevolent, neutral language gives way to an attitude of reproach. The crowds in the streets now seem to be made up exclusively of refugees and vagabonds recently admitted to Paris, former prisoners of the Châtelet released by the rioters, and "criminals, sharks, rogues, and good-for-nothings." The same was true in Bruges, Montpellier, and Béziers. It was even claimed that some Tuchins indulged in cannibalism. In England the workers were not to blame for all the violence, for we are told that social outcasts were present in large numbers in both the London and the rural mobs. In Bohemia the Taborite troops recruited many tramps and homeless peasants who had moved to the cities. Finally, in Lyons in 1436 the crowd in the rebeyne also received undesirable reinforcements. Following the typical pattern, the vandals arrived on the scene after the protest of the poor was over and compromised their cause. By the end of the fourteenth century the idea of the poor as a "dangerous class" had come close to supplanting the image of the pauper as God's chosen and a symbol of Christ.

Vandalism by rioters was not the only reason for this change. Various "prophets" had attempted to superimpose the new image of the pauper upon the old. Here I am not referring only to the official teaching of the Church on the subject of poverty, which one writer has characterized as "morally revolutionary and socially conservative." The influence of Taddeo Dini in Florence may have been greater than has been thought. He preached temporal as well as spiritual advancement for the poor and thus heightened popular awareness of the differences between *popolo minuto* and *popolo grasso*. It has been observed that the name Dominic became common among the *minuti* in the latter part of the fourteenth century. It was at San Lorenzo that the program of the Ciompi was hammered out, by night, in July of 1379. On 27 August five thousand people gathered in front of the Dominican convent in the piazza San Marco. And it was at the house of the Camaldolites that the wool carders chose their leadership committee, which adopted the significant name of Eight Saints of the People of God. Finally, it was to Santa Maria Novella, with the Dominicans, that the Ciompi intransigents retreated with their headquarters, and there that they were pursued by the forces of reaction. Two of the Eight Saints were killed. The Popolo di Dio was reduced to yielding up its martyrs.

Moral and social issues were inextricably intertwined. The teaching of Taddeo Dini and his followers fell on fertile ground wherever poverty prevailed, wherever millenarian hopes continued to flourish and opposition to the social and ecclesiastical order continued to grow.

The poor received the good word in a variety of ways. The most powerful preaching raised the glimmering hope of happiness in this world and looked forward to the imminent end of time. It praised the holy force of the "people of God" and likened use of that force to the work of the Exterminating Angel. What all this meant to a simple man or woman is indicated once again by a Florentine source: "The time will come," said one of the Ciompi rebels, "when I no longer have to go begging, because I expect to be rich for the rest of my life, and if you will join me, you, too, will be rich, and we will all live in splendor."

God's chosen, the pauper, assumed many guises in propaganda literature. William Langland is a case in point. His revolutionary reputation is based not on his known intentions but on inferences from his novel *Piers Plowman.* For Langland, Christ was incarnated in the person of the pauper, and the philosophy that underlies his work is made explicit in a sort of iconography of Christ the worker. The tools of the peasant and craftsman are substituted by one artist for the instruments of the Passion and by another for the usual elements in the nimbus of Christ the Redeemer. The sublimation of the pauper's suffering and labor, the humanization of Christ, and the idea of a Communion of Saints were all quite traditional and at the same time quite characteristic of fourteenth-century spiritual ideals. Still, the psychological content of the theme was powerful indeed; and it was exploited. Piers Plowman became the judge of the wealthy and with his fellow paupers constituted the chosen people.

The influence of Wycliffe on the preachers who hailed the workers' rebellion as the dawn of a new age is still a matter of controversy; it has, in my judgment, been greatly overestimated. Wycliffe did not condemn wealth as such, nor did he encourage subversive activities; he did approve of common ownership and regarded poverty as a sign of predestination. Others went much further. One such was a rabble-rousing priest by the name of John Straw, who stirred up the people of Suffolk. The preaching of John Ball found a wide audience. Ball described himself as the Herald of the Apocalypse. According to Froissart's vivid and informed account, Ball gave Sunday sermons in the villages in which he preached equality, community ownership, and social subversion, stirring up the peasantry: "Good people, things cannot go well in England and will not go well until property is held in common and neither a villein nor a gentleman remains."

‡ In Flanders the situation was similar. The Ghent artisans, like the Ciompi, saw themselves as the people of God; in seven Sunday sermons lasting an hour and a half each, Minorite friars likened them to Israel fighting the Pharaoh or to the Maccabee heroes fighting Rome. This kind of preaching reached its height in Bohemia, of course, not so much with John Huss himself as with his more fanatical disciples. Perhaps we can best gauge the importance of public oratory in the late Middle Ages by considering the case of Bohemia or England. The oratorical violence of a John of Zeliv is reflected in a popular song which, after describing the unhappy lot of the serf, concludes as follows: "Such is the torment suffered by the poor everywhere, but especially by the Czechs." We know, of course, what came next: not only armed rebellion but also an extraordinary experiment in communal, egalitarian poverty.

That so much bloodshed and so many utopian ideas ultimately compromised the cause of the poor, whose contemporaries never really understood what the problem was, is hardly surprising. Some ambitious politicians and demagogues realized that they could profit from the disorders. Finally the poor, after having been exploited and misled, suffered frustration and disillusionment. Of the disturbances in Bourges in 1474 Louis XI said, "The poor did not do all that themselves." Others might have made the same observation much earlier.

‡ Popular social movements did not always find the messianic leaders appropriate to their biblical ideals and eschatological concerns. In the period that interests us here, there were hardly any such leaders out-

side Bohemia, for in England none of the popular leaders had the stature of a Zeliv, a Chelčiky, or a Huska. What popular leaders do we find propelled from poverty onto center stage in the years 1378–1430? To begin with there were the three Hussites just mentioned, whose fanaticism was a guarantee of their integrity and inflexibility. There were also Wat Tyler and the dyer Geoffrcy Litster, as well as Henry of Roye in Amiens. The Rouen draper Jean Le Gras can hardly be considered a leader: he was a mere puppet, whom the rioters "placed on a wagon in the posture of a king and who, in fear for his life, had to obey them." What is more, he wasn't even poor. As for Michele di Lando, who was indeed an authentic artisan, he allowed himself to become intoxicated by his honors, accepted the gift of a knight's equipment, turned his back on his friends, and allowed them to be massacred in the streets or sent into exile. This abrupt about-face brought him no good fortune, for less than four years after the rebellion he, too, was exiled. But he ended his life in comfort as an employer, a *lanaiolo*.

Paradoxically, peasants on occasion sought leaders among the minor nobility. This occurred in the Jacquerie in France as well as in England and Bohemia. In the cities the middling bourgeoisie often made common cause with the poor, whose unrest provided an opportunity to settle scores with the *grands bourgeois*. An instance of this can be seen in Florence, where some wealthy *popolani* joined forces with the Ciompi. In France a change in the tone of the chronicles is once again revealing. Popular agitators were joined by citizens and nobles. In Rouen comfortable bourgeois took the lead in opposing the new taxes. In Paris a goldsmith and a number of drapers attended a secret meeting at Saint-Sulpice in early October 1382. Some became extemporaneous orators: one of these later pleaded that he had climbed the platform "out of fear of the people, and to please them." Another, a tawer, was described as "quite obscene and completely out of control."

A similar scene unfolded in Lyons in 1436. A bourgeois by the name of Jean de Condeyssie, the son of a notary, well married, a vehement orator and man of action, had been the deus ex machina of the rebellion before openly declaring his colors. A demagogue who "drank easily with the common people" in the taverns of the Saint-Nizier district, he had drawn up a list of demands for the rioters while refusing to accept a position of leadership. He was nevertheless thrown into prison and his followers were persecuted.

The great demagogues were rather different from these politicians who hoped to benefit from social unrest, but the poor were no less their dupes. Philip Van Artevelde opened the municipal assembly "to the poor as well as the rich," requisitioned grain to hand out to the populace, and served as an arbitrator in wage disputes. Did he do these things out of political necessity or for demagogic reasons? The *Chronicle of Flanders* assures us that Francis Ackerman "abused the people with his fallacious, duplicitous, deceptive speeches." The greatest demagogue of all was Salvestro de' Medici, the instigator of the Ciompi rebellion. Determined to attack the Guelph practice of banishing enemies from the city, he took advantage of the opportunity provided by a lawsuit against a dyer and a tanner. With the support of other aristocrats from the Dini, Strozzi, and Alberti families, he posed as a spokesman for the *popolani*, for "the poor and weak who want to live in peace on what they earn." In this way he secured popular support. The few chronicles favorably disposed to the Ciompi are the only ones to praise him: the Squittinatore Chronicle calls him "the good Salvestro, good and dear citizen, enemy of the powerful and of the voracious wolves." The demagogue Salvestro pressed his advantage with a theatrical gesture, resigning his post as gonfalonier, while Benedetto Alberti exhorted the crowd from the palace balcony, shouting "Long live the people." According to his enemies the "instigator of all the troubles and scandals," Salvestro even renounced his rank in order to share power with a former wool carder; he had himself dubbed a "knight of the people." Finally, out of cautious self-interest, he abandoned the hard-core of the Ciompi, but his reward was no better than that of Michele di Lando: he, too, was exiled. Demagogy was a tactical weapon in clan rivalries. After being abandoned by the Medici-Alberti-Strozzi group, the Ciompi received the equally dubious support of another, equally histrionic, demagogue, Luca da Panzano (who was apparently not, whatever else one may say about him, motivated by self-interest). He too cast aside the gold spurs that were the symbols of nobility and begged to be made a knight of the people. It was too late. Having followed one demagogue after another, the Ciompi had lost the battle, victims of their leaders and of themselves.

Contempt and punishment were in store for all the common folk who had served as the rebels' shock troops. The judgments of contemporary observers are almost uniformly severe. Ten years after the Maillotin uprising, the term *Maillet* was still used as an insult, as was *vilain jacques* (vile peasant) in the wake of the Jacquerie. Alongside this emotional vocabulary, the cool judgment of the author of *Chemin de Povreté et de Richesse* (Path of poverty and wealth) seems even more harsh:

> For such people truly
> One should have little pity.

There were of course a few people—Gerson, Eustache Deschamps, Christine de Pisan—who could tell the peaceful poor apart from the troublemakers: "The crocodiles are the enemies of the true poor," wrote Deschamps. But the general attitude was one of suspicion: every indigent was a delinquent or a potential criminal. But guilty of what? The *Rhymed Chronicle of Flanders* gives one answer:

> Their mouths still water
> For the property of the rich.

Covetousness is basic, the chronicle went on to say.

Froissart voices a similar opinion: "The wicked people . . . envied the wealthy and the nobles." With the word *envy* Froissart was of course denouncing one of the fundamental vices of the Middle Ages and indeed of any time when luxury and misery coexist side by side. Envy was a serious matter because in a society of orders it represented a threat to stability: in other words, it was a revolutionary sin. Worse still, the rebellious poor might enter into collusion with heresy, as was suspected in England and manifest in Bohemia in the late fourteenth century. Even those most favorably disposed toward the poor were troubled by this.

An example was Thomas Brinton, who was bishop of Rochester at the time of the workers' rebellion (1373–89). A Benedictine monk, he remained faithful to his vow of poverty despite his rank. More than half of his 103 surviving sermons are devoted in whole or in part to the virtues of poverty and charity. Before 1381 he occasionally treated the essential equality of rich and poor, lord and serf, in terms similar to those used by Langland. Then came the events of 1381. Rochester was right in the middle of the area that succumbed to rebellion. Riot broke out in the city on 6 June. The nearby castle was seized and the royal constable taken prisoner. The preaching of John Ball and Thomas Brinton was coming true. Simon Sudbury, archbishop of Canterbury, whom Thomas served as suffragans, was assassinated in London on 14 June. Subversion and heresy had compromised the cause of the poor. Brinton became a member of the investigative commission that con-

demned the rebel workers of Kent; then, in the following year, he sat
on the Blackfriars Council that condemned Wycliffe. The orator suddenly found himself without a voice. The theme of social charity
disappeared from his sermons. Perhaps this means nothing: Brinton's
habits and attitudes do not seem to have changed. Perhaps it was
ambition or opportunism, though it seems doubtful that this former
monk, who remained faithful to the rule of Saint Benedict and had
never flattered the powers-that-be, who had criticized Edward III for
his loose living and John of Lancaster for his ambition and greed, would
have renounced his deepest beliefs at more than sixty years of age.
Thomas Brinton belonged to a generation frightened by the rise of
pauperism; his charity never came to grips with the complexity of
actual poverty, and he never succeeded in distinguishing the "real"
poor from the slackers, vagrants, and vagabonds. The plaint of the poor
had become an uproar. Men needed to know just who it was that they
were dealing with.

AN ATTEMPT AT
CLASSIFICATION

Thomas Brinton's confusion was
characteristic of his generation.
Most of those who made their
voices heard as representatives of the poor did not fit the traditional
definition of the pauper. And many who did fit that definition remained silent. As Boucicaut said, in Paris there were "many great and
secret poverties."

*Beggars in Search of Their Daily
Bread*   The influx of refugees fleeing the ravages of war in the open
country, together with unemployment in a period of recession, greatly
increased the number of people living in desperate poverty. Administrative records and the archives of charitable institutions confirm
that this was the case. We see the faces of these miserable wretches in
chronicles, literature, and iconography. "The pauper," writes Gerson,
"is the person who, raging with hunger, shouts, 'God's alms for the
pauper!' He goes from street to street, begging from door to door." Tens
or even hundreds of paupers followed the funeral corteges of the
wealthy, waiting for their posthumous handout. The poor waited at
the doors of the churches, occasionally entering and disturbing the
services within. They ate no meat and drank no wine. They were sick,
blind, crippled, maimed, covered with sores. They were dirty and
smelled bad. They were ugly and fearsome to look at. They were

deemed nasty. Even dogs chased after them. Dante wrote, "With that fury and with that storm, with which dogs run out upon the poor wretch, who where he stops, suddenly asks alms."[1] Miniatures showed the poor as despicable and despised wretches (as in one annotated Bible dating from around 1390).[2] The pauper's lowered head, disheveled hair, bushy beard, and pug or hawk nose connoted crudeness and bestiality. In a picture representing a gift of alms, every detail establishes a contrast between donor and recipient: the respectful distance, the disproportion in size, the contrasting colors of the clothing (vivid red and blue for the donor, somber brown and gray for the beggar). Even the composition reflects the difference: the pauper is rarely alone. Usually he is shown huddled in a corner with his fellows. The attitude of the wretched beggar is one of uselessness, worthlessness, and guilt. To touch him was to suffer a humiliation. But it is significant that he is shown as a member of a group. Iconography was intended to be edifying, to arouse compassion and set an example of charity. It also aroused horror and disgust, as well as fear of the large number of the poor.

Fiscal Paupers Common as working poverty was, its image is nowhere to be found in the iconography of the time. The scholastics, slow as they were to accept the teachings of Thomas Aquinas, in doing so adopted the principle that "mercenaries who hire out their labor are paupers, because they depend on their toil for their daily bread."[3] In contrast to iconography, tax rolls did include the working poor but generally omitted beggars. The search for the poor, at best a highly approximate enterprise, must constantly move back and forth between quantitative and qualitative approaches. Surviving tax rolls, most of which date from the fifteenth century, include only those wealthy enough to pay taxes, not the insolvent.

Three important points stand out: (1) the number of poor increased between 1350 and 1500; (2) the scene of poverty shifted from the countryside to the cities; and (3) short-term difficulties masked the effects of long-term structural change.

In the fifteenth century, the poverty rate in Ile-de-France, an especially fortunate region, was only 10 to 12 percent among agricultural laborers in the grain-growing plains and only 1 percent among the vintners of Hurepoix. The Paris tax rolls for 1421, 1423, and 1438 mention only those residents of the city who were subject to taxation. Wage earners and domestic servants were not included. These sources have nothing to say about people in modest occupations. At best they tell us that the sections of the city along the Right Bank of the Seine were the least heavily taxed.

Nor do we have accurate figures for the areas north of Paris or for the parts of the Low Countries then under the domination of the Duchy of Burgundy. Even the most extensive of the tax rolls, that of 1469, does not include the insolvent. Georges Sivery has estimated that the proportion of paupers receiving assistance in Hainault ranged from 20 to 30 percent of the population. André Bocquet has arrived at similar estimates for Artois and Boulonnais. Almost the same results emerge from the study of fifteenth-century tax rolls from Brabant (where 23–24 percent of all households were poor in 1437 and 27.3 percent in 1494) and certain parts of Holland (25–26 percent in 1494). It is impossible, however, to generalize the figures from one province of the Low Countries to the others. In rural Brabant poor households accounted for a quarter to a third of the population. The numbers of the poor in Louvain, Brussels, and Antwerp grew steadily over the course of the fifteenth century.

In Burgundy a distinction was made between households classed as "miserable" and others classed as "mendicant." These two categories accounted, respectively, for 29.5 and 48 percent of all households surveyed in 1375 in the *bailliage* of Dijon (not including the city itself). In Dijon in 1397 83 percent of all households were classed as "miserable." By 1431 this figure had dropped to 58 percent and by 1433 to 54 percent, with, respectively, 27 and 34 percent of all households classed as "mendicant." Thus overall, more than 80 percent of all households in the city and 75–80 percent of all households in the country were not subject to taxation. Now, the difference between "miserable" households and "mendicant" ones was surely the difference between, on the one hand, the precarious condition of the working poor and, on the other, indigence so severe that, without work, survival was impossible without outside assistance. For once, the tax classifications seem to correspond to the social realities. The case of Chalon-sur-Saône is similar. Henri Dubois found the following figures:

Year	1381	1394	1400	1406
Total households	492	485	348	395
"Miserable" households	113	180	207	230
"Mendicant" households		120	51	75

The number of miserable households increased by more than 100 percent in twenty-five years, owing to problems in certain occupational groups: cordwainers, tailors, mercers, and hoopers. Thus the figures reflect an increase in what we have been calling working poverty. In Avallon in 1380 almost half the households (50 out of 110: 25 miserable and 25 mendicant) were not subject to the hearth tax. In Lyons lists of those in arrears on payment of tax debts reflect an increase in poverty.

While there were variations from one region to the next, the number of paupers seems to have increased almost everywhere. In Basel the proportion of citizens unable to pay a tax of twelve florins was 25 percent in 1424, 29 percent in 1439, 32 percent in 1453, and 26 percent in 1484. A poverty rate of close to one third of the population appears to have been common. To be sure, it was only 10 percent in Cologne in 1476, but in Strasbourg in 1473 it was 29 percent. In Augsburg in 1475, of a list of 4,700 taxpayers E. Maschke has found that 3,378 were *nihil habentes*, of whom 2,700 were artisans, mainly in the textile trades. Based on a study of wills in the same city, the poverty rate ran as high as 80 percent of the population in the fifteenth century; in Lübeck in 1350 it was 64 percent. The number of paupers in Germany has been found to have increased in the fourteenth and fifteenth centuries.

Abundant data concerning Savoy and Dauphiné suggest that the proportion of paupers in the population was fairly high, although the valleys seem to have fared better than the highlands. In Chablais in the latter third of the fourteenth century a third to a half of the population was poor, although the poverty rate declined to 10 percent at the beginning of the fifteenth century in some areas (for example, in Les Bauges in 1432). The number of vagabonds increased over the course of the century. Large numbers of them began flowing into Geneva as early as 1459. Fifteenth-century poverty in Dauphiné is reflected in revised administrative lists of households in the region. In 1474 50 percent of the households in Valentinois were classed as miserable. In upper Dauphiné 60 percent of the households were miserable and 20 percent more were classed as mendicant, but only 14 percent of the households in the foothills were so categorized. In certain mountain parishes the majority of the population lived at or below the poverty line and could not have survived without alms. War and epidemic only exacerbated economic distress.

In Italy, we may add to our previous discussions of Florence, Siena, and Orvieto the fact that in Genoa in 1464 a third of the population was too poor to pay taxes of more than one florin. When a hearth tax was levied in Palermo in 1442, 23 percent of the households were classed as poor.

The sources for Provence are also abundant and precise: 33 percent of the population of Puget-Theniers was classed as poor in 1364, and 50 percent in Sisteron in 1371. By contrast, the figures for Carpentras in 1390 and 1394 show a poverty rate of only 8–9 percent, but at Pourières in 1330 and in Arles in 1462 the figure was 33 percent. Philippe Wolff has studied estimates for Toulouse which suggest that *nichils* accounted for more than half the hearths counted in that city in the late fourteenth and early fifteenth century and that the figure declined only slightly in 1431. In Périgueux in that same year 60 percent of the population was too poor to pay taxes, not even counting mendicants and vagabonds. But in Nantes at the end of the century the figure was only 15–20 percent.

Data from the other side of the Pyrenees show an equal diversity. In Barcelona in 1378 12–13 percent of all households were poor. In Castille tax documents yield figures of 6, 30, and 20.7 percent for 1433, 1476, and 1493, respectively. In Utrera, in the mountains near Seville, 12.3 percent of all households were poor, not counting disabled persons and an apparently large number of vagabonds. In the fifteenth century the proportion of paupers in the countryside near Valladolid varied from 10 to 20 percent. It is difficult to draw any firm conclusions.

Surviving tax rolls for the hearth tax in Normandy from the fourteenth and fifteenth centuries reveal the combined effects of war, epidemic, food shortages, and taxation. Upper Normandy was especially hard hit, and historians are much given to evoking the misery of the Caux region at the end of the Hundred Years' War. What is striking is the dwindling of the taxable population due to impoverishment, emigration, or death. In a village of thirty households it was not uncommon for ten of them to be headed by widows of limited means. The number of poor in Rouen increased dramatically with the influx of refugees during the siege years of 1418–19. Even after the surrender, three parishes in the center of the city contained only 93 households that were required to pay the hearth tax compared to 207 that could not pay: thus the poverty rate was more than 66 percent. The figures for lower Normandy were less disastrous, especially in the fifteenth century. To be sure, the tiny port of Agon, which in 1328 was prospering with 246 households, was down to 10 only three years later and 20 twelve years after that. But in general the coastal area seems to have had fewer paupers than the *bocage* (or region of enclosed fields in the interior), to judge by tax rolls at any rate. Langrune, for example, had only one poor household in 1433 but 5 out of 55 in 1461 and 10 out of 69 in 1473; Luc-sur-Mer was even more prosperous, with no poor households in 1433, 2 in 1452, and 4 in 1497. It is reasonable to extrapolate backward from what is known to have been the case in the seventeenth century and assume that the coastal population benefited from a high-calorie diet that even the poor could afford, thanks to the ready availability of places to fish along the coast. By contrast, in Caen, only fifteen kilometers from the ocean, the proportion of paupers seems to have increased steadily from 1434 to 1515 in the city's twelve parishes, more in the central ones than in the semirural parishes on the outskirts. Pauperization, a serious matter in rural Normandy during the Hundred Years' War, seems to have slowed in the second half of the fifteenth century only to begin again at the beginning of the following century.

POVERTY IN THE COUNTRYSIDE   Rural poverty and urban poverty seem to be closely related, and to some extent I agree with Bronislaw Geremek that, while poverty's deep roots are in the countryside, its most spectacular tragedies are played out in the cities. Rural poverty, already in evidence in the early fourteenth century, increased in intensity over the next hundred years in the wake of a series of crises. But the crucial episode involved the loosening and finally the breaking of the tie between the peasant and the land, which in many ways serves as a test of the peasant's impoverishment. In examining this question I shall atempt to classify the various types of rural poverty.

Though rural poverty varied somewhat from region to region, certain common characteristics can be isolated, especially if we focus primarily on France and England. It is worth pausing a moment to compare the portrait of the English peasant in *Piers Plowman* (circa 1380), which was cited earlier, with the portrait of the French peasant drawn by the Englishman Fortescue almost a century later: the French peasant, Fortescue tells us, is a poor man, badly dressed, dead tired from work, who lives in "the most extreme misery."

When a plot was divided upon the death of its owner, the resulting subplots were often too small to support a family, so that some children had to seek work on other men's land and the youngest were forced to move on. One solution to this problem, tried almost everywhere, was joint exploitation of farms by a group of brothers (*fré-rèches*), with multiple households living on the same plot. On the estates of St. Hubert's Abbey in Hainault, for example, there was a large number of small farms, sometimes little more than vegetable gardens and far too small to support a family. Among men who hired themselves out as laborers to other farmers, how could a sense of attachment to the soil survive? Those whose farms were too small could not pay the head tax and other temporary taxes. They went into debt and ran afoul of the law, with the result that they were forced to leave their land. In the late fourteenth century this was a common occurrence in Hainault and Provence. Elsewhere, particularly in England with the beginning of "enclosures," peasants were simply evicted from their lands by force. Increased breeding of livestock was both a cause and an effect of rural migration, depending on the region. The hard life of an agricultural laborer may be judged from the case of one hay mower employed by the *hôpital* Saint-Julien in Cambrai: in order to buy a hectoliter of wheat in 1380 he had to harvest 1 hectare, in 1400 2 hectares, and in the period 1430–40 4 hectares. Things improved somewhat in the period 1466–76, when 2.65 hectares sufficed, but it was back up to 4 by the end of the century. A 1469 census in Artois mentions large numbers of unskilled workers, or "working people" earning unspecified wages. One father of eight children from Marchy-le-Breton went from village to village repairing old shoes. A similar form of poverty is revealed in certain posthumous inventories of property from the countryside around Toulouse. In 1369 a rural shoemaker left his only son little in the way of possessions but forty-five livres in debts, no clothing, and what is even more peculiar, no tools of his trade. In 1390 one farmer left a small plot of land and a few wooden casks. Occasionally the documents touch on the very depths of poverty, as at Gye near Bar-sur-Seine in 1396, where a deceased pauper left "a wife and children, very poor people who beg for their bread at the oven and the mill." He also left his wife debts that finally drove her to suicide: "Said woman did away with herself on the grave of her aforementioned husband." In the fifteenth century poor peasants accounted for only 5–10 percent of the population of this region, yet the worst off owned as little as half an acre of vineyard.

Vineyard workers were paid by the day or by the job, a practice that lent itself to easy exploitation. Events in the Auxerre region in 1390–93 illustrate the tensions that could readily result from this. Employers complained that workers, "grown fat on delightful luxuries" made possible by wages deemed excessive by those who paid them, were now also demanding that the working day be shortened. Rather than work from dawn till dusk workers were quitting at three in the afternoon, holding meetings, and trying to induce other tradesmen to join their cause. These group pressure tactics succeeded in bringing the case to the attention of Parlement, which in settling the dispute in favor of the workers advanced a number of arguments with a singularly modern cast: "Every man should be paid a wage in keeping with the nature of his occupation," and "even though they are poor men, still they are men, and one cannot ask them to perform the kind of toil and labor that one might ask of an ox or a horse. . . . One cannot compel a free person to work against his will, for to do so would be contrary to nature and liberty." It is worthy of note that arguments derived from both Christian doctrine and humanist principles concerning the dignity of labor found champions as early as the end of the fourteenth century.

In some regions the millers' case is comparable to that of the vine-yard workers. In Ile-de-France mills were owned by lords or bourgeois and leased or subleased to the actual millers. Some of the subcontractors found themselves hard pressed. In the Toulouse region millers and donkey drivers were bound by one-year contracts that provided fixed remuneration for them and their employees. In 1426 they found their compensation under the terms of the contract inadequate and went on strike, but the seneschal ordered them back to work in the public interest.

Even workers whose labor was of vital importance were often quite poor. Many of the trades associated with the forest fell into this category. Carpenters, wheelwrights, and makers of baskets, brooms, and bowls were so poor that the official in charge of the Chaux forest in the county of Burgundy reduced the fines for various sorts of fraud. Charcoalmen and tilemakers lived a precarious existence. As for shepherds, Jean de Brie had tended sheep as a child. As an adult he dedicated to King Charles V his treatise *The Good Shepherd* (1379). Tending the flocks thus became an art, indeed a vocation through association with the Good Pastor of the Gospels and the shepherds of Bethlehem. The shepherd was sanctified in the iconography of the Annunciation and Adoration. But in reality the shepherd was hardly a sacred figure. Like the forest workers, his presence was troubling. Working alone, he communicated only with his animals, whose bestiality he shared. He was thought to possess evil powers. Many shepherds were odd or mentally retarded and therefore despised. No one would marry his daughter to a shepherd. People looked upon shepherds as lazy, because their work required little physical effort. They were badly paid. Thus shepherds were poor mentally, socially, and economically—and their filthy appearance only confirmed this general perception.

Another occupational group that lived on the fringes of society was the salt workers. Salt was a commodity of little value that enriched no one but speculators and the public treasury. The work of extracting salt from the mines was so onerous that ever since antiquity it had been used as a punishment for criminals. Salt was also produced by drying salt marshes: those who made salt in this way were at the mercy of the sun. The method was used along the Adriatic Coast, on the Greek Isles, around Cagliari in Sardinia, from Hyères to Peccais in Provence, in the vicinity of Ibiza and La Mata near Valencia, in Setubal, and along the French coast from Royan to Guérande. There were some who speculated in salt, such as Francesco Datini in the late fourteenth century in Provence and, in Spain a century later, Santangel, who helped to finance the discovery of the New World. But behind these wealthy speculators, and behind the collectors of the *gabelle*, or salt tax, in France, humble people toiled to maintain the mines or to scrape up the salt from the marshes and store it in open-air piles. These salt workers were known by a variety of names: *fachiers* along the Mediterranean coast of France, *laboureurs salinans* and *paludiers* (marshmen) along the Atlantic. They were aided by mule drivers and bargemen. Salt production was so variable that any tax increase could easily crush the salt makers. In 1383 an ordinance imposed a tax on salt in Poitou and forced hundreds of salt workers to leave Guérande. To head off a similar tax in 1451 the Estates of Poitou prepared a memorandum minutely detailing the harsh working conditions of the "very poor people" who earned their livelihood in the salt trade, some eight to ten thousand salt workers along the coast and ten to twenty thousand poor carters who hauled the salt inland.

Sailors, fishermen, and other maritime workers shared the seaside marshes with the salt workers and also shared their position at the bottom of the social hierarchy. Jacques Bernard's work on Bordeaux has revealed the poverty of the apprentice seaman, "that pauper among the poor," whose wages were too low to provide a decent living: in the late fifteenth century an apprentice seaman earned less than three sous per day, compared with up to six for a laborer. Sailors went from ship to ship in search of better pay. Even allowing for any propensity they may have had to squander their hard-earned cash while in port, it remains true that many were forced to sell their clothing and beg for meals. In the sources sailors are classed together with other "poor mechanics." Surviving records of one investigation shed light on the career of a poor mariner: Robert Dufay learned the sailor's trade "in his youth" from a man by the name of Vitou of Jumièges, with whom he worked for two years before going to work for his father at Vatteville. In 1435 he moved to Rouen, in the company of many other refugees from the war. Rouen was still his home port in 1452. Sailors earned little and worked long hours up to the age of sixty and beyond. Fishing, an inherently risky business made even riskier by the dangers of war, yielded a poor living at best. In Dieppe, for example, where fishmongers paid fishing crews by weight of catch, sixty percent of the populous Saint-Rémy district did not pay taxes in the fifteenth century. The nearby fishing village of Le Pollet had always been quite poor. Conditions along the English and Mediterranean coasts were similar. Something of the life of the needy in the tiny fishing villages of the Low Countries is revealed by the life of the blessed Lydwine (1383–1433), a humble resident of Schiedam. Her father's illness plunged his large family into hardship, and even common household items had to be sold.

At this point it may be in order to say a word or two about aristocratic poverty. Like the poverty of peasants and fishermen, aristocratic poverty stemmed from problems in the agricultural economy as well as from the ravages of war. To be sure, the costs of providing military equipment and ransoming captives were a heavy burden on the families of knights. They, too, borrowed and fell into debt, particularly when they felt honor-bound to maintain their rank in society. Seigneurial rents declined and labor costs increased. French nobles hard pressed by the Hundred Years' War were not the only aristocrats to experience monetary difficulties, however. In the fifteenth century the English and Imperial aristocracies also fell upon hard times. In the Namur region it was the custom that if a man could not pay the costs required for knighthood, he and his family were classed as "impoverished gentlemen" and no longer regarded as noble. This was a widespread problem, and the Italian jurist Baldo degli Ubaldi offered the opinion that a nobleman unable to provide for his daughters' dowry was entitled, as an indigent, to receive aid from his bishop, "father of the poor." In Venice, poverty among the nobility was regarded as a debility of state, since the function of the aristocracy was to defend the Republic. Derogation from nobility was unquestionably a symptom of the spread of poverty.

Poverty among the clergy is also worthy of note. The words *pauper* and *paupertas* sometimes occur in the sources alongside the names of those granted exemption from the payment of university dues or chancery taxes upon grant of an ecclesiastical benefice, but this was probably the result of an indulgence or special favor of some sort. From the time of Robert de Sorbon on, however, scholarships were deemed a necessity for truly needy students, of whom there were six in Paris's Ave Maria College in the fourteenth century. Gerson was the eldest of twelve children, and Nicholas of Cusa, who studied at Heidelberg, Padua, and Cologne, was the son of a Moselle boatman. The proportion of poor students in northern Europe was high: more than fifteen percent in Cologne and nineteen percent in Leipzig (in the late fourteenth and early fifteenth century). The same can be said of Louvain or of the college founded by Albornoz in Bologna. Nor was poverty among the clergy limited to students. Some parish clergy lived on meager resources in conditions close to genuine hardship: this was the case, for example, with certain vicars in the dioceses of Strasbourg, Geneva, and Dauphiné. Others had to make do with a half-prebend (known as a *paupertas*) or with one of the innumerable chaplaincies established in the fourteenth century. Still others had nothing and, especially in England in the time of the Lollards, formed a starving clerical plebs whose rootless bitterness is not difficult to understand.

Flight was always a natural reaction of people reduced to poverty. Ruined nobles—younger sons without title or fief—looked to the mercenary companies and bands for a way out of their troubles. Humbler people were forced, as the sources tell us, to "flee," "decamp," "run away," and "abandon" their land owing to the "great poverty in which they find themselves." The following passage describes the situation near Tournai in 1443: "Just as animals and birds head for soil that is fertile and freshly plowed, and abandon the wasteland, so do mechanics and laborers who live by their toil. For they go where there is a living to be earned . . . and flee places where the people are hobbled by servitude and subsidies."[4]

Flight was sometimes the only way to escape legal action, seizure of one's property, and unmitigated hardship. Some were "so desperate from the great poverty that they suffered" that they hanged or drowned themselves. Research has focused on deserted villages and other aspects of the mobility of the poor. In Artois and Boulonnais in the fifteenth century the last inhabitants of several villages of the Hesdin region "were on the point of abandoning the place and going off to beg and wander through the countryside." In Dauphiné revisions of the hearth tax reveal the depth of peasant poverty. In Brignais in 1398–99 thirty-eight tenants failed to meet their obligations to their lord, and the collector noted that six were fugitives and seven others too poor to pay what they owed. Those who fled went to the cities in the hope of finding work. But therein lay the crux of the problem: Could the economy absorb this additional labor?

THE CITY, POVERTY'S CROSSROADS A newcomer to the city could find work by appearing at an early-morning "hiring." Hirings were generally held on the main square or fairground, near a bridge or church. This is known to have been the practice in the cities of Flanders and Artois as well as certain cities in Italy (Trentino, Lodi) and France (Bourges, Chartres, Troyes). Paris was large enough to have had, on the Right Bank of the Seine, several labor markets, each serving a different group of trades. The best known was the hiring on the place de Grève for the building trades and unskilled laborers. It was difficult for new arrivals to find work in trades organized by the guilds. Few were lucky enough to be hired as valets for a year's service. Many found work for a day at a time or for the duration of a job.

The difficulties that the working poor faced in finding housing brought them into contact with society's outcasts. Although there was no real segregation, some districts were predominantly poor. In Venice, for example, there were the sordid *contrade*. In Genoa the poor were forced to live in the hills surrounding the city. In port cities there was always a disreputable district or street near the waterfront, as in Marseilles, Barcelona, Nantes, Rouen, London, Antwerp, and Lübeck. In an inland city like Lyons, on the peninsula known as the Empire (which was flanked on both sides by rivers), the old "burg" of Saint-Nizier was the center of the *rebeynes*, while in Tours, Poitiers, Rouen, and Toulouse the poor were pushed toward the outskirts where they lived in the vicinity of tanneries or dye shops whose odors made living there undesirable. In Paris, apart from the tiny parishes of the City, the poor lived on the Right Bank near the place de Grève and along the city walls, both inside and outside, especially in the parishes of Saint-Laurent and Saint-Nicolas-des-Champs near the porte Saint-Martin.

It is hard to know what the standard of living of the working poor was. It varied from city to city. What information we have about wages is disparate and discontinuous. The sources depend on the season and rarely mention supplemental benefits such as room and board (except for apprenticeship contracts). It is especially difficult to relate the wage data to the supply of labor and to the cost of food and housing. There is a basic distinction between the skilled and unskilled trades, as between the trades generally and domestic service. Laborers in Tours, though less well off than apprentices and journeymen, are known to have had enough to eat in the second half of the fifteenth century; they did not suffer physically. In Poitiers during the same period the annual wage of an assistant in the building trades has been estimated at about thirty livres tournois, whereas the cost of food alone was at least fifteen livres per person. How could a man raise a family under such conditions? What is more, these figures are from a relatively prosperous period. For at least half the population of the city, then, it was but a short step from poverty to misery. The situation in Toulouse was somewhat different. Wages remained stable or rose only slightly from the middle of the fourteenth to the middle of the fifteenth century, while the cost of living fluctuated considerably. In general labor was scarce in Toulouse, as opposed to Poitiers and Tours, where there were many unskilled people seeking jobs.

In Göttingen, W. Abel has found that 74 percent of those who arrived from the countryside in the period 1330–60 had no skills. The oversupply of unskilled labor in Paris in the fourteenth and fifteenth centuries accounts for the wide variations in wages there. Using municipal and hospital records from Lille and methods first developed in connection with the study of Florence, G. Pierret has been able to analyze the condition of Lille's workers. Eighty percent of all laborers experienced hardship in the fourteenth century, particularly those with families. Wages fell at times to below the vital minimum of one thousand calories. Poverty even affected half of the more highly skilled workers. In the fifteenth century a rise in nominal wages suggests that some improvement had occurred. Single workers could now make ends meet and only 25 percent of laborers with families—that is less than five percent of the work force as a whole—fell into the indigent category. Thus in Lille, the working poor were mainly married men (between 25 and 35 years of age on the average), with children, and for the most part unskilled. This was discreet, almost invisible poverty, characterized by chronic malnutrition, poor housing and clothing, hopelessness, and discomfort, largely deprived even of forms of assistance available to more notorious indigents such as beggars, tramps, and other social pariahs.

Even those who found work enough to keep them alive were sorely tempted to quit. "We would rather have a gay time than work and still have nothing."[5] The cities harbored a swelling population of the rootless, in which the poor mingled with the criminal, fallen, and degraded. Some of this group were better integrated into society than others, however.

The councillors of Lausanne in 1450 and of Tours around 1460 found that "some (of the idle) go begging daily for lack of work and the rest are in danger of falling into wicked ways and criminal activity." Of the professional beggars some wanted to work and some did not, but all went begging in the same places, in courtyards or covered marketplaces, by bridges, or in the vicinity of the haylofts in which they often slept. Some feigned blindness or lameness, simulated wounds, or played on the pity of passersby by moaning or holding up half-naked babies borrowed or rented from some other indigent. Charity-related extortion and fraud were so commonplace that Eustache Deschamps considered the problem in his plays and poems. The vagrant was regarded as a parasite but not yet as an asocial creature.

The same might be said of prostitutes, whose openly acknowledged role brought them into close contact with men of every rank. Their poverty was moral as well as material. The low wages paid to laundresses, seamstresses, and the like encouraged the development of prostitution, as the Bourgeois of Paris observed in 1419: "good maids and good, proud women . . . of necessity have become wicked." Some prostitutes established themselves in brothels or bathhouses on which they paid rent, in some cases, to wealthy bourgeois, nobles, and even clerics, not to mention the Hôtel-Dieu of Paris; their rent was proportional to the number of clients they served. In Paris there were brothels in every district, for example, in the rue de Mâcon on the Left Bank, the rue de Glatigny on the Ile de la Cité, and the rue Saint-Martin on the Right Bank. Lyons's brothels were in the center of town, near Saint-Nizier. Dijon had seven of them, Avignon six, and Cologne ten. The situation was not much different in Venice, Genoa, Florence, Bologna, Rome, Antwerp, and London. Prostitution was considered an occupation and one theologian, Thomas of Chobham, offered the opinion that "prostitutes must be counted among the mercenaries and they provide . . . labor." But the procurers and madams who recruited, abducted, and exploited unfortunate young girls were closely involved with the criminal element.

Indeed, an extensive fringe element lived outside of, and in conflict with, organized society. This group recruited its members among the poor. It swelled to unusual size in the late Middle Ages, though numbers are hard to come by. It is unlikely that there were eighty thousand beggars in fifteenth-century Paris, as one chronicler maintains, but the municipal authorities may not have been far off when they put the number at thirty thousand at the beginning of the sixteenth century. In general, it has been estimated that a city can sustain a fringe element of up to 10 percent of its population without danger to law and order. Contemporaries liked to compile lists of odd characters—some of them rather picturesque—belonging to these fringe groups. It was no accident that the first French ordinance against the "idle" was issued in Paris in 1351 shortly after the Black Plague and not long after the *Notatenbuch* of Dithmas of Merckenbach (1346–48). The latter is the oldest of a series of catalogues that describe and classify various suspect types, the best known of which are the *Speculum Cerretanorum* (Mirror of Charlatans, circa 1485) and the *Liber Vagatorum* (Book of Vagabonds, circa 1509–10).

Taverns and cabarets (the word dates from this period) were the places where the poor mingled with this dubious element. A beggar might easily become a vagabond, wastrel, good-for-nothing, crook, or tramp, moving from begging under false pretenses to petty theft to skilled burglary. Plots were hatched by tipplers in the taverns. The Sunday drinking bouts deplored by Nicolas of Clamanges often ended in fistfights or ambushes in a dark alleyway. The drinkers might then wind up in court and at best receive a royal pardon. Collective criminal ventures are perhaps more significant than individual ones. Court decisions shed much light on the sociology of crime. François Villon's observations are corroborated by the documents. In Paris there appears to have been a change in the types of crime committed: 70 percent of the cases heard by the high court of Saint-Martin-des-Champs between 1332 and 1357 involved crimes of violence, whereas 68 percent of the cases heard by the Châtelet between 1389 and 1392 involved various types of theft. Crimes of violence were again on the rise in the fifteenth century. Of those involved in violent crimes in the latter period, Jacqueline Misraki has found that 44 percent were repeat offenders, mostly young men who worked sporadically; generally they stole in order to survive, usually shoes and clothing, selling what they stole to rag dealers who acted as "fences." Occasionally they resorted to murder. Ms. Misraki adds that "every judgment contained the same phrase: 'and had no property.'" Letters of remission often justified mercy to an accused on the grounds of poverty: one man was pardoned, for instance, because he was "responsible for a wife and small children" who would be "reduced to poverty and mendicity" if pardon was not granted.

Not all the guilty were beggars—far from it. Poorly paid workers also became involved in crime. B. Geremek has looked at the occupations of persons accused in the Châtelet between 1389 and 1392. Of a total of 127 accused, 50 were artisans, 27 were domestics, and 22 were farmers. A case of theft in 1400 involved 12 accused, 8 of whom were artisans: 3 tailors, 2 ditchdiggers, 2 farm workers, 1 blacksmith, 1 carpenter, 1 hosier, 1 furrier, and 1 porter. The needy and the unemployed were not the only people who took to crime. Discharged soldiers made up the "companies" of the fourteenth century and "bands" of the fifteenth whose crimes were noted by the Bourgeois of Paris. The affair of the "caymans" in Paris in 1448, the trial of the Coquillards in Burgundy in 1453, and that of the Crocheteurs in Languedoc nine years later are well known examples. But if the talent of François Villon has served to immortalize the delinquents of the fifteenth century, their crimes blackened the reputation of the far larger number of nameless indigents whom Eustache Deschamps baptized the "law-abiding poor."

THE VAGABONDS   People tolerated the beggar but hated the vagabond. Guillaume du Breuil, in his treatise on parliamentary practice, defines vagabondage as "the absence of a domicile." Others put it more picturesquely: "living everywhere," "without hearth or home." In French the phrase *sans aveu* (meaning vagabond) aptly captures the vagabond's lack of a place in society. [Literally, *sans aveu* means "without avowal," that is, without a lord and master to acknowledge—*Trans.*] In a society still organized largely in terms of direct, man-to-man relations, not to recognize ties between oneself and anyone else was a sign of extreme isolation. In a final phrase that sums up all the rest, the vagabond was also referred to as a man of "ill repute." People were instinctively and automatically suspicious of any stranger without employment, a potential delinquent or criminal and possible carrier of disease. This suspicion was only heightened when many vagabonds were about, and people no longer bothered to distinguish between the quiet ones and the troublemakers any more than they bothered to distinguish among beggars. Once again court documents are a useful source of information. In 1425 a young man from Mians in Dauphiné allowed his animals to graze on his neighbor's property. Afraid of being beaten for this offense, he left his father's house and fled to Lyons. After wandering about the city, he obtained work as a valet with a resident of Vourles. But along with two other young men he stole some clothing, a knife, and two ducks to eat; once again he fled to Lyons. He was arrested, beaten, and driven almost naked through the streets. His case was typical, as was his punishment. And the course of events was predictable: from flight to vagabondage to delinquency to crime. A letter of remission from 1382 tells of a beggar couple living in concubinage and "traveling about living on alms" and on what the man could earn "by making fine speeches." They left Mont-Saint-Michel in the company of another beggar, a Breton, a "strong, quite stocky man who wore an iron band around his body against his bare flesh and said that he was a penitent." They traveled together through Bazoches-en-Dunois. The Breton earned a little at odd jobs. But things turned sour as a result of a quarrel, quite naturally over the woman. There was a fight and the Breton was killed. The couple were arrested and thrown into prison. The man was executed, his wife received a pardon. She was "heavy with child . . . and had nothing to live on but for the courteousness of good people."

There were as many types of vagabonds as there were kinds of poverty: some had taken flight, some liked the loose life, and some disliked work; others had been evicted from their land or their homes or been thrown out of work. Many were banished from their native cities or sentenced to exile. In the Italian cities the parties in power exiled their adversaries. In Germany an average of ten people a year were banished in Stralsund and fourteen in Speyer in the period 1350–60. During the Diet of 1397, 450 vagabonds were present in Frankfurt. Following famines or periods of economic distress, families were forced to desert their villages. In 1440–50 a mass exodus of this kind occurred in Dauphiné, which was at the same time the destination of a stream of immigrants from Ile-de-France, Burgundy, Lorraine, and the Rhineland. The newcomers were as poor as those who departed: the wretched crossed paths on the highways.

Ever since Fernand Braudel's work on the Mediterranean coast, the study of vagabondage and migration in that region has been an important topic of research. The devastation of the Caux region at the end of the Hundred Years' War sent many people into vagabondage, where they were joined by discharged soldiers and false pilgrims. Also vagabonds were those new Wanderprediger known as Lollards.

The arrival of Gypsies in central Europe around 1416 and then in France in 1419 added still further complexity to the already complex world of the vagabond. These "Bohemians" or "Egyptians," as they were called, astonished people by their "horrible posture," their habit of living in tents "like men of war," and "hair as black as a horse's tail." Few contemporaries can rival the Bourgeois of Paris in his expression of that melange of fear, repugnance, and pity that the Gypsies aroused when they arrived at the gates of the capital in 1427: "In a word, they were the poorest people ever seen in France since the age of man. And yet their poverty had for company witches who looked into people's hands." The Gypsies moved into central and northern France, but when they asked for money they were dealt with harshly, as at Tournai in 1442. By that time they had covered southern France, Italy, and Catalonia—like the Wandering Jew, people said, with a misplaced tinge of anti-Semitism.

‡ Some of the poor who wandered the highways went in search of work. Unemployment in textiles, for example, added to the flow of workers from Flanders and Brabant to Italy, England, and France that began in the thirteenth century. Artisans in late fourteenth-century Paris were highly mobile. One shoemaker, born in Tournai, had practiced his trade in Laon, Soissons, Noyon, Rheims, and Chartres before settling in Paris. A journeyman tailor had spent three years working in Rouen, Nantes, Bourges, Le Blanc, Paris, Melun, Brie-Comte-Robert, Compiègne, Crépy-en-Valois, and Montdidier. Artisans were just as mobile in other countries, for example, in Frankfurt, Konstanz, and Gdansk. Augsburg figures in one exceptional story in the history of poverty: Burkard Zink, born in 1396 the son of an artisan, was an apprentice and student in various places before becoming a merchant's assistant in Augsburg and then in Nuremberg. He returned to Augsburg to conclude his career as a wealthy and honored man. Simonnet Salignet, of Dun-le-Roy in Berri, was not so lucky. He moved to Paris where he found work tending a butcher's sheep. Then he lost his job and had to take odd jobs. For a while he worked as a domestic at Savigny-sur-Orge but finally left his master and returned to Paris, where he worked for eight days as a porter. Then he went to Meaux and worked as a stable boy before returning to Paris, where instead of

finding work he was arrested and thrown into prison. The fluctuating labor market outweighed the obvious desire to live in Paris. Another factor in Salignet's case was that employers were not free to hire "passing" laborers at will; this made it particularly hard for poor vagabonds to find work. What was to become the customary "tour of France," in which apprentices would travel to various towns "to improve their knowledge of their trade," as we hear in the case of one goldsmith from Tours, was then just getting under way. Not everyone had such legitimate reasons for moving about, and court records mingle the names of paupers and artisans indiscriminately with those of vagabonds. How many people clogged the roads! And how many suspect faces appeared in the crowds along with the suffering poor. It was for society to choose between draconian measures on the one hand and just and compassionate concern on the other.

CHAPTER TWELVE ‡
FROM CHARITY TO POLICING OF THE POOR

Some people were outraged, others dismayed, by the development of pauperism after the second half of the fourteenth century—and not without reason. More than ever there was a sharp contrast between the idealization of spiritual poverty and the visibly sordid realities of material poverty.

Between Fear and Contempt We saw earlier how Thomas Brinton was left speechless by the events of 1381. Those who, like Brinton, felt genuine compassion for the wretched had their work cut out for them. Less sensitive observers were simply outraged. What did hideous tramps and fierce bandits have in common with Christ? How could people tolerate rebellion and violence against the established order and the will of God? What justification allowed able-bodied men to go begging, contrary to the natural law of labor? How was society to cope with the destabilizing threat of vagrancy? And why should unconscionable sums be given as alms to the indigent, perpetuating their abasement and prolonging the offense to human dignity? The evidence suggests that for a period of at least three generations the new forms of poverty continued to perplex people of all stations and to encourage harsh attitudes toward the poor.

It is but a short step from mistrust to fear, from suspicion to accusation. People were afraid not so much of the beggar's indigence as of his idleness, his rootlessness, and his anonymity. They no longer knew with whom they were dealing.

Mistrust stemmed not only from ignorance of the beggar's identity but also from fear of what he was capable of doing: stealing, setting fire to barns, raping women, killing animals and people, poisoning the wells, casting spells. But such crimes were really the least of people's worries, isolated acts committed here and there by individuals or small groups. A more serious concern was the possibility of rebellion. Signs that such fears were indeed common can be found in various rumors and in the belief in omens foretelling violent uprisings. In connection with the disturbances that took place in Paris in 1382, for example, the Religious of Saint-Denis recorded various items of gossip with a mixture of doubt and credulity. He reports, for instance, that on the eve of the riot a calf had been born near the abbey with two heads, two tongues, and three eyes. In Paris, at the *collège* of Cardinal Lemoine, the students had found a dead animal, larger than a cat, buried in the courtyard. Each of the animal's limbs was different from the others, its eyes sparkled, and it gave out horrible moans. Finally, during the week prior to the disturbance, a ball of fire had rolled from door to door, even though the skies were clear and there was no wind: an early instance of an unidentified flying object! It was said that the wickedness of men knew no bounds, that a sort of natural disaster had unleashed untold horrors. Froissart, as we saw earlier, described the uprising as "devilishness." For was not poverty the result of sin, and were not paupers predisposed to sin repeatedly? Literary denunciations of poverty by Eustache Deschamps in France or Ruy Paez de Ribera in Spain were not much better than maledictions on the poor.

Thus the problem was not simply that the poor were importunate and embarrassing, though they were that: Philippe de Mézières viewed Cairo as a model city because it had no beggars, or so he said. People were really afraid of the numbers and the anonymity of the poor. And yet if the term *pauper* and its synonyms suggested vast masses of the indigent when used in the plural, in the singular the word tended to acquire an abstract meaning that even more strongly evoked the collective character of poverty. Compare the Ciompi manifesto's reference to the opposition between *il ricco e il povero* with the placard displayed in Lyons a century and a half later, during the Grande Rebeyne of 1529, which was signed "Le Povre" and addressed to "all the common people of the city of Lyons." Le Povre speaks in the singular but in the name of all; he says "we" in every line. Does this suggest an emerging class consciousness? Since the middle of the fourteenth century social fear had inspired defensive reactions on the part of the wealthy (which I shall discuss later on), so that it is not surprising to find Machiavelli advising the Prince to keep the people poor in order to keep them quiet. Villon said "the mountains do not move for a pauper, neither forward nor backward." Had fear of the pauper—and of his companion, the criminal—dried up the sources of charity? Gerson himself spoke harshly of the "occupation of begging and panhandling." Others went further still. "Mendicity is contrary to the common good," said *Le Songe du Vergier*. The general public found it difficult to believe that a man with a job could be poor. With memories of crisis still fresh, people were slow to perceive the problem of working poverty. It was no accident that tax records listed the homes of the poor and struggling as "useless hearths" (*feux inutiles*). The meaning of the terms *pauper* and *poverty* underwent a change. The mendicant orders, which should have set an example for the rest of society, only made matters worse: they disagreed over the meaning of poverty, and the manner in which many mendicants lived the poor life left them open to criticism. Thus paradoxically the champions of poverty helped to confirm many of the complaints against the poor.

The accusations against the mendicant orders, particularly the Minorites, were more serious than one might suppose from satires depicting friars as impresarios of relics and brokers of indulgences or from the caricature of the mendicant with his cowl pulled down over his eyes in feigned indifference to the money accumulating in his purse. The reproaches addressed to one cleric by a knight in *Le Songe du Vergier* shows that criticism of the mendicants was already quite fully developed in the time of Charles V. Mendicity, the knight tells us, is a "very shameful thing." It is contrary to the law of labor set forth in the Bible, at odds with the practices of the apostles as set forth by Saint Paul, and discordant with the teachings of the Church Fathers. What is more, the mendicancy of the friars impedes spiritual progress, the knight argues, because "a man always thinks of living, of where he will sleep and what he will eat: it is a natural thing." And his concern only increases with the uncertainty of his resources. If a man is fit for work, begging is inimical to the "common good." This argument already has a humanist cast. Begging is unworthy of man: "When one sees a man asking publicly for alms, one fears that he has come to such misery by his own guilt." Misery and guilt: the very words suffice to show how the mendicants were judged. In response to the knight, the cleric protests that Christ himself led a life of poverty, as did the mendicant saints; he also invokes the old argument that Mary, symbol of the contemplative life, is better off than Martha, symbol of the active life. As a parting shot the knight offers the malicious observation that among the sons of Saint Francis there are some who "preach one thing and do another." The author of *Le Songe du Vergier* was not the only one who thought so. Nicolas Oresme, too, held that poverty was harmful both to the state and to its subjects: to practice poverty voluntarily was to tempt Providence and violate God's laws, hence to sin. He therefore concludes that the mendicant orders should be forced to work. Such thinking is less explicit in Philippe de Mézières, but it lies just beneath the surface of his work. In his view, work makes possible the virtue of giving alms.

The mendicants were often blamed for appropriating that which belonged to "the indigent and wretched who have good and true title to mendicancy" (*jus et verus titulus mendicandi*): these were the terms used early in the fifteenth century by one indubitable authority, Cardinal Pierre d'Ailly.

Criticism of voluntary poverty was common in the fifteenth century, and it was not altogether silenced by the reform of the Observance and the success of strict orders such as the Poor Clares and the Carthusians. The non-Observants were denounced. Criticism was directed especially to the Minorites, because the Preachers, as we saw in the case of the Ciompi in Florence, had an audience among the poor. By the end of the fifteenth century the Conventuals were as discredited as many *béguinages*, with the exception of those houses engaged in true charitable activities. This was the case in the Rhineland, where the Conventuals had rendered all mendicancy suspect in the eyes of the authorities. In Strasbourg, for example, the authorities did not have to look far for arguments to justify their long-standing hostility to begging by the mendicants and *béguines:* they merely cited treatises by the Dominican Johann Mülberg and the canon Felix Hemmerlin and later works by the Franciscan Thomas Murner and Sebastian Bruant. A fierce satirist, Murner could not find terms harsh enough to castigate the "tramps and hypocrites who abscond with the money of the poor." More moderate as well as more influential was Johann Geiler of Kaisersberg, who preached in Strasbourg for thirty-two years (1478–1510). He combined current doctrine with a caricatural critique of the unreformed mendicants. Further criticism was voiced by the leading figures of the pre-Reformation; but even without citing their strictures it should be clear that, in spite of the efforts of the Observants, the abuses of voluntary poverty had cast discredit on all forms of mendicity.

Even this would not have sufficed to undermine voluntary poverty altogether without the rise of humanism. Poverty, at first feared, then discredited, was now derided. On what grounds? Contempt for the poor was surely nothing new. It was a natural reaction on the part of the powerful during the feudal period and on the part of the wealthy during the period of economic expansion of the later Middle Ages. Most fourteenth-century chroniclers were indifferent to poverty. Poverty was not Froissart's subject, although he was able to describe its extent without great emotion. In France and Italy only Jean de Venette and the anonymous chronicler of the Ciompi were much interested in the people from whose ranks they had emerged. By contrast, Jean le

Bel, after alluding to the misfortunes of the poor, icily adds: "Little did it matter to us."

With humanism, contempt for the poor took a subtle and perfidious turn, becoming disdainful and philosophical and—height of irony—invoking the dignity of man as justification. The social failure of poverty stood at the opposite extreme from personal self-fulfillment; to those who exalted success and *fortuna* it made no sense. Eulogy of poverty gave way to praise of wealth. No one challenged the idea that poverty was an evil, a consequence of original sin. The *Roman de la Rose* had painted a horrifying portrait of poverty and of the pauper, a portrait capable of arousing repugnance as well as pity. It also suggested that poverty was intimately related to sin. Jean de Meung substituted an allegory for the story of original sin, portraying poverty as one of the disturbing influences that upset man's idyllic existence. Corruption came into the world when Poverty and his son Larceny were let loose on the earth. It is surprising to find a charitable woman like Christine de Pisan writing as follows about Meseur, Poverty's husband:

> Large, fat, wrinkled,
> Black and hairy, his
> Hideous, disagreeable face takes me back.
> . . . .
> His great beard hangs
> Almost to his belt.
> Never, I think, was so ugly
> A creature given form.[1]

The typical servant has the back of a donkey, the better to bear his burdens, the ears of a cow, the better to hear, and the snout of a pig, the better to gobble up whatever comes his way. To conclude this survey, consider the following passage, much read by several generations, from the *Chemin de Povreté et Richesse* (The Path of Poverty and Wealth):

> In truth one should have
> Little pity for such people.
> . . . .
> It is right to be suspicious of them.

That such harsh—perhaps shocking—attitudes could have coexisted with genuine charity is surprising, but this was often the case.

The vulgarity and ridiculousness of the poor and the infirm became a common theme of literature. On the stage, almsgiving was extolled in the mystery plays and yet the poor were held up to ridicule in farce. Inconsequential though it may be, it is nonetheless surprising that in the first third of the sixteenth century Juan Luis Vivès included in his program of good works—so appropriately entitled *De subelevatione pauperum*—a theological treatise on poverty followed by a sordid account of misery, which he describes as a sewer of which servitude is the drain.

Contradictions, paradoxes, and flashes of wit abound in the writings of Leon Battista Alberti (1404–72). Alberti had experienced difficulties in youth, and it is therefore hardly surprising that in his treatise *On the Family* he recommends that poverty be avoided. It is more surprising to find him advising against education for the poor, on the grounds that the poor man cannot hope to escape his condition. Is the condemnation of the beggar in *Paupertas* a product of Alberti's bitter memories of youth or an expression of self-satisfaction at having "made it"? For Alberti, poverty is the worst of all evils: "Even the gods," he says, "do not love the poor." From this he draws the conclusion that "it is better to die than to live in poverty." But this opinion was subject to later revision, for in *Theogenio*, and especially in his little-known *Momus*, Alberti imagines a dialogue on Olympus in which poverty, mendicity, and even vagabondage are praised. Was this merely a literary exercise, a game, a paradox in which the author's true beliefs are the contrary of what he explicitly states? Vagrancy is the most agreeable way of life, Alberti says, because it requires no apprenticeship, can be practiced freely without a master, involves no risks, and enables a man to thumb his nose at all the world and to live without responsibilities. Alberti's cynicism may have classical roots, or it may express a changing society's awareness of a moral dilemma.

Instead of Alberti we might have looked at such other humanists as Coluccio Salutati and his reflections on the law of labor, or Lorenzo Valla and his condemnation of begging, or Robert Gaguin and his *De validorum per Franciam mendicantium astucia*. We might even have looked to eastern Europe, especially Poland, for evidence of the influence of humanist attitudes in discrediting poverty. For the humanists, poverty was unworthy of man: in the words of Agrippa d'Aubigné, poverty "makes men ridiculous." This was perhaps the unkindest cut of all: poverty lost its sacred status.

Between Charity and Justice The
critics of poverty had their limitations—the limitations, in part, of
common sense. Even in troubled times people were perfectly capable
of distinguishing between the truly poor, whose misfortune was the
result of some accident, and those who were out to profit from disorder. The Religious of Saint-Denis, for example, drew a distinction
between paupers and criminals in his account of the riots of 1482.
Later, Jouvenel des Ursins, a bishop, to be sure, yet the son of a provost
of merchants, acknowledged that the poor sought tax relief by peaceful
means. Christine de Pisan, who showed such harshness to anyone who
fell by his own fault into poverty, draws a tender portrait of the "poor
varlets carrying firewood" whom Charles V did not disdain to hail
from his palace window, asking after them and their families and
offering them a gift. Chroniclers and memoir writers were no less
perceptive in dealing with the confusion of poverty: Oresme, Jean de
Faucomberge, Nicolas de Baye, Alain Chartier, Jouvenel des Ursins,
and especially the Bourgeois of Paris all noticed subtle points that
Villon had somehow missed. Although none of the *Canterbury Tales*
is entirely devoted to the poor, Chaucer frequently describes the
wretched life of the pauper in the most vivid of terms. For example, the
Man of Law has this to say:

> O hateful harm, condicion of povrete!
> With thurst, with coold, with hunger so confounded!
>
> . . . .
>
> Maugree thyn heed, thou most for indigence
> Or stele, or begge, or borwe thy dispence!
> Thou blamest Crist, and seist ful bitterly,
> He mysdeparteth richesse temporal;
> Thy neighebor thou wytest synfully.
>
> . . . .
>
> Herkne what is the setence of the wise:
> "Bet is to dyen than have indigence."
>
> . . . .
>
> "Alle the days of povre men been wikke."[2]

As for the theater, how could it have been as popular as it was had it not
been truthful? When an actor in the *Mystery of the Passion* uttered the
line "There is nothing that money cannot do" in a period of rampant
speculation and stark contrast between wealth and poverty, he was

certain of striking a responsive chord in his listeners. Later, in 1541, a morality play entitled *Church, Nobility, and Poverty Do the Laundry* and performed in Rouen described poverty as follows:

> I am Poverty, simple and frail,
> In whom famine and mourning, care,
> Labor and desolation come together.

No one made the mistake of confusing this poverty with vagrancy and shirking.

The study of vocabulary is, as was mentioned earlier, quite revealing. In literature, sermons, chronicles, and even ordinances and court judgments the word *poor* was usually applied only to the truly indigent, disabled, and underprivileged. We hear of "poor mechanics and laboring people," "poor people of hunger and poverty," "poor and pitiful individuals." The word *poor* was still used as an adjective with nouns that conveyed a significant connotation of either affliction (labor, debt, indigence, hunger, mendicity, fatigue) or feeling (pity, mercy). The words applied to criminals and social outcasts were quite different.

Theory ratified the conclusions of common sense. Only the cultivated could, with reference to Boethius, define poverty as "gilded mediocrity"—a definition that owed more to intellectual speculation than to observation of reality. Similarly, the Franciscan Observance, which restored strictness to the practice of the order, emphasized spiritual rapture over material destitution. The Observance was inspired in part by the *devotio moderna* and related to the "spiritual mendicity" so dear to Gerson. Poverty was reinstated but as a means of spiritual advancement rather than as an end in itself. This did not limit the notion of poverty but sharpened the distinction between its voluntary and involuntary forms. Of all the contrasts that marked the waning Middle Ages, that between the desanctification of ordinary wretchedness and the sublimation of Christlike suffering was not the least striking.

The phrase *pauperes Christi* was extended beyond the cloister and applied to indigents. Wills, charters, and gifts to hospitals are more eloquent on this point than sermons and educational treatises. The use of certain, apparently conventional formulas may indicate deeply rooted beliefs. Wills, for example, frequently speak of the "poor limbs of God." Toward the end of the fourteenth century a knight by the name of de la Tour Landry taught his daughters that "poor people . . . are servants and lambs of God and representatives of his person." In keeping with tradition, Brinton characterized the poor as God's heirs and "most beloved": "Every day," he went on, "we see Christ crucified in his members." Gerson described the spiritual life of the pauper. Poverty, he said, was not a virtue in itself, much less a form of perfection. The pauper was subject to various temptations: envy, dreaming of inaccessible things (such as meat), wrath, and rebellion against God. He had his models and his protectors, his guardian angels who "guide the blind man through the great streets from door to door" and his saints, notable for their labor, patience, charity, and alms. In the late Middle Ages cults grew up around Saint Joseph, the patron of labor, Saint Yves, the advocate of the humble, and Saint John the Almsgiver, patriarch of Alexandria in the seventh century, whose cult became especially popular in Poland and Venice and began to attract followers in France as well.

Charity was not the only reason for treating the poor decently; prudence was another, especially given late medieval man's concern with the hereafter. It was often repeated that charity wipes away sin. The craze for accurate accounting was reflected in detailed computations of purgatorial punishments. Alms were like a bill of exchange drawn on Heaven. Bishops advised the faithful to amass a treasure safe from the worms and the mites, and preachers repeated the message in forms that had become popular in the previous century. As impressive as the sheer number of surviving anthologies of sermons and manuals for preachers is the monotony of their contents: both facts are significant and call for a scholar with the stamina to undertake a systematic study. Some work has already been done on the *Tabula Exemplorum*, on John Bozon's *Stories with Morals* addressed to a rural audience in England, and on the *Quadragesimale* by the German Johann Gritsch. One of these manuals, by John of Werden, carries the unwittingly ironic title *Dormi secure*, which may have comforted oratorically untalented preachers with the thought that their audiences would remain tranquil throughout the sermon. More inspiring examples of the genre are the sermons of Thomas Brinton and especially of Jean Gerson, which shed light on the relationship between a Parisian pastor and his flock.

Fifteenth-century crowds were kept rather more awake by the devices of the popular preachers, whose techniques are worthy of today's mass media. Among them were many speakers of renown, including Bernardino of Siena, Vincent Ferrier, Bernardino of Feltre, Francis of

Paola, and, of course, Savonarola. Less illustrious preachers attracted attention in particular regions: for example, the Lollards in England and the Hussite sermonizers in Bohemia, as well as men like Jean of Varennes in Champagne, Brother Richard in Paris and Orléans, Thomas Conecte in Flanders, Olivier Maillard in Brittany, and Alonso of Mella in Portugal. The mere fact that I set down all these names together should not be allowed to obscure the differences among them. Yet all shared the goal of producing instantaneous conversions, of leading their listeners to renounce the wealth and vanities of this world and donate all their belongings to the poor. Bernardino of Siena did not mince his words: "You do not hear the cries of the poor! Why not? Because you are not shivering. Because you fill your bodies with plenty to eat and plenty to drink. Because you have clothes to wear and a fire to warm you. And beyond that you do not think, you well-filled bodies and contented souls." Occasionally popular enthusiasm produced more than just individual conversion, generating social pressures that bordered on the subversive. In Paris a contagious frenzy led many people to throw baubles, jewels, and playing cards into the fire or the Seine. Stirred up by Thomas Conecte, children followed fashionable ladies through the streets with shouts of "To the hennin! To the hennin!" And the auto-da-fés of Savonarola's would-be cultural revolution are too well known to recount here. Without indulging in undue speculation, it seems fair to say that the constant appeals to the Sermon on the Mount, however novel their formulation, were not heeded as fully as the preachers may have hoped.

It was quite another matter to base the duty to give alms on the principle of Justice. Influenced both by economic change and by humanism, late medieval thinkers did look at the problem from this angle, however. It is hardly surprising that this kind of speculation flourished mainly in great commercial centers such as Florence, Lyons, Flanders, and Germany. Christian regard for the pauper and humanist admiration of man converged in Saint Antonino, the archbishop of Florence (1389–1459). But his was not the only ecclesiastical contribution to new theological, canonical, and ethical ideas about justice in a cash economy. Bernardino of Siena, a Franciscan, followed Duns Scotus. Antonino, a Dominican, was the disciple of Raymond of Peñafort and Thomas Aquinas. The son of a Florentine notary, he was at home among the business bourgeoisie as well as with such mendicant friars as Fra Santi Rucellai and Fra Piero degli

Strozzi. But Antonino was the most remarkable of them all. His doctrine and casuistry are summed up in a *Summa theologica* and a *Manual of Confession*. Having first set an example by giving all of his possessions to the poor, Antonino felt free to teach men of his own station how they ought to behave. It was a duty, he said to give alms. Superfluous property was anything in excess of what one needed for oneself and one's family, with due allowance for one's estate. The natural human instinct for brotherhood, together with Christian compassion, made it incumbent upon each and every man to aid the needy. Alms must be given to the truly poor with righteous intention and must be drawn from lawfully acquired property. As a disciple of Saint Thomas, Antonino believed that charity should follow a preferential order: assuming equal poverty, the saved were to be favored over sinners and relatives over strangers. The pauper's need established an absolute obligation without regard to his person, provided only that the recipient make good use of the gift and not waste it or use it to live in idleness. That poverty was an evil and mendicity deplorable were simple facts, but these in no way altered the duty to give alms. The only purpose of casuistry was to judge the degree of poverty and to regulate accordingly the size of the gift. Antonino is a representative figure of his age by virtue of the clarity of his thought and his concern for efficiency. He has wrongly been credited with designing a program of poor relief. He did, however, stress the value of mutual help in confraternities and trade organizations. Here again he was combining the old traditions of the family clans and parish communities with the new corporate solidarities associated with the development of the *arti* in his native city. It is only natural that Antonino should have been greatly concerned with the problem of usury. This was a persistent issue: as early as 1363, in the time of that mystical merchant Giovanni Colombini, founder of the poor order of Gesuati, Florentines had asked themselves whether a confraternity could accept a bequest from a banker who had been a notorious usurer. The theologians consulted on the matter had declared that in the absence of proof (the banker's books having been lost) the bequest could be accepted as a restitution to the poor. This case points the way toward a new development. Antonino and Bernardino (and other lesser known clergymen) were as uncompromising on the evil of usury as they were on the duty to give alms: the latter, they said, could not excuse the former. Soon, voices were heard calling for the establishment of legitimate sources of credit (as distinct from gifts) to the poor. New ideas for helping the poor were born of the encounter between Christian charity and humanist philanthropy.

CHARITY OVERWHELMED *The Inadequacy of Alms* It is impossible to know the extent of direct alms, that is, alms handed directly by the donor to the recipient—to a beggar going from door to door or soliciting in a public place or to a "shamefaced" pauper waiting discreetly at home or to a "holy" pauper awaiting his due. Apparently a great deal of money, bread, and clothing was given in this way. The sources suggest that almsgiving was customary with people of every condition. It was permissible to violate the injunction to rest on the Sabbath provided one worked "for God," that is, for the poor. In the late fourteenth century, a great lord, the marshal of Boucicaut, even when detained at some distance from Paris often sent "very large amounts of money to use in this way [that is, for alms] to people he charged with this responsibility." His contemporary, the Prato merchant Francesco di Marco Datini, gave much more than the paltry sum he donated when he made his pilgrimage to Rome in 1399 (and for which he has been the butt of so much ridicule). Federigo Melis's study of his correspondence and accounts reveals that he also provided dowries, room and board for the poor, and even purchased a home for a blind pauper "for the love of God." In the following generation the capital of Christendom marveled at the charity of Santa Francesca Romana, "the poor woman of Trastevere." Examples could easily be multiplied. In iconography, especially in miniatures, direct almsgiving was depicted as a routine occurrence, and almsgiving remained a regular topos of hagiography. Engraved in the south porch of the Bourges cathedral in the fifteenth century was a poem intended to encourage charity. In six strophes it sums up the moral theology of alms. Underneath these lines the beggars waited and allowed the poet to speak for them:

> Those who cry and are poor
> In spirit will always be happy,
> For they shall laugh.
> In the end Heaven will hold
> The poor who endure,
> And many of the rich shall perish.

Those who beg and of whom no evil
Can be said, and who ask for the
Love of God and cry for alms will be happy,
If they pray for those who give
And for him who has made this place.

The poor who have patience
And live according to their conscience
In keeping with love and harmony,
If they endure their indigence
And hold that it is enough,
Then they shall have mercy.

Therefore, poor people, endure
And suffer all evils
Patiently and willingly,
For by so doing you will gain
Beatitude and eternal Paradise.

And everyone give, for God's sake,
Generously to the poor, for at the
Judgment Our Lord will pay us back.
Giving alms usually will
Not impoverish a living man
Who gives with an open heart.

Give, you who pass this place,
Alms for sinners
To free them from Purgatory.
By means of the good and alms
That each man does and gives to them,
They will receive the glory of Heaven.

About posthumous almsgiving we know more than we do about direct almsgiving. Wills were drawn up by even the humblest families, and thousands of these wills have survived. Documentation of legacies is therefore relatively plentiful, and we are less dependent than for some earlier periods on the chance survival of certain documents. Yet generosity does not seem to have kept pace with the growing numbers of wills or, for that matter, with the growing numbers of the poor.

Anxiety over sin, fear of death, and the uncertainty of salvation—characteristic features of the religious attitudes of the late Middle

Ages—are reflected in the way in which those who made wills called upon the prayers of the poor. The wealthy continued to view the poor primarily in the light of services the poor might render. This attitude was shared by the not-so-wealthy; even peasants and artisans frequently had wills drawn up. In a study of 950 wills from the Lyonnais, 750 were prepared for peasants or artisans. A majority of the 7,000 wills from the Forez region studied by E. Perroy also pertained to those two categories. Aware, as Pierre de Giac put it in 1399, that "full restitution could never be made," people made bequests to repair some of the wrong they believed they had done. If one hoped to move God, it was not enough to call on the Redeemer, the Virgin, or the many saints of the Catholic Church. As the study of wills in Valladolid has revealed, something was required beyond their suffrages, namely, the support of "Christ's paupers," "the limbs of God." In wills the members of this group are rarely referred to as beggars but as "paupers in the habit of soliciting alms." When a wealthy person died, a hue and cry through town and country brought tens or even hundreds of the poor running from as far as fifteen or twenty kilometers away, depending on the wealth and rank of the deceased. Paupers would join the funeral cortège, attend the burial mass, and participate in subsequent anniversary masses. The holy water was contributed by the poor. At a somewhat higher level of spirituality, some people wished to be treated as paupers after death, and we have no right to suspect them of demagogy merely because they wished to make a posthumous display. Paupers clothed in the garb of penitents (at the expense of the deceased) would carry candles in the funeral procession or even, according to the custom of the confraternities, carry the body to the grave. Some people asked to be buried with the poor. Among the wills registered with the Parlement of Paris between 1392 and 1421 are some expressing the wish that the maker's body be "thrown into the pauper's grave in the Cemetery of the Innocents." One of these is the will of a dealer in skins in the rue Saint-Denis. Another is that of Elie de Tourettes, a former *premier président* of Parlement, who adds that he wishes to be buried "in front of the image of the Passion." Some people bequeathed their own beds to hospitals and thus not only joined the poor in death but also enjoyed the purifying effects of poverty.

Wills rarely named specific paupers as beneficiaries, though occasionally we find a widow or young girl in need of dowry mentioned by name. More commonly, wills referred to "wretched persons" generally or to some specific group, such as orphans or patients of a particular hospital. The common formula was: *pauperes Christi heredes nostros instituimus*. The voluntary poor of the mendicant orders and monasteries were seldom forgotten, nor, in some localities, were the *béguins* and *béguines*. Of twenty-odd wills from Valladolid in the fifteenth century, half leave something to the black monks and only two to the mendicant orders. In some cases bequests to the poor are entrusted to the wardens of a particular parish. But increasingly the custom was to leave bequests to hospitals and other charitable institutions. By the beginning of the fifteenth century such institutions occupy second place, after the parishes and mendicant orders, in 60 percent of all wills in Paris, Douai, Toulouse, and Florence and around 25 percent of wills in the Lyonnais.

It is difficult to evaluate or even estimate how much relief such bequests actually brought to the poor. At best we can offer only a few qualitative observations. Wills, no matter what the rank of the testator, generally favored large numbers of recipients, perhaps in order to express gratitude to many people, perhaps in order to secure the suffrages of as many intercessors as possible. This observation fits in rather well with what we know of religious attitudes in this period; salvation, like investment, was a matter of debits and credits, and in neither the temporal nor the spiritual realm were people willing to put all their eggs in one basket. In one will, for instance, we find bequests for twenty-eight different hospitals, twenty-four of them in Paris. Some gifts were of course quite small, a few livres or even a few sous in cash, a bed, clothing, food, wood, or, in one will from Douai, a kettle for "warming the bathwater of poor women in childbirth." Scholarships were established for poor students. The names of the Ave Maria and Dormans *collèges*, both in Paris, might be mentioned in this connection. Wills also provided for distributions to the poor, which E. Perroy has aptly named the "pauper's perquisites." The fact that news of a funeral brought paupers running shows that such occasions were of some importance to the poor, for whom frequent burials were a great boon. At some funerals the crush was so great that people were killed. For that reason some testators specified that, on the day of burial, alms were to be handed out discreetly, to individual paupers one at a time or at various distribution sites scattered around the town. From the total amount set aside for alms and the amount specified for each individual gift, it is sometimes possible to evaluate the number of recipients: a few hundred or a few thousand, usually, with Parisian wills ranging between 960 and 3,800, compared with a poor population of between

8,000 and 20,000. B. Geremek has studied the will of Denis de Mauroy (d. 1411), *procureur général* in the Parlement of Paris, and identified eighty-eight designated alms-distribution points around the city, where alms were to be handed out on the Day of the Dead and during Holy Week. Included were various churches, chapels, and hospitals around the city, with a particular concentration in the Ile de la Cité, where there were nineteen sites, compared with forty-seven for the Right Bank (especially along the rue Saint-Denis and rue Saint-Martin) and twenty-two on the Left Bank.

The amount given as direct alms cannot be evaluated; what is important about direct almsgiving is that it was a social custom. Nor can we estimate the amount of aid collected in the parishes. By contrast, hospital records sometimes include the amounts collected from poor-boxes. For example, in 1416 the two poor-boxes of Paris's Hôtel-Dieu received, again according to Geremek's research, gifts whose varying sizes reflect the whole social spectrum. The poor-box located inside the hospital and used primarily by poor visitors to the hospital's poor patients received some 500 small silver coins of between one and one-and-a-half deniers in value out of a total of 940 coins in all. In the twelfth century Maurice de Sully said that Notre-Dame had been built with the gifts of old women, and it seems that in the fifteenth century the poor of Paris perpetuated the evangelical spirit of those old widows by giving aid to their poor brethren.

Other traditional forms of charity, though less methodical and more frequent than direct or posthumous alms, nevertheless fell short of meeting society's new needs. The regular benevolence of the professional confraternities often sufficed only to meet members' needs, with small sums allocated as alms for selected indigents. Clans also assisted their members, especially in Italy, but this again was a closed system. In Genoa the *alberghi* invested in the public debt funds allocated for the upkeep of designated paupers; the income was used to pay board for the inmates of certain hospices, to defray the expenses of students attending universities outside the city, and to provide dowries for poor girls. That not all paupers were beggars seems to have been acknowledged, but charity did not extend outside the clan.

Charitable institutions organized along traditional lines also proved inadequate to cope with the new forms of poverty, and the increase in the number of paupers made the problem all the more serious. Monastic almonries continued to function as they had always done; the office of almoner tended, as a result of fourteenth-century legalism, to be regarded increasingly as a benefice. Bishops also continued the tradition of episcopal assistance to the poor, but this depended largely on circumstances and on the individual bishop. The Pignotte became a full-fledged department of the papal bureaucracy, as its records reveal. Under Benedict XII almost a fifth of the annual expenditures of the papal court were devoted to providing several hundred meals a day to the poor, and some twenty hospitals were subsidized in Avignon.

The princely almonries, though traditional in their methods, proved relatively effective in aiding the poor. The almoner of the king of France received each year a fairly constant sum of money to distribute to the various royal hospitals, mainly in the Paris area. Kings and queens reserved the right to make occasional gifts on their own. Princes with appanages and other sovereign princes did the same. Much information is available about the charitable activities of Edward III, Isabeau of Bavaria, King René of Anjou, Louis XI, and Charles the Bold. The office of almoner was established in Aragon in the fourteenth century and, later, in Castille. Pedro the Ceremonious, concerned that the unemployed should find work, appointed officials to oversee the daily "hiring" in certain cities. In general, however—as the accounts of Isabella the Catholic prove—royal almsgiving was more in the nature of a private benefaction than a public agency.

I do not wish to take an unduly pessimistic view or to deny that the hospitals were useful. Still, the poor frequently did not receive the help they needed. This was not because there were not enough hospitals. On the contrary, there were so many small hospitals with just a few beds that none could really develop as an institution. What is more, gifts to the hospitals seem to have declined just as the number of patients increased. With the coming of economic hardship many hospitals found it difficult to survive. Mismanagement, poor staff, and misuse of the facilities were deficiencies that cried out for reform. All of this occurred against a tragic background of "desolation," numerous accounts of which have been collected by Denifle.

A study carried out in the diocese of Paris in 1350 found that the number of hospitals was fairly large but that the operation of many of them left much to be desired. This is not the place to consider the leprosariums, which had only an indirect bearing on poverty. In any case, many of these were nearly empty thanks to the decreasing incidence of leprosy. Some twenty-eight hospitals were visited by the investigators, or about half of all hospitals in the area, the others falling under the jurisdiction of the abbeys or hospital orders rather than the bishop. These twenty-eight institutions were subject to various legal forms; Jean Imbert has classified these into four groups, according to whether the founder was an ecclesiastic, a lay person, a king, or a parish or confraternal community. Apart from the different legal status of the various hospitals, there were also differences in resources. Smaller hospitals both in the city and outside stood in marked contrast to the large Hôtel-Dieu or *hôpital* Saint-Jacques-aux-Pelerins. Yet despite these disparities in size, all these hospitals were vulnerable to economic difficulty. A petition to the pope in 1360 led to the establishment of the Holy Spirit hospital to serve the suffering young people of the city. Three years later, the bishop of Paris, addressing a gathering marking the establishment of a confraternity, pointed out the deficiencies of his city's hospital system. At the beginning of the fifteenth century Paris seems to have had only 1,000–1,200 hospital beds (excluding beds for lepers), including the hundreds of beds in the large hospitals and the dozens in smaller ones, and almost as many places for pilgrims, travelers, and "passing paupers." This was by far too few for the size of the city. These figures of course say nothing about the homeless or about the living conditions of the working poor. Yet Paris was far better off than many other cities. Lyons had only 200 beds in twenty hospitals.

The great misfortune was that hospital resources declined as poverty increased. Most of the hospitals depended on income from land. Rents and head taxes declined steadily from the middle of the fourteenth century through the first third of the fifteenth. Payments in kind, which had provided supplies for hospitals and almonries, had been converted into cash payments, often in devalued currency. Donors, too, were affected by the crisis and reduced their gifts of alms and bequests. Some were more concerned for their own salvation than for the fate of the poor and gave to establish masses rather than alms for the poor. They were afraid that their instructions would not be followed after their death, that nothing would be given to the poor on their behalf, and therefore that the poor would not pray for their souls.

It was primarily in France that charitable institutions encountered difficulties due to wartime devastation. But in all countries the fluctuations of the economy had an impact on older institutions and threatened the survival of new ones. The Teutonic Order and the Hospitallers, wealthy as they were, had a less than unblemished record when it came to discharging the tasks for which they had been founded. A papal investigation of the Order of Saint John in 1373 discovered that progress in the area of charity had come to a halt. Although some commanderies in southern France devoted from 5 to 15 percent of their revenues to triweekly distributions to the poor (for example, in Toulouse, Uzès, and Elne), these were the exceptions that proved the rule. The chapters of the Order were on several occasions (in 1344, 1358, and 1383) obliged to remind their subsidiaries of the duty to help the poor. Excuses for the failure to fulfill this duty ranged from the scarcity and high cost of labor to the decline of revenues, the shift in agriculture from crops to livestock, and especially unwillingness to resort to the practice of farming. Whatever the cause, it was obvious that the Order found itself unable to adapt its mission of hospitality to the altered circumstances. This was true of all the priories. In 1373, in the diocese of Besançon where the Order maintained thirty-two houses, thirteen stood empty and only six discharged their mission of aiding the poor. In Douai the Hospitallers were able to provide food and lodging for eight paupers per night. The unique children's hospital that the Order maintained in Genoa encountered serious operational difficulties even though it housed only eight pensioners.

The hospital at Montbrison has been thoroughly studied by E. Perroy. The revenues of the Aubrac hospital declined sharply in the middle of the fourteenth century. In 1466 it proved necessary to end the practice of offering free lodging to travelers, in order to maintain free facilities for the sick. In Aix hospital revenues declined to the point where survival was threatened. No new hospitals were founded after 1444 (so far as we know), and the number of existing hospitals decreased from eight in the thirteenth century to six in the fifteenth. In Meaux the dramatic events of 1358 dealt a serious blow to the city's three hospitals. The case of the *hôtel-Dieu* of Tonnerre is typical: income exceeded expenditures until the middle of the fourteenth century, after which deficits persisted until the end of the fifteenth. Even the tiny rural almonries of Poitou and Anjou had to battle for survival during the Hundred Years' War. Even so, new rural almonries continued to be established.

In Germany, despite the traditional vigilance of communal authorities, some hospitals experienced difficulties. The hospital of Lüneburg, which lived chiefly on the income from salt mines, suffered from fluctuations in the international market for salt, due largely to competition from salt produced in the bay of Bourgneuf. English charitable institutions experienced a serious crisis at the end of the fifteenth century. Of forty-six almshouses that had operated in Yorkshire in the Middle Ages, twenty were in ruins by 1480. Yet Yorkshire fared better than most other countries. Norfolk and Birmingham together had at most ten almshouses. Of the thirty-six almshouses surviving in the three countries just mentioned, fourteen found themselves in dire straits and six were close to ruin. The situation was still worse in London, where only eight of twenty-two almshouses were still in operation. Henry II found at the beginning of his reign that "untold numbers of the needy die miserably every day for want of assistance."

Temporary economic hardship was not the only reason for the crisis. Not all the abuses identified in 1311 by the council of Vienne had been stamped out, and further abuses were encouraged by the negligence, lack of skill, and inexperience of those who staffed the hospitals, many of whom were lay persons or families that held their positions as though they were prebends. In some large establishments such as the Hôtel-Dieu in Paris, disputes between the sisters and the master of the hospital had revealed the need for reform as early as the reign of Charles V.

A common abuse was restriction of the use of hospital facilities to residents of a particular locality or region. This was probably a measure intended to exclude false beggars and vagabonds. The result, however, was that hospitals were no longer open to all victims of misfortune and served only fixed "quotas" of certified paupers. In Valencia hospitality turned into hostility against foreigners, who were accused of stealing bread from the mouths of the city's poor. Corrupt misuse of hospitals and hospices was a far more serious matter. In England and to a lesser degree in France the royal government assigned protégés to the hospitals as administrators and pensioners. In Portugal in 1427 King John I was accused by the clergy and by his brother Dom Pedro of misusing alms and of substituting his protégés for the poor. Elsewhere bourgeois citizens purchased life annuities that guaranteed them a place in a hospital for their old age. This is known to have been done in Narbonne as early as 1298. It became a fairly common practice in the Low Countries and in Germany. The hospital at Aire-sur-la-Lys, for example, could accommodate some forty individuals. Little by little it became the custom for people to pay for accommodations by the month or the year; by the fifteenth century the practice was commonplace.[3] In the Empire, particularly in northern cities such as Rostock, it was common for people of means to purchase a hospital bed for their old age; this was refered to as a *prebend* (*Prufronta, Pfründe*). The end result was that charitable institutions were turned into retirement homes. Foreigners were excluded from the hospital of Saint Mary Magdalen in Munster in 1360 and later from hospitals in Ulm and Erfurt. And that was not all: the city council of Bremen received the Saint George Hospital for the use of the bourgeoisie, excluding the poor. In Gdansk in 1432 a protest was raised against the practice of refusing admission to the Holy Spirit Hospital to all but bourgeois possessing property valued at between one hundred and two hundred marks. In Lübeck and Gosslar the sick were no longer admitted to hospitals, all the beds having been taken by prebendals. Even those lucky enough to enjoy the privilege of a hospital bed were treated differently according to their wealth. In Wismar, for example, the poor were housed in small buildings on the hospital grounds, each accommodating twenty-five to thirty individuals. Old people and invalids were lodged in the basement. More is known about conditions in northern German cities than about conditions elsewhere in Europe, but the former were not atypical. In Portugal, for example, a 1459 charter of Alfonso V takes note of complaints from the poor that the hospitals are no longer willing to take them in.

We should be careful not to generalize unduly. Some signs suggest that the hospitals continued to serve as homes for the poor. For example, nineteen out of twenty paupers who died at Saint Julian's Hospital in Cambrai between 1377 and 1413 left no money or other possessions after their death. At the Hôtel-Dieu in Paris, between 1428 and 1444, the average value of the clothing of the three hundred to six hundred people who died each year barely came to three sous.

Yet many hospitals were no longer primarily devoted to the poor, even though both custom and law dictated that they should be, as did the earliest known work on the subject of hospitals, the *Tractatus hospitalitatis*[4] by Lapo of Castiglionco. This change accounts for the observation made in Tours in 1501–02, that "the unfortunate are about town day and night because the almonries refuse them lodging."

Thus the traditional charitable institutions failed to achieve their goals or achieved them only partially. All suffered from economic difficulties. Many were ill adapted to the new forms of poverty. Created mainly to serve the abject and the disabled, these institutions failed to recognize the existence of the working poor and were overwhelmed by the growing numbers of vagabonds and other social outcasts. Some were corrupted in their purposes. Renewal, reform, and new leadership were needed.

The Search for Efficacy   The Church, which in many regions found itself unable to cope with poverty unaided, turned for help to the civil authorities. Charitable institutions remained under the control of the bishops, however. When we speak of a "secularization" of charity, therefore, the term is not to be understood in a modern sense. But in any case, new ways of thinking about charity encouraged a search for more effective means of aiding the poor. Emerging city and national governments took part in this effort, supervising or supplementing older private and church institutions. The change occurred relatively smoothly.

There were two reasons why change came easily. First, in the cities the same men who belonged to the confraternities and met in the vestries also administered the Poor Tables, gave alms, left bequests to the poor, and sat on city councils and boards of aldermen. These various activities were not narrowly compartmentalized. For example, in 1373 a hermit at Vallombrosa wrote to a friend who held a municipal office in these terms: "Know how to turn your face and spirit toward the honor of God, the good of the commune, and the needs of the poor."

Second, it was quite logical for the prince, in keeping with his traditional role as guarantor of justice and guardian of the common good, to assume a supervisory role over the distribution of charity. Assistance to the poor was one of the areas in which the state found it possible to extend its authority. The men around Charles V and Richard II were well aware of this. Philippe de Mézières recommended that royal officials exercise stricter control in order to eliminate oppressive practices and encourage assistance to the poor. His humanist views, bolstered by ancient precedents, inspired the work of the next generation. Dom Pedro of Portugal examined the state's duties to the poor in his treatise *Virtuosa Benefeitoria*. Among other things he argued that the king must administer hospitals after their founders have died, at which time they cease to be private property. In 1498 King Manuel of Portugal ordered a reform of relief institutions. From then on it was generally acknowledged that the state had a duty to look after the poor. Geiler of Kaysersberg stated the point quite explicitly. The same point was also made by his anonymous compatriot, the author of the *Book of One Hundred Chapters*, which is preserved at Colmar and which celebrates the advent of a new society in the eighth phase of world history: "If sovereigns do not assume responsibility for establishing a harmonious social order, the Lord will unbridle the poor, who will be the instruments of his wrath and the artisans of their own liberation."[5]

Thus the temporal authorities joined the church in maintaining, supplementing, and promoting works of charity in order to maintain civil peace as well as to meet the needs of the poor.

‡ Confraternities and "poor tables" established and administered by laymen helped the poor in the parishes as best they could. In so doing they supplanted the old monastic almonries, which had lost touch with the needs of society. In the fourteenth century the growth of confraternities was facilitated when they came under a canonical statute and, in civil law, were held to be moral persons. Confraternities served the rural as well as the urban population. The Lyonnais region, for example, was served by the community for the parish of Saint-Cyr-au-Mont-d'Or, for which we possess an inventory of property in land for the period 1416–1513. In parishes around Geneva distributions were made two or three times a week, and in Geneva itself the confraternity of the Holy Trinity assisted 2,000 to 2,950 paupers annually in the period 1439–43. The Parisian confraternity of Saint-Jacques-aux-Pelerins not only gave lodging to "passing paupers" but devoted a considerable portion of its resources to providing poor relief. In the modest town of Coulommiers the confraternity of Sainte-Foy served some 500 paupers through its annual distributions. In Normandy at the end of the Hundred Years' War *charités* were revived in places like Honfleur and Le Bourg-Achard, a town of fifty hearths, of which twenty-five were poor, "some having come from the Caux area to wait for alms each day at the priory (in 1443)." Assistance from the authorities was frequently required. In Narbonne in the fourteenth century it proved necessary to combine the two existing *charités* of the city and burg. The Marseilles almshouse was reorganized in 1319 by a commission made up of four city councillors. In hard times the influx of beggars everywhere overwhelmed the confraternities, which appealed for help to communes and princes in every country in Christendom. Without help from the pope and the cardinals the Roman confraternities would not have been able to meet the demands placed on them in the fifteenth century. For example, the almonry of Campo Santo dei Tedeschi was besieged every Monday and Friday by 2,000 indigents, while the confraternity of the Annunciation took care of poor young girls. In Florence the Buonomini di San Martino began to serve the "shamefaced poor" in 1441 under the inspiration of Saint Antonino and continued their work into the next century. And in Turin we see a sign of change in 1375, when at the end of a hard winter the bishop of

that city requested the commune to organize the distribution of bread and wine to the poor.

Often it is difficult to distinguish between the work of the confraternities and that of the poor tables. The poor tables seem to have attracted, even more than the confraternities, the attention of the communal authorities, perhaps because their purpose was specifically charitable rather than spiritual and thus gave them an essential role to play in the maintenance of law and order. In any case both the ecclesiastical and the civil authorities took an early interest in the operation of the poor tables. I stress this point not merely because evidence for it happens to have survived but because the role of the poor tables became increasingly important in the last 150 years of the Middle Ages, as examples from Catalonia and the Low Countries—two widely separated parts of the continent—make clear.

Archives of the Plats dels Pobres in several parishes of Barcelona have survived. Established by laymen and administered by *probi homines* who were elected annually, the Plats dels Pobres were financed by endowments and by Sunday contributions. The royal and papal authorities took no interest in the operation of these institutions beyond granting or confirming certain privileges. The communal authorities played a more active role. The Plats dels Pobres practiced traditional forms of charity: they distributed food, clothing, shoes, and money, organized public dinners, and gave assistance in the home. In addition, low-interest loans were made available to the poor, particularly in Santa Maria del Mar. But the Plats dels Pobres served not only the traditional needy but also the working poor, who by the fifteenth century required occasional assistance. Assistance was limited to the poor of the parish, excluding beggars and "vicious" individuals. Eventually the administrators (*baciners*) of the Plats established criteria that paupers had to meet in order to qualify for relief. Well endowed during Barcelona's years of prosperity in the fourteenth century, the Plats suffered with the city's decline (late fourteenth to fifteenth century), and the poor, whose numbers had in the meantime increased, suffered with them. Reform was needed and the city was forced to intervene. Still, the Plats were an effective relief agency. The Pia Almona de la Seo helped 178 paupers in 1317, and throughout the fifteenth century it regularly assisted some 288 paupers annually. The Plat of Santa Maria del Pi helped 791 men and 758 women in 1423, and 935 men and 375 women in 1428. The number assisted each month rarely dropped below 100, with the maximum occurring in February of both years. Almost all the men had families. Their occupations were diverse and show no obvious pattern. The Plat dels Pobres Vergonyantes of Santa Maria del Mar enjoyed a considerable income derived primarily from bequests of real property in this wealthy district of the city. In 1379 Pedro IV praised the institution for its social role, which had been preserved by a reform. The detailed nature of the accounts kept in the fifteenth century, which indicate the personal background and even the address of those receiving assistance, shows awareness of the need for good administration as well as a desire to insure that the assistance made available to the poor did not fail of its purpose.

Turning now to the poor tables of northern Europe, we find that these too were lay institutions with close ties to local authorities. Rural poor tables were administered by *mambours* chosen from among local residents; their accounts were examined by the curate and aldermen. This was the practice in Boussoit (Hainault) and Walcourt (Namurois). At Pittem in Flanders the lord took a hand in the administration of the poor table, and at Jodoigne in Brabant the mambours were appointed by officers of the Duke of Burgundy. At Marbaix in Hainault, a village of thirty hearths in 1453, only six families required assistance (by 1540, this number had risen to sixteen). The income of the poor table came from "poverty lands" bequeathed to it in the fourteenth century; the communal treasury also provided funds. Only paupers residing in the commune's *finage* (administrative area) were entitled to relief. In 1447–48 the amount offered to each recipient came to barely two livres tournois, which supplemented wages earned in seasonal employment—yet another instance of what we have been calling working poverty. It is worth noting that in this same year the poor table enjoyed a surplus of six livres.

The urban poor tables, about which a good deal is known, operated in much the same way. The communes tightened their control over the poor tables in the fourteenth and fifteenth centuries. This control involved more than just the power to appoint administrators. In Huy in 1377 a commission investigated frauds associated with the poor table there. In 1444 the communal council of Liège specified how poor table accounts were to be kept. Mambours took an oath before the minicipal magistrates. In some towns the aldermen were allowed to use income from the poor tables. In Fosses, for example, poor table revenues were used to restore town monuments in 1429. Local authorities frequently attempted to regulate such things as criteria for distribution of relief (Antwerp, 1434) or the number of recipients and amount of bread allotted to each (Louvain, 1459). On the other hand, the administrators of the poor tables could themselves be adamant: in Mons, for example, the administrators threatened to resign in 1425–26 unless the aldermen provided from the communal treasury funds sufficient to meet the "needs of the Alms." In general, however, poor tables were not authorized to borrow and adjusted their distributions as required by their revenues. Aldermen insisted on strict management: in 1463, for example, the collector of the Louvain poor table was admonished to tighten his administration.

With such strict management controls, were the poor tables effective in their relief mission? Surviving records, mainly from the fifteenth century and from such places as Mons, Louvain, Brussels, Antwerp, and Lierre, give the impression that poor table administrators knew what they were doing, made wise purchases, and managed their property and distributions quite well. They knew how to increase poor table revenues by buying additional land and rents, and they put idle funds to work by making low-interest loans to people of modest means. The role of the poor tables as lending institutions is worthy of further study. Generally well administered, the poor tables seem to have fulfilled their purpose. Unfortunately their assistance was too limited, going only to the needy of a specific locality, to those who received or purchased a modest stipend and who carried a token that enabled the authorities to verify their eligibility. Those fortunate enough to be entitled to such a stipend did receive considerable help, even if it was only a supplement to other sources of income. Distributions were made for the most part on specified days of the week and on major holidays and consisted of bread, clothing, shoes, meat, dried herring, peas, oil, wine or beer, and firewood. In Brussels reserves were stored in the cellars and lofts of the Gheesthuis, which also housed a kitchen, a dining hall, and a room for distributing alms. In different localities the content of distributions was similar but the amount varied. The quantity seems to have been greater at Sainte-Gudule, the most important of the six poor tables in Brussels, than at the Great Table in Louvain, which in turn gave out larger quantities than the poor tables in four other parishes of that city. In Brussels bread amounting to 1,448 calories was distributed, compared with 567 calories in Louvain. The annual stipend in Louvain in 1480 was as follows: 384 rye breads of 205 grams (or more than 78 kilograms per year), 20–30 herrings, 26 liters of beer, 2.3 liters of rape oil, 100 faggots, approximately 138 liters of charcoal, a pair of shoes, and 2 meters of linen cloth. We have no specific figures for the amount of meat (usually pork) distributed. In Brussels in the fifteenth century meat never accounted for less than 30 percent of total food distributions (exclusive of bread). Early in the century the figure was as high as 46 percent. Although the alms dispensed by the Tables of the Holy Spirit were not inconsiderable, recipients were still obliged to beg, and were authorized to do so by the insignia that they wore.

In times of crisis, especially in the period of 1480–90, rations were reduced or eliminated because of the increased demand. It is difficult to know just how great the increase was. In Lierre some recipients of aid were entitled to a full share and others to a half share, as indicated by the insignia they wore. Lists of families receiving aid in Lierre have survived. We know that at various points between 1463 and 1480 up to eight hundred people received assistance in Louvain. One good way of studying fluctuations in public assistance is to examine the amounts spent by the poor tables for supplies. Hermann van der Wee has done this for Antwerp and Lierre. In Leyden in 1425 a quarter of the population found itself in need of assistance, but the poor table was unable to cope with such hardship. The years 1437–38 were a time of famine almost everywhere in the Low Countries. In 1445 the streets of Malines were overrun by beggars. In Brussels in 1472 unemployment and declining purchasing power forced the Table of Sainte-Gudule to offer assistance to the unemployed and unskilled. The penultimate decade of the fifteenth century was a period of widespread hardship, and traditional forms of relief proved inadequate. In 1481 the Magistrate of Leyden compiled a list of families able to contribute to a weekly collection on behalf of the poor. In Amsterdam collectors went from door to door. The same thing was done in Brussels fifteen years later. In extraordinary circumstances municipal authorities would purchase grain and distribute it to the poor.

In order to see just how enterprising the poor table administrators were, consider the rather impressive case of William of Nijmegen, collector of the Great Table of Louvain from 1427 to 1450. A man who "knew how to look at poverty," he was responsible for the decision to switch from wheat bread to rye bread and to deliver extra provisions to the homes of the sick and the blind. He was not a man to allow himself to become bogged down in routine procedure. He helped poor people to pay their rent, repair their homes, buy clothing, and redeem garments held in pawn by usurers. He also helped people to pay doctors' fees, helped a priest obtain a breviary, and helped still another man to buy a

casket. Charity bred more charity: the generosity of William of Nijmegen was matched by an increase in bequests to the poor. Unfortunately William was in the habit of acting without authorization from
the mambours of the poor table, and this habit worried the aldermen. It
was said that the collector failed to make distinctions among the poor
and that he gave to people "who had no provisions," perhaps even to
scoundrels fit for work.

Considerable space has been devoted to the work of the poor tables
in the areas where they prospered. In part this is because a good deal of
useful research has been done on this topic by Belgian and Spanish
historians. More importantly, however, the case of the poor tables
shows that the men and women of the cities felt a deep need to deal
effectively with poverty.

Another indication of this was the spread of the *monti di pietà*, or
public pawnbroking establishments. Under the influence of humanism, many people came to regard loans as morally preferable to alms,
because a man could accept a loan and still maintain his dignity or
even regain dignity that he had lost. Loans were also a more effective
means of dealing with poverty, since experience had shown that it was
easier to ward off economic disaster in the first place than to rehabilitate a man once he had lost his place in society. Certain other developments preceded the advent of the pawnshop. As early as the fourteenth
century Durand de Saint-Pourcain advised city magistrates to be sure
that credit was available to all at a low and legally fixed rate of interest.
In the middle of the same century in Salins an official lending institution offered loans at a reasonable rate in competition with Lombard
and Jewish lenders. One of the earliest experiments with credit for the
poor was the work of the bishop of London, Michael of Northbury. In
1361 he left a legacy of one thousand silver marks to be used to finance
interest-free one-year loans. The amount of each loan was to be apportioned to the status of the borrower: a common man might borrow ten
pounds, a bourgeois twenty, and a bishop fifty. This schedule of loans
shows that men at every level of society might find themselves in
need. A short while later Philippe de Mézières recommended the establishment of a state bank that would lend to the poor at no interest
against collateral and to others in return for an optional gift to the
institution of 10 percent of the amount of the loan, intended to support
the bank's continued operation. The bank's capital was to have been
provided primarily by the king, that is, by the state.

It is of little importance to know where, but of considerably more importance to know why and for whom, the first "mount of piety" was established. Richard C. Trexler is right in thinking that the problem has too often been studied in relation to the peasant poverty of the twelfth century; he shows that the pawnshops aided impoverished nobles and bourgeois. But most clients of the monti di pietà were very modest people; this was particularly true of the *monti frumentari* of southern Italy, which lent seed to peasants.

In 1432, before the advent of the monti di pietà in Italy, an earlier system of credit existed in Sibenik in Illyria, then under Venetian domination. But this was too different from the pawnshop system to offer any basis for comparison. In the same period in Castille we find the *arcas de limosnas*, which were established at the behest of the Count of Haro and approved by Eugene IV in 1431 at the request of King Juan II. The purpose of these institutions was to snatch the needy from the jaws of the usurers by offering one-year interest-free loans repayable in quarterly installments. Managed by governors elected by local residents and supervised by Minorite friars, the arcas de limosnas were found in various places in the provinces of Burgos, Palencia, Logrono, and Calahorra. In Spain less than fifty years later and only a few years before the monti frumentari were organized in Italy, we find so-called *positos de trigo*, or grain depositories, which made commodity loans. The first was established in Molina in 1478. Subsequently Cardinal Cisneros encouraged the establishment of similar depositories in Toledo, Torre Laguna, Cisneros, and Alcala de Henarcs.

Italy, the birthplace of humanism and banking, was a natural place for the development of the monte di pietà. The movement was begun by socially conscious Franciscans of the Observance and powerfully promoted by one man in particular, Bernardino of Feltre. In 1428 Ludovico of Camerino made an early attempt to establish a pawnshop at Arcevia in the Marches but failed owing to opposition from the commune. Success invariably required the cooperation of the municipal authorities and frequently followed a set course of events: a sermon during Lent aroused public opposition to usury, whereupon the urban authorities undertook to raise, or to approve the raising of, funds to finance a pawnshop, which was finally established by an act of the town council. Loans were then granted against collateral valued at twice the amount loaned. A small interest fee was charged, generally around 5 percent, to cover administrative costs. If the pledged collateral was not redeemed by the time the period of the loan elapsed, the pawned item was sold at auction.

Whether the first monte di pietà was established in Perugia in 1462–63 or in Orvieto or Gubbio, the idea quickly caught on throughout Umbria, Tuscany, the Marches, Lazio, and Abruzzi. Bernardino of Feltre arrived on the scene in 1484 and "like a hurricane" descended upon northern and central Italy, where he delivered more than three thousand sermons in years of constant travel. He overcame all obstacles thrown up by usurers and speculators in such places as Mantua, Piacenza, Padua, Vicenza, and Venice. In Verona he was especially successful: the monte di pietà there did more than two hundred thousand ducats worth of business in its first year, thanks to a graduated system of loans at rates of interest ranging from zero to six percent (*monti piccolo, mezzano,* and *maggiore*). Florence proved more difficult to conquer. A first attempt ended in failure in 1473. Bernardino arrived in 1488 and stirred up a great deal of emotion with a sermon on the poor; he is said to have received four hundred visits in a single day. But the Signoria deemed the event *inconveniente e scandaloso* for law and order and asked him to leave. He returned five years later and despite official opposition proved so popular that no church was large enough to hold his audience and six stout men armed with clubs were needed to protect him from the enthusiasm of the crowd. A monte di pietà began operation in Florence in the following year, but Savonarola used it as an instrument in his purge of the city and by so doing damaged its reputation in the eyes of the Florentines.

There was no lack of controversy surrounding the question of interest on loans. Even though some Dominicans and Augustinians helped to establish pawnshops in such places as Modena and Reggio di Emilia, both orders were opposed—at times vociferously—to the charging of interest. One Augustinian, Nicola Bariano, challenged Bernardino of Siena in a treatise whose title is a play on words: *De monte impietatis.* Invoking the lessons of experience, Bernardino argued that a low rate of interest was indeed moral as well as necessary for the survival of the monti and far more tolerable than the rates of 30, 40, or even 50 percent charged by the usurers. In practice, of some forty pawnshops in the Marches, only half a dozen offered interest-free loans. The strategy of combining the preaching of the Observants with the support of the municipal authorities ultimately proved successful.

Even as Bernardino of Siena was doing his work in the towns, another Observant, Andrea of Faenza, proposed that so-called monti frumentari be set up in rural areas to lend seed and distribute grain in time of famine. Much is known about the monti frumentari that Andrea established in Foligno, Spoleto, Rieti, and Bologna, but another, located at Sulmona near Naples and associated with the orphanage of the Annunziata, played a particularly important role in helping the indigent.

By 1500 the principle of the pawnshop was established in Italy and Spain. The institution developed later in other countries. In the Low Countries, where the poor tables were active, it is not surprising that the first public pawnshop was not established until 1534, in Ypres. In Nüremberg, whose government had asked the Emperor in 1473 to expel Jewish usurers and establish a nonusurious bank, a pawnshop was opened in 1498. But none was established in Lyons before the sixteenth century, and the first experiments in that city met with no success. The Tables of the Holy Spirit, the Banco di Santo Spirito, and the monti di pietà are all members of the same family of institutions, twice consecrated by the popes: first by Julius II, who set forth the purpose of the monti di pietà in 1503, and then by Leo X, who granted official recognition in 1515.

‡ The same concern with efficacy prompted the civil authorities to undertake hospital reform, usually in concert with the church hierarchy. Hospitals that had ceased to give priority to the treatment of the poor needed to be encouraged to do so once more; facilities had to be improved where necessary; and in keeping with the spirit of the times the two principles of efficient management and competent care had to be instilled into hospital staff. The reform efforts of state and commune did not interfere with the application of the Council of Vienne's decree, Quia contingit, as the case of Saint Antonino makes clear. The archbishop of Florence held that hospitals were not automatically or exclusively subject to episcopal supervision. Laymen were free to endow new hospitals and therefore to assume responsibility for their operation. Lapo of Castiglionco agreed with this position.

We can learn a great deal about state intervention in hospital affairs by considering the case of France. The royal almoner, in theory responsible only for hospitals endowed by the king, received the title of Grand Aumônier in 1519. The king assumed responsibility for certain hospitals, such as the one in Langres (1501), and the Parlements began to take an increased interest in hospital management. The situation was similar in the principalities, for example, the Duchy of Burgundy, where major hospitals like the one at Beaune were first established in the fifteenth century.

Municipal interest in hospital affairs naturally developed earliest in highly urbanized regions such as Italy and the Low Countries. Three men delegated by the city government of Mons administered the Common Alms, the hospitals, and infirmaries of that city in 1318. The hospital of Dinant, which was placed under the control of the commune in the late thirteenth century, began less than one hundred years later to use its own seal as a mark of independence. In Mézières aid from the city council enabled the hospital to surmount persistent financial difficulties. Municipal governments supervised or ran hospitals in Mirecourt, Senlis, Saint-Omer, Tournai, and Ypres in the fourteenth century, and, in the fifteenth century, in Lille, Caen, and Rennes, where the *hôpital* Saint-Yves was dependent on city subsidies from 1461 and was finally placed under the control of the commune in 1522. In Nantes, which until the middle of the fifteenth century suffered with too few hospital facilities (having only the two almonries of Saint-Jacques and Saint-Clément and the small hospice of Saint-Julien), the city government built a 140-bed hospital at the end of the fifteenth century. Hospitals in Aix in southern France fell on hard times in the middle of the fourteenth century. The city established a new hospital in 1437 and paid for its upkeep. Dijon reorganized its charitable institutions in 1481; in the following year a census turned up 1,500 indigents.

In some places city governments intervened in hospital affairs more for disciplinary than for financial reasons. In Lyons, for example, the consuls took possession of the hospital in 1478 to make up for "the deficiencies of the religious authorities" that had supervised it previously. The Hôtel-Dieu in Paris met with a different fate: the chapter, unable to maintain orderly operations or to quell discontent among the staff over the removal of the hospital's master, turned for help to the city government. From 1505 on, temporal administration of the hospital was entrusted to eight bourgeois appointed by the provost. Spiritual matters remained under the control of church authorities. To this episode we owe one of the finest documents in all hospital history, the *Book of the Active Life* with its many miniatures, the purpose of which was to remind the nuns of their duties to the sick and the poor.

Countries other than France also provide innumerable examples of the same phenomenon. In 1391 the city council of Porto named a commission to look into the care given the sick and poor in the city's hospitals; regulations were established and an inspector appointed. Throughout Portugal the beginnings of public assistance were marked by the spread of so-called *gafarias*. In Castille, where confraternal hospitals played an important role, the city councils or *consejos* supervised their operations in conjunction with the royal authorities. In England the accounts of the steward of Southampton tell us a great deal about the relationship between charitable institutions and city politics. And the story was similar in the cities of Switzerland.

In Italy laymen were involved in the affairs of even the smallest hospitals in the rural communes and occasionally came into conflict with the bishops as a result. The civil authorities claimed patronage of the hospitals, and especially the right to name a new master after a hospital's founder died, which contradicted the custom whereby patronage passed to the bishop after a founder's death. The problem was complicated by the necessary, though controversial, distinction between canonically instituted confraternal hospitals (for example, in Bitonto and Bologna in the fourteenth century) and professionally instituted hospitals: the bishops controlled the former while the secular authorities controlled the latter. In the fifteenth century a modus vivendi prevailed, as the bishops sought to avoid conflict. Francesco Sforza, the Duke of Milan, ingeniously sought to keep the bishops out of hospital affairs in his city, though he did not go so far as to provoke an open break with the Church on the question.

In the Empire it was common for cities to assume control of hospitals within their walls. A study of 424 hospitals has shown that one third dated from the fourteenth century; 109 were endowed by city governments, 94 by private individuals, and 28 by confraternities. In other words, half of all hospitals had been built at the behest of bourgeois citizens belonging to the governing classes. The secular clergy were responsible for 65 hospitals, and the monastic orders (mendicants and hospitallers) for 50. It is uncertain who endowed the remainder of the hospitals. City governments assumed control over 80 hospitals in addition to those that they had endowed. This occurred especially in northern parts of the Empire, where endowments by lay groups were particularly numerous. The city of Gdansk forced the Teutonic Order to relinquish control of the Hospital of the Holy Spirit in 1382. Generally speaking, municipal control was accepted without protest by the confraternities, for example, in Hamburg, where the hospital was jointly managed by lay and ecclesiastical authorities. In the fourteenth century it was so widely accepted that hospitals were communal institutions that episcopal intervention in administrative matters was looked upon as illegitimate. In 1341 the city council of Halle excluded ecclesiastics from any role in the administration of the hospital. And the following statement concerning the *hôpital* Saint-Nicolas in Metz is rather astonishing: 'The hospital is not a house of God.'' Perhaps this was a complaint against the usurpation of the rightful place of the sick and the poor by healthy persons receiving stipends from the Church, in view of which cities such as Cologne, Freiburg-im-Breisgau, Goslar, Lüneburg, Bremen, Lübeck, and Frankfurt-am-Oder established *Gasthaüse* and *Gotteskeller* for the poor in the fifteenth century. In Switzerland it was held in 1491 that each canton should as a matter of principle assume responsibility for the poor.

Another significant indication of the concern to provide effective relief was the amalgamation of small charitable institutions into larger ones. The smaller hospitals were inefficient and hard to supervise, so that assistance was spread too thin. The need for amalgamation was widely felt. Approval from church authorities, perhaps even from the pope, was normally required if the hospitals involved enjoyed special privileges. The support of the prince was also needed. In practice, city and national governments simply required smaller hospitals to associate with a larger one or established a large new hospital to replace a number of older, smaller ones.

The need for amalgamation arose as a result of economic difficulties, an increase in the poor population, and demands on government to maintain order. In France it was felt as early as the fourteenth century in Aix-en-Provence: the *hôpital* Saint-Jacques annexed the *hôpital* Sainte-Marie-Madeleine some time between 1370 and 1380 and around 1400 was itself absorbed by the *hôpital* Saint-Sauveur. But all the hospitals of the city were not combined until 1581.

In the Iberian peninsula, Portugal began to regulate its hospital facilities in 1430. When a new hospital was built in Tomar in 1437, Dom Duarte obtained Eugenius IV's permission to combine all the hospitals of that city. Further bulls in 1479, 1486, and 1499 facilitated operations in such major cities as Lisbon, Coïmbra, Santarem, and Evora. The establishment of *misericordias* and *mercearias* open to impoverished individuals from the upper strata of society reflects the same trend toward larger institutions. In Castille and Aragon events followed a similar pattern. In the middle of the fifteenth century six hospitals in Barcelona merged. Bishops frequently petitioned Rome for authorization to merge several hospitals: for example, the bishop of Lerida applied for permission to merge six hospitals in his city. Many mergers were delayed until the sixteenth century.

Mergers began in Italy in the fourteenth century, when, for example, the hospital of the confraternity of Santa Maria Novella in Ferrara merged with the older hospital of the Montini to form, in 1354, the Ospedale dei Battuti Bianchi. By the fifteenth century mergers had taken place in all the major cities, for example, in Genoa in 1423, Turin in 1430, Florence in 1436, Como and Crema in 1468, Piacenza in 1471, Rome in 1475, and Ferrara in 1478. Somewhat belatedly, Venice established a sort of reception center for the poor at Campo Sant'Antonio in 1471.

There were other reasons for mergers beyond the obvious administrative and financial advantages. The improvement of roads favored the growth of hospitals in major urban centers, as did advancements in the art of medicine. Then, too, this was a period during which the scale of state services generally tended to increase. In addition, the major cities vied with one another for prestige and philanthropic renown. Finally, the growth in the size of hospitals accorded well with Renaissance ideas of architecture and urban design. Milan is in many ways typical. The proposal for a new hospital originated with the archbishop, Cardinal Enrico Rampini, and won the support of the citizenry. Francesco Sforza assumed responsibility for the project, and the pope encouraged the idea. The result was a sort of hospital complex, the Ospedale Maggiore, whose cruciform plan was organized around a central court onto which all departments of the hospital opened. The architect was no less a figure than Filarete (Antonio Averlino). "In thy glorious city of Milan, I built the celebrated inn of Christ's paupers, whose first stone thou thyself hast laid," said the architect in dedicating his *Trattato di Architettura* to Francesco Sforza. The pauper thus took his place in the ideal city of the Renaissance. The example was not without its imitators. Similar renovations had already been made at the Hôtel-Dieu in Paris, but there the final building had drawbacks due to its having evolved from a series of additions. In Bourg-en-Bresse, however, the cruciform plan was adopted with a chapel at the center, and fifty years later the well-known architect Enrique de Eguas used it in Toledo. Building large hospitals soon became fashionable. In 1486 Galeotto Malatesta incorporated the eleven hospitals of Rimini in the Ospedale di Santa Maria della Misericordia. Also worth mentioning is the Ingolstadt Hospital in Bavaria, begun at the behest of the duke in 1434. The Todos os Santos hospital was begun in Lisbon in 1492, while in Spain two hospitals Del Rey were built in Burgos and Seville, the Santa Maria de la Piedad Hospital was built in Medina del Campo, and the Vitoria Hospital was established in Santiago da Compostella. Henry VII of England investigated Florentine models in planning the transformation of the Savoy Palace in London into an almshouse for a hundred paupers.

The reorganization of public assistance was governed by a spirit of rationality, signs of which are also evident in the tendency toward greater specialization and in the insistence on professional competence. In the interest of improving care the authorities insisted on tighter management of hospitals and supervised the work of hospital administrators. Specialization also affected other areas: the physical management of the hospital was increasingly separated from the spiritual ministry of the chaplains. For the first time the hospitals began to make therapy one of their main goals. Gone were the days when the sick and the poor went into hospitals merely to be fed, to grow old, and to die. Men began to believe that diseases could be cured. Saint Antonino held that specialization was indispensable. While it was well and good that brothers and sisters holding "letters of fraternity" granted by bishops should live under a rule inspired by the rule of Saint Augustine, they also needed special virtues if they were to succeed in the hospital setting, namely, patience and kindness.

Antonino also believed that one hospital could not treat many different kinds of patients. Ever since the thirteenth century, attempts had been made to assign specific hospitals or parts of hospitals to specific types of patients, and experiments of this sort grew more frequent in the fourteenth and fifteenth centuries. We need not concern ourselves with the rather special case of leprosariums, which in any case were everywhere on the wane (except in Scotland). In Paris the Quinze-Vingts was devoted to the care of the blind, who continued to receive royal favors; other hospitals were also set aside for the blind, such as the *hôpital* Rose (after the name of its founder) established in Meaux in 1356. A new and less censorious attitude developed in relation to the mentally ill, who, in the words of Michel Foucault, had previously lived "on the periphery of medieval man's concern." Did the number of lunatics increase in the fourteenth and fifteenth centuries, or was it simply that more attention was paid to them? The mad were still kept in chains at St. Mary's of Bedlam in London, the first mental hospital, of which the earliest mention dates from 1370. The second known asylum was the Tollkiste of Hamburg, established in 1375. In Nüremberg lunatics were arrested and banished from the city in the middle of the fifteenth century. Sailors were sometimes hired—as in Frankfurt in 1399—to relieve society of the burden of the mad, by what means we do not know. The number of houses of detention for the mad increased, with new ones established in Valencia in 1410, Saragossa in 1425, and Seville and Valladolid in 1436. Certain wards were set aside for lunatics at Saint Revilian's Hospital in Cologne, and there were lunatic asylums in Bamberg, Lübeck, and Esschingen. In the late fifteenth century the Tables of the Holy Spirit in Brussels were ordered to give help to the insane until construction could be completed on a special building known as the Simplehuys. And there was yet another malady that became the object of specialized medical attention at the end of the fifteenth century: syphilis, for whose victims so-called Hospitals of the Incurables were opened in Strasbourg (1496), Nüremberg, Erfurt, Lüneburg, and various cities in Italy.

There were also institutions specialized in the treatment of certain occupational groups and people in unusual situations. Persistent suspicion of sailors led to the establishment of special institutions devoted to their care. Venice established a sailors' home inside the walls of the Misericordia in 1385; from 1500 on, sailors were entitled to retire to the San Nicolò di Castello hospital. For additional examples we may turn to the Iberian peninsula at the time of the first major discoveries: En Bou, a Valencia merchant, founded a hospital for fishermen in 1396. The Hospital of the Holy Spirit in Porto was managed by *pilotos, mestres e mareantes*. At Puerto Santa Maria a confraternity maintained a hospital for galley slaves (which we know to have been in operation in 1512). Abroad there were many such institutions: sailors' homes in Madeira (established in 1479 and 1484) and homes for wounded soldiers and prisoners escaped from Saracen jails at Ceuta (1450). In London in 1454 a Salter's Almshouse was opened for men and women who worked in the salt trade.

There were also specialized hospitals serving people in unusual situations. In Cologne, for example, there was a hospital for Jewish converts and catechumens, a change from the usual anti-Semitism. For the sake of completeness, mention should also be made of hospitals set aside for members of specific occupational groups, generally run by guilds or confraternities: in Florence, for example, there were hospitals for porters, dyers, and blacksmiths, and in Strasbourg for cobblers.

Less novel were shelters for penitents, such as those at Avignon (1374), Marseilles (1381), Venice (1357), Strasbourg, Worms, Regensburg, and Erfurt (all in the fifteenth century), and the *hôpital* Sainte-Madeleine in Paris (1483). Some of the *béguinages* played a similar role, though most served as retirement homes. Old men usually found homes in the general hospitals, though there were a few special homes for the aging poor (for example, in Augsburg in 1353 and Bremen in 1366). Women in labor went to special wards nearly everywhere, and the popularity of this custom grew steadily.

‡ New concern was shown for the well-being of orphans and foundlings. Northern cities such as Lille, Saint-Omer, and Douai appointed officials known as *gard'orphènes* to protect orphans and their inheritances, possibly in conjunction with a guild or confraternity if the child's father had been a member of one of these organizations. From the middle of the fourteenth century on, foundling hospitals and orphanages were established all over Europe. There were fewer, apparently, in the northern countries than in western and southern Europe, though the sources mention such institutions in Vienna, Ulm, and Cracow. In London the Orphan Court and Chamberlain were responsible for the safety of orphans. In France the *hôpital du* Saint-Esprit-en-Grève was established by a Parisian confraternity in 1363 to take in abandoned children of legitimate birth as well as children under the age of nine who had lost both father and mother. The hospital was home to some fifty boys and girls in 1409 and two hundred a century later. Children whose parents were patients of the Hôtel-Dieu or who died there were also supposed to be accepted by the Saint-Esprit, but since this was not the case the Hôtel-Dieu kept the children in horrible conditions until 1536, when François I established the *hôpital des Enfants-Dieu*, later known as the Enfants Rouges because of the red uniform the children wore. Other cities had similar hospitals: e.g., Marseilles (1371). In Aix a *charité*, probably a confraternity, took care of orphans. In the fifteenth century there were apparently more orphanages in Italy than in France. The orphanage in Genoa is well known, but even more celebrated was the Innocenti of Florence (1444).

As for foundlings, children whose parents were unknown, it took some time before attention was paid to their unhappy lot. Theirs was truly a miserable existence: in some years the infant mortality rate ran as high as 80 percent, even at the Hôtel-Dieu in Paris. The Bourgeois of Paris tells of being horrified at this fact. Neglected by the civil authorities, foundlings were generally cared for by church officials. There were beds or altars in some churches where unwanted babies could be left: in Paris there was the "bed of Our Lady" at Notre-Dame and in Poitiers the "bed of Our Lady of the Straw" at Saint-Cyprien. In the early sixteenth century the Paris chapter appointed a "children's guardian," who was responsible for some sixty children. In Rouen, Poitiers, and Lausanne the city paid for the nurse. In Germany there were homes for foundlings in Cologne, Augsburg, Munich, Nüremberg, and Ulm. The home in Ulm housed two hundred foundlings in 1500. In Italy there were foundling homes in Pavia and Florence and, in Naples, the celebrated Annunziata.

On the whole, there seems to have been a tendency toward increased specialization in hospitals whose primary clientele was poor. Progress in medicine was slow, but efforts were made to make hospitals places that truly cared for the ill. The food given to patients shows how little was known about proper diet. It was a long while before beds ceased to be assigned to two or three people at a time, but by the fourteenth century some hospitals had begun to isolate patients with contagious diseases. The need for a period of in-hospital convalescence (for example, a week was allowed in Rheims) was increasingly accepted. It took a long time, however, for the idea to take hold that hospital personnel should have medical or paramedical training. The Hôtel-Dieu in Paris had a surgeon on its staff in 1328. Guy de Chauliac practiced at Saint-Just in Lyons in 1367. The Children's Hospital at Genoa had a physician, a surgeon, and a barber on its staff in 1373. In 1396 the city of Basel paid a physician to examine lepers. Around the same time John of Mirfield was attached to St. Bartholomew's Hospital in London. In 1434 a barber was employed by the Hôtel-Dieu in Lyons as well as Marseilles. In the mid-fifteenth century the council of Dijon paid a physician to visit poor patients in their homes. At the end of the century the council of Nantes hired two apothecaries, a surgeon, and a physician for its Hôtel-Dieu. And finally, to look ahead just a bit, one can hardly fail to recall that the great François Rabelais practiced medicine at the Grand Hôtel-Dieu in Lyons in 1532. As the principles of specialization, competence, and efficacy gradually took hold, the hospital came into its own as a therapeutic institution. And no doubt André Vauchez is right to add the following observation: "No sooner did hospitals cease to accept the vagabonds, beggars, and pilgrims who had accounted for a considerable portion of their clientele . . . than they began to exhibit the first signs of a growing tendency toward medical specialization." Thus to complete our analysis of those late medieval attitudes that survived to become a model for early modern medical care, we must now look at how the "bad" paupers were evicted from the hspitals so that the "good" ones might receive more effective treatment.

‡ Social attitudes from the middle of the fourteenth century on were shaped by the idea that some people deserve charity, namely, those who through no fault of their own are unable to live by the fruits of their labor. Society's pity was reserved for them alone. The increase in the number of "able-bodied beggars" after the middle of the fourteenth century aroused instinctive, unthinking defensive reactions intended to "reduce beggars and vagabonds to obedience." Even before the plague was over, countries all over Europe, from Poland to Portugal, took steps to suppress begging and vagabondage, acting with remarkable simultaneity in the brief period 1347–51. National and city governments repeatedly promulgated laws against begging, indicating that these laws were often ineffective or unenforced or else that the seriousness of the begging problem had in the meantime increased. Begging posed a serious threat to order, society, and morality. It was not enough to establish criteria for distinguishing between those paupers deemed worthy of assistance and others dismissed as reprobates, for to do so was to make social outcasts of large numbers of the wretched, against whom drastic measures might then be required. Repression was coupled with would-be correction in the form of rules and regulations governing the behavior of beggars and vagabonds: the "idle" were required to work, for example, and the homeless were required to live in shelters for the poor. Thus the men of the late Middle Ages in some ways anticipated the future policing of the poor.

In the view of contemporaries, measures designed to preserve order were in the interest of all the poor. By distinguishing between the deserving poor and the rest, such measures protected the reputation and the rights of the deserving. Those who were not deemed worthy were offered the opportunity to mend their ways and regain their place in society. For some, no doubt, this kind of reasoning was nothing more than face-saving rationalization, but there is no reason to doubt the sincerity of others in making such arguments.

The measures actually taken were remarkably similar from country to country and city to city. The idle and the homeless were the principal targets. Though impossible to prevent, begging was made subject to various regulations. In England in 1350 begging was made illegal for all but those over sixty years of age or unable to work. Beggars in many cities were required to wear insignia, often regarded (perhaps wrongly) as badges of infamy. Or San Michele in Florence and the Poor Tables in the North gave such insignia to their clients. In Lille in the fifteenth century patients at the Countess Hospital who wore the hospital badge were allowed to beg in the streets. Even authorized begging could not be carried on just anywhere. In Paris, for example, beggars were assigned specific places; this was also the case in Malines and Mons. Begging in churches was generally forbidden. England was especially strict: on several occasions (in 1388, 1405, and 1509) paupers were forbidden to leave their place of birth or residence.

Beggars who wished to travel in England after 1388 were required to obtain passes from the county justice of the peace. Vagabondage was even more severely restricted than begging. By 1350 the English authorities were tracking down fugitives. By the end of the fifteenth century French roads were also closely watched. In 1473 the Paris Parlement established a system for the control of begging and vagabondage, capping an array of penalties including imprisonment, branding with a hot iron, and banishment—penalties that had been steadily increased since 1351. In England a tramp caught on the road without a highway pass was branded with a hot iron. Municipal laws were just as strict. Some towns refused to allow "passing" vagrants to stay for more than one night, on pain of death by hanging for all violators. Hostels were carefully watched in all countries—in England, in the Empire, in Spain, and in France (for example, Tours and Poitiers). In Venice in the fourteenth century, beggars were required to sign up for distributions at a hospital or else to leave the city. In the following century Genoa did not even allow them this option: beggars were simply expelled. London did the same in 1359. And punishments were not merely meted out to unauthorized beggars and tramps: in England, for instance, anyone who gave illicit alms could also be sent to prison. In Mons in 1403 and later in Louvain in response to an ordinance promulgated by Philip the Good in 1458, the Poor Tables were forbidden to distribute charity indiscriminately to all comers.

In the middle of the fourteenth century ordinances were passed in many countries to force able-bodied paupers and vagabonds to work. Ways of creating new work were sought. In 1367, Hugues Aubriot, the provost of Paris, offered the "idle" money for dredging the city's moats and repairing its fortifications. The seneschal of Toulouse tried the same experiment twenty-eight years later. These initiatives were distant precursors of the "charity workshops." Aubriot's ordinance also included a provision that vagabonds could be sent to work "in other places where someone may want to hire them." In Castille at about the same time private landowners were authorized to arrest vagabonds and put them to work without pay for one month. The idea of forced labor was in the air and gradually extended its influence. Compulsory workers were not upset in 1486 when they were asked to dredge the Morin River to make it fit for navigation or to clean the streets of the capital. They had already known better and worse treatment elsewhere. Jacques Coeur is said to have initiated the idea of sending vagabonds to the galleys, which benefited from this supply of cheap labor. This practice is referred to in an ordinance of 1400, which mentions the embarkation of "worthless men," In 1456, the Estates of Languedoc followed Jacques Coeur's lead by suggesting that the region could be cleared of vagabonds "by putting them in the galleys." The Duke of Savoy, in making preparations for an expedition to Cyprus in 1462, found galley slaves ready to hand among the vagabonds of Geneva.

Forced laborers and galley slaves call to mind one final group of poor men and women with which the Middle Ages had always had to contend and which it bequeathed to the Europe of the Age of Discovery: the slaves. Present in large numbers in cities along the Mediterranean, slaves lived in a variety of conditions. Legally, all were the property of their masters. But some enjoyed relatively good treatment as domestics or scribes, while others formed a wretched proletariat. In Genoa, for example, at the end of the fifteenth century, several thousand slaves were employed as manual laborers and in the galleys. Many slaves were natives of the Black Sea region. By the middle of the fifteenth century, however, these slaves began to be replaced by others, imported from Africa in the most frightful of conditions. The chronicler Zurara has left us a description of a slave market in Lagos in which apparently sincere compassion for the plight of the slaves is offset by the traditional idea that their slavery is somehow justified by disbelief in Christ. It took centuries for humanist attitudes to make any difference in the way people thought about certain matters, such as slavery.

Both in converting the slaves to Christianity and in controlling the behavior of beggars and vagabonds the intention was the same: to encourage moral and social rehabilitation. The idea of bringing vagabonds and beggars together in poor shelters began to gain popularity at the end of the fourteenth century. Gerson refers to "enclosed" and "unenclosed" paupers, but by this he meant those who lived in hospitals as opposed to those who lived by begging. He took no position as to which kind was preferable. But some charitable individuals saw no way of providing food, shelter, and work for the indigent other than grouping them together in huge hospices. Siena and Milan—to name only two examples—had already begun to confine the poor. In 1396 Giangaleazzo Visconti asserted that the pauper's place is in the hospital, and he appointed a commission to find the poor and intern them. The danger of such an approach was that it might well overwhelm hospital facilities, at a time when the trend in many cities was to allow beggars and vagabonds into hospitals only when necessary to receive distributions. On the other hand, the idea of locking up the poor accorded well with the trend toward building large hospices. These conflicting tendencies point up the magnitude of the problems faced by a society which, unable to eliminate poverty, had to content itself with alleviating indigence and hiding its miseries.

CONCLUSION ‡

Perhaps nature made those people to be tramps.
—Erasmus

Is this book too long or too short? Probably both. In any case, I have attempted to trace, over the course of a millennium, the history of people who have left no records and who remain largely unknown. We found the poor anonymous and hidden from view when we began, and we leave them still in obscurity as we near the end of our survey. But we have observed important changes in the poor as a group as we worked our way toward the present. For one thing, there are more of them by the year 1500 than there were when we began. Still on the bottom rung of the social ladder, their presence is more keenly felt than ever before.

We also found a greater variety in poverty as time went by. The poor were not all alike and yet all shared the same inability to cope with adversity without assistance, the same moral and physical dependency. Consider for a moment the paupers of Europe arrayed in a great procession. In the vanguard remains the traditional pauper, to whom the monk lent his title as "Christ's pauper" and his position as a suffering member of the Communion of Saints: he is the man struck down by sickness, age, or misfortune, physically or mentally incapable of earning his own living. Next in line, and sharing the same religious connotation of the word *pauper*, are the victims of violence of all kinds, from the most barbarous ages of feudalism to the waning years of the Middle Ages. No one ever challenged the right of these victims to be called poor. First come the weak who lived overshadowed by their powerful neighbors, then the humble who faced disaster with the aid of their brethren in the faith, and finally the indigent whose work did not bring them enough to survive.

In effect it was labor—or the function corresponding to a man's social estate—that determined the pauper's character: his worthiness to receive aid from others depended on whether he was unfit for work, unable to find work, or unwilling to engage in work. It took a long time before inadequate income or the inability to find work were recognized as signs of a new and growing form of destitution, which we have called "working poverty." The reason why society was slow to recognize this new type of poverty was that many people were worried about the problem posed by social outcasts, vagabonds, slackers, and fake beggars, collectively designated as "tramps." Distinctions were drawn between the "true pauper" and the "unworthy beggar," between the "peaceful" and the "threatening" poor.

How did the importance of poverty as a social fact vary with the number of paupers? In medieval history we can have quantitative understanding even without the magical precision of numbers. The impressionistic responses of the chroniclers to figures they glean here and there are often more revealing than raw numbers painstakingly extracted from the sources. It would be hard to interpret these data without indications of a qualitative order. Poverty changed its nature often and existed in many forms. Prior to the eleventh century the general level of economic development was low and everyone lived in precarious conditions, so that dependency rather than wealth determined who was a pauper and who was not. The number of peasants was large, but their influence on society was ordinarily negligible. Only a disaster of some kind could increase the number of the starving (who came from all strata of society) to levels perceived as dangerous. For the late Middle Ages, careful analysis of census data and tax rolls can be used to verify qualitative estimates of the number of people belonging to various categories of indigents. It may be that the number of paupers declined relative to the early Middle Ages, but the nature of poverty had meanwhile changed and many found even its existence a troubling phenomenon. By the fourteenth or fifteenth century a poverty rate of 30–40 percent in a city might pose a greater problem than did an 80-percent poverty rate among tenth-century peasants. How do we account for this?

It is unnecessary to point out that misery and the economy follow similar cycles. We see a striking example of this in the fourteenth century and again at the beginning of the sixteenth century. Aberrations in wage and price levels, primarily in the cities but also in the countryside, were further accentuated by serious food shortages in the years after 1520, as has recently been conclusively demonstrated in several regional studies. All the age-old elements of poverty seem to have converged. But the pauper's lot depends on more than just the economic, social, technological, and political circumstances. What we somewhat pedantically refer to as structures, infrastructures, and superstructures mutually interact. And since every human being's lot depends in part on the way his condition is seen by others, the situation of the poor depends on how the poor themselves, and society at large, view poverty.

It is not always easy to guess how the poor see themselves. At times they have left it to others to express their resignation and weariness. At other times they have shown themselves to be angry, aggrieved, or rebellious but have left it to others to proclaim their anger to the world. Occasionally we glimpse the first glimmerings of collective consciousness of shared adversity, for example, in the peace movements of the eleventh century or with the rebels of 1380 or, later, among the Hussites. Signs of dawning collective consciousness are still more obvious in the Peasant Wars of 1520. And recall the abstract significance of the signature "Povre" on a manifesto that appeared in Lyons in 1529, which reads, "Know that we are four to five hundred men and that we are allied."[1] The disinherited might of course choose to reject society, to threaten it and rebel against it rather than to live at its expense. But in reality the poor often behaved like eternal children, dependent on others and even defined by external perceptions. The economy and the social structure were not alone responsible for misery, for responsibility is always a matter of conscience.

We have not come close to resolving the many problems that the subject of poverty poses for the historian. The question of the physical condition of the poor remains unresolved, in part because we lack the resources to settle it definitively. Beyond that, the moral and social implications of poverty are largely untouched. Part of the difficulty is that poverty, in all its forms, is still but one aspect of the problem of evil, and the men and women of the early sixteenth century seem to have experienced a heightened consciousness of evil. What had been an individual affliction became a social scourge. Poverty, once seen as a consequence of, and punishment for, individual sin, was later considered a form of social parasitism or even (as in the case of beggary) a crime. It should be kept in mind that people were frightened of the sheer numbers of the poor and that old disputes about the religious importance of voluntary poverty had for many people detracted from the spiritual value of poverty. For example, Poggio, in his *De Avaritia*, stigmatized the mendicant friars as "worms who live in idleness thanks to our labor." Yet Poggio was a contemporary of the Observance. Humanist praise for success, with its concomitant exaltation of wealth, eventually contaminated the poor themselves, who were rightly or wrongly accused of giving in to the natural tendency of the poor man to envy or desire the comforts of the rich.

What was the good, then, of centuries of charity, if the number of the poor increased and their situation worsened? Was Saint Francis's view of the poor forgotten by a generation that still continued to pay homage to his name, the generation of Francesco Sforza, Francis of Paola, King Francis I, and François Rabelais? Was humanism, which aimed to be a philosophy of men thinking about men, nothing but a game for the intellectual elite, a philosophy that could find no place in its scheme of things for the unfortunate, whom it did nothing to rehabilitate but rather condemned to a life of wretchedness and confinement? Writers drew hideous portraits of tramps who would one day become models for grotesque sculpture and painting. Even Erasmus finally conceded that "perhaps nature made those people to be tramps." Thomas More's knowledge of the problem of pauperism enabled him to speculate about it in *Utopia*, but he did not feel it.[2] And what about the efforts to rationalize and upgrade charitable institutions and to bring them under the auspices of city and national governments? Did these ultimately rob charity of its sacred character? Francis Rapp has rightly denounced the "deep disparity between charity, which gives without asking to what use its generous gifts will be put, and (public) assistance, which calculates and gives aid only for reasons of its own." Rapp also points out another disparity, in which "being poor" becomes primarily a state of mind and "giving to the poor" is transformed into an institution.

Once again, changes in language reflect changing ideas and misrepresent changing attitudes. A new word came into use as a rival to *charity* and *mercy: beneficence* (with its equivalents in other languages), a precursor of the more modern *benevolence*, which first came into use (in French) in the eighteenth century, along with *philanthropy*. Did profane reason win out over religious sentiment? Did humanist concern for the dignity of man blind humanists to the plight of the poor? And meanwhile, governments guided by the principle of *raison d'état* invented the idea of policing the poor—an idea more rational than it is charitable.

Did medieval charity ultimately end in failure? And did the Church fail in its oft-invoked and oft-affirmed mission to protect and rehabilitate the poor? Were the protests that developed in the name of poverty within the Church itself and in order to remind that institution of its exemplary role and to call the faithful to charity—were those protests insufficient, and did they fail to achieve their goal? Were the serenity of the Benedictines and the goodness of the Franciscans eroded by time and diverted from their original purpose? Did Christians neglect the poor and make themselves and their own salvation the chief focus of their almsgiving? Were not the hopes of the poor allowed to dilute themselves in the form of millenarian illusions, whose indefinitely postponed day of reckoning cost the wealthy but little anxiety? And were not the protests and agitations of the poor often left to heterodox voices and thus confounded with heresy?

The final balance would appear to be negative. The economy developed in such a way that society could no longer ignore the presence of the poor. The poor occupied the lower rungs of the social ladder, and before long even the most intractable of tramps would be confined in poor houses and assigned a place at once outside and inside the social structure. But was this outcome really a failure of charity, or rather a momentary lapse? The Church no longer had the wherewithal to cope by itself with problems that had grown too large for it to handle. But the legacy of the Middle Ages also had its moral component, without which benevolence in all its forms is mere bureaucracy. In the thirteenth century William Peyrault had taken as a sign the reversal of fortunes of the "pauper" and the "wicked rich man" of the Gospels. Even in the Renaissance this antithesis preserved its value: the pauper, received into the bosom of Abraham, was immortalized and given his own name, Lazarus, whereas the Eternal One refused to give a name to the miser relegated for all eternity to Gehenna. Social and economic change affected the fate of the downtrodden. Change was like a litmus paper that revealed men's deepest attitudes toward poverty. Through the accumulated crust of centuries medieval Christendom's old mental infrastructures reemerged in each critical phase. The return to the Gospel animated the hermits of the eleventh and twelfth centuries and inspired the mendicant friars in their efforts to rehabilitate poverty. Christian humanists scoured the Bible and the Fathers to restore the tarnished luster of old ideas. Natalie Zemon Davis has shown how the thinking of Augustine, Jerome, and Gregory Nazianzen was revived in humanist social theory and practice. In Geneva, bound together in one old binding, are two works, each quite different from the other though both deal with the same subject and both were printed at Lyons by Sebastien Grypheus in 1539: one is a translation of Gregory Nazianzen's treatise on the love of the poor, printed under the title *The Care and Feeding of the Poor*, while the other is a copy of *The Policy of Alms*. Here we see two sources of inspiration with but one objective. It would be pleasant to be able to say that fear of the poor marked the beginning of wisdom. It is more certain that the idea of the pauper as an image of the suffering Christ remained alive. To be sure, Protestantism would do away with the Catholic idea that good works and the suffering of the poor cooperate to bring about redemption. But both Catholic and Protestant traditions, nourished in the same soil, hold that charity is the primary instrument for the rehabilitation of the poor. It was not for nothing that Juan Luis Vivès in 1526 bestowed the title *De sub-elevatione pauperum* upon a program that bears a remarkable similarity to a celebrated sermon preached by Jean de Vauzelles in Lyons in 1532. For our purposes it is of little importance that contemporary criticism of individual alms and praise for institutionalized public assistance resulted in charges of heresy against both of these documents. It was prophetic of things to come that Catholics in Spain and early Protestant reformers in Lyons should have reacted in similar ways: in Lyons, where the street in which Waldo had lived still attracted pilgrims, we find a Poor Office, a General Alms, a General Hospital, and a Supreme Charity—these are the names given to the new forms of public assistance that began to develop around 1520. In fact they are direct descendants of traditional medieval institutions. What better proof could there be of the close relationship between sixteenth-century "beneficence" and medieval "mercy." The poor are now more numerous, more diverse, more insistently present. The name and face of mercy may have changed, but by nature it is still Charity, which like Poverty is always with us.

REFERENCE MATTER ‡
LIST OF ABBREVI-
ATIONS; NOTES;
NOTE ON SOURCES;
BIBLIOGRAPHY;
INDEX ‡

ABBREVIATIONS ‡

AHR	American Historical Review
Ann. ESC	Annales: Economies, Sociétés, Civilisations
ASBHH	Annales de la Société belge d'Histoire des Hôpitaux
Atti Sett. La Mendola	Atti delle Settimane internazionali di Studio de La Mendola
Atti Sett. Spoleto	Atti delle Settimane di Studio del Centro Italiano di Studi sull' Alto Medioevo di Spoleto
BCRH	Bulletin de la Commission Royale d'Histoire de Belgique
BEC	Bibliothèque de l'Ecole des Chartes
B. Phil. Hist.	Bulletin de Philologie et d'Histoire
BSFHH	Bulletin de la Société française d'Histoire des Hôpitaux
Cah. Fanjeaux	Cahiers de Fanjeaux, Toulouse
Cah. Sorb.	Cahiers de Recherches sur l'Histoire de la Pauvreté, 10 vols., Paris-Sorbonne, 1962–77.
CCSL	Corpus Christianorum Series Latina
CESO	Atti del primo congresso europeo di Storia Ospitaleria, Reggio Emilia, 1960 (ed. 1962)
CISO	Atti del primo congresso italiano di Storia Ospitaleria, Reggio Emilia, 1965 (ed. 1967)
Conv. Pov. Todi	Povertà e Richezza nellà Spiritualità dei secoli XI e XII (8° Convegno del Centro di Studi sulla Spiritualità Medievale, Todi, 1967 (1969)
CR Acad. IBL	Comptes Rendus de l'Académie des Inscriptions et Belles-Lettres
Ec.H.R.	The Economic History Review
Et. Pauvr.	Etudes sur l'Histoire de la Pauvreté, 2 vols., ed. M. Mollat, Paris, 1974
M.A.	Le Moyen Age
MAHEFR	Mélanges d'Archéologie et d'Histoire de l'Ecole Française de Rome

Mém . . . SAN	Mémoires de la Société des Antiquaires de Normandie
MGH	Monumenta Germanige Historica
P.L.	Patrologiae Cursus, series Latina (Migne)
Pobreza . . . Ibérica	A Pobreza e a Assistência aos Pobres na Peninsula Ibérica durante a Idade Média, 2 vols., V. Rau and F. Saez, eds., Lisbon, 1973
Pov. M.A.	Poverty in the Middle Ages, D. Flood, ed., Paderborn, 1975
R.A.M.	Revue d'Ascétique et de Mystique
R.B.S.	Rerum Britannicarum Scriptores
R.H.	Revue Historique
RHDFE	Revue d'Histoire du Droit Français et Etranger
RHEF	Revue d'Histoire de l'Eglise de France
RHMC	Revue d'Histoire moderne et contemporaine
R.H.S.	Revue d'Histoire de la Spiritualité (a continuation of *R.A.M.*)
R.I.S.	Rerum Italicarum Scriptores
R.N.	Revue du Nord
Spec.	Speculum

NOTES ‡

INTRODUCTION

1. *PL* 187.365G and *pl* 207.575–79.

2. *Scriptores Ord. Grandim.* (De confirmatione), J. Becquet, ed., *CCSL* 8 (1968), 366.

3. The Hebrew word *anawim* (sing. *ani*), which refers to the poor in general, acquired a connotation of humility meaning "one who did not try to outwit the Lord." See M. Gelin, *Les Pauvres de Yahvé* (Paris, 1953), p. 65.

CHAPTER TWO

1. Michel Rouche, "La Faim à l'époque carolingienne," *RH* 508 (1973), pp. 295–320.

2. Homily 41.

3. Homilies 152, 182.

4. *Formulae Turonenses* 43, *MGH, Formulae,* I, 258 (Hanover, 1882).

5. 836, Canon 3.

6. It is not beyond the realm of possibility that in a time of overpopulation some poor peasant families were forced to resort to infanticide, especially of baby girls. See R. Coleman, "L'Infanticide dans le haut Moyen Age," *Ann:ESC* 29 (1974), pp. 315–35.

7. Anségis Collection 827.

8. Capitulary of 850.

9. *MGH, Passiones,* III, 323–24.

10. Sixth Council of Paris, 829, c. 53, Mansi XV, 570 E.

CHAPTER THREE

1. *Habous,* or *waqfs,* are mortmain properties established by pious or charitable gift.

2. Council of Agde of 506; Council of Orléans of 546.

3. Homily 277.

4. Council of Mâcon of 585.

5. The terms *matricula, matricularius* were still in use in the fourteenth century. The former referred to the poor list or poor house, the latter either to the person responsible for distributing relief or to the person receiving relief (Lausanne, 1377). See A. Briod, *L'Assistance des pauvres au Moyen Age dans le pays de Vaud* (Lausanne, 1926, repr. 1976).

6. I borrow this phrase from Jean Devisse, *Hincmar, archévêque de Reims (845–882),* 3 vols. (Lille-Geneva, 1976).

7. *PL* 119.703–26, XV, chap. 33.

8. Ibid.

9. *PL* 87.533.

10. Better known now than they were in the past, the Benedictine customaries for the most part take their inspiration from the regulations for Aix established by Benedict of Aniane in 817–20, even those drafted in the wake of the reforms sponsored by Cluny (founded in 909). There are several groups of customaries: the Anglo-Norman group, which show signs of Lorraine influence spread by Lanfranc; the Cluniac group, related to the customaries of Farfa in Italy and of the Spanish abbeys; the Fleury-sur-Loire and Dijon group, affiliated with Italy through William of Volpiano; and the imperial group (with Treves and Regensburg), with which Saint-Vanne in eastern France was associated. W. Witters, "Pauvres et pauvreté dans les coutumes monastiques du Moyen Age," *Et. Pauvr.,* 177–216.

11. Witters, "Pauvres et pauvreté," 210, Council of Libelli, c. 14.

12. Ed. U. Chevalier (Paris, 1884), pp. 25–27.

CHAPTER FOUR

1. Ed. F.-J. Tanquerey (Paris, 1922), p. 52.

2. In twelfth-century Iceland, the Church followed the curious practice of permitting divorce in couples where one spouse was responsible for very poor relatives (*omagi*) and did not have enough property to provide for them. *Omagi* could be minors, aged persons, invalids, indigents, or vagabonds. See R. Boyer, "La vie religieuse en Islande (1116–1264)," Ph.D. diss., University of Lille, 1972, I, 26–27, (382–83).

3. Peter the Chanter, *Verbum Abbreviatum,* in *PL* 205.279.

4. Archives of the Eure *département,* H 506.

5. Following up the early work of R. Genestal, *Le rôle des monastères comme établissements de crédit, étudié en Normandie du XIe à la fin du XIIIe siècle* (Paris, 1901), R. Fossier, *La Terre et les Hommes en Picardie jusqu'à la fin du XIIIe s.,* 2 vols. (Paris-Louvain, 1968), has noted the use of mortgages by the priory of Hesdin (pp. 614–15). A Chedeville, *Chartres et ses campagnes, XIe–XIIIe s.* (Paris, 1973), notes opposition to the prohibition (pp. 463–68), and P. Toubert (see bibliography) discusses the importance of rural credit in Lazio (pp. 615–19).

6. *MGH, SS,* VI, 453.

7. Cited by A. Luchaire, *La Société française au temps de Philippe Auguste* (Paris, 1909), p. 412.

8. J. de Garlande, "Dictionnarius," ed. T. Wright, *A Volume of Vocabularies* (1873), I. 128–35.

9. Chrétien de Troyes, *Yvain ou Le Chevalier au Lion*, ed. Foerster (Halle, 1891), at 5300–01, 5318–19.

CHAPTER FIVE

1. M.-C. Wintrebert, "L'Aumône du chevalier dans la littérature du XIIe siècle," Ph.D. diss., Paris, 1965.

2. Robert of Clari, *Conquête de Constantinople*, ed. P. Lauer (Paris, 1924), and *Devastatio Constantinipolitina, MGH, SS*, XVI. See also Alphandéry and A. Dupront, *La Chrétienté et l'idée de Croisade* (Paris, 1959); J. Le Goff, "Riches et pauvres à la quatrième croisade," *Cah. Sorb.* 4; G. Miccoli, "Dal Pellegrinaggio alla conquista: Povertá e Ricchezza nella prima Crociate," *Conv. Pov. Todi*, pp. 43–80.

3. *PL* 207.1069.

4. This stick, which was buried with Robert of Arbrissel, is preserved in the priory of Saint Mary at Chemillé (Maine-et-Loire). It was shown in two public expositions of French ecclesiastical treasures, one at Angers in 1960, the other in Paris in 1965.

5. BEC 5 (1854), 225–35.

6. The Tafurs were a band of marauders whose crimes were notorious in Islamic as well as Christian countries.

7. Chronicle of William of Newburgh, *RBS* 82, (London, 1885),2:466–73.

CHAPTER SIX

1. E. Magnou-Nortier, *La Société laïque et l'Eglise dans la province ecclésiastique de Narbonne (zone cispyréenne) de la fin du VIIIe siècle à la fin du XIe* (Toulouse, 1974).

2. Magna vita S. Hugonis, episc. Lincolnensis, ed. J.-F. Dimock, *RBS* 37 (London, 1884).

3. Charter 2112.

4. Chap. 29.

5. Sermon 30, to the nuns of Paraclet.

6. *PL* 205.90, 145.

7. *PL* 207.285–88.

8. *PL* 207.168, 212.

9. *PL* 205.147–53.

10. Sermon "De Cruce," ed. M.-T. d'Alverny (Paris, 1965), p. 283.

CHAPTER SEVEN

1. R. Manselli, *Studi sulle Eresie del secolo XII*, 2d. ed. (Rome, 1975).

2. See M. H. Vicaire, "Les Origines dominicaines de la mendicité religieuse et la condition d'humilité mendiante selon saint Dominique," *La Vie dominicaine* 34 (1975), 195–206, 259–79.

3. Justinian code, Council of Tours of 567, capitulary of 806.

4. Philippe Grand, "Gérard d'Abbéville et la pauvreté volontaire," *Et. Pauvr.*, pp. 389–410.

5. *De emptione et vendicione. Contra impugnantes.*

CHAPTER EIGHT

1. A. Vauchez, "Charité et pauvreté chez sainte Elisabeth de Thuringe, d'après les actes des procès de canonisation," *Et. Pauvr.*, pp. 163–73.

2. M. Candille, "Les Statuts de la maison-Dieu de Vernon," *BSFHH* 24 (1970), 11–33.

3. On Florence cf. Charles de La Roncière, *Et. Pauvr.*, p. 699.

4. Bernard Guénée, *Tribunaux et gens de justice dans le Bailliage de Senlis à la fin du Moyen Age (vers 1300–vers 1550)* (Strasbourg, 1963).

5. R. Favreau, "La pauvreté en Poitou et en Anjou à la fin du Moyen Age," *Et. Pauvr.*, pp. 589–620.

6. J. Avril, "Clercs et laïcs devant la richesee d'après les statuts synodaux d'Angers de la fin du Moyen Age," *Et. Pauvr.*, p. 563.

7. This is the opinion expressed by Lester K. Little in *Et. Pauvr.*, pp. 447–48.

8. R. C. Texler, "Charity and the Defense of Urban Elites in the Italian Communes," *The Rich, the Well-Born and the Powerful*, ed. F. Jaher (Urbana, 1974), pp. 63–107.

CHAPTER NINE

1. Economic historians have expressed considerable skepticism about King's Law, as it is called, according to which rises in grain prices parallel—and magnify—shortages in the harvest. Recent work has been much more detailed and subtle. Among the studies that promise to help increase our understanding of living standards of the poor, in addition to works by H. Neveux, G. Sivéry, and H. Van der Wee cited in the bibliography, is the very recent work by M. J. Tits-Dieuaide, *La Formation des prix céréaliers en Brabant et en Flandre au XVe siècle* (Brussels, 1975). See also P. Chaunu and R. Gascon, *Histoire économique et sociale de la France*, vol. 1 (1450–1600) Paris, 1977).

2. Published in *Pobreza . . . Ibérica*, pp. 610–11.

3. Gene A. Brucker, *Florentine Politics and Society* (Princeton, 1962), pp. 54–109.

4. G. Sivéry, *Structures agraires et vie rurale dans le Hainaut à la fin du Moyen Age* (Lille, 1977), vol. 1.

5. Fossier, *La Terre et les hommes.*

6. G. Fourquin, *Les Campagnes de la région parisienne à la fin du Moyen Age* (Paris, 1964).

7. At 1111–13, ed. E. Martin (Halle, 1869), cited by Jean Batany in *Et. Pauvr.*, p. 478.

8. Published by J.-L. Martin in *Probreza . . . Ibérica*, p. 611.

9. P. Desportes, "Les Pauvres à Reims au début du XIVe siècle," *Cah. Sorb.* 7.

10. R. Lavoie, "Pauvreté et criminalité en Provence à la fin du Moyen Age," notes from a seminar held at the Sorbonne in May 1974 and published in *Provence historique* (1977).

11. L. Génicot, "Sur le nombre des pauvres dans les campagnes médiévales," *RH* 522 (1977), 273–88.

12. J. Heers, *Fêtes et jeux dans les sociétés d'Occident à la fin du Moyen Age* (Montreal-Paris, 1971).

13. C. Gaignebet, "Le combat de Carnaval et de Carême de P. Bruegel (1559)," in *Ann: ESC* (1972), 313–46.

14. *Bulletin de la Société Néophilologique d'Helsinki*, ed. A. Langfors (1947).

15. *Renart*, sec. 1, 532–33.

16. P. Bonnefant, "Hôpitaux et bienfaisance publique dans les Anciens Pays-Bas," *ASBHH* 3 (1965), 1–194.

17. Génicot, "Sur le nombre des pauvres."

18. A. Langfors, ed., *Miracles de Gautier de Coincy*, (Helsinki, 1937).

19. P. M. Dufeil, *Cah. Sorb. 6*.

20. T. Manteuffel, *Naissance d'une hérésie: Les Adeptes de la pauvreté volontaire au Moyen Age* (Paris, The Hague, 1960).

21. Jacques Le Goff, ed., *Hérésies et sociétés dans l'Europe préindustrielle, XIe–XVIIIe siècles* (Paris, 1968), esp. pp. 171–98.

22. N. Guglielmi, "Hérésie et marginalité," *Cah. Sorb. 9*, pp. 71–79.

23. Quodlibet XIV.

CHAPTER TEN

1. The six hundredth anniversary of this event was celebrated with an international congress at Dubrovnik, proceedings of which are currently in publication.

2. *Ordonnances des Rois de France*, II, pp. 350–80.

CHAPTER ELEVEN

1. Dante, *Inferno*, XXI. 68.

2. Bibliothèque nationale, French ms. 167.

3. *Summa Theologica*, Ia, IIae 105, a^2.

4. Cited by J.-L. Roch, "Esquisse d'un vocabulaire français de la pauvreté à la fin du Moyen Age, 1330–1480," Master's thesis, Paris, 1970, p. 73.

5. Cited by Gerson in his sermon *Vivat Rex*, 1405.

CHAPTER TWELVE

1. In *Mutacion de Fortune* V, 172.

2. F. N. Robinson, ed., *The Complete Works of Geoffrey Chaucer* (New York, 1933), p. 75, ll. 99–118—*Trans.*

3. Thanks to this custom we obtain a glimpse of one woman who expresses an interest—rare for this time—in nature with a request that she be allowed to

occupy a "room with a view on the lake" in the hospice of Moudon (Vaud) until she dies. See Briod, *L'Assistance*, p. 63.

4. Chap. 59.

5. Francis Rapp, *Réforme et Réformation à Strasbourg: L'Eglise et la société dans le diocèse de Strasbourg (1450–1525)* (Paris, 1974), pp. 461–62.

CONCLUSION

1. Municipal archives of Lyons, BB 47, published by J.-P. Gutton, *La Société et les pauvres: L'Exemple de la généralité de Lyon, 1534–1789* (Paris, 1971).

2. R. Aulotte, "Les Gueux dans la littérature française du XVIe siècle," in *Misère et gueuserie au temps de la Renaissance: Colloque sur les gueux et gueuserie*, M. Jones-Davies, ed. (Paris-Sorbonne: Center for Renaissance Research, 1976), pp. 109–42.

NOTE ON SOURCES ‡

I. There are few document collections that pertain specifically to the poor who, numerous as they were, left no archives. Historians have their work cut out for them, for they must be constantly on the lookout and gather information wherever it is to be found. Following is a list of the most useful kinds of sources.

A. Sources relating to poor relief: hospital archives, generally stored on the hospital premises; documents of abbatial almonries (in France, series H of the Archives départementales); chapter archives (series G); statutes and accounts of confraternities and poor tables; wills and donations preserved in cartularies and notarial records (series E).

B. Administrative and judicial sources: papal bulls, royal ordinances; minutes and accounts of city councils; census data, cadastral surveys, estimates. Chancellery acts, especially letters of remission. Judgments of the Parlements (especially the Parlement of Paris) and of the penal and criminal courts (*baillis, sénéchaussées*, the Châtelet).

C. Religious sources: besides those listed under *A*, sermons, confessors' manuals, texts, spiritual works, works of theology and canon law, biographies, hagiographies, collections of exempla, florilegia.

D. Chronicles, literary sources, and iconography: the list of possibilities is endless.

II. The study of poverty has been greatly facilitated in recent years by the work of centers for the study of social history that have been established in a number of countries. A number of centers and societies have specialized in the history of poverty and poor relief, especially in France and Belgium, where there are sister societies devoted to this line of research, and in Italy. For several years now there have been increasing numbers of conferences and colloquia devoted to the history of poverty and held in France, Italy, Spain, Portugal, the United States, and Canada. Proceedings of some of these conferences have been published, adding substantially to the literature in the field.

Clearly, it is impossible to give a comprehensive bibliography of so vast a subject. What follows is a brief guide to further reading about the subjects covered in each chapter of this book.

BIBLIOGRAPHY ‡

On the terminology of the poor, see *Et. Pauvr.* 14–15, 35–45, 275–295, 841–842; J. Leclercq, "Pour L'Histoire du vocabulaire latin de la pauvreté," *Mél* . . . *Dib, Melto,* 1967 (Kaslik, Liban), 293–308; J.-L. Roch, *Esquisse d'un vocabulaire français de la pauvreté à la fin du Moyen age, 1330–1480,* Master's thesis, Paris, 1970. Repr. in *Cah. Sorb.* 8, pp. 91–98.

Abel, A. M. "La Pauvreté dans la pensée et la pastorale de saint Cesaire d'Arles." *Et. Pauvr.,* 111–124.
Abel, W. *Agrarkrisen und Agrarkonjunktur.* Hamburg-Berlin, 1935, 1956. Trans. *Crises agraires en Europe, XIIIe–XXe siècle.* Paris, 1973.
Actes du 97e Congrès National des Sociétés Savantes. Nantes, 1972.
Aragoneses, M. J. *Los movimientos y luchas sociales en la baja Edad Media.* Madrid, 1949.
Ariès, Ph. "Richesse et pauvreté devant la mort." *Et. Pauvr.,* 519–34. Repr. in *Essais sur L'histoire de la mort en Occident du Moyen Age à nos Jours,* Paris, 1975.
———. *L'Homme devant la mort.* Paris, 1977.
Arnaud, M. "Les Comptes de l'aumônerie pontificale de la Pignotte d'Avignon au XIVe siècle." Ms. Paris, 1963.
Atti Sett. La Mendola. 1959. *La vita comune del clero nei sec. XI e XII.* Milan, 1962.
———. 1962. *L'eremitismo nei sec. XI e XII.* Milan, 1965.
———. 1965. *I Laici nella "societas christiana" dei sec. XI e XII.* Milan, 1968.
———. 1968. *Il Monachesimo e la Riforma ecclesiastica (1049–1142).* Milan, 1971.
Aubineau, M. "Zoticos de Constantinople, nourricier des pauvres et serviteur des lépreux." *Analecta Bollandiana* 93 (1975), 67–108.
Aulotte, R. "Les Gueux dans la littérature française du XVIe siècle." In Jones-Davies, ed., *Colloque Gueux,* 109–42.
Aureggi, A. "Ospedali e Vescovi." *CESO* (1960), 38–56.
Autrand, F. Notes taken at a lecture on the wills registered at the Parlement de Paris in the fourteenth and fifteenth centuries, 25 avril 1973.

————. *Naissance d'un grand corps de l'Etat: les Gens de Paris (1345–1454)*. 5 vols. Ph.D. diss., Paris: Université Paris-Sorbonne, 1978.

Avril, J. "Clercs et laïcs devant la richesse d'après les statuts synodaux d'Angers de la fin du Moyen Age." *Et. Pauvr.*, 563.

Balard, M. "Les Orientaux à Gênes: Un Exemple de classe inférieure." *Cah. Sorb.* 9.

Baratier, E. *La Démographie provençale du XIIIe au XVIe siècle*. Paris, 1961.

Barrière, B. *L'Abbaye cistercienne d'Obazine en Bas-Limousin: Les Origines, le patrimoine*. Forthcoming.

Batany, J. "Les Pauvres et la pauvreté dans les revues des 'Estats du Monde.'" *Et. Pauvr.*, 469–86.

Battle, C. "La Ayuda a los pobres de la parroquia de S. Justo de Barcelona." *Pobreza . . . Ibérica*, 59–72.

Baucells i Reig, J. "La Pia Almoina de la Seo de Barcelona." *Pobreza . . . Ibérica*, 73–136.

Bavoux, P. "Les Orphelins et les enfants trouvés à Paris à la fin du Moyen Age." Master's thesis, Paris, 1967. A summary appears in *Cah. Sorb.* 5.

Bec, C. *Les Marchands écrivains à Florence, 1375–1434*. Paris-La Haye, 1967.

Beck, H. G. S. *The Pastoral Care of Souls in Southeast France during the Sixth Century*. Rome, 1950.

Bernard, J. *Navires et gens de mer à Bordeaux, 1400–1550*. 3 vols. Paris, 1968, pt. 2.

Bienvenu, J.-M. "Pauvreté, misères et charité en Anjou aux XIe et XIIe siècles." *M.A.* 72 (1966), 389–424; 73 (1967), 5–34, 189–216.

————. "Fondations charitables laïques au XIIe siècle: L'Exemple de l'Anjou." *Et. Pauvr.*, 563–69.

————. "Préhistoire du Franciscanisme: Aspects préfranciscains de l' érémitisme et de la prédication itinérante dans la France de l'Ouest." *Pov. M.A.*, 27–36.

Binz, L. *Vie religieuse et réforme ecclésiastique dans le diocèse de Genève (1378–1450)*. Geneva, 1973.

Biraben, J. N. *Les Hommes et la peste en France et dans les pays européens et méditerranéens*. 2 vols. Paris, 1975–76.

Blanc, Y. *Les Hôpitaux lyonnais au Moyen Age*. Master's thesis. Lyon, 1968.

Bligny, B. "Les Premiers Chartreux et la pauvreté. *M.A.* 57 (1951), 27–60.

————. "Monachisme et pauvreté au XIIe siècle." *La Povertà del sec. XII e Francesco d'Assisi. Atti. 2 Conv. Intern. Assisi.* 1974–75, 99–147.

Bocquet, A. "Recherches sur la population rurale en Artois-Boulonnais pendant la période bourguignonne." *Mém. Com. Dép. Ant. Pas-de-Calais* 13. Arras, 1969.

Bois, G. *Crise du féodalisme: Economie rurale et démographie en Normandie orientale au début du XIVe siècle au milieu du XVIe*. Paris, 1976.

Bonenfant, P. "Hôpitaux et bienfaisance publique dans les Anciens Pays-Bas." *ASBHH* 3 (1965), 1–194.

Bonnassie, P. *Croissance et mutation d'une société: La Catalogne du milieu du Xe à la fin du XIe siècle*. Toulouse, 1975.

Bosl, K. "'Potens' und 'Pauper'. Begriffsgeschichtliche Studien zur gesellschaftlichen Differenzierung im frühen Mittelalter und zum 'Pauperism' des Hochmittelalters." *Festschrift für O. Brünner.* Göttingen, 1963, 60–87.

Boulet, M. "La Criminalité dans la baille de Moustiers-Sainte-Marie, d'après les comptes de la première moitié du XIVe siècle." Master's thesis. Québec: Université Laval, 1972.

Bouvier, L. *Le Précepte de l'aumône chez saint Thomas d'Aquin.* Montreal, 1935.

Boyer, M. N. "The Bridgebuilding Brotherhood." *Spec.* 39 (1964), 635–50.

Boyer, R. "La Chartreuse de Montrieux XIIe–XIIIe siècles." 3 vols. Thesis. Aix-en-Provence, 1973.

Brandt, V. "Philippe de Mézières et son projet de banque d'Etat." *Rev. Cath. Louvain* (1880).

Bresc, H. "Images et réalités de la pauvreté dans la Sicile méridionale." *Cah. Sorb.* 9.

Brinton, Th. *The Sermons of Ths. Brinton, bishop of Rochester (1373–1389).* Ed. M. A. Devlin. 3d ser., vols. 85–86. London, 1954.

Briod, A. *L'Assistance des pauvres au Moyen Age dans le pays de Vaud.* Lausanne, 1926, rev. ed., 1976.

Brucker, G. A. *Florentine Politics and Society.* Princeton, 1962, 54–109.

Burns, R. I. "Los hospitales del reino de Valencia en el siglo XIII." *Anuario de Estudios Medievales* 2 (1965), 144–54.

Cabestang, J. F. and S. Claramunt. "El 'Plat dels Pobres' de la Parroquia de Santa Maria del Pi de Barcelona." *Pobreza . . . Ibérica,* 157–218.

Caille, J. *Hôpitaux et charité publique à Narbonne au Moyen Age (fin XIe–fin XVe siècle).* Toulouse, forthcoming.

Candille, M. "Les Statuts de la Maison-Dieu de Vernon." *BSFHH* 24 (1970), 11–33.

———. "Pour un précis d'histoire des institutions charitables." BSFHH 30 (1974).

Capitani, O., ed. *La concezione della povertà nel Medioevo.* Bologna, 1974.

Cardwell-Higonnet, E. "Spiritual Ideas in the Letters of Peter of Blois." *Spec.* 50 (1975), 218–44.

Carolus-Barré, L. "Benoît XII et la mission charitable de Bertrand Carit dans le pays dévastés du Nord de la France, 1340." *MAHEFR* (1950), 165–232.

Caron, P. G. "L'evoluzione della *quarta pauperum* alla pia fundatio . . ." *CISO* (1960), 287–99.

Carpaneta de Langasco, C. "L'intervento papale nelle concentrazioni ospitaliere del Rinascimento." *CISO* (1956), 130–37.

Carpentier, E. *Une Ville devant la Peste: Orvieto et la Peste noire de 1348.* Paris, 1962.

———. "Orvieto et son contado: Etude du cadastre de 1292." 3 vols. Thesis. Paris, 1975.

Castieau, E. "Les Aumones du Roi René." Master's thesis. Paris, 1973.

Cazelles, R. "La Peste de 1348–1349 en Langue d'oïl, épidémie prolétarienne et enfantine." *B. Phil. Hist.* 1962 (1965), 293–305.

Caesarius of Arles. *Sermons.* Ed. G. Morin. *CCSL* 103. Maredsous, 1953.

Chapelot-Leclerc, O. "Les Matériaux de construction en Bourgogne: Aspects techniques et économiques, 1340–1475." Ms. Paris, 1975.

Chatillon, J. "Nudum Christum Nudus sequere." *S. Bonaventura (1274–1974).* Pt. 4, Grottaferrata, 719–72.

Chenu, D. "Civilisation urbaine et théologie: L'Ecole de Saint-Victor au XIIe siècle." *Ann. ESC* (1974), 1253–63.

Cherubini, G. *Signori, Contadini, Borghesi, Ricerche sulla societa italiana del Basso Medievo.* Florence, 1977.

Chevalier, B. "Alimentation et niveau de vie à Tours à la fin du XVe siècle." *B. Phil. Hist.* 1968 (1971), 143–58.

――――. *Tours, ville royale.* Louvain-Paris, 1973.

Chiffoleau, J. "La Comptabilité de l'Au-delà: Les Hommes, la mort et la religion comtadine à la fin du Moyen Age (vers 1320–vers 1490)." 2 vols. Thesis. Paris: Université Paris-Sorbonne, 1978.

Cohn, N. *Les fanatiques de l'Apocalypse: Pseudo-Messies, prophètes et illuminés du Moyen Age.* Trans. S. Clement. Paris, 1962.

Congar, Y. "Les Laïcs et l'ecclésiologie des *ordines* chez les théologiens des XIe–XIIe siècles." *Atti 3a Sett. La Mendola* 1965 (1968), 83–117.

――――. "L'Eglise et l'Etat sous le règne de Saint Louis." *Septième Centenaire de la mort de Saint Louis.* (Conference proceedings 1970.) Paris, 1976, 257–71.

Contamine, Ph. *La Vie quotidienne en France et en Angleterre pendant la guerre de Cent Ans.* Paris, 1975.

Coste Messelière, R. de la. "L'Importance réelle des routes dites de Saint-Jacques dans le pays du sud de la France et de l'Espagne du Nord." *B. Phil. Hist.* 1, 1969 (1972), 451–70.

Courtenay, W. J. "Token Coinage and the Administration of Poor Relief during the Late Middle Ages." *Journal of Interdisciplinary History* 3 (1972–73), 275–95.

Couvreur, G. *Les Pauvres ont-ils des droits? Recherches sur le vol en cas d'extrême nécessité depuis la "Concordia" de Gratien (1140) jusqu'à Guillaume d'Auxerre († 1231).* Rome-Paris, 1961.

Coville, A. "Ecrit contemporains sur la peste de 1348–1350." *Hist. Littér. France* 37 (Paris, 1937), 325–50.

Coyecque, E. *L'Hôtel-Dieu de Paris au Moyen Age.* Paris, 1889–91.

Cruz, A. "A Assistência na cidade do Porto e seu termo durante a Idade Media." *Pobreza . . . Ibérica,* 329–44.

Cruz Coehlo, M. H. de. "A acção dos Particulaires para com a Pobreza. . ." *Probreza . . . Ibérica,* 329–44.

Curschmann, F. "Hungersnöte im Mittelalter." *Leipziger Studien* 6 (1900), 1–218.

Dagron, G. *Naissance d'une capitale: Constantinople de 330 à 451.* Paris, 1974.

Dainton, C. *The Story of England's Hospitals.* Springfield, 1962.

Darmery, C. "La Société rémoise au début du XIVe siècle." *Mém. Soc. Agric. Marne* 88 (1973), 37–70.

Davis, N. Z. "Gregory Nazianzen in the Service of Humanist Social Reform." *Renaissance Quarterly* 20 (1967), 455–64.

———. "Assistance, humanisme et hérésie: Le Cas de Lyon." *Studies in Medieval and Renaissance History* V (1968), 217–75. Repr. in *Et. Pauvr.*, 761–822.

Defermont, J. C. "Pauvres et pauvreté d'après les sources insulaires du VIIe au IXe siècle." Master's thesis, Lille, 1967. Summary in *Cah. Sorb.* 5, 1966–67.

Delafosse, M. "Les Vignerons d'Auxerrois XIVe–XVIe siècle." *Ann. Bourgogne* 20 (1948), 8–14.

Delaruelle, E. "Jonas d'Orléans et le moralisme carolingien." *Bull. Litt. Eccl. Inst. Cath. Toulouse* (1954), 129–43, 221–28.

———. "Erémitisme et pauvreté dans la région de Toulouse au XIIe siecle." *Cah. Sorb.* 6, 40–44.

———. *La Piété populaire au Moyen Age.* Turin, 1975.

Delisle, L. *Et. condition agricole.* . . Evreux, 1851, 197.

———. *Enquêtes administratives du règne de saint Louis, 1248–1270.* Rec. Hist. France 24. Paris, 1904.

Delumeau, J. *La Peur en Occident, XIV–XVIIIe siècles.* Paris, 1978.

Desportes, P. "Les Pauvres à Reims au début du XIV siècle." *Cah. Sorb.* 7. *2000 Ans de Christianisme.* Pt. 3, XIIe–XIIIe siècle. Paris: Soc. Hist. Chrét., 1975.

Devailly, G. "La Pastorale en Gaule au IXe siècle." *RHEF* 59 (1973), 23–54.

Devisse, J. "'Pauperes' et 'Paupertas' dans le monde carolingien: Ce Qu'en dit Hincmar de Reims." *R.N.* 48 (1966), 273–89.

———. "L'Influence de Julien Pomère sur les clercs carolingiens: De la pauvreté aux Ve et IXe siècles." *RHEF* 56 (1970), 285–95.

———. *Hincmar, archévêque de Reims (845–882).* 3 vols. Lille-Geneva, 1976.

Dhuoda. *Manuel pour mon fils.* Ed. P. Riché. Sources chrétiennes 225. Paris, 1975.

Dijck, W. Van. "Rapports de saint François d'Assise avec le mouvement spirituel du XIIe siècle." *Etudes franciscaines* 12 (1962), 129–42.

Dijk, W. Van. "Une Pauvresse aux Pays-Bas aux XIVe–XVe siècles, sainte Lydwine de Schicdam." *Cah. Sorb.* 9, 30–36.

Douët d'Arcq, L. *Choix de pièces inédites relatives au règne de Charles VI.* 2 vols. Paris, 1863–64.

Dubois, H. *Les Foires de Chalon-sur-Saône et le commerce dans la vallée de la Saône à la fin du Moyen Age (vers 1250–vers 1430).* Paris, 1976.

Duby, G. "Les Pauvres des campagnes." *RHEF* 49 (1966), 25–32.

———. *Guerriers et paysans (VII–XII siècle): Premier essor de l'économie européenne.* Paris, 1973.

———. et al. *Histoire rurale de la France.* Vol. 2. Paris, 1975.

Dumont, L. "Les Pauvres dans la prière de l'Eglise." *Cah. Sorb.* 7.

———. "Les Pauvres dans la piété populaire à la fin du Moyen Age (XIVe–XVe) principalement en France." Master's thesis. Paris, 1976.

Duval-Arnould, L. "Une Apologie de la pauvreté volontaire par un universitaire séculier (1256)." *Et. Pauvr.*, 411–46.

Elsener, F. "Le Pauvre dans le droit de procédure des comtes et ducs de Savoie." *RHDFE* (1971), 703–04.

Faure, C. "Les Pauvres et la pauvreté dans la pensée de Chaucer." Master's thesis. Paris, 1969.

Favier, J. *Les Contribuables parisiens à la fin de la guerre de Cent Ans.* Paris, 1970.

Favreau, R. "Le Commerce du sel en Poitou à la fin du Moyen Age." *B. Phil. Hist.* 1966 (1968), 185–223.

———. "La Ville de Poitiers à la fin du Moyen Age: Une Capitale régionale." 5 vols. Ms. Paris, 1974.

———. "La Pauvreté en Poitou et en Anjou à la fin du Moyen Age." *Et. Pauvr.*, 589–620.

Fédou, R. "De Valdo à Luther: Les 'Pauvres de Lyon' vus par un Humaniste lyonnais." *Mélanges A. Latreille.* Lyon, 1972, 417–21.

Flood, D. "Petrus Johannus Olivi." *Wissenschaft und Weisheit Zeitschrift* 34 (1971), 130–41.

———. "Armut und Erneuerung im Franziskanenorden: Zur Geschichte der Gentile von Spoleto." *Pov. M.A.*, 79–83.

Flood, D., ed. *Poverty in the Middle Ages.* (Conference held in Möndchen-Gladbach in 1973.) *Franziskanische Forschungen.* Paderborn, 1975.

Fonseca, C. D. "Canoniche e Ospedali." *CISO* (1960), 482–500.

Fontette, M. de. "Villes médiévales et Ordres Mendiants." *RHDFE* (1970), 390–407.

Fossier, R. "La Terre et les hommes en Picardie jusqu'à la fin du XIIIe siècle. 2 vols. Paris-Louvain, 1968.

———. "Aspects sociaux des institutions de paix." *Cah. Sorb.* 9, 91–99.

———. "Les Mouvements populaires en Occident au XIe siècle." *CR Acad. IBL* (1971), 257–69.

Fourquin, G. *Les Campagnes de la région parisienne à la fin du moyen age.* Paris, 1964.

———. *Les Soulèvements populaires au Moyen Age.* Paris, 1972.

Fragonard, M. "Le Thème de l'identité du Christ et du pauvre dans les textes et l'iconographie relatifs à 'Piers the Plowman.'" Master's thesis, Paris, 1966. Summary in *Cah. Sorb.* 4.

François, O. "La conception de la pauvreté chez saint Siran." Ms. Paris, 1967.

Freed, J. B. "The Mendicant Orders in Germany (1219–1273)." Thesis. Princeton: Princeton University, 1979.

Gabriel, A. L. *Students in Ave Maria College.* Notre Dame, Ind., 1955. 105–09.

Garra, R. M. "Aspetti della povertà a Firenze nel sec. XV–XVI, attraverso lo studio del libro nell' entrata e uscita dell'Opera della Carità 1496–1508." Thesis. Florence: Inst. Econ. Univ.

Gascon, R. "Economie et pauvreté aux XVIe et XVIIe siècles: Lyon, ville exemplaire et prophétique." *Et. Pauvr.*, 747–60.

Gautier-Dalché, J. "Recherches sur l'histoire urbaine en León et en Castille au Moyen Age." 3 vols. Thesis. Paris, 1971, 380.

Geest, G. de. "Les Distributions aux pauvres assurées par la paroisse Sainte-Gudule à Bruxelles au XVe siècle." *ASBHH* 6 (1969), 41–84.

Genet, Ph. "Economie et société rurale en Angleterre au XVe siècle, d'après les comptes de l'Hôpitale d'Elme." *Ann. ESC* (1972), 1449–74.

Génicot, L. "Sur le nombre des pauvres dans les campagnes médiévales." *R.H.* 522 (1977), 273–288.

Geremek, B. "I salari e il salariato nelle città del Basso Medio Evo." *Rivista Storica Italiana* 78 (1966), 368–86.

———. La popolazione marginale tra il Medioevo e l'era moderna." *Studi Storici* 9, 3–4 (1968), 623–40.

———. *Le Salariat dans l'artisanat parisien.* Paris, 1968.

———. "La Lutte contre le vagabondage à Paris aux XVIe et XVe siècles." *Richerche storiche ed economiche, Memoria* di C. Barbagallo. 1970, 2:211–36.

———. "Renfermement des pauvres en Italie (XIVe–XVIIe siècle): Remarques préliminaires." *Mélanges F. Braudel* 1. Toulouse, 1972, 205–17.

———. "Les Migrations de compagnons au bas Moyen Age." *Studia historiae oeconomicae* 5 (Poznan, 1920), 61–79.

———. "Il pauperismo nell' età preindustriale (sec. XIV–XVIII)." *Storia d'Italia* 5 (I documenti). Turin 1973, 667–98.

———. "Criminalite, vagabondage, paupérisme la marginalité à l'aube des temps modernes." *RHMC* XXI (1974): 337–375.

———. *Les Marginaux parisiens aux XIVe et XVe siècles.* Paris, 1976.

Giardini, M. *I banchieri ebrei.* Florence, 1970.

Gieysztor, A. "La Légende de Saint Alexis en Occident." *Et. Pauvr.*, 125–40.

Goglin, J.-L. *Les Misérables dans l'Occident medieval.* Paris, 1976.

Goncalvès, I. "Formes medievais de assistencia num meio rural estremenho." *Pobreza . . . Ibérica*, 439–54.

Gonthier, N. *Lyon et ses pauvres au Moyen Age (1350–1500)* Lyon, 1978.

Goubert, D. "Recherche sur le culte de saint Martin . . ." Master's thesis, Paris, 1966.

Granata, A. "La Dottrina dell'Elemosina nel Sermone 'Pro Sanctimonialibus' de Paraclito di Abelardo." *Aevum* 47 (1973), 32–59.

———. "Un problema ancora aperto: Pietro di Blois come difensore dei 'Pauperes.'" *Contrib. Istit. Stor. Medioev.* 2. Milan, 1972 (*Raccolta S. Mochi Onory*), 429–37.

Grand, Ph. "Gérard d' Abbeville et la pauvreté volontaire." *Et Pauvr.*, 389–40.

Graus, F. *Dejiny Venkovského Lidu v Cechách v dobe predhusitské.* Vol. 2, XIIIe–1419. (Czech.) Prague, 1957.

———. "Pauvres des villes et pauvres des campagnes." *Ann. ESC* 16 (1961), 1053–65.

———. "La Pauvreté dans l'hagiographie mérovingienne." *Cah. Sorb.* 3 (1964–65).

———. "Social Utopias in the Middle Ages." *Past and Present* 38 (1967), 3–19.

———. "Littérature et mentalité médiévales: Le Roi et le peuple." *Historica* (Prague) 16 (1969).

Grégoire, R. "La Place de la pauvreté dans la conception et la pratique de la vie monastique médiévale latine." *Atti 4a Sett. La Mendola* 1968 (1971), 173–92.

Gual, M. "La assistência a los pobres en la corte de Pedro IV el Ceremonioso." *Pobreza . . . Ibérica*, 445–81.

Guenée, B. *L'Occident aux XIVe et XVe siècles: Les Etats.* Paris, 1971.

Guiral, J. "L'Assistance aux pauvres à Valence (Esp.) du XIIIe au XVIe siècle." Master's thesis, Paris, 1967. Summary in *Cah. Sorb.* 5.

Gutowski, C. "Le Traité 'De Avaritia' extrait de la 'Summa de Viciis' de Guillaume Péraut. Edition critique et commentaire." 4 vol. ms. Summary in *Pos. Th. Ec. Chartes.* (1975), 103–12.

Gutton, J. P. *La Société et les pauvres: L'Exemple de la généralité de Lyon, 1534–1789.* Paris, 1971.

Guy, J. C. *Jean Cassein: Vie et doctrine spirituelle.* Paris, 1961.

Heers, J. *Le Clan familial au Moyen Age.* 1974.

Heupgen, P. "La Commune-Aumône de Mons (XIIIe–XVIIe siecle)." *BCRH* 90, 319–72.

Hippeau, C. "Quelques Observations à propos d'une enquête en 1297 par le bailli de Caen sur les chaussées de Corben, Troarn et Varaville." *Mem. Soc. Ant. Normandie* 20 (1953), 367.

Hisard, B. "La Pauvreté dans la prédication populaire franciscaine aux XIVe–XVe siècles." Master's thesis, Paris, 1963. Summary in *Cah. Sorb.* 1.

Hocquet, J. C. "Venise et le commerce maritime du sel du milieu du XIIIe siècle au commencement du XVIIe siècle." 2 vols. Ms. (1974), 1:283.

Holzapfel, H. *Le origini dei Monti di Pietà (1462–1515).* Rocca S. Casciano, 1905. *Hommage au Prof. P. Bonenfant.* Brussels, 1965.

Houtte, J. van. "Pauvreté et assistance aux Pays-Bas au XIVe siècle." *Cah. Sorb.* 8.

Huizinga, J. *Le Déclin du Moyen Age.* Paris, 1948, repr. 1968.

Ibanès, J. *La Doctrine de l'Eglise et les réalités économiques du XIIIe siècle.* Paris, 1967.

Imbert, J. *Les Hôpitaux en droit canonique.* Paris, 1947.

———. "L'Eglise et l'Etat face au problème hospitalier au XVIe siècle." *Et. hist. Droit canonique dédiées à G. Le Bras.* Paris, 1965.

Jones-Davies, M., ed. *Misère et gueuserie au temps de la Renaissance: Colloque sur les gueux et gueuserie.* Paris: Center for Renaissance Research, Université Paris-Sorbonne, 1976.

Jordan, W. K. *The Charities of London, 1480–1660.* London, 1960.

———. *The Charities of Rural England, 1480–1660.* London, 1961.

Kayser-Guyot, M.-T. *Le Berger en France au Moyen Age.* Paris, 1974.

Kloczowski, J. "Les Hôpitaux et les Frères Mendiants en Pologne au Moyen Age." *Et. Pauvr.,* 589–620.

Labande-Mailfert, Y. "Pauvreté et Paix dans l'iconographie romane." *Et. Pauvr.,* 319–46.

Lacroix, M-.Th. "L'Hôpital saint-Nicolas du Bruille à Tournai (1230–1611)." Thesis. Université Louvain, 1975.

Laga, T. W. "The English Villainage in England." *Amer. Hist. Assoc.* (1900), 44–46, 59–65.

Lagos Trindade, M. J. "Notas sobre a intervençâo regia na administraçâo des instituições de assistencia nos fins da Idade Media." *Pobreza . . . Ibérica,* 873–82.

Lallemant, L. *Histoire de la Charité.* Pt. 3. Paris, 1906. *La Pauvreté: Des So-*

ciétés de pénurie à la société d'abondance. Vol. 49, Collection of the Catholic Center for French Intellectuals. Paris, 1964.

Lapo de Castiglionco. "Tractatus hospitalitatis." *Tractatus Universi Juris* 14. Venice, 1589, 162–67.

La Roncière, Ch.-M. de. *Un Changeur florentin du Trecento: Lippo di Fede del Sega (env 1285–env 1363).* Paris, 1973.

———. "Pauvres et pauvreté à Florence au XIVe siècle." *Et. Pauvr.*, 661–67.

———. *Florence, centre économique régional au XVIe siècle.* 4 vols. Paris, 1977.

Lavoie, R. "Pauvreté et criminalité en Provence à la fin du Moyen Age." Notes taken at a May, 1974, lecture on the history of Provence. Paris: Université Paris-Sorbonne, 1977.

Lazzarino del Grosso, A. *Armut und Reichtum im Denken Gerhohs von Reichersberg.* Munich, 1973. Repr. in *Società e Potere nella Germania del XII secolo: Gerhoch von Reichersberg.* Florence, 1974.

Le Brozec, F. "Saint Yves, avocat des pauvres." Master's thesis, Paris, 1967.

Leclère, F. "La Charité des bourgeois de Douai envers les pauvres au XIVe siècle." *R.N.* 48, 139–54.

Le Goff, J. "Les Archives des monts-de-piété et des banques publiques d'Italie." *Rev. Banque,* Brussels, 1957, 21–46.

———. "Pauvreté et pauvres dans les manuels de confesseurs du XIIIe siècle." *Cah. Sorb.* 1.

———. "Le temps du travail dans la crise du XIVe siècle." *M.A.* (1963), 597–613.

———. "Les Paysans et le monde rural dans la littérature du haut Moyen Age (Ve–VIe siècle)." *Atti 13a Sett. Spoleto* 1965 (1966), 723–70.

———. "Apostolat mendiant et fait urbain." *Ann. ESC* 23 (1968), 335–52.

———. "Ordres Mendiants et urbanisation." *Ann. ESC* 25 (1976): 939–40.

Le Grand, L. *Les Statuts d'Hôtels-Dieu et de léproseries (XIe–XIVe siècles).* Paris, 1901.

Legras, A.-M. "L'Enquête pontificale de 1373 sur l'Ordre des Hospitaliers de Saint-Jean de Jérusalem." 4 vols. (Annotated collection of documents relating to Le Grand Prieuré de France.) Thesis, Paris: Université Paris-Sorbonne, 1976.

Leistikov, D. *Hospitalbauten in Europa aus Zehn Jahrhunderten.* Ingelheim-am-Rhein (RFA), 1967.

Lejean-Hennebique, R. "'Pauperes' et 'Paupertas' aux IXe et Xe siècles." *R.N.* 50 (1968), 169–87.

Le Mené, M. "Les Pauvres et l'hospitalisation à Nantes à la fin du Moyen Age et au début du XVI siècle." *Cah. Sorb.* 9, 214–20.

Leroy, P. "L'Hôtel-Dieu de Tonnerre." *Cah. Sorb.* 2.

Le Roy-Ladurie, E. *Montaillou: Village occitan.* Paris, 1975.

———. *Les paysans du Languedoc.* 1 Paris, 1966.

Lesne, E. *Histoire de la propriété ecclésiastique en France.* Vol. 6. Lille, 1943.

Little, L. K. "Saint Louis' Involvement with the Friars." *Church History* 33 (1964), 1–24.

————. "Pride Goes before Avarice: Social Changes and the Vices in Latin Christendom." *AHR* 76 (1971), 16–49.

————. "Social Meaning in the Monastic and Mendicant Spiritualities." *Past and Present* 63 (1974), 1–24.

————."Evangelical Poverty, the New Money Economy, and Violence." *Pov. M.A.*, 11–26.

Longère, J. *Œuvres oratoires des Maîtres parisiens au XIIe siècle.* 2 vols. Paris, 1975.

Lopez Yepes, J. and F. Sagredo Fernandes. "Las arcas de Limosnas del Conde de Haro y las instituciones de préstamo benéfico (s. XV–XVI)." *Pobreza . . . Ibérica*, 547–74.

Lorcin, M. T. "Les Clauses religieuses dans les testaments du plat-pays lyonnais aux XIVe–XVe siècles." *M.A.* (1972), 287–323.

————. *Les Campagnes de la région lyonnaise aux XIVe–XVe siècles.* Lyon, 1974.

Lottin, O. "La Nature du devoir d'aumône chez les prédécesseurs de saint Thomas d'Aquin." *Ephemeridas theologicae Lovanienses* 15 (1938), 613–24.

Lucas, H. S. "The Great European Famine of 1315, 1316, and 1317." *Spec.* 5 (1930), 343–77.

Luce, S. *Histoire de la Jacquerie,* 2d ed. Paris, 1894.

Luis Martin, J. "La pobreza y los pobres en los textos literarios del siglo XIV." *Pobreza . . . Ibérica*, 587–636.

Macchi, C. "La pauvreté en Lorraine (XIe–XIIe siècle) d'après les cartulaires monastiques." Master's thesis, Paris, 1970. Summary in *Cah. Sorb.* 8, 8–15.

Magnou-Nortier, E. *La Société laïque et l'Eglise dans la province ecclésiastique de Narbonne (zone cispyréenne) de la fin du VIIIe siècle à la fin du XIe.* Toulouse, 1974.

Manselli, R. *La Religion populaire au Moyen Age.* Albert le Grand Lecture. Montreal-Paris, 1973.

————. *Studi sulle Eresie del secolo XII.* 2d ed. Rome, 1975.

————. "Divergences parmi les Mineurs d'Italie et de France méridionale." *Cah. Fanjeaux* 8: 355–74.

Manteuffel, T. *Naissance d'une hérésie: Les Adeptes de la pauvreté volontaire au Moyen Age.* Paris-La Haye, 1960.

Martin, H. *Les Ordres Mendiants en Bretagne vers 1320–vers 1530.* Rennes, 1975.

Maschke, E. "Pauvres urbains et pauvres ruraux dans l'Allemagne médiévale." *Cah. Sorb.* 1.

Mathieu, Cl. "Les Hôpiteaux de Meaux." Master's thesis. Paris, 1972.

Matteo Villani. *Cronica.* Ed. L. A. Muratori. *R.I.S.* 14, c. 15–16.

Mattoso, J. "O Ideal de Pobreza e as Ordines monasticas em Portugal durante os seculos XI–XIII." *Pobreza . . . Ibérica*, 638–70.

May, A. N. "An Index of XIIIth Century Peasant Impoverishment? Manor Court Fines." *Ec.H.R.* 26 (1973).

Melis, F. *Aspetti della vita economica medievale.* Siena, 1972, 1:88–92, 100–03.

Menini, C. "L'Ospedale dei Battisti Bianchi a Ferrara (1354–1784)." *CESO* (1960), 828–35.

Mertens, J.-A. "Les Confiscations dans la châtellenie du Franc après la bataille de Cassel." *BCRH* 134 (1968), 239–84.

Metz, B. "La Pauvreté dans le *Liber de diversis ordinibus*." *Et Pauvr.*, 247–55.

Michaud-Quentin, P. "Les sermons 'Ad pauperes' au XIIIe siècle." *Cah. Sorb.* 5.

Miqueau, R.-M. "Aumônes et fondations charitables d'Alphonse de Poitiers." Master's thesis. Paris, 1971.

Mirot, L. *Les Insurrections urbaines au début du règne de Charles VI (1380–1383)*. Paris, 1905.

Misraki, J. "Criminalité et Pauvreté en France à l'époque de la guerre de Cent Ans." *Et. Pauvr.*, 535–46.

Mollat, M. *Le Commerce maritime normand à la fin du Moyen Age*. Paris, 1952.

———. "Le Problème de la pauvreté au XIIe siècle." *Cah. Fanjeaux* 2, 23–47.

———. "Pauvres et pauvreté à la fin du XIIe siècle." *R.A.M.* 41 (1965), 304–73.

———. *Genèse médiévale de la France moderne*. Paris, 1970, repr. 1977.

———. "Les Moines et les pauvres." *Atti 4a Sett. La Mendola* 1968 (1971), 173–92.

———. "Hospitalité et assistance au début du XIIIe siècle." *Pov. M.A.*, 37–51.

Mollat, M., et al. *Le Rôle du sel dans l'histoire*. Paris, 1968.

Mollat, M., and Ph. Wolff. *Ongles bleus, Jacques et Ciompi*. Paris, 1970. Trans. as *The Popular Revolutions of the Late Middle Ages*. London, 1973.

Moreau, L. *Recherches sur l'origine et la formation du diocèse royal en France*. Strasbourg, 1975.

Mornet, E. "*Pauperes scolaires* . . . scandinaves, XIVe–XVe siècles." *Cah. Sorb.* 9, 109–15; *M.A.* (1978), 53–102.

Mundy, M. "Hospitals and Leproseries in XIIth and Early XIIIth Century Toulouse." *Essays . . . in honor of A. P. Evans*. New York, 1965.

Najat el Khatib. "L'Organisation des hôpitaux dans l'Islam médiéval en Irak, en Syrie et en Egypte." Thesis. Paris: Université Paris-Sorbonne, 1976.

Nasalli-Rocca, E. "Pievie ospedale." *CISO*, 493–507.

———. *Il diritto ospedaliero nei suoi lineamenti storici*. Milan, 1956.

Neveux, H. "La Mortalité des pauvres à Cambrai (1377–1413)." *Annales de Démographie historique* (1968), 73–97.

———. *Les Grains du Cambresis (fin XIVe–début XVIIe): Vie et déclin d'une structure économique*. Lille, 1974.

Nortier, M. "Inventaire des rôles de fouage paroissiaux 1368–1482." *Cahiers Léopold Delisle* 9, 20, 22, 24 (1970–75).

Nucé de Lamothe, M. S. "Piété et charité publique à Toulouse de la fin du XIIIe siècle au milieu du XVe d'après les testaments." *Ann. Midi* 76 (1974), 5–40.

"*Ordres et Classes*": *Colloque d'Histoire sociale*. St. Cloud, 1967, Paris-La Haye, 1973.

Pacaut, M. "La Notion de Pauvreté dans la règle de saint Benoît." *Economies et Sociétés au Moyen Age: Mélanges offerts à E. Perroy*. Paris, 1973, 626–33.

Paravy, P. "L'Eglise et les communautés dauphinoises à l'âge de la dépression." *Cah. d'histoire* 19 (1974), 227–31.

Patlagean, E. "La Pauvreté à Byzance au temps de Justinien: Les Origines d'un modèle politique." *Et. Pauvr.*, 59–82.

_____. *Recherches sur les Pauvres et la Pauvreté dans l'Empire Romain d'Orient (IVe–VIIe siècles)*. 2 vols. Lille, 1974. Published as *Pauvreté économique et pauvreté sociale à Byzance (IVe–VIIe siècles)*. Paris-La Haye, 1977.

_____. "Un Prédicateur errant du Xe siècle à Byzance: Nikon 'repentez-vous.'" *Cah. Sorb.* 9, 25–28.

Patzelt, E. "Pauvreté et maladies." *Conv. Pov. Todi*, 163–87.

Paubert, A. "Recherches sur la mendicité religieuse avant saint François d'Assise." Master's thesis, Paris, 1965. Summary in *Cah. Sorb.* 3.

Pellistrandi, Chr. "La Pauvreté dans la Règle de Grandmont." *Et. Pauvr.*, 229–47.

Pento, A. "Institution hospitalière en Angleterre au XIVe siècle. Master's thesis, Paris, 1972. Summary in *Cah. Sorb.* 9

Perroy, E. "Les Crises du XIVe siècle." *Ann. ESC* (1949), 167–82.

_____. "L'Hôtel-Dieu de Montbrison aux XIIIe–XIVe siècles." *Bull. de la Diana* 26 (1937), 103–37.

Pezzi, G. "L'assistenza ospitaleria ai Naviganti." *CISO*, 548–55. *Picenum Seraphicum* 9 (1972). Special issue on pawnshops.

Pichon, J., ed. *Le Ménagier de Paris (1393)*. 2 vols. Paris, 1846. Repr. 1968.

Pierret, G. "Pauvres et pauvreté à Lille à la fin du Moyen Age." Master's thesis, Paris, 1972. Summary in *Cah. Sorb.* 9.

Piget, J.-L. "Aspects du crédit dans l'Albigeois à la fin du XIIe siècle." *Castres et les pays tarnais*. (Actes XXVIe Congrès Etudes regionales, Castres, 1970.) *Revue du Tarn* (1972), 1–50.

Plessier, M. "La Pauvreté à Cluny d'après le Receuil des Chartes." Master's thesis, Paris, 1966. Summary in *Cah. Sorb.* 4.

Plouin, R. "Les Hôpitaux dans la France de la Renaissance." Jones-Davies, ed., *Colloque Gueux*, 117–26.

Poulet, F. "Les Pauvres et la pauvreté dans l'oeuvre de l'œuvre de Gerson." Master's thesis, Paris, 1963. Summary in *Cah. Sorb.* 2.

Poulin, J. C. *L'Idéal de sainteté dans l'Aquitaine carolingienne d'après les sources hagiographiques (750–950)*. Quebec, 1975.

Pound, J. *Poverty and Vagrancy in Tudor England*. London, 1971.

Pourrière, J. *Les Hôpitaux d'Aix-en-Provence au Moyen Age*. Aix, 1969.

_____. *La povertà del secolo XII e Francesco d'Assisi. Atti del IIo Convegno Internationale*. 1974. Assisi, 1975.

Pullian, B. "Poverty, Charity, and the Reason of State." *Boll. Istituto di Storia della Societa et dello Stato Veneziano* 2 (1960), 17–61.

Rapp, F. "Les Mendiants et la societé strasbourgeoise à la fin du Moyen Age." *Pov. M.A.*, 84–102.

_____. *Réforme et Réformation à Strasbourg: L'Eglise et la société dans le diocèse de Strasbourg (1450–1525)*. Paris, 1974.

Rapp, R. "L'Eglise et les pauvres à la fin du Moyen Age: L'Exemple de Geiler de Kaysersberg." *RHEF* (1966), 39–46.

Rau, V. "Conclusions." *Pobreza . . . Ibérica*, 925–43.

———. *Sesmarias portuguesas*. Lisbon, 1946.

Reneaux, J. "Le Thème de la Pauvreté dans les miniatures au XIVe siècle." Master's thesis, Paris, 1963.

Renouard, Y. "La Peste noire de 1348–1349." *Etudes d'Hist. médiévale*. Paris, 1968, 1:143–64.

Renucci, P. "Un Précédent italien du *Liber Vagatorum*." Jones-Davies, ed., *Colloque gueux*, 85–95.

Revel, M. "Recherche sur l'hôpital du S. Spirito à Rome." Master's thesis, Paris, 1967. *Summary in Cah. Sorb*. 8.

RHEF 52 (1966). Special issue on poverty.

Riché, P. *La Vie quotidienne dans l'Empire carolingien*. Paris, 1973.

Riu, M. "La ayuda a los pobres en la Barcelona medieval: El 'Plat dels pobres vergonyants' de la parroquia de Santa-Maria del Mar." *Pobreza . . . Ibérica*, 783–811.

Roberts, S. "Testamentary Bequests and the Laicization of Charity in the Rouergue, 1280–1350." Ms. Wooster, Oh.: College of Wooster, 1973.

———. "Charity and Hospitality in the Rouergue, 1100–1350." Thesis. Boston: Harvard University, 1975.

Rodolico, N. *I ciompi: Una pagina di storia del proletario operaio*. Florence, 1945.

Rondeau, M. J. "La Pauvreté chez les Peres de l'Eglise au IVe siècle." *Cah. Sorb*. 3.

Roover, R. de. *S. Bernadino of Siena and S. Antonio of Florence, the Two Great Economic Thinkers of the Middle Ages*. Boston, 1967.

———. *La Pensée économique des Scolastiques*. Montreal-Paris, 1971.

Rouche, M. "La Faim à l'époque carolingienne." *R.H.* 508 (1973), 293–303.

———. "La Matricule des pauvres: Evolution d'une institution de charité du Bas-Empire jusqu'à la fin du haut Moyen Age." *Et. Pauvr.*, 83–110.

Roux, S. *La Maison dans l'Histoire*. Paris, 1976.

Salin, E. *La Civilisation mérovingienne*, vol. 2. Paris, 1952.

Sanselme, E. and L. Oeconomos. "Les Oeuvres d'assistance et les hôpiteaux au siècle des Commènes." *Actes 1er Congrès de l'Art de Guérir*. Anvers, 1921.

Scaramella, G. "I Tumulto dei Ciompi, Cronace e Memorie." *R.I.S.* 18 (1917), pt. 2.

Schmitt, J.-C. "La Mort d'un hérétique: L'Eglise et les clercs face aux beguinés et aux béghards dans la région du Rhin supérieur (XIVe–XVe siècle)." Thesis. Paris, 1973.

Schneider, J. *La Ville de Metz aux XIIIe et XIVe siècles*. Nancy, 1950, 419–20.

Severino, G. "Appunti su 'Poverta' e Ricchezza nella Spiritualità dei sec. XI e XII." *Boll. 1st Stor. per il Medio Evo* 79 (1968), 149–65.

Shahar, S. "Les Pauvres et la pauvreté dans 'la Songe du Vergier' et dans les œuvres de Nicolas Oresme et Philippe de Mézières." *Cah. Sorb*. 3.

Sicard, G. *Les Moulins de Toulouse au Moyen Age*. Paris, 1953.

Sigal, A. "Pauvreté et charité d'après quelque textes hagiographiques." *Et. Pauvr.*, 141–62.

Sigal, P. A. "Pauvreté et charité aux XIe et XIIe siecles" *Et. Pauvr.*, 141–62.

———. *Les Marcheurs de Dieu*. Paris, 1974.

Simon, N. "La pauvreté à Caen et dans la vicomté de Caen au XVe siècle." *Cah. Sorb.* 1

Sivéry, G. *Structures agraires et vie rurale dans le Hainaut à la fin du Moyen Age*. Lille, 1977.

———. "La Pauvreté dans les villages du Sud du Hainaut à la fin du Moyen Age." *Cah. Sorb.* 6, 89–93.

Sontag, A. "Les Hôpitaux dans l'Empire au XIVe siècle." Master's thesis, Paris, 1969. Summary in *Cah. Sorb.* 7.

Sousa Costa, A. D. de. "Hospitais e albergarias na documentação pontificia da segunda medade do sec. XV." *Pobreza . . . Ibérica*, 259–328.

Spiciani, A. "L'archivo Fiorentino dei Buonomini di S. Martino." *Studi Storici in memoria de N. Caturegli*. Pisa, 1976, 427–36.

Stra, Cl. "Les "Exempla" source pour l'histoire de la pauvreté." Master's thesis, Paris, 1973. Summary in *Cah. Sorb.* 9.

Tenenti, A. "La Mendicité dans le 'Momus' de Leon Battista Alberti." *Cah. Sorb.* 4.

Texler, R. C. "Charity and the Defense of Urban Elites in the Italian Communes." *The Rich, the Well-Born, and the Powerful*. Ed. F. Jaher. Urbana, 1974, 63–107.

Thérel, M.-Th. " 'Caritas' et 'Paupertas' dans l'iconographie médiévale . . ." *Et. Pauvr.*, 295–318.

Thomson, J. A. F. "Piety and Charity in the Late Medieval London." *The Journal of Ecclesiastical History* 16 (1965), 178–95.

Tits-Dieuaide, M. J. "L'Assistance aux pauvres à Louvain au XVe siècle." *Hommage au Prof. P. Bonenfant*, Brussels, 1965.

———. "Les Tables des pauvres dans les anciennes principautés belges au Moyen Age." *Tijdschrift voor geschiedenis* (1975), 562–83.

Toubert, P. *Les Structures du Latinum médiéval*. 2 vols. Rome-Paris, 1973.

Toulon, F. "Les Maladies dans les récits de miracles . . . du centre de la France (Xe–XIIe siècle)." Master's thesis. Paris, 1971.

Valdéon Baruque, J. "Problematica para un estudio de los pobres y de la pobreza en Castilla a fines de la Edad Media." *Pobreza . . . Ibérica*, 899–920.

Vauchez, A. "Une Campagne de pacification en Lombardie autour de 1233: L'Action politique des Ordres Mendiants d'après la réforme des statuts communaux et les accords de paix." *MAHEFR* 78 (1966), 503–49.

———. "Sainteté laïque au XIIIe siècle: La Vie du Bienheureux Facio de Crémone (vers 1196–1272)." *MAHEFR* 84 (1972), 11–53.

———. "Assistance et charité en Occident (XIIIe–XVe siècle)." Paper given at the *6a Settimana . . . del Istituto Francesco Datini*. Prato, 1974.

———. *La Spiritualité du Moyen Age occidental*. Paris, 1975.

———. "Charité et pauvreté chez sainte Elisabeth de Thuringe, d'après les actes des procès de canonisation." *Et. Pauvr.*, 163–73.

Vaux de Foletier, F. de. *Les Tsiganes dans l'Ancienne France*. Paris, 1961.

Verger, J. *Les Universités au Moyen Age*. Paris, 1973.

Verlinden, C. "L'Esclavage dans l'Europe méridionale." Pt. 1. (Iberian Peninsula, France.) Bruges, 1955.

Vicaire, M.-H. "Recherches sur le premier siècle des Ordres Mendiants." *Rev. des Sciences philos. et théol.* 57 (1973), 675–91.

———. "Les Origines dominicaines de la mendicité religieuse et la condition d'humilité mendiante selon saint Dominique." *La Vie dominicaine* 34 (1975), 195–206, 259–79.

———. *Dominique et ses Prêcheurs.* Friburg, 1977.

Vicens Vivès, J. *Historia de los remensas en el siglo XV.* Barcelona, 1945.

Vilar, P. "Le Déclin catalan au bas Moyen Age: Hypothèse sur sa chronologie." *Estudios hist. mod* 4. Barcelona, 1956.

Villages désertés et hist. écon., XIe–XVIIIe siècle. Paris, 1965.

Vincent-Cassy, M. "L'Envie en France du XIII au XV siècle." Thesis. Paris, 1974.

Violante, C. "I laici nel movimento patarino." *Atti 3a Sett. La Mendola* 1965 (1968), 597–704.

———. "Hérésies urbaines et hérésies rurales en Italie du XIe au XIIIe siècle." *Hérésies et Sociétés.* Paris-La Haye, 1968, 171–98.

———. "Riflessioni sulla Povertà nel secolo XIe." *Studi . . . R. Morghen.* Rome, 1974, 2:1061–81.

———. "Pauperes e Povertà nella societa carolingia." *Cultus et Cognitio.* Warsaw, 1976, 621–30.

Vismara Chiappa, P. *Il tema della Povertà nella Predicazione di Sant'Agostino.* Milan, 1975.

Vogüé, A. de. "Honorer tous les hommes: Le Sens de l'hospitalité bénédictine." *R.A.M.* 40 (1964), 129–38.

Volney, J. "La Pauvreté et les pauvres dans les sermons de Peregrinus d'Opole." *Cah. Sorb.* 2.

Wee, H. van der. *The Growth of Antwerp Market and the European Economy, XIV–XVI.* 3 vols. La Haye, 1963.

———. "Les Archives hospitalières et l'étude de la pauvreté aux Pays-Bas du XVe au XVIIe siècle." *R.N.* 48 (1966), 5–16.

Werner, E. *Pauperes Christi: Studien zu sozialreligiösen Bewegungen im Zeitalter des Reformpapsttums.* Leipzig, 1956.

———. "Ricchezza e povertà nelle idee degli eretici della Chiesa orientale e occidentale XI–XII sec." *Conv. Pov. Todi,* 81–126.

Werveke, H. van. "De Middeleeuwse Hongersnood." *Medelingen van de Koninklijke Vlaamse Academia . . . van België* 29 (1967), 3–22.

———. "La famine de l'An 1316 en Flandre et dans les régions voisines." *R.N.* 61 (1959), 5–14.

Wintrebert, M.-C. "L'Aumône du chevalier dans la littérature du XIIe siècle." Master's thesis, Paris, 1965. Summary in *Cah. Sorb.* 3.

Wolff, Ph. *Estimes toulousaines.* Paris, 1952.

———. *Commerces et marchands de Toulouse . . .* Paris, 1954.

——— et al. *Histoire du Languedoc.* Toulouse, 1967.

———. "Fortunes et genres de vie dans les villages du Toulousain aux XIVe–XVe siècles." *Miscellanea G. F. Niermeyer.* Groningue, 1967, 325–32.

Wolff, Ph., and F. Mauro. L'Age de l'artisanat (Ve-XVIIIe siècles). Pt. 2, *L'Histoire générale du Travail,* ed. L. H. Parias. Paris, 1960.

Wolff, Ph., et al. *Documents Hist. Languedoc.* Toulouse, 1969.

Zanaldi, L. "Storia documentaria dell'Ospedale civile in Venezia." *CESO,* 1365–90.

Zerbi, P. "Pasquale II e l'ideale della povertà della Chiesa" *Annuario Univ. Cattolica.* Milan, 1964–65, 205–29.

Zink, M. *La Prédication en langue romane avant 1300.* Paris, 1976.

INDEX ‡

Blindness, 17, 27, 151–52, 179, 286
Blue Thumbs, 225
Bohemia, 75, 193, 207, 219, 221, 222, 226, 228, 229, 260
Bologna, 107, 111, 126, 136, 158, 162, 210, 242
Bonaventure, Saint, 131, 133, 158
Boniface, Saint, 25, 38, 42
Bourges, 110, 136, 228
Bridges, 92–93
Brie, Jean de, 239
Brinton, Thomas, 231–32, 251, 259
Brittany, 77, 85
Brothers of the Penitence of Jesus Christ ("Bags"), 124
Bruges, 60–61, 147, 151, 159, 164, 165, 188, 223, 226
Bruno, Saint, 75, 77
Brussels, 140, 142, 147, 150, 152, 153, 182, 209, 234, 276–77, 287
Burchard of Worms, 104–05
Burgundy, 27, 92, 97, 195, 207, 234, 247
Burials, 145, 149, 150, 161, 196–97
Byzantine poverty, 18–23, 38

Cade, Jack, 219
Caesarius, Saint, 23, 27, 29, 30, 38, 39
Calixtus, 211
Canonical movement, late eleventh to early thirteenth century, 90–93, 119, 120, 125
Capetians, 65, 165
Cappadocian eremites, 22
Caradoc, Saint, 79
Carmelites, 124
Carolingian era, 20, 23, 24–25, 40, 42, 89; development of poverty in, 32–37
Carthusian order, 66–67, 75, 81, 120, 122, 254
Cash economy, growth of, 57, 61, 95, 120, 154, 155–56, 158
Cassian, 23, 39, 45
Castille, 121, 161, 202, 236, 267, 279, 283, 284, 292
Catalonia, 36, 61, 64, 168, 197, 211, 218, 221, 226, 274
Champagne, 53, 62, 68, 117, 147, 161, 166, 207, 260
Charity and charitable institutions, 11, 300; almonries, 48–52; aristocratic, 71–72, 96–98, 137; Christian concepts of, 21–23, 38, 39, 44–45, 71, 88–90, 95–96, 99, 104–13, 258–63; of Dark Ages, 38–53; of late antiquity, 19–20, 21–23; late eleventh to early thirteenth century, 58, 59–62, 66–67, 71–72, 81, 87–113; mid-thirteenth to mid-fourteenth cen-

tury, 135–58, 179–90; mid-fourteenth to early sixteenth century, 196, 199–200, 232, 252–53, 256, 258–93; municipal supervision of, 100, 152–53, 201–03, 272–91; papal, 136–37, 267; parish, 139–42, 154, 155, 266, 273–76; royal, 71–72, 96, 136–39, 267, 281. *See also* Hospitals; Lay charity; Monastic charity
Charles the Bald, 44
Charles the Good, 96–97, 111
Charles VI, King of France, 215, 216
Chartres, 85, 91, 101, 105, 152, 167
Chaucer, Geoffrey, 257
Chauliac, Guy de, 193–94
Children, 6, 7, 20, 28, 93, 151, 288–89.
Chrétien de Troyes, 69
Christ, pauper as representative of, 9, 22, 24, 76, 77, 78, 112–13, 119, 121, 258–59
Christian of Alms, 77, 78
Christine de Pisan, 255, 257
Chrodegang of Metz, Saint, 41, 42
Chrysostom, 21, 22, 104
Cicero, 21, 104
Ciompi rebellion (1378), 211, 213, 223, 224–25, 227, 229, 230, 254
Cistercians, 66–67, 104, 122
Clement of Alexandria, 21, 22
Clement VI, Pope, 196, 197
Clergy, poverty among, 242
Climatic disasters, 6, 10, 16, 51; late eleventh to early thirteenth century, 57, 59–63, 75, 125; mid-thirteenth to mid-fourteenth century, 158–62
Clothing of the poor, 17, 64, 195–96
Cluny, 49, 87, 88, 96, 135
Colomban, Saint, 45
Colombini, Giovanni, 261
Common Alms, 139–42, 145, 153, 206, 282
Compostella, 91
Confessors' manuals, 128
Confraternities, 93, 98, 99, 120, 125, 127, 139, 142–45, 152–55, 175, 179, 180, 261, 266, 272–73, 283
Constantinople, 73, 85; ancient poverty in, 15–16, 17, 18, 19, 22
Contempt for the poor, 72–74, 85, 112, 189, 197, 247, 251, 254–55
Conventuals, 254
Council of Aix (816), 41
Council of Chalcedon (451), 40
Council of Charroux (989), 53
Council of Clermont (1095), 59
Council of Orléans (511), 27, 38
Council of Paris (829), 33, 34–35, 42
Council of Paris (1212), 151

76, 80, 82, 91, 93, 97, 99, 101, 121–27; mid-thirteenth to mid-fourteenth century, 117, 135, 140, 142–43, 146–48, 152, 155–64, 168, 169, 174–75, 180, 182, 183, 189; mid-fourteenth to early sixteenth century, 193–95, 199–201, 206–10, 213, 216, 217, 222–31, 235–36, 241, 243, 245, 248, 249, 260–61, 273, 279–83, 285, 287, 289, 291. *See also* *specific cities*

Jacquerie, 204–05, 229, 230
James of Vitry, 85, 102, 103, 105, 109–10, 124, 181
Jean André, 128–29
Jerome, Saint, 22–23, 104, 299
Jerusalem, 15, 18, 73
Jews, 21, 45, 67, 170, 181, 197, 278, 281, 287
John, King, 203, 206
John I, King of Portugal, 270
John of Zeliv, 228, 229
Jonas of Orléans, 43
Jordan of Limoges, 53
Joseph, Saint, 259
Julius II, Pope, 281
Justice, 260; twelfth-century concepts of, 106–12
Justinian, Emperor, 18, 19, 20

Labor. *See* Working poor *and specific occupations*
Land. *See* Property ownership
Langland, William, 227
Languedoc, 99, 121, 168, 174, 201, 206, 212–13, 215, 247
Lateran Council of *1179*, 67
Latin Christendom, 21–23, 24, 38
Lay charity: early eleventh to mid-thirteenth century, 88–100, 104, 117, 119–34; mid-thirteenth to mid-fourteenth century, 136–39, 142, 148, 152–56, 179–81; mid-fourteenth to early sixteenth century, 267–90, 293; vs. mendicant orders, 126–34. *See also* Aristocratic charity; Charity and charitable institutions; Hospitals; Royal almonry
Lazarus, 103, 112
Legal systems, and poverty, 17, 20, 33–35, 97, 103, 110, 144–45, 150, 171
Leo the Great, Pope, 39–40
Leo X, Pope, 281
Leprosariums, 98–101, 146, 267, 286
Leprosy, 15–16, 17, 27, 60, 63–64, 79, 87, 98, 146, 267
Limousin, 77, 78, 92
Lollards, 219, 242, 249, 260

Lombards, 58, 67, 170
London, 58, 85, 152, 164, 214–15, 217, 221, 223, 243, 270, 286, 287, 288
Louis VII, King of France, 96
Louis IX (Saint Louis), King of France, 96, 117, 126, 137–38, 144, 171, 222
Louis XI, King of France, 219, 228, 267
Louis the Pious, 35, 42
Low Countries, 61, 81, 98, 139, 141, 142, 159, 165, 169, 189, 208, 217, 234, 241, 270, 274, 277, 281, 282. *See also specific cities and countries*
Lull, Raymond, 184, 186–87
Lyons, 42, 91, 93, 142, 145, 215, 219, 226, 229, 235, 243, 245, 252, 281, 282, 289, 300

Mahaut of Burgundy, 138–39, 140
Maillotins, 215, 223, 226, 230
Malnutrition, 17, 27–28, 194–97, 244
Manuel of Portugal, King, 272
Marbode, 79, 80
Marcel, Etienne, 203, 204, 205
Marseilles, 26, 27, 164, 171, 243, 273, 287, 288
Martin, Saint, 23, 24, 112, 122
Mathurins, 95
Matilda, Empress, 97
Medici, Salvestro de', 209, 213, 230
Medicine, 91, 152, 194–96, 289–90
Mendicant orders, 117, 119–34, 136, 139, 155, 158, 182, 185, 190, 253–54, 265. *See also specific orders*
Mental illness, 152, 286–87
Merovingian era, 20, 38, 40; development of poverty in, 25–32
Metz, 29, 40, 100, 101, 124, 165, 201, 284
Mézières, Philippe de, 252, 253, 272, 278
Michele di Lando, 229, 230
Migration of the poor, fourteenth to fifteenth century, 242–50
Milan, 80, 101, 147, 158, 285, 293
Military service, 35
Millau, 101, 141
Minorites, 124, 126, 130, 253, 254
Monastic charity, 38, 41–42, 45–53; of late antiquity, 21–23; late eleventh to early thirteenth century, 59–62, 66–67, 81, 87–88; mid-thirteenth to mid-fourteenth century, 135–36, 181; mid-fourteenth to early sixteenth century, 196, 266–67, 273, 283. *See also* Mendicant orders; Religious aspects of poverty; *specific orders and saints*
Monastic estates, 41–44, 52, 66–67
Money alms, 155–56
Monte di pietà, 278–81
More, Thomas, 298

Mortgages, peasant, 67
Municipal supervision of the poor, 100, 152–53, 201–03, 272–91
Murner, Thomas, 254
Mutual aid, 98, 99, 156, 179, 261

Narbonne, 36, 100, 101, 145, 148, 149, 151, 153, 193, 197, 270, 273
New Testament, 21, 45, 74
Noble alms, 71–72, 96–98, 137
Normandy, 65–66, 67, 75, 77, 142, 150, 195, 215, 236, 237, 273
Norway, 197

Observance, 254, 258, 279, 280
Odila, Saint, 28
Odo of Tournai, 103
Old Testament, 21, 45, 74
Olivi, Giovanni, 131, 133
Order of Mercy, 95
Order of Saint John, 268–69
Order of the Holy Sepulchre of Jerusalem, 94, 95
Orphans, 20, 28, 99, 288–89
Or San Michele, 143–44, 156, 162, 163, 180, 200, 224

Pachomius, Saint, 45
Papal almonry (Pignotte), 136–37, 267
Paris, 41, 42, 62, 85, 91, 100–02, 117, 124, 137, 138, 146, 147, 149, 150, 155, 160, 165, 167, 176, 194–95, 199, 204, 215–16, 219, 222–23, 226, 233–34, 243–47, 251–52, 260, 265–68, 282, 288–89, 291
Parish charity, 139–42, 154, 155, 266, 273–76
Pascal II, Pope, 79
Pastoral missions, 89–90, 123–27, 135
Pastoureaux, 158, 187
Patarine movement, 53, 80
Paul, Saint, 78
Paulinus of Aquileia, 42
Pauper and peasant, distinctions between, 31–32, 33, 70
Pauperism, rise of mid-fourteenth to mid-fifteenth century, 211–50
Pawnshops, 278–81
Peasant Wars of 1520, 297
Pedro Dom, of Portugal, 270, 272
Pedro the Ceremonious, 139
Peregrine of Oppeln, 129, 130
Personal charity, meaning of, 153–56
Peter Lombard, 111, 112
Peter of Blois, 4, 68, 73–74, 107, 108, 110, 113, 119
Peter of Poitiers, 111
Peter of Roissy, 85

Peter the Chanter, 77, 84, 102, 103, 107, 108, 109, 111
Peter the Hermit, 57, 58, 60, 73, 74, 75
Petronilla of Chemillé, 80
Peyrault, William, 128, 133, 144, 299
Philip Augustus, 62, 66, 96, 137
Philip of Alsace, Count of Flanders, 96–97
Pilgrims, late eleventh to early thirteenth century, 91–94
Plague, 26, 161, 193–97, 206, 207, 212; social and moral consequences of, 197–210, 212
Plantagenet, Geoffroy, 97
Plats dels Pobres, 274–75
Poland, 75, 130, 147, 256, 259, 271
Poll tax, 214, 222
Pomerius, Julianus, 23, 42
Poorhouses, 41
Poor-lawyers, 144–45
Poor list, 38–42
Poor Tables, 139–42, 272–78, 281, 291
Popular uprisings, 53, 58, 82, 159, 160, 187–89; fourteenth to fifteenth century, 188–89, 203–05, 209–32, 251–52
Population growth, 7, 11, 24, 52; late eleventh to early thirteenth century, 57, 61, 66, 121; mid-thirteenth to mid-fourteenth century, 148, 166; mid-fourteenth to early sixteenth century, 197
Portugal, 60, 91, 101, 139, 148, 161, 179, 202, 217, 260, 270, 271, 272, 282–83, 284
Posthumous charity, 154–55, 199–200, 232, 263–66, 268
Potentes, Carolingian, 32–37
Poverty rates, 18, 296; mid-fourteenth to early sixteenth century, 233–37
Prague, 218–19
Prisoners of war, 27, 65, 95
Property ownership, 24, 52, 107; of Dark Ages, 32–37, 41–44; late eleventh to early thirteenth century, 66–68, 107, 110, 111; mid-thirteenth to mid-fourteenth century, 166–70, 174; mid-fourteenth to early sixteenth century, 198, 218, 237–38, 242; monastic estates, 41–44, 52, 66–67
Prostitution, 65, 79, 85, 122, 137, 245–46
Provence, 99, 161, 168, 171, 176, 195, 196, 201, 206, 207, 236, 238, 240
Puig, Bernat, 184, 185

Quarta, 90

Raoul Ardent, 103, 104, 107, 108–09, 110, 113

Ratherius, 45
Raymond of Peñafort, 128, 260
Rebellion. *See* Popular uprisings
Reform, hospital, 181–82, 281–90
Registration of the poor, 38–42
Religious aspects of poverty, 8–9, 11, 57, 298–300; of Dark Ages, 25–26, 38–53; of late antiquity, 19–23; late eleventh to early thirteenth century, 58, 87–113, 119–27; mid-thirteenth to mid-fourteenth century, 123, 135–36, 139–42, 150–53, 180, 181, 185; mid-fourteenth to early sixteenth century, 197, 211, 239, 253, 256, 258–63, 272, 283–84; poverty as path to god, 21–23, 46, 71, 81, 89–90, 94, 103–06, 119–23, 258–59, 264. *See also* Crusades; Mendicant orders; Monastic charity
Remensa movement, 218, 221
Rémi, Saint, 29, 34
Rheims, 41, 51, 68, 90, 99, 101, 151, 176
Rhône River, 92–93
Richard II, King of England, 214–15, 222, 272
Rivers, 92–93
Robert of Arbrissel, 60, 74, 75, 76, 77, 79, 80, 81, 99, 103, 106
Robert the Pious, King, 96
Rock, Saint, 197
Rodez, 101, 141, 149, 150
Roman Empire, 15, 17, 20, 23, 24
Rome, 39, 40, 91, 93, 101, 102, 150, 186, 262, 273
Rouen, 124, 135, 150, 159, 164, 188, 204, 215–16, 221, 226, 229, 236, 243
Rouergue, 140, 141, 161
Royal almonry, 71–72, 96, 136–39, 267, 281
Rule of the Master, 46, 47
Rural poverty, 24, 296; of Dark Ages, 24–37, 41, 45; late eleventh to early thirteenth century, 57, 61, 65–68; mid-thirteenth to mid-fourteenth century, 140, 148–49, 166–73; mid-fourteenth to early sixteenth century, 195, 196, 198, 199, 206, 207, 212, 218–19, 233, 234, 237–43, 269, 273, 275, 280–81

Sailors, 152, 164, 180, 240–41, 287
Saint Anthony's fire, 63, 94
Salt makers, 207, 219, 240, 287
Savonarola, 260, 280
Schism in the Church, 211, 213
Sebastian, Saint, 197
Second Council of Aix-la-Chapelle (836), 32
Self-help by the poor, 179

Seneca, 21, 104
Servile homage, 169–70
Sesmarias law, 202
Sforza, Francesco, 283, 285
Sharecropping, 169
Shepherds, 7, 172, 187, 239–40
Siena, 209–10, 293
Sigebert of Gembloux, 60–61, 63
Simplicius, 38
Sin, 255, 259
Siran, Saint, 32, 37
Slavery, 30, 33, 180, 199, 292
Smaragdus of Verdun, 46
Social aspects of poverty, 5, 6–7, 53, 295–300; of Dark Ages, 30–37, 40, 43–44; distinctions between peasant and pauper, 31–32, 33, 70; of late antiquity, 17–21; late eleventh to early thirteenth century, 57–58, 63, 65, 70–113, 125; mid-thirteenth to mid-fourteenth century, 121, 135, 152, 153–57, 158–90; mid-fourteenth to early sixteenth century, 193–210, 211–93. *See also* Rural poverty; Urban poverty; *specific classes and occupations*
Soissons, 90, 91, 101
Spain, 23, 25, 145; Carolingian, 36; late eleventh to early thirteenth century, 65, 75, 95, 100, 101; mid-thirteenth to mid-fourteenth century, 117, 136, 138–42, 148, 159, 161, 172, 184; mid-fourteenth to early sixteenth century, 201–02, 218, 221, 222, 236, 240, 267, 274–75, 279, 281, 284, 285, 287. *See also specific cities*
Spirituals, 182, 185, 186
Stephen of Bourbon, 129
Stephen of Obazine, 76
Structural poverty, 26, 30–32
Suicide, 242

Tafur, King, 73
Tafur affair, 81
Taverns, 246
Taxation, 6, 9; of Dark Ages, 30, 36; of late antiquity, 16, 17, 19; mid-thirteenth to mid-fourteenth century, 158, 165, 174–77, 188; mid-fourteenth to early sixteenth century, 203, 204, 206–07, 212, 214–17, 222, 223, 233–38, 240, 243, 268
Technological development, 11, 24, 92, 105, 170
Templars, 136, 221
Terminology for poverty, evolution of, 1–5, 21, 30, 31, 32, 33, 51, 57, 123, 139, 252, 253, 258, 298